Market Driven Strategy

Processes for Creating Value

George S. Day

THE FREE PRESS
A Division of Macmillan, Inc.
NEW YORK

Maxwell Macmillan Canada
TORONTO

Maxwell Macmillan International
NEW YORK   OXFORD   SINGAPORE   SYDNEY

The Free Press
A Division of Macmillan, Inc.
866 Third Avenue, New York, N.Y. 10022

Maxwell Macmillan Canada, Inc.
1200 Eglinton Avenue East
Suite 200
Don Mills, Ontario M3C 3N1

Macmillan, Inc. is part of the Maxwell Communication
Group of Companies.

Printed in the United States of America

printing number

3 4 5 6 7 8 9 10

Library of Congress Cataloging-in-Publication Data

Day, George S.
    Market driven strategy : processes for creating value / George S.
    Day.
        p.   cm.
    ISBN 0-02-907211-5
    1. Marketing—Management.   2. Strategic planning.   I. Title.
HF5415.13.D368   1990
658.8'02—dc20   89–71473
                                                                      CIP

Contents

iii

PART

FIVE

Renewing the Strategy

PART

SIX

Issues in Implementing Market-Driven Strategies

Preface

The arguments for a new perspective on competitive strategies remain compelling. Old ways of competing and much of the conventional wisdom about organizations are being overturned by a convergence of forces: markets are fragmenting into narrower customer segments while competition is globalizing. Information technologies are blurring traditional demarcation lines between markets and organizations while accelerating the pace of decisions. Technological change continues to shorten product life cycles and customers are demanding ever-higher levels of responsiveness and quality. Add to this a rich mixture of organizational arrangements that create networks and partnerships among suppliers, channel members, and customers, and managers find they have less room for error than ever before. The rate of change in the market has clearly outstripped the speed at which a conventionally managed organization can respond.

Few businesses are exempt from these pressures—but each has to develop its own response, in the form of a strategy that specifies how the business intends to compete in the markets it elects to serve. There are no formulas to guide this choice of direction, but there are three distinctive features of successful responses. These are the integrating themes woven together throughout this book to shape its distinctive character.

The first theme is the necessity for an adaptive planning process to harness the power of bottom-up understanding of market and technology opportunities and competitive realities, with top-down vision and leadership. Effective strategies are the product of motivated teams of managers continually addressing joint issues and challenges. But what is the glue that gives shared meaning to the activities of each team member? This is the role of competitive advantage. The second theme of this book is the continual creation and renewal of new sources of competitive advantage, as the surest route to sustained profitability.

The final thread that pulls this book together is the necessity for an external orientation. Every part of the organization must be market-driven, by consciously working to put customers first while staying ahead of the competition. This primacy of decision values will channel the energies of people, and gives meaning to functional activities.

Market-driven businesses that instill commitment with team-planning processes to secure a sustainable edge over competitors also reap economic rewards. The appropriate measure of a strategy is whether it credibly promises to create shareholder value. While this is a useful litmus test of a sound strategy it still does not have priority over the imperative of creating customer value, without which there is no shareholder value.

Acknowledgments.   A book proposing to marry the softer-edged qualitative process approaches that facilitate organization change with the harder-edged substantive approaches that describe and explain the content of strategy, accumulates many debts of gratitude. It is a pleasure to acknowledge them, although that is still inadequate recompense for their contributions. While I can't begin to recognize all the scholars and practitioners whose thinking has influenced mine, there are six whose ideas have been especially important. At the head of the list is Peter Drucker, whose seminal writings on the nature and purpose of organizations and sheer mastery of the intricacies of a strategy and its execution remain a continuing inspiration to anyone trying to make sense out of a market. Next is Michael Porter, whose pioneering work on the structural analysis of industries and competitive advantage is frequently utilized throughout this book. Many marketing scholars will also recognize their ideas in this book, with Philip Kotler and Ted Levitt having the biggest role. Finally, harsh experience has taught me that strategies are no more than elegant and impractical constructions unless they change the direction of the organization. The work of James March and Karl Weick has constantly challenged my tendency to think otherwise.

It has been my good fortune to work with many people whose insights into strategy helped me separate the important from the merely interesting. In this influential group is Steve Burnett of the Allen Centre at Northwestern, Bill Brandt of the Impact Planning Group, John Cady of the Centre for Executive Development and Brad Gale and Robert Buzzell of the Strategic Planning Institute. My association with SPI has been especially rewarding for the opportunity to confront my ideas with data and analysis.

Unquestionably my greatest intellectual debt is to the friends and co-authors whose joint work often appears here. Robin Wensley helped me unravel the layers of meaning in the slippery notion of competitive advantage. Liam Fahey was a continuing source of insight during our joint investigation of value-based planning methods and freely shared his thinking on current developments in strategy. Allan Shocker has collaborated with me on studies of market structure analysis and positioning strategies and continues to make important contributions to this area. Finally Bart Weitz, Adrian Ryans, and David Aaker never let our friendship get in the way of roundly criticizing my loose thinking, while stimulating me to push my thinking further.

Demanding consulting clients have also played a big role in forming these ideas. The pressure of their continuing stream of challenging problems and their unwillingness to accept facile prescriptions has greatly strengthened this work. In particular the General Electric Company has had a major formative role. It has been a privilege to have been associated with an organization so deeply committed to achieving advantage in global markets. I'd like to single out Dick DiPaolo and Steve Mercer for special thanks.

These ideas have been tested in numerous executive programs and strategic planning sessions. The patience of those unsung participants, and their willingness to straighten out any errant thinking has been extremely useful.

Many students and faculty at the University of Toronto contributed to this book. Some were reviewers of early drafts, while others were in the PhD program, and alerted me to new sources of thinking. Mike Mayo, Mary Lambkin, Saul Klein, Alexandra Campbell, Ena Garmaise, and Jonathan Freeman get special thanks for this help. The University of Toronto went out of its way to provide a supportive environment. Dean Roger Wolff has done more than I deserve to make this work possible. In an important respect the university made this book possible by honoring me with a Connaught Senior Fellowship and a year free of the normal academic responsibilities.

A second organization, the Marketing Science Institute, has provided enormous help at many stages in the intellectual journey that preceded this book. The continued interplay of problems and ideas that is the hallmark of this unique marriage of managers and academics, jointly dedicated to advancing the practice of marketing, is reflected in many of these pages.

This book is dedicated to the person who made it possible and worthwhile. My wife and best friend, Marilyn, has blessed me with a wonderful family that has been a continuing source of inspiration. Her own patience, enthusiasm, and unfailing support gave me both momentum and incentive.

GEORGE DAY
Cambridge, Massachusetts

ONE

Strategic Choices in Competitive Markets

Managing in
Turbulent Markets

*There is no resting place for an enterprise in a competitive
society.*

—ALFRED SLOAN, JR.

*Unless we change our direction we are likely to end up where we
are headed.*

—ANCIENT CHINESE WISDOM

Benetton and Sears, Roebuck both compete for a piece of the retail apparel
market. Otherwise there are few similarities. The differences between
these two firms are more interesting for they illustrate the richness and
complexity of competitive strategies, as well as the adverse consequences
for performance when a strategy drifts out of touch with the market. Their
stories are also apt metaphors for some of the forces that will be sweeping
the markets of the 1990s.

Sears is a classic example of what happens when a firm becomes complacent in its market.[1] Until 1986 Sears was the dominant retailer in the
United States, before being challenged by K-Mart and Wal-Mart. By 1989
it was struggling to reverse a decade-long decline in its share of general
merchandise sales from 18 percent to 13 percent, overcome bloated selling
and administrative costs of 30 percent of sales, and raise pretax margins
from 3.7 percent to a level closer to the 7 percent of their competitors.

The problems with apparel were symptomatic of Sears's difficulties.
The traditional key success factors in this department were quality of presentation and assortment. Both were major problems to manage because of

the number of stores and diversity of product lines in each store. Many suppliers of branded apparel didn't like Sears's sloppy presentation or considered a mass market outlet inappropriate. Changes to overcome these problems proved difficult to make. One proposal was to create "neighborhood stores" that would sell only apparel and home furnishings. However, the executives representing "hard goods" such as appliances, electronics, and automotive products argued they shouldn't be left out of the stores, and killed the proposal.

Despite Sears's problems, its standing with consumers remained strong. Consistently it was picked as a company associated with high quality, and 75 percent of Americans visited a Sears store at least once a year. Unfortunately, this reservoir of goodwill was being dissipated by a ponderous and noncompetitive culture, antiquated systems, and excessive in-fighting. Customers were being siphoned off by trendier specialty retailers, such as The Gap or The Limited, or superdiscounters such as Circuit City or Toys R Us who dominated specific merchandise types.

Benetton was anything but complacent. In just 10 years this Italian-based fashion retailer opened 5,000 shops in 79 countries. Each shop offered brightly colored sportswear with a distinctive flair, presented in basic color and design configurations, with lots of excitement and ever-changing variety.

The contrasts with Sears were telling; Benetton was focused, global. It competed with a distinct strategy that provided a stable platform for managing in a turbulent fashion market where life cycles were often less than a season. Not surprisingly, their net profit margins were also three times those of Sears.

The most noticeable difference was their "customer draw" system[2] that electronically tied the 5,000 stores directly to their factories—so closely that turnaround from order to delivery was only two to six weeks. Store managers didn't have to guess in advance what to order, they could monitor what was selling and reorder the "hot" items. The highly automated factories produced only to order. If a new style or fabric emerged unexpectedly, a sophisticated computer-aided design (CAD) system could compress the time from design to production of a full range of sizes and colors. Not only had they broken the traditional constraints of time with this system, they were also able to avoid being penalized by costs that typically rise with increasing variety (see Figure 1–1). This gave them a distinct competitive advantage.

While it is tempting to dismiss Sears as a dinosaur, ill-equipped to match fleet-footed competitors in fast-changing global markets, and celebrate Benetton as a prototype of innovative winners in the future, that would be

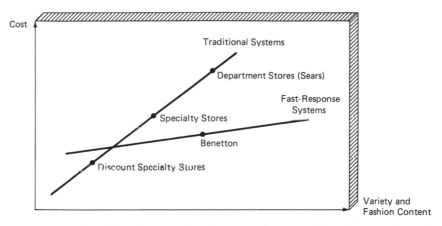

FIGURE 1-1 Traditional versus Fast-Response Systems: Why Benetton Prevails

terribly misleading. Their respective positions reflect past strategic choices and intentions, but their future performance hinges on how well they adapt to the future environment. If Sears management can shake loose from their bad habits, they have enormous strengths to exploit. Conversely Benetton must keep innovating or be surpassed by eager emulators. Their futures are very much in their hands, depending on the wisdom and commitment their management brings to the critical choices any business must make to successfully manage its markets. This chapter introduces the strategic choices that collectively determine whether the rules of their competitive game are defined to their advantage and not preempted by their rivals. The rest of the book is about how to make these choices.

CHOICES AND CHALLENGES
IN TURBULENT MARKETS

A competitive strategy specifies how a business intends to compete in the markets it chooses to serve. This strategy provides a conceptual glue that gives shared meaning to all the separate functional activities and programs. Effective strategies are straightforward in their intent and direction. Too much subtlety and complexity, and the essential ingredients won't be consistently understood or acted upon by the organization. This is damaging to performance in the market because it sends erratic and confusing signals to customers.

Strategies are directional statements, rather than detailed step-by-step plans of action. The direction is set by four choices:

Arena: the markets to serve and customer segments to target

Advantage: the positioning theme that differentiates the business from competitors

Access: the communication and distribution channels used to reach the market

Activities: the appropriate scale and scope of activities to be performed

These choices are highly interdependent—change one and all the other elements of the strategy have to be changed. The result of these choices is an integrated pattern that collectively specifies the strategy in Figure 1–2.

A fifth and final set of choices deals with the adaptation of the strategy to impending threats and emerging opportunities. Winning strategies don't change every year or at the whim of new management, because if they did the customers and the organization would soon become confused. This

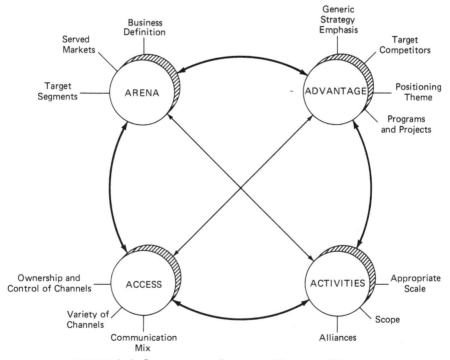

FIGURE 1–2 Strategy as an Integrated Pattern of Choices

doesn't mean a sound strategy can be static, for that would stifle innovation and lead to stagnation. Successful adaptation requires a clear sense of the growth direction to pursue that will best capitalize on the competencies of the business.

The choice of the best direction depends on making sense of a myriad of events, trends, and cross-currents, and placing bets on how the environment will unfold. If the bets are wrong, and the business can't change course quickly, the penalty is below par performance and foreclosure from future opportunities. Each of the critical strategic choices will be more difficult in the future because of the challenges posed by an accelerating rate of change and competition of unprecedented intensity.

ARENA: CHOOSING MARKETS AND TARGET SEGMENTS

As soon as the market arena is chosen management loses many of their degrees of freedom. This single choice largely dictates the customers to be served, the rivals to surpass, and the key success factors (KSFs) they must master. These KSFs are the functions and activities that must be managed well for the business to outperform the rivals. Conversely if these are done badly then failure is almost assured. Each market has a distinctive profile of KSFs, shaped by the attributes of the market. In mature industrial markets, for example, the defining attributes are technology—whether it is small or large batch or continuous processing—and transaction complexity, which reflects the frequency of purchase, risk of failure, and size of the decision-making unit.[3]

Despite the importance of choosing target segments, this is often done by default; a failing attributable to the misguided logic that says that since we make hydraulic hoses, semiconductors, or frozen food, we serve all the customers for these products. Serving every segment with a common strategy is seldom the best choice. Alternatively, the business may serve the broad market with distinct, tailored strategies for each segment, or limit coverage to a single segment to the exclusion of the others. The merits of these coverage alternatives will be dealt with further in Chapter 8.

Challenges. Firms are reconsidering their choice of market arena under pressure from three trends that cannot be ignored.

First, there is increasing market fragmentation. New segments with distinct needs and requirements are emerging and being served by specialist competitors with tailored offerings. In markets from soup to cars, sweeping demographic and life-style changes are rendering mass marketing obsolete and eroding brand loyalties. This trend breeds product diversity that encourages further fragmentation. The automobile market, for example, is rapidly becoming a collection of niche markets in which customers can personalize their choice with specific models, designs, and features, rather than take a standard design and add accessories and options.

Second, traditional market boundaries are blurring as a result of a barrage of substitutes that result from new technologies. Today there are auto springs from plastic, telephone lines of glass with awesome channel capacity, engines made of ceramics that promise to run efficiently at high temperatures, minerals mined by microbes, and holes being drilled cheaply and accurately by pinpoint, high-pressure jets of water. Worse, these changing market structures usually bring new competitors. To name a few: telecommunication companies have entered the computer industry and vice versa; more management and technical education is done within companies than by universities and some of these companies grant academic degrees; and some churches own television stations.

The third and most compelling market-shaping trend is the transformation of previously self-contained national markets into linked global markets. Many forces underlie this trend: increasing homogenization of buying patterns for products from sweaters to audio-disc players; the challenge from global competitors who gain scale or skill advantages from coordinated country strategies; the emerging economic prowess of the Pacific Rim countries; the upheavals triggered by Europe 1992 and the opening of the Communist block of countries; and technology change that makes it feasible to coordinate far-flung operations and easily communicate with customers across national boundaries.

The challenge for management is to find the right balance of global reach and standardization of activities, versus local adaptation. For example, Nabisco is unlikely to launch their Grey Poupon family of Dijon mustards, which leads the premium segment in the United States, into other markets where tastes may differ or competitors are already solidly entrenched. Their challenge is to use the skills and scale gained in the U.S. market to develop products suited to the unique needs of other markets. This is such an important issue that Chapter 10 will be devoted entirely to managing globally.

ADVANTAGE: POSITIONING
FOR COMPETITIVE SUPERIORITY

When a new management team inherits or acquires a business, the market arena has already been chosen for them by the actions and commitments of their predecessors. Initially their emphasis has to be on strengthening their competitive advantages within that arena. This involves achieving demonstrably superior performance on attributes that are important to the target customers at a competitive cost. Points of superiority that cost more than the customer is willing to pay are a profit sink that can't be endured for long.

The essence of competitive advantage is a positioning theme that sets a business apart from its rivals in ways that are meaningful to the target customers. The most successful themes are built on some combination of three thrusts: better (through superior quality or service), faster (by being able to sense and satisfy shifting customer requirements faster than competitors), and closer (with the creation of durable relationships). The task for management is to simultaneously find a compelling theme and ensure continuing superiority in the skills, resources, and controls that will be the source of this advantage over target competitors. This issue is so central that Chapters 5 and 6 are devoted to the process of finding and achieving a position of advantage.

Successful businesses can't afford to stop and celebrate their current advantages. They have to be paranoid about competitors and move aggressively to defend their position. As important as a strong defense might be, it can only delay the inevitable erosion. This means continuously innovating to build new sources of advantage before rivals overtake. Thus Kodak reasserted itself in the film market by introducing its best film ever, Ektar, just two years after introducing another world-class product, Kodacolor Gold film. Kodak management has pledged to keep making these improvements ahead of their arch-rival Fuji.

Challenges. During the eighties it became increasingly difficult for firms to be complacent about the durability of their advantages. By one estimate 70 percent of all product innovations were matched within a year.[4] Process knowledge was easier to protect, but 60 to 90 percent eventually diffused to competitors. Price and advertising moves could be readily matched because they are so visible.

The trends that have quickened the rate of erosion of advantages will continue to intensify. Overshadowing everything is the compression of product life cycles which puts a premium on getting to market first, or imitating quickly to avoid missing a short-lived profit window. This trend can be appreciated only by looking back to markets like refrigerators that took 30 years to fully mature, and comparing them to the market for microwaves that took only 10 years to get to the same place, or compact disc players that matured in three years.

Further pressure on advantages will come from supply gluts. Markets as diverse as commodity petrochemicals, automobiles, and electronics presently suffer chronic global overcapacity of 15 to 40 percent. Why?

- There are too many firms competing. Besides traditionally established firms there are new players from other geographic areas, including the newly industrialized countries, and others that are subsidized by their host government.
- Customers may back integrate by making their requirements rather than buying them. This first reduces the volume of market demand relative to supply. Then these customers may sell their excess capacity in competition with their one-time supplier.
- All firms are increasingly productive as technology improvements diffuse rapidly. The ubiquity of the experience curve is evidence of the extent of productivity improvements.[5]
- Because of significant legal, physical, technological, and financial barriers that block their exit, not enough firms are leaving.

Customer bargaining power also works to narrow the differences between competitors—or at least, to erase the possibility of capturing superior profits for long periods. This is particularly evident in industrial markets, where large customers are bent on eliminating all but a few of their suppliers by raising the acceptable quality and performance requirements even as they demand price concessions.

ACCESS: SELECTING CHANNELS TO REACH THE ARENA

Until recently, channels were not seen as a matter of strategic choice—they were a fact of life that came with the market. A propensity for inertia was reinforced by a perceived absence of good alternatives, and the justified fear of the conflicts that would be unleashed by any changes.

A great deal of attention has been devoted to managing the channel to keep costs in line, motivating the sales force to improve their productivity, and instituting tighter controls over key channel relationships. But basic choices over the form of the channel have seldom been confronted by most firms; they have elected to go directly to their markets with their own sales force if tight control was essential, or opted for intermediaries such as distributors when they could benefit from their superior efficiency and coverage. Seldom was there any debate, for example, over whether to appoint only an exclusive handful of dealers versus pushing for intensive distribution. These issues were not viewed as important, as they were largely ordained by the characteristics of the product or service.

This view of channels obscures the contribution the choice of a channel makes to the firm's competitive advantage. In most markets, distribution strength (coverage, cost, and closeness of relationships) plays a distinct role in reinforcing superior product performance and maintaining a strong position in end-user markets. Industrial firms in particular cannot maintain market leadership without having a strong distribution system. This applies equally to consumer goods firms, as Procter & Gamble found in the soft drink market. After nine frustrating years in which the U.S. market share of their subsidiary Crush International declined from 1.3 to 0.8 percent in 1989, they finally gave up and sold the brand. They were crippled by not being able to get adequate access to the local bottlers who buy concentrate from the marketers, such as Coke and Pepsi, and then bottle the product and stock the shelves. The overwhelming presence of the two soft drink giants eventually forced P&G to try an alternative store-to-warehouse distribution system. This move not only cut them out of nongrocery store outlets—such as vending machines—but so angered their remaining bottlers that they retaliated.

Challenges. Passive acceptance of existing channel arrangements will be increasingly risky for a number of reasons.[6] Companies in all markets are facing greatly increased direct sales costs with little evidence of improved productivity to offset these costs. Meanwhile, customer demands for closer relationships and information technologies that permit direct order-entry links and rapid information flows from buyer to seller and back are forcing companies to reconsider traditional channels.

Companies that use intermediaries are encountering an unwelcome shift in the balance of power. In consumer markets, the retail trade is forcing major concessions on their national brand suppliers. The pressure for trade allowances, deals, and discounts has substantially reduced the funds available for franchise-building advertising. Many industrial markets are seeing rapid concentration among previously fragmented distributors, who bring unprecedented purchasing power, sophistication, and new forms of value-adding services to their dialogue with their suppliers. In response there is an increasing tendency for firms to create hybrid arrangements, and use a variety of channels to reach distinct segments. This escalation in the complexity and scale of channel arrangements has certainly raised the strategic visibility of this area. In recognition of this trend, Chapter 9 is devoted to the choice and management of the appropriate channel.

ACTIVITIES: CHOOSING THE APPROPRIATE SCALE AND SCOPE

The next set of strategic choices is the selection of the strategically central and distinct activities to be performed to convert inputs into outputs that customers will value. Among the potential activities are purchasing, manufacturing or processing, design, sales, distribution, and service. When these activities are assembled together, with the necessary organizational structures, controls, and technology linkages, they establish the value chain for the business.

Few businesses choose to be fully "integrated," that is, to carry out all possible activities starting with raw materials and culminating in a finished product sold and delivered to the end user. Instead, their value chain is limited to only those activities that have to be done very well in order to achieve a competitive advantage—the key success factors. Surrounding this value chain is a set of value chains that links suppliers at one end to the channels and end-users at the other end.

Challenges. Until recently the choice of appropriate scale and scope was guided by two rules of thumb: bigger is better, and keep as many activities as possible under one roof to maintain control. Adherence to these beliefs led to big companies characterized by sprawling plants, extensive vertical integration, a continuous striving for economies of scale, hierarchical and functional organizations, and mass marketing with a strong volume orientation.[7]

A wrenching era of global competition, resulting in restructuring and cost control to generate cash flow, and market share losses to more agile, entrepreneurial specialists, is changing the rules. Today, large corporations are behaving as though the old organization structures are obsolete. The benefits of specialization, scale, and the control they promised have been nullified by inefficiencies and lack of flexibility. Meanwhile, the imaginative use of information technologies is overcoming the control problem. A company that once might have acquired a key supplier to get more control over component quality may now feel it can do better simply by tracking the supplier's performance by computer. Increasingly, large companies are trying to create autonomous, small, entrepreneurial units to find responsive solutions to customer problems in well-defined market niches.[8] Long-term advantages are sustained by simultaneously investing heavily in core competencies, such as microprocessor controls or digital imaging, that are common to families of business units. Other activities, such as public relations or managing the computer system that are not central to the strategy are increasingly farmed out to independent contractors.

Structures are also changing to accommodate long-term alliances that come in many guises: joint ventures for co-development of technology or entering new markets, supply and service agreements, and sundry licensing agreements. Even IBM, which once felt strong enough to go it alone, had arranged more than 40 active alliances by 1990, including several major partnerships with Japanese firms. They created links with Ricoh in the distribution of low-end computers, with Nippon Steel in systems integration, and NTT in value-added networks.

The move to alliances reminds us that the same forces are often working on several strategic choices at the same time. Globalization has already presented a challenge to thinking about the choice of arena and the directions for growth. But this force puts equally insistent pressure on the need to form alliances. Their appeal lies in the way they help defray the immense fixed costs that must be borne because of the broadened market base.[9] Few companies can afford the costs of building and maintaining a brand name, while investing in automated factories, distribution networks, and communications networks to serve a global market at a pace that will keep them ahead of their rivals. But alliances are only one of a number of means to this end. The essence of strategy is knowing which choices to make, and then making sure they happen.

ADAPTATION AND RENEWAL: GROWTH DIRECTIONS TO PURSUE

Sooner or later all market arenas lose their luster, as sales growth stagnates, profit margins are squeezed, and competition intensifies. Management can't wait until this has happened before taking action, for then they will surely be too late to capitalize on emerging market opportunities. Delay means attractive positions will already be staked out by competitors, and the best opportunities for alliances and acquisitions are likely to have been preempted.

Vigilant companies constantly seek new opportunities in related markets, products, and services, where their distinctive competencies can be effectively utilized. When senior management is committed to finding new sources of growth, the rest of the organization is energized to innovate and propose new directions with some confidence they will be heeded. However, unmanaged growth can be just as dangerous as complacency and inertia, if it leads the business into diverse markets that management doesn't understand, where the available competencies can't be used, and unanticipated competitors are better situated. Such unproductive directions distract management and diffuse their scarce resources. Thus, the choices of where to look for new opportunities, and how aggressively to move, have to be made very carefully. These choices are specified by a growth strategy that gets major attention in Chapters 11 and 12. This growth strategy specifies the growth paths worth pursuing, the purpose of new products and markets, the size of the risks to be taken, and the alternative entry strategies to be used to reduce the risks of internal development.

Challenges.[10] Managers will find that charting new directions for their business will be increasingly difficult. Each market has its own sources of uncertainty and opportunity—but few will be exempt from the three megaforces of demographic and life-style changes, technology change, and environmental concerns.

At the heart of demographic and life-style changes are population aging, and seemingly insatiable demands for convenience and service. By the year 2000, the baby boom generation will be 36 to 54 years old, and their households include more than half the U.S. population. Japan and Germany will have even older populations, all with tastes that will be difficult for youth-oriented firms to satisfy. Whole new markets are being created to satisfy the fastest growing of all demographic groups that is over 85 years old.

Technological change will be the main impetus behind new market opportunities. The possibilities range from so-call "super" technologies such as superconductors, fusion power, and robotics, to "appropriate" technologies including micro refineries and photovoltaics, "bio" technologies that promise designer genes, and "information" technologies that are being created by advanced generations of lightning-fast microprocessors coupled to modern computer networks.

The least predictable influence on new market directions is environmentalism. Escalating concerns about acid rain, ozone depletion, water quality, and waste disposal foreshadow the future. The global plastics and petrochemical industry is one of the most likely to bear the brunt of these concerns. West German chemical companies are already devoting about half of their capital spending to the environment and safety. While few industries will be as exposed as this, it is also unlikely that many will entirely escape the growing social and political forces at work to deal with the public consequences of private consumption.[11]

SUCCESSFUL MARKET MANAGEMENT

There are three kinds of companies: those that make things happen, those who watch things happen, and the rest who wonder what happened.
— ANONYMOUS

Strategic choices have wide-ranging ripple effects through the organization. They determine the key success factors, dictate the programs and projects to initiate and continue, define the skills and resources to mobilize or acquire, and shape expectations for profit and growth performance. In short, they give meaning and direction to the myriad activities of the business. Yet without effective implementation the clearest strategic thinking will be for nought—mired in functional conflicts, ill-conceived programs, budget overruns, missed schedules, and poor follow-through. The penalties are loss of confidence, missed opportunities, diminished capabilities, and poor performance.

While strategy guides implementation, it is equally true that implementation has a steering effect on the strategic choices. No strategy is so prescient that it can anticipate all eventualities and opportunities. Instead, there must be enough latitude to permit wide-ranging adaptation and learning at the operating level where the changing market reality is continually encountered. These bottom-up experiments, initiatives, and adjustments, continuously made by informal problem-solving groups and ad hoc task forces, go a long way toward deciding the future strategic choices. As we'll see in Chapter 3, these inputs are a crucial ingredient to a robust planning process.

Some firms are consistently better at managing the process, making the right strategic choices, and ensuring superior execution. They can be contrasted with their lagging peers along two critical dimensions—each of which will be woven throughout the succeeding chapters. Winners are:

- guided by a shared strategic vision,
- driven to be responsive to market requirements and continuously strive to satisfy their customers.

THE ROLE OF STRATEGIC VISION

A vision is a guiding theme that articulates the nature of the business and its intentions for the future. These intentions are based on how management collectively believes the environment will unfold, and what the business can and should become in the future. Visions are not vague expressions of goodwill, but explicit systems about what it takes to succeed in the future.

Without a vision, and the leadership to rally others around the vision, the organization is likely to be reactive in its present arena and aimless in pursuit of new directions. One well-known strategy typology[12] calls them "Reactors" to highlight an organizational mind-set that dwells solely on how to protect past gains. A reactor's world is full of threats, while opportunities are filtered through a haze that is like glaucoma. New directions are pursued with little relish by individual contributors responding to customer requests, new findings in the lab, or preemptive moves by competitors. Broad-based encouragement for initiatives is hard to find since the organization lacks guiding principles to help distinguish between sensible moves that might support a future direction versus tangential undertakings that dissipate effort.

While there is abundant evidence that successful businesses are guided by a meaningful vision, it is unclear whether the losers suffered because they simply lacked a vision or were following a misguided vision. To avoid being misguided, however, there are four defining characteristics of meaningful visions: they are informed, shared, competitive, and enabling.

Informed. A vision must be grounded in a solid understanding of the business, and the ability to foresee how the forces operating in the market will change in the future. Here vision is equated with insight, of the sort that distinguishes Perrier from its competitors. Perrier has become almost a generic term for mineral water, by understanding that their business was neither water nor soft drinks, but natural beverages. This may seem a subtle distinction, but it has a profound impact on how the market is approached, and was missed by some formidable competitors including Anheuser-Busch and Nestlé, who have largely abandoned the market.

Shared. Visions will motivate organizations when they are created through collaboration, with the leader serving as the articulator and sponsor of the vision that emerges from the team's collaboration. The vision must reflect the leader's view of opportunities, values, and important trade-offs. However, as one CEO put it,

> Visions are more powerful when they are inspired by strong personal conviction and motivation. They are richer when they flow from an internal source that can constantly respond with different aspects of the vision as new and changing circumstances arise. And yet visions are powerless unless they are derived from and embraced by those individuals in the organization who will collectively achieve them.[13]

If the leader's vision is not accepted, the price is likely to be high. In fact, Charles Parry, who became CEO of Alcoa in 1983, was deposed because his vision was rejected by a deep-seated, conservative company culture.[14] For years Alcoa, the largest U.S. producer of aluminum, had suffered through boom-bust cycles in the industry. By the early eighties the combination of chronic excess capacity to produce ingots, and several state-owned competitors who were more concerned with job protection than profits, reduced profits to a break-even level. In response Parry articulated a vision of Alcoa as the preeminent producer of highly engineered alloys, using ceramics, composites, and plastics. His eventual aim was to derive 50 percent of revenues from nonaluminum markets. Unfortunately, Parry had already alienated most of his management with a series of shutdowns to cut costs and they were in no mood to fund diversification adventures with aluminum profits. Meanwhile the board, which generally endorsed the need to reduce dependency on primary aluminum, were uneasy with the 50 percent goal which had never been explicitly justified. They were further disenchanted with the logic of the acquisitions being proposed, and by 1987 withdrew their support.

Competitive. Powerful visions are also statements of intent that create an obsession with winning throughout the organization. By focusing attention on a desired leadership position, measuring progress against that achievement, and continually searching for new ways to gain competitive advantage, the actions and aspirations of the organization are given meaning.

Audacious intentions can be powerful, in light of evidence that they are often realized even when they outrun the current capabilities and resources. It is unlikely that so many Japanese firms like Honda, Matsushita, and NEC would have achieved global leadership had they been content to tailor their intentions to their resources of 10 to 15 years ago.[15]

Aggressive intentions are most likely to be realized when the target competitor has low aspirations, and is willing to concede its leadership position under pressure. This nearly happened to Caterpillar, when they suffered global losses of shares to Komatsu who had an avowed intent of "encircling Caterpillar." By 1986 Komatsu had gained 12 percent of the U.S. market, despite starting in 1970 with revenues that were only 35 percent of Caterpillar's and mostly from the sales of small bulldozers within Japan. But unlike many of its American peers Caterpillar intended to do everything possible to protect market share.[16] When Komatsu began underselling it by as much as 40 percent in the early 1980s the company cut prices heavily in markets around the world. Although some market share was lost, the company would have fared far worse had they not stood their ground. Their intention to maintain leadership by beating back Komatsu also benefited from the high quality of their product. By comparison with U.S. automakers, their machines had set the world standard for workmanship for decades.

Visions that merely strive to catch up to the competition and match "best" practices that are visible in the market are usually flawed and unproductive. The flaw lies in the transparency of the resulting strategic moves to competitors that have already mastered them, and are already preparing the next generation of moves that will continue to keep them ahead. Imitative moves are also unproductive because they won't create competitive advantages. This is not to say that efforts to rationalize product lines to improve global economies of scale, institute quality circles to improve quality, or follow the lead of other banks to institute "relationship" banking programs, are not worthwhile. But if all the energy of management is expended to reproduce the cost and quality advantages their competitors have already achieved, there won't be much energy left to devote to finding meaningful ways to be different.

Enabling. Visions flourish within organizations where individual managers have enough latitude to make meaningful decisions about strategies and tactics. These individuals are empowered to use the general framework articulated by the vision to decide which opportunities or threats to respond to, and which to ignore. They have confidence that they will not be second-guessed by their superiors, who realize they are unable to anticipate every twist and turn in the market environment and must delegate downwards.

MARKET-DRIVEN MANAGEMENT

Compelling visions are best nourished in market-driven organizations. While there are many views on what this means, all start with Drucker's original formulation[17] of the marketing concept as a general management responsibility. This concept holds that, "There is only one valid definition of a business purpose: to create a satisfied customer. . . . It is the customer who determines what the business is." While being customer-oriented is an essential condition it is not sufficient, for there has to be an equally intense emphasis on outperforming the competition. This keeps the business focused on well-defined market segments and the continual enhancement of their competitive advantages. Thus it pervades all the strategic choices made by the business.

The rewards that come from being market-driven are an integrating theme of this book. Virtually every chapter is a demonstration of why responsiveness to customers is a prerequisite to superior performance. Yet many firms continue to behave otherwise, by emphasizing internal concerns and short-term financial performance rather than long-run customer satisfaction.

Recently there has been a "rediscovery" of the marketing concept as firms wrestle with new or intensifying environmental challenges.[18] The growing acceptance of the need to be market-driven closely parallels the evolving role of the marketing function:

- Until the mid-1950s marketing was equated with sales. The marketer's job was to convince prospects to want what the firm could most readily produce.

- The 1960s and early 1970s was the golden era of acceptance of the marketing concept as the driving philosophy for a business. Volume, production, or sales orientations toward the market were seen as less profitable than satisfying the needs of attractive customer segments with appropriately tailored products. The role of marketing was seen as persuading the firm to have what the customer wanted—not the other way round.

- Throughout the 1970s the commitment to a customer-orientation waned, as strategic planning ascended in the favor of top management. Only retrospectively was it realized that these approaches to setting strategic direction were overweighted with top-down financial imperatives, and analyses of industry structures as guidelines to action. The main emphasis was on managing share, and allocating cash flows to conserve scarce financial resources. Even firms that had been market-driven lost their focus on the customer, and marketing was relegated to short-run tactical concerns.[19]

An unfortunate and costly side effect of the enthusiasm for strategic planning was a deflection of attention away from customer satisfaction as the main source of long-run competitive advantage and profitability. This lapse was adroitly exploited by off-shore competitors who invested heavily to bring new products and processes to segments that had been smugly underserved by domestic competitors. Indeed, much of the economic history of the eighties was shaped by the successful global conquests of Japanese and European firms and the efforts of American firms to redress their shortcomings and become market-driven. There are many manifestations of American resurgence, including greater emphasis on customer value through quality enhancement, leaner and more flexible organizations that are closer to their markets, a search for innovative strategies to combat competitive incursions—and ultimately the recognition that marketing is everyone's job.

SUMMARY: WHEN STRATEGY MATTERS

The need for a forward-looking competitive strategy, that specifies how a business intends to compete in its chosen markets wasn't always as pressing as it is today. When markets are stable or slowly evolving in predictable ways, and the rules of competition are accepted by all the players, it is possible to prosper with a trial-and-error approach. This puts a premium on maintaining programs and activities that seem to be working and dropping those that have stopped working. In effect, the business is reacting to events, and the strategy is only understood after the fact by looking for consistent patterns in the stream of decisions taken piecemeal through the year.

The implicit assumption of a reactive strategy is that the organization can adapt faster than the environment is changing. This was never a very good assumption, but is increasingly dangerous in light of the intensifying forces impinging on competitive markets:

- markets are fragmenting, and traditional boundaries are blurring,
- previously self-contained national markets are being transformed into linked global markets,
- competitive advantages are harder to sustain as product life cycles shorten, and global competitors contest more markets,
- supply gluts further intensify competitive pressures by giving customers more bargaining power,
- customer relationships are changing as customers reduce the number of suppliers and information technologies permit closer links,
- new market opportunities are being created from demographic and life-style changes, technological changes, and rising environmental concerns,
- old organization arrangements are suffering at the hands of more agile, entrepreneurial specialists.

Three ingredients are necessary for a business to successfully steer a strategic course through market turbulence and become proactive in shaping events and competitive behavior to its advantage. The first is a strategic vision or theme that articulates the nature of the business and focuses the energies of all parts of the organization toward the task of outperforming the competition. The second ingredient is a market orientation in which the beliefs and values that pervade the organization emphasize the need to put the customer first. Finally, a successful business needs a robust process for formulating and choosing the best strategy in light of the issues facing the business. The next three chapters deal with the design and cultivation of planning processes that will yield effective strategies.

TWO

Strategies
for Competing

S trategy is like trying to ride a bicycle while you're inventing it.
—IGOR ANSOFF

Strategy is a very elastic term, with so many meanings in common use it has almost lost meaning. But if we didn't have the term we'd have to invent it, for it gives purpose and direction to organizations. A strategy is both an explanation of the pattern of past actions, and a guide to future initiatives and programs. The emphasis is on guidance, for good strategies are not detailed prescriptions for dealing with all conceivable eventualities and contingencies. Turbulent markets are simply too unpredictable and efforts to codify everything usually result in rigidity and myopia.

What is needed from a strategy is a statement of direction that serves as a central theme guiding and coordinating functional actions. We are seeking a compass, not a detailed road map. The metaphor is telling, for a compass-user needs ingenuity and teamwork in overcoming unforeseen obstacles and exploiting unanticipated opportunities that open the way to a destination. Road maps give detailed instructions that are of little use when the topography is unknown or fast-changing.

This chapter is designed to give meaning to the concept of strategy as *integrated actions in the pursuit of competitive advantage.* We will examine both the anatomy and pathology of strategy: what has to be considered in a meaningful statement of strategy, and how a superior strategy can be distinguished from one that is flawed. The next two chapters deal with the planning process that yields an effective and adaptable strategy. Later chapters will put these ideas to work and argue the necessity of a pervasive market-orientation if winning strategies are to be conceived and implemented.

Throughout this book we will be concerned with business strategies executed by strategic business or market units (SBU's). These are organizational units that compete in well-defined markets: they serve distinct *customers* with close families of *products* or *services* and have distinct sets of competitors they are trying to surpass. They are strategically autonomous to the extent the management of an SBU has control over the key factors that determine success in their served markets. This means the management can be assessed on how well they used the resources of the business, and held accountable for the performance results—good, bad or indifferent.

SBUs are not completely independent or stand-alone entities. They function within a *corporate context* that ties them to the parent with an umbilical cord of resource flows, financial and human resource policies, operating controls, and the broad corporate direction or mission. They may also share assets, including plants and warehouses as well as functions such as pooled sales forces, with sister businesses. This corporate context will be left in the background until we come to the question of negotiating the objectives.

Strategy in Layers. The top layer of a business strategy is a core statement of direction that guides the detailed tasks of converting management intentions into specific actions. To be useful the core of the strategy should include the following:

- a *business definition* that describes the market arena where the business has chosen to compete (especially the customer needs to be satisfied, the technologies used to satisfy these needs, and the customer segments to target), the scale and scope of activities in the value chain, and the channels to be used to gain access to the market arena
- the *strategic thrust* that specifies how the business intends to gain and sustain a competitive advantage and the pattern of investments and cash flows that will be required to support the strategy
- the *objectives,* which are commitments to performance results the business team expects to achieve in the future.

The top layer is necessarily general and long-term. The core of the strategy should not be shifted every year unless circumstances are drastically altered and basic assumptions have to be abandoned. The layer below this core gives further meaning to the basic strategic direction, by detailing the supporting functional strategies—from R&D, to manufacturing, distribution, sales force, pricing, and so on—as well as new product development programs and major investment projects such as new plants or systems

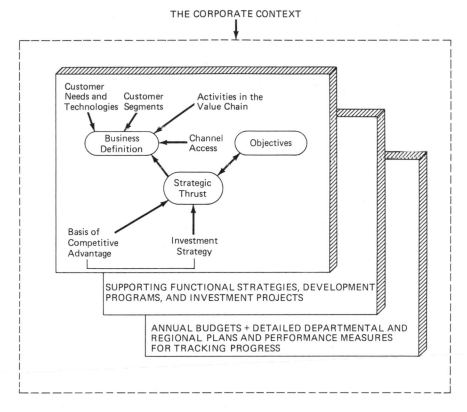

FIGURE 2–1 Elements of a Competitive Strategy

modernization. At this second layer the emphasis is on specific actions where expenditures of time, money, and energy will have the greatest leverage on the strategic thrust. This will only happen when the myriad elements of the functional strategies reinforce rather than contradict each other. The third and lowest level is the detailed tactical planning, including budgets and planned activities for the coming year. The three stacked layers are shown in Figure 2–1.

Strategies as Integrated Actions. Otis Elevator (a division of United Technologies) illustrates the benefits of clear thinking about strategic direction.[1] The essence of their strategy is revealed by two managers who observed

"... our business is moving people and materials horizontally and vertically over relatively short distances"

"... when elevators are running really well, people do not notice them ... our objective is to go unnoticed."

Otis Elevator serves two closely related markets: the design, manufacture, and installation of elevators, escalators, and moving sidewalks, and the subsequent service of the equipment. Otis competes with technological leadership (they were first to incorporate microprocessor controls to dispatch elevator cars according to load), high reliability due to superior quality, and a superior service force. These attributes offer significant benefits to customers who willingly pay a premium for Otis equipment and service.

Elevator sales are very cyclical, going up or down depending on the building cycle. Servicing of the elevators, however, is both stable and profitable. Manufacturers often take low margins on the sale of an elevator to lock up the initial elevator service contract. This means they usually win 60 to 80 percent of the service contracts for new elevators they have installed. However, as the building ages and competition for tenants increases, the cost of service looms larger to the building owner and subsequent contracts are likely to be given to the lowest bidder. Most low bidders are local companies offering an acceptable speed of response to a call for service, especially during the sensitive, "trapped-in-an-elevator" emergency.

To regain an edge over the small local service companies Otis capitalized on its size and investments in technology to enhance the quality of its service in two areas of prime importance to customers:

- speed of response to call backs (the time it takes for the service mechanic to arrive after being called). The problem in the past was their reliance on commercial answering services; all service companies were using the same answering services and they often lacked a sense of urgency in forwarding requests for service. To overcome this problem Otis developed a dedicated customer service center with 60 dispatchers responding to incoming calls on dedicated lines and quickly finding service mechanics. The result was a much faster and more accurate response.
- minimizing callbacks. Otis estimated that reducing the number of callbacks to a building by one per year would mean a saving of $5 million annually. More important, out-of-service elevators were irritating to customers and eroded their perception of service quality. One solution was remote elevator monitoring where a microprocessor on board the elevator transmitted performance information to a central computer that could identify potential problems and then dispatch a mechanic to prevent the problem.

This was a winning strategic move for the service business. The new technology was proprietary and tied the customer to the company, while reducing the costs of delivering the service. The advantage Otis gained over the small players was large and sustainable. Substantial investments in dedicated systems, hardware, and software were needed, along with training and deployment of central dispatchers and cooperation across many functional areas. The glue that held the new strategy together was a shared strategic thrust, dedicated to differentiating Otis on the basis of performance attributes that were important to their customers.

BUSINESS DEFINITION

A favorite question for management consultants to ask of new clients is "what business are you in?" Thoughtful answers are a good starting place for a productive strategy dialogue. On the other hand, if the answer is a superficial description of the product line, or—what is more likely—the management team can't agree on the answer, a problem has already been identified.

Why is the business definition regarded as the foundation of a strategy? First, it reveals the *true function or purpose* of the business. This is why business definitions are sometimes called mission statements (a term we prefer to reserve for the corporate parent). If we follow Peter Drucker,[2] who argued the only purpose of a business is to "create a customer," there has to be an explicit recognition of the ways the business satisfies the needs of its target customers.

A company making noise abatement materials and coatings for heavy machinery decided it was in the business of "protecting people's hearing from noise." This definition created more problems than it solved, for now it was not clear whether the business intended to expand its offerings to include noise protectors (ear muffs) for workers, or offer devices to test compliance with noise standards. Each definition implied very different resource requirements and customers to serve.

Second, the business definition *sets the boundaries of effort* and the horizons for growth. This is the arena in which the business wants to compete. For Snap-On Tools, this arena is narrowly defined as hand tools for professional mechanics, a market reached by direct sales to the work location: factory, garage, or machine shop. Most of their competitors, such as Sears, Roebuck, serve a broader array of customer segments through retail or direct mail channels.

The business definition is also *the starting point for strategy development*. A change in business definition may trigger dramatic changes in strategic thrust, resource allocation priorities, performance indicators to watch, and places where profits are taken.

Some years ago Courage Breweries in the U.K. was mired in a sagging, oligopolistic brewing industry with excess capacity and declining profits. They broke away from their competition by redefining their business from the brewing of beer to being a seller of beer in English pubs.[3] Under either definition the assets, products, and markets were virtually the same. The new strategy required a shift from a supply-side emphasis on producing and delivering beer, with pubs simply a conduit for the output, to a consumer's life-style mind-set emphasizing the experience in the pub, with beer only one of the ingredients of that experience.

Multidimensional Business Definition. A useful definition helps an organization break away from an internal orientation, that emphasizes the characteristics of the products or services being offered, to reveal what the business does for its chosen customers. To aid this shift in perspective it helps to portray the business definition as a set of choices along four dimensions:

- *Customer needs.* We start here on the grounds that customers satisfy their needs or solve their problems by seeking a package of benefits, rather than the products or services themselves. The usage situation or application the customer has in mind will shape the pattern of benefits that are sought. Manufacturers then provide a package of functions, including augmented services, to deliver these benefits. This opens up a host of questions that help clarify where the organization has chosen to compete. If we make adjustable speed controls, are they going to be used for all applications regardless of size and precision? and what kinds of environments (toxic, abrasive, dusty, or not)?

- *Customer segments.* A customer segment is a group of customers with similar needs, sharing characteristics that are strategically relevant. A business can elect to serve all possible customers, or focus on a distinct and protected segment within the broad market. Geography is one of the most difficult choices. Many firms limit themselves to regional or national markets because of resource constraints or freight cost and perishability considerations. Tariffs and other impediments to international trade may also constrain the geographic scope.

- *Technology/materials.* A technology describes one way that a customer need can be satisfied, or a function performed. A discrete product is the consequence of applying a technology to a customer need. Often a generic need can be satisfied by several technologies. Customers with a need for a 1/4″ hole will normally use a metal twist drill, but some segments are finding lasers or high-pressure water jets to be a better solution. Companies that refine cane sugar wrestle with this question often. Their product is a sweetener, but the needs of soft-drink and candy manufacturers for sweetening can be satisfied with sugar made from corn (fructose), or sugar beets. Depending on market conditions these alternatives may be cheaper. Should they offer all sweetening materials?

- *Activities in the value-added chain.* The fourth dimension poses the question of the appropriate scale and scope of activities. How far forward toward the end customer or backward to the raw materials and components should the business participate? Some businesses do everything from start to finish: Xerox makes or sources all components to its own designs for copiers, does the assembly manufacturing and all sales and service. Some of Xerox's competitors are simply assemblers of standard components and rely on distributors to sell, install, and service their copier. Included with this dimension is the choice of how to access the market—the communication and distribution channels—and whether they are owned by intermediaries or the firm.

A display of the scope of the business, along the three most relevant dimensions, is a valuable aid to strategic thinking. As a framework for communicating assumptions about the scope of the business it can cut down the areas of disagreement within the management team, and helps ensure that energies are not dissipated on pursuing different definitions. Figure 2–2 shows such a display for Otis Elevator, without the fourth dimension of value-added activities.

Business definitions tend to evolve slowly as the organization expands its capabilities to serve new needs or related market segments, develops or acquires new technologies, responds to changing customer expectations, or matches competitors' offerings. They are most likely to be reviewed when performance is lagging, new competitors are emerging, or a change in senior management leads to questioning old beliefs or conventional wisdom. Rather than wait for trouble, it is better to recognize that evolutionary expansions or contractions in business definition have profound strategic implications and that the current definition may reflect only an uneasy compromise in the continuing trade-off between the benefits of breadth versus narrowness of scope:

- a broad definition along the customer segment dimension usually achieves manufacturing cost advantage, but may fragment the sales, distribution, and service activities if the differences in needs across segments are significant.
- a broad definition of the business along the customer needs dimension, with the intention of offering integrated systems, runs the risk

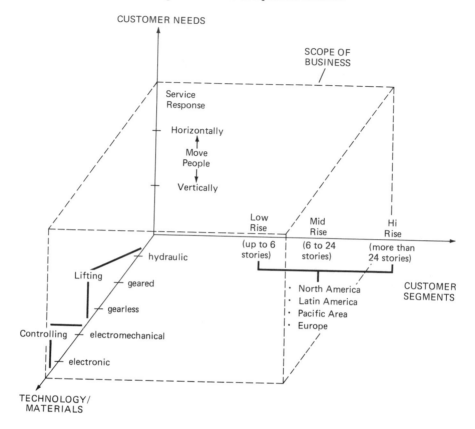

FIGURE 2-2 The Dimensions of Business Definition: Otis Elevator

that technological and manufacturing resources will be spread thin, leaving the business open to attack by a narrowly specialized competitor.

These trade-offs are a reminder that the questions of where to compete and how to compete cannot be separated. For the moment, however, we are going to fix on one business definition, and look at how the business competes within that arena.

STRATEGIC THRUST

High-performing businesses are distinguished by all seeming to have a compelling theme that knits together otherwise independent activities and focuses the energies of functional groups on things that matter in the market. The essence of these themes is a shared understanding of why the business is better than the competition, and what has to be done to keep in front. Otis Elevator parlayed their technological resources into superior service response and preventative maintenance to reduce elevator failures—attributes that customers appreciated and were willing to pay a premium to secure. To gain and hold this advantage management had to invest substantially and then commit to ambitious performance objectives. Taken together, the competitive advantage and the pattern of investments allocated to build, hold, or harvest these advantages direct the thrust of the strategy into the served market.

COMPETITIVE ADVANTAGE

Competitive superiority is revealed in the market as some combination of superior customer value and lowest delivered cost. These generic positional advantages are derived from relative superiority in the skills and resources the business can deploy. These in turn are the consequence of past investments made to enhance the competitive position. In practice most firms put greater emphasis on one dimension over another, because the skill and resource requirements may be quite different. Superior profit performance, however, requires that the firm be perceived as offering superior customer value to its target market while holding a cost advantage over the competition.

Superior Customer Value. A business is differentiated when it is perceived as superior on attributes that are important to customers. Superior value is created when the benefits these customers derive from this superior performance are worth more than the price premium they have to pay.

There are a myriad of ways to favorably distinguish a business or its products. Providing superior service, utilizing a strong brand name, offering innovative features or providing superior product quality are some of the favored routes. Thus Procter & Gamble is regaining lost share in the disposable diaper market with a new super-absorbent contoured model; Salomon has gained a dominant position in the market for ski bindings with a stream of innovations such as step-in bindings that meet the needs of average rather than expert skiers, and Digital Equipment Corp. has enhanced its position in the microcomputer market with an artificial intelligence system that dramatically reduces the time required to fill orders and increases accuracy. This view of differentiation goes beyond physical product attributes to embrace all activities and linkages of the business, including the kind of comprehensive support that Salomon provides its dealers to ensure they actively promote the superior features of their boots and bindings.

Lowest Delivered Cost. An overall edge is gained by performing most activities at a lower cost than competitors. NUCOR has achieved an enviable steel cost position by making extensive use of scrap metal instead of iron ore and producing all its steel by the efficient continuous-casting method, to eliminate the intermediate step of making ingots.

This strategy can also be focused on a distinct market segment. For example, Fort Howard Paper uses only recycled pulp, rather than the more expensive virgin pulp, to make toilet paper and other products. The quality, however, is only acceptable to the away-from-home market such as office buildings, hotels, and restaurants—so the company doesn't try to sell to the home market through grocery stores.

A cost leader must be able to offer at least a parity product, in order to achieve above-average profitability. If the product or service is perceived as poor quality, or deficient on important attributes, the customers will demand a price discount that may offset the cost savings. So long as an average price can be obtained for the standard or no-frills product, the low costs will be translated directly into higher profits.

The pursuit of competitive advantage is given lip service by most firms—it is viewed as a "good thing to have." Yet there are relatively few competitors within each market that have been able to hold a profitable advantage. For the rest, the processes of competition quickly eat away at their transitory edges. Effective response is impeded by uncertainty over what advantages have been gained, how long they can be sustained, and by what means they can be enhanced. These issues are at the heart of this book, and will be dealt with in detail in Chapters 5 through 8.

INVESTMENT STRATEGY

A business with a differentiation advantage doesn't have to extract all the extra value it has created for customers by asking a large price premium. Instead it can choose to shrink or even eliminate the premium to increase market penetration and customer loyalty. The price might even be set low enough to discourage competitive entries. The trade-off is between taking profits now or building a long-run market position. Conversely, a weak business that lacks discernible cost or differentiation advantages, while living off the momentum of past investments in customer relations, might push for higher prices. They may also cut back on spending on R&D, human resource development, and promotion, where the payoffs are long-term. These harvesting decisions make a deliberate trade-off in favor of short-run profits and cash flow at the expense of erosion in the future market position.

The broad choices of build, defend, or harvest market position are guided by an investment strategy that specifies: (1) the requirements for funds needed to achieve the competitive advantage, and (2) the outcomes expected from the allocation of these funds. These funding requirements are determined by the patterns of anticipated cash flows the business has negotiated with the corporate parent. There are many possible patterns; the following boxed insert describes the most common categories.[4] In the next two chapters, we will look at the process for negotiating the investment strategy and the corresponding objectives.

INVESTMENT STRATEGIES
(arranged in descending order of need for investment funds)

a. *Invest to enter.* Here, resources are allocated to enter a business segment that is new to the company. This might mean a separate unit or may be undertaken within the structure of an existing unit. When a new market is being created, the investment requirements and corresponding risks are especially large.

b. *Invest to build.*
 aggressively
 gradually

A business or segment in this category uses resources both to expand the market and to enhance or gain a leadership position. The rate and breadth of building may be aggressive with a view to preempting competition, or may be more gradual to moderate the risk exposure.

c. *Invest to rebuild.*
 aggressively
 gradually

This investment strategy is indicated when the goal is to reestablish a leadership position that has been allowed to erode. These "catch-up" efforts are often costly, especially if results are expected soon.

d. *Build selectively.* In this category, the goal is still overall growth, but the investment will be highly focused in selected areas in which

---

differential gains can most readily be obtained. The business may be expected to fund the necessary investments from current earnings.

e. *Protect current position.* This thrust implies taking aggressive steps to maintain a strong position but not to grow any faster than the market. Depending on the competitive and technological turbulence and rate of growth of the market, the investment demands may be substantial.

f. *Selectively manage for earnings.* Here, the business will limit and focus its investments on a few specific segments, with the priority given to maintaining and improving current earnings.

g. *Harvest.* Investments in these businesses will be limited, with the emphasis on generating maximum short-term cash flows. Modest harvesting is typical of leaders in maturing and declining industries in which competitive pressures have abated or stabilized. Harvesting can be rewarding because it contributes cash and profits that can be used elsewhere.

h. *Exit/divest.* Here, managers conclude that their long-run problems overwhelm any promise of profits and wish to channel their efforts and resources elsewhere. This is normally a zero investment option, although selective investments may enhance the selling price.

PERFORMANCE OBJECTIVES

Objectives are not fate: they are direction. They are not commands; they are commitments. They do not determine the future; they are means to mobilize the resources and energies of the business for the making of the future.

— PETER DRUCKER

Objectives are desired and needed performance results to be achieved by a specific time. Because they are stated very specifically they are valuable for translating the general statements about competitive advantage and investment strategy into implementation tasks and programs. Objectives can be set for virtually all areas of performance of the overall business unit as well as the lower levels of cost centers, product groups, and teams within a group or department. Thus it is useful to think of a hierarchy starting with the broad objectives of the business and spreading down to increasingly specific short-term measures of performance at the lower levels.

Heading the list of objectives for a business unit is the creation of shareholder value. While this is widely accepted as a guiding principle for the overall firm, it has only recently been applied to the business or division level.[5] The rationale is straightforward; investors willingly invest in a firm only when they expect management can get a better return on their funds than they could on their own. But for the firm to reach this objective each business unit or division must make a proportionate contribution. This is estimated by discounting the forecast cash flows by the appropriate cost of capital. Here cash flow is net (after tax) profits plus depreciation, less investments in working capital and fixed assets.

In terms of specific performance objectives, the management team of a business unit that commits to a shareholder value creation objective is also committing to the component parts. These comprise the rate of profitability, in terms of gross and net margins, and return on assets utilized. The benefits and pitfalls of this approach to setting objectives and valuing strategies will be dealt with thoroughly in Chapter 13.

The drawback of purely financial targets is their remoteness from the actions in the market that actually create value. Profits and cash flows are the outcomes—not the determinants—of performance and cannot be managed directly. This also means that they have little relevance to most employees, because they can't see how their day-to-day actions influence the financial results. This certainly undercuts their motivational impact. This is why businesses have to translate their financial expectations into performance targets that can be more readily managed, as listed below:

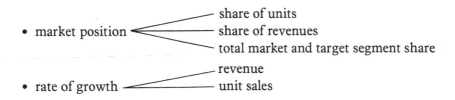

- market position
  - share of units
  - share of revenues
  - total market and target segment share
- rate of growth
  - revenue
  - unit sales

- customer satisfaction (overall as well as for individual attributes)
- reliance on new products or new markets (usually expressed as the percent of sales from new offerings in the next five years)
- risk exposure (proportion of sales from a specific product, market, or customer)
- cost reduction (overhead as a percent of sales)
- accounts receivable (days outstanding)

As a rule of thumb few businesses can successfully strive to reach more than three or four performance objectives in a planning period without creating confusion. Thus, the election of the overriding objectives is a fundamental strategic choice.

Once these broad requirements have been agreed upon, they can be decomposed into finer detail. An overall objective of sales growth or market share gain has implications for each component of revenue: prices, sales of individual product types, sales by region or distribution outlet as seems necessary. Once a warehouse manager or regional sales manager sees what is expected of his or her department, then the necessary action plans and budgets can be put in place. This is not a one-way process, for it is obviously futile and usually counterproductive to ask the impossible. If the market doesn't exist or people can't be hired and trained in time, and these realities are ignored when the objectives are set, the resulting aspirations will be ignored. At the same time, setting the hurdles too low is equally self-defeating, for the organization will be functioning below its capabilities. Strategy formulation, and especially the setting of objectives, will be viewed in the next chapter as an iterative, trial-and-error process that requires inputs from all levels of management.

ATTRIBUTES OF A SOUND STRATEGY

The premise of this book—and an article of faith among strategists—is that the acid test of a proposed strategy is whether it will gain a competitive advantage.[6] This belief is well-founded, for companies that have maintained a return on equity (ROE) of 20 percent or more for long periods clearly have something unique. It might be patents for pharmaceutical companies like Merck, Smith Kline Beckman, or Eli Lilly, a consumer franchise such as that "owned" by the *Wall Street Journal*, or the strong brand names of Kellogg's, Coca-Cola, and Maytag. However, a sound strategy has many other attributes. Their role is revealed through the tough questions typically used to review a business strategy—to help decide whether it should be funded, and reveal where changes have to be made.

The lessons of failure usually teach us more about the attributes of a sound strategy than those of success. If this is so there is a lot to learn from the demise of the Workslate portable computer.[7] The initial reception left no doubt this was an outstanding product and there were no direct competitors in sight. The designers had managed to package a powerful small computer into a shape the size of a piece of letter paper and one inch thick.

Soon after introduction the Workslate appeared on the covers of three major computer magazines, was featured in the American Express Christmas catalog, and touted in various mailings. One computer retailing chain forecast they could sell everything that could be made. When the company saw this reception it made ambitious plans to sell 100,000 units in the first year, at a retail value of $90 million.

The first cracks in the plan emerged when the project ran into production difficulties. The company, Convergent Technologies, a manufacturer of workstations for large computer suppliers, was unused to large-volume production of standard units. As a result, the factory soon fell a month behind schedule and missed most of the Christmas season. Lack of production wasn't the real problem; customers weren't buying what was available. In fact, it wasn't clear this was a consumer product that could be sold as an ordinary personal computer. Unfortunately, the company used a totally new sales force to reach a mass market consumer, and ignored the existing sales network of business sales teams and distribution that might have delivered steady sales. Confusion was also created in the market by frequent price changes; starting at $900, the retail price soared to $1,300, but soon dropped to $1,100 in face of buyer resistance. It appeared the accountants were responsible for the price hikes after they discovered that even at the most optimistic production levels it was not profitable at a unit price of $900. Costs were high, because of very high expenses, including 50 engineers in the R&D budget.

Despite the excellence of the Workslate product, the prospects for implementation of the strategy were never good. What kinds of questions should have been asked to help reveal these problems and possibly avoid a crippling $15 million write-off?

EVIDENCE OF SUSTAINABLE ADVANTAGE

The first question that should have been used to probe the Workslate strategy—and must be asked of any proposed strategy—is whether there is an effective match of the competencies of the business with the threats and opportunities in the environment. The purpose of this question is to see whether there is a basis for a competitive advantage that is sustainable in light of probable competitive moves. Will that advantage be gained by achieving the lowest delivered cost, or offering superior customer value?

The Workslate product was clearly superior to anything the competitors had, and the edge was likely to last as long as any computer product. The problem was that the Workslate team believed deep in their hearts that the excellence of the product would sell itself to all comers. This belief is sel-

dom warranted, no matter how good the product, but is especially dangerous when it obscures the need to take the product to the right market and
distributors. Because neither the Workslate team nor the parent management had ever dealt with retail chains they didn't appreciate the lack of
match between what their product could do, and the needs of the market
they were trying to reach.

Other useful questions about sustainability include:

- Will the strategy put the business in a position to ward off known
  threats, exploit opportunities, enhance current advantages, or provide new sources of advantages?
- Can the strategy adapt to a broad range of foreseeable environments—
  is it robust, or only likely to work under specific conditions of inflation, industry demand, and currency relationships?
- How difficult will it be for competitors to match, offset, or "leapfrog" the expected advantages?

These questions give the flavor of the kind of probing a strategy must be
given. In subsequent chapters these questions will be expanded in the context of the process that yields the strategy.

An assertion of advantage—or even rave reviews of product excellence—
is not a sufficient test of the soundness of the strategy. The assertions must
be valid; that is, grounded in reliable and thorough evidence of advantage.
This is so vital an issue that we will devote most of Chapter 6 to the question of how organizations come to know their advantages.

Are the Assumptions Realistic? Choices among alternative strategies are
among the least structured of all decisions a manager must make.[8] To cope
with this ambiguity assumptions are made about how competitors and
markets will respond, costs will behave, and how well the organization can
implement the programs. These assumptions are pieced together from informed judgments, analyses of historical patterns, forecasts, and other bits
of evidence that either confirm or refute the assumption. Seldom is there
hard data on which to rely, and different members of the management team
may have very different assumptions that reflect their particular vantage
point and experience.

How can sound assumptions be distinguished from faulty, uninformed
guesses? One must be especially vigilant for assumptions that are accepted
as conventional wisdom, but have never been thoughtfully examined or
cannot be justified in light of past events or probable trends. Whenever a
major departure from past performance is anticipated, it is important to ask
whether there is evidence to support the forecast. Exhibit 2–1 shows how

Exhibit 2-1 Testing Key Strategic Assumptions 1983–1987 ($ in million)

Sources of Change	Sales	Net Income	Key Assumptions/ Actions	Validity
Price increase	$23	$12	• 5.5% per year (inflation rate forecast = 6%)	• 7.6% increase in 1981 • 5.3% increase in 1982 • 80% industry capacity and Japanese threat • Simultaneous growth in share
Share improvement	$17	$4	• 31 to 34% in industrial segment • 20 to 27% in commercial segment	• 0.6% per year increase in 1979–1982 but with minimal price increase • Industrial segment is a high price sensitivity market • New products in the commercial segment are catch-up
Real market growth	$10	$2	• 7% per year	• 2% per year, 1980–1982 • 20% from unproven new market X
Cost productivity	$1	$1	• 3% per year	• 70% of annual productivity increase (3% per year, 1978–1982) was a single technical process breakthrough
Compensation		($12)	• 24% increase in head count	• 1983 head count same as 1980 with 10% less volume
Total change	$51	$7		

this was done in the case of a proposed strategy for an industrial components business that forecast an increase of $51 million in sales and $7 million in net income between 1983 and 1987.

The first step in the validity test is to isolate each of the assumptions about the reasons for the forecast changes. For example, sales and profits were expected to benefit from a combination of price increases close to the rate of inflation, real market growth of 7 percent per year in the forecast period, and substantial share gains in both market segments. The next step is to evaluate the evidence used to support each assumption. Here the basis for the assumptions about share gains and real market growth appears especially tenuous. How can any share gains be realistically justified when the new products in the commercial segment do not appear to offer a competitive advantage, and the business is trying to hold prices in the industrial segment close to inflation while countering potential Japanese competition? On this evidence, one has little confidence the proposed strategy will deliver the promised results. New evidence has to be provided and the forecasts adjusted to fit market realities and reflect trade-offs between conflicting performance objectives.

Vulnerability: What Are the Potential Risks? The promised advantages may be unappealing if they expose the business to excessive risks. The overall level of risk reflects the vulnerability of key results if pivotal assumptions are wrong or critical tasks are not accomplished. For example, an aggressive build strategy that increases investment intensity also elevates the break-even point. This makes the strategy alternative more sensitive to revenue shortfalls than a "manage for current earnings" strategy.

Overall risk reflects the combined threats from *environmental* uncertainties (can competitors match, offset, or leapfrog the prospective advantage? will the target customers respond as anticipated? will the government regulations be more restrictive than expected?) and the *internal* ability of the business to implement the strategy. Both sources of risk proved too much for the Workslate computer. Either would have crippled the undertaking; in combination they were lethal.

PROSPECTS FOR SUCCESSFUL IMPLEMENTATION

Three conditions must be satisfied before a strategy can achieve the promised results or avoid ignominious failure.

Feasibility: Does the Business Possess the Necessary Skills and Resources? If not, is there time to acquire or develop them before the window of opportunity closes? Financial resources (capital funds or cash flow requirements) and physical resources are the first constraints against which a strategy alternative is tested. If these limitations are so restrictive that undertaking a strategy would actually jeopardize the competitive position, then the strategy has to be modified to overcome or live within the constraint or perhaps be rejected. Imaginative solutions may be necessary, such as innovative financing methods using sale and leaseback arrangements or the tying of plant mortgages to long-term contracts.

The next constraints to be tested are access to markets, technology, and servicing capabilities. Do we have adequate sales force coverage? Is the sales force capable of the selling job demanded by the strategic alternative? Is the advertising effort likely to be sufficient? What about the cost, efficiency, and coverage of the present distribution system—including order handling, warehousing, and delivery? Are relationships with jobbers, distributors, and/or retailers strong enough that they will support the proposed new strategy? Negative or uncertain answers should trigger a search for modifications to overcome problems, and may lead to eventual rejection of the strategy. Clearly, the Workslate project failed these tests.

The most rigid constraints stem from the less quantifiable limitations of individuals and organizations. The basic question is whether the organization has ever shown it could muster the degree of coordinative and integrative skills necessary to carry out the change in strategy. Any strategy that depends on accomplishing tasks outside the realm of reasonably attainable skills is arguably unacceptable.

Supportability: Do the Key Implementers Understand the Strategy and Are They Committed to It? A broad-based commitment to successful implementation requires two conditions:

- The premises and elements of the strategy must be readily communicable. If they are not understood, then not only will the strategy likely be flawed, but its capacity to motivate support will be seriously compromised. A good strategy is one that can be easily understood by all functions, so they are are not working at cross-purposes. For this reason a good strategy is one that can be adequately explained in two or three pages.

- The strategy should challenge and motivate key personnel. Not only must the strategy have a champion who gives it enthusiastic and credible support, but it must also gain acceptance by all key operating personnel.

If managers have serious reservations about a strategy, are not excited by its objectives and methods, or strongly support another alternative, the strategy must be judged infeasible.

Consistency: Does the Strategy "Hold Together?" To achieve consistency there should be minimal conflict within each level of strategy, and between the levels. The first question is the fit of the elements of strategic thrust with the supporting functional strategies. Table 2–1 is an example of how the functional elements might mesh with the alternative investment strategies. This chart was developed by a manufacturer of process equipment to aid in testing the suitability of individual functional programs.

The second level of fit is concerned with the couplings among the functional strategies. Without an acceptable degree of fit at either level, effective coordination cannot be achieved. The obvious price is management energy needlessly devoted to organizational conflict and functional "finger pointing" to shift blame. A less obvious price is the diffused and uncertain impression of the business in the market. The customer has the best view of the inherent contradictions in the strategy—a quality claim contradicted by shoddy packaging, or a service-intensive selling program without the essential back office support to expedite deliveries and troubleshoot problems.

The "consistency test" is seldom pivotal in that few strategies are conclusively rejected for inconsistency. But it can be useful in improving and refining the strategy to ensure that all elements are pointing in the same di-

Table 2–1 Alternative Functional Strategies

	Investment Strategies				
FUNCTIONAL ELEMENTS	*Invest/ Build*	*Selectivity Growth*	*Maintain/ Protect*	*Selectivity/ Manage for Earnings*	*Harvest/ Divest*
Product Design	Lead, Differentiated ....Cost Reduction				
Product Line	Proliferate ....Prune				
Pricing	Value Oriented, Build Experience .... Generate Margin				
Distribution	Exclusive, Selective .... Margin Oriented				
Promotion/ Sales	Create Demand, Capture Share.............................Least Cost				
Service	Quick Fix, Applications.................................. Only for Profit				
Technology	Innovate...Minimum Necessary				
Costs	Pursue Scale Benefits .... Ruthless Cutting				
Capacity	Lead Demand ....Divest for Utilization				
Inventory	Anticipatory ....Minimum Response				
Risk	Accept, Contain ....Avoid				

rection. This test may also indicate that the degree of change necessary to bring the elements into line is simply not feasible with the available resources. Functional managers can only cope with a few changes simultaneously while trying to maintain continuing operations. Thus it may not be possible to upgrade old product lines, enter new markets, modernize the costing system, and build a new manufacturing plant all at once.

SUMMARY: THE PAYOFF FROM A SOUND STRATEGY

The new theology of strategic management has been succinctly captured by Jack Welch, the CEO of General Electric, in his idea of a good manager: "Somebody who can develop a vision of what he or she wants their business, their unit, their activity to do and be. Somebody who is able to articulate to the entire unit what the business is, and gain through a sharing of the discussion—listening and talking—an acceptance of the vision. And [someone who] then can relentlessly drive implementation of that vision to a successful conclusion."[9]

A sound business strategy is an articulation of a vision. It provides identity and direction by specifying how a business intends to compete in the markets it wants to serve, and the results it wants to achieve. The formal statement should describe: (1) the business definition, (2) the strategic thrust, comprising the basis of competitive advantage, and the investment strategy that specifies the funding sources and uses, (3) the specific performance objectives, and (4) the functional strategies and programs to support the basic strategy.

The soundness of a competitive strategy depends on how well it can satisfy the following tests:

Test One: Will the strategy as described, create and maintain a competitive advantage, through some combination of lowest delivered costs, or superior customer value?

Test Two: Are the assumptions valid?

Test Three: Is the strategy vulnerable to unacceptable environmental and internal uncertainties? Can these risks be avoided or contained?

Test Four: What are the prospects for successful implementation?

- feasiblity?
- supportability?
- consistency?

The fifth and final test asks whether the forecast financial results are acceptable compared to the probable risk. Ultimately there must be evidence that the business will eventually enhance shareholder value. Lack of acceptable results will cool enthusiasm for funding the strategy and trigger a search for another strategy for the business. However, a forecast of substantial creation of economic value cannot be taken as an automatic endorsement. There is no alternative to persuasive evidence of competitive advantage, for this is what produces the profits and revenues.

Processes for Developing Market-Driven Strategies

THREE

Making Strategic Decisions

*S*trategy: *good luck rationalized in hind-sight.*

—EDWARD DE BONO

Planning means designing a desired future and identifying ways to bring it about.

—GEORGE STEINER

How are strategies actually developed? The quotations suggest two possibilities. One is that strategies are the *deliberate* consequence of an analytical "top-down" process of matching opportunities with capabilities. This is the strategic planning model, so fashionable in the 1970s. The alternative view posed by de Bono is that strategies *emerge* from piecemeal, interim responses to events over which management has little control.[1] These events may be threats from new competitors, unexpected shortages of materials, production problems, or technological improvements that offer opportunities for new products or new ways of reaching the market. Eventually the pattern of "bottom-up" actions and reactions taken by those closest to the situation coalesces to reveal a change in overall strategy.

Both approaches are needed if a business is to successfully adapt. A top-down, deliberate strategy imposed unilaterally on lower levels of an organization seriously limits the possibilities for learning and may be badly implemented if the assumptions and objectives are not understood or accepted. But solely bottom-up strategies that emerge from a series of incremental moves are no guarantee of success either—especially when the environment is changing rapidly. The pace of change may be too leisurely, the elements of the strategy that finally emerge may not fit together into a coherent whole, and the resulting strategy may leave the business poorly positioned against more aggressive competitors.

An adaptive planning process combines the benefits of deliberation with the need for flexibility and organizational learning. The framework for this process is the familiar sequence of steps taken to cope with any ill-structured problem. Start with *intelligence* (the situation assessment), then *design* the possible responses (develop alternatives) *choose* the best alternative, and *implement* the decision. Flexibility is added to this tidy, linear sequence by: shifting the focus of planning activities away from the process to the issues and projects that have been uncovered, broadening management participation in planning activities, treating objectives as negotiated outcomes rather than as the starting point, and continuously tracking performance against objectives and assumptions. These and other practices come from the trial-and-error experience of managers who have learned to subordinate the mechanics of planning to the need to keep adapting to shifting and unpredictable competitive markets. The rest of this chapter builds on this theme.

APPROACHES TO STRATEGY DEVELOPMENT

An experienced but cynical management consultant claims the number of possible ways to plan is some multiple—greater than one—of the companies that have tried disciplined approaches. Recent research suggests the seeming variety is illusory. Most approaches have an affinity to either a "top-down," command mode, or a "bottom-up," incremental mode. Yet his point shouldn't be ignored, for many companies follow both these extreme approaches to planning at the same time, but at different levels in the organization. This is a sure recipe for confusion and inhibited strategic responses. The point of adaptive planning is to have the top-down and bottom-up influences complement rather than contradict each other.

The directory publishing subsidiary of a large telecommunications company recently hit a serious impasse because of conflicting planning approaches. The managers of the subsidiary were aggressive incrementalists. One feature of their strategy was the introduction of new services to help their mid-sized, local, or regional space advertisers do a better job of attracting and retaining customers. There were lots of ideas for these services that the managers had seen in other markets or were testing in various local markets. They were confident these new services would add an additional 12 percent to their revenues within five years.

On the corporate level there was unwillingness to accept this growth objective, on the grounds that the strategies weren't clear, the profit potential hadn't been documented, and it wasn't clear the sales force could sell the new services. Top management felt the subsidiary should be concentrating on earnings from the existing business, instead of being distracted by new directions. This was both galling and demoralizing to the managers of the subsidiary who wanted a stretch growth objective so they could begin to commit resources to testing and launching the new services. Both sides of the controversy have good points, but this will not ensure either a productive strategy dialogue or the selection of the best strategy. Before this impasse can be resolved we need to understand how the two approaches to planning contributed to this problem.

THE TOP-DOWN COMMAND MODEL

Command strategies are devised by a few visionary thinkers at the top— led by the CEO as chief architect—and handed down to the lower echelons for implementation. This model assumes that there is time for exhaustive analysis before taking action, that the CEO and the planning staff have the necessary information, and that the lower echelons are waiting for their orders from above. As Richard Leam, president of the Scott Paper Co. tissue-products operations described the company in 1985, "We used to make all the decisions from Philadelphia: here's the strategy, you guys figure it out."[2]

This autocratic approach to planning was given a boost during the era of strategic planning that lasted through the 1970s. Senior managements of diversified firms were preoccupied with managing a capital crunch in a slow-growth, inflationary setting marked by numerous discontinuities. Typical was the plight of General Electric, competing in a range of businesses, including jet engines, computers, nuclear power, electronics, and plastics; each with a prodigious need for cash the company lacked. Their emphasis necessarily shifted to sorting out winning businesses from losers that were draining cash, and consolidating strong competitive positions. The main tool for guiding these choices was a portfolio matrix that displayed all businesses in terms of their market attractiveness and competitive position. Depending on where a business was positioned, there were well-defined strategic options to consider.

The era of strategic planning left a number of positive contributions to planning practice. Organizations were sensibly formed into SBUs with control over the strategic factors that affected their performance, SBU objectives were tailored to reflect differences in their profit prospects (instead of every division or unit having similar objectives), and the explicit understanding of competitors' strategies and intentions became a high priority. Indeed, the whole premise of this era was that finding an unassailable competitive positioning within a favorable industry envirionment was the recipe for success. Strategic change then could be based on the promise of projected results.

The top-down command model still works in the right conditions.[3] (1) the company or business should be in a steady state situation, where good execution of a few key variables is important, (2) the CEO either wields a great deal of power, perhaps because of an authoritarian style, or the proposed strategy poses little threat to the managers who will have to implement it, because the results won't challenge their values or cause layoffs, (3) the appropriate systems are in place to support the proposed strategies, and (4) it helps if the business is in a strong financial position with slack resources it can mobilize.

The Attack on Strategic Planning. By the mid-1980s top-down strategic planning was in disarray: line managers either tolerated it or dismissed it as irrelevant, the strategic actions often couldn't be implemented, and the intrusions of strategic planning were widely resented. Many companies enthusiastically dismantled their planning groups. What happened?

- the necessary conditions of stability that made a command approach feasible were out of step with the turbulence most businesses were facing;
- the fuel for strategic planning is valid and timely information. But in fast-moving markets the filtered information about new market opportunities or nascent threats may be obsolete or biased before it can be fed into the top-down decision process.
- companies found that the simplistic prescriptions of the planning tools, such as portfolios, experience curves, and "changing the game strategies," were often misleading or wrong. Frequently the premises did not hold true. The largest market share did not always assure the most profitable position; the risks of high growth markets eroded their attractiveness; and portfolio position wasn't necessarily a guide to cash flow.

The most damaging attacks were directed at the absolutist assumption that strategy and creative energy were the prerogative of the CEO and the planning staff, and the results could be forced downward. Instead, as Quinn and others[4] found, strategy was often the result of individuals below the top championing an initiative. Studies of innovation[5] uncovered lower-level managers who resisted or flouted company policy to bring about strategy changes. There was growing recognition that top-down planning didn't tap the contributions from informal problem-solving groups close to the market or operations.

The influence of bottom-up strategic decisions and initiatives was given further credence when the "real" story of Honda's success in the U.S motorcycle market was reported.[6] The strategy was brilliant in *retrospect:* Honda was the low-cost producer, and used its dominant position in Japan to buy entry into the United States. They expanded the traditional macho market for big bikes, by identifying an untapped leisure segment for smaller bikes. Remember the advertising theme, "You meet the nicest people on a Honda" that appealed to this segment. Honda's advantages with the group were sustained with aggressive advertising and pricing. The payoff was a 50 percent market share.

The *reality* of Honda's entry was a story of miscalculation, mistakes, and serendipitous events. They started with the wrong product, pursued the wrong channels, and tried to straddle all segments with their advertising. But instead of doggedly pursuing the big racing bike strategy favored by the company president, Honda adapted to the market as it emerged. In fact, a relatively junior sales director in the United States was given the latitude to overturn his bosses' preference and pursue the "Nicest people" campaign. An openness to learning and a long-term commitment to the market counted for more than the original flawed analysis of the opportunity.

Fixing the Command Model. By 1985 Scott Paper was well on its way to transforming the command approach to strategy that had mired the company in mediocrity. In their core facial and toilet tissue market they had suffered a 20-year slide in share from over 50 percent to the mid-20s. On one side they suffered from P&G's aggressive marketing campaigns for its branded products. Low-cost producers such as James River Corp. put added pressure on the price-sensitive segments. As a result, Scott's products were perceived as too expensive to be bargains, but not good enough for the quality segment.

To turn the business around the company began to look for strategies from the lower echelons, who would then have a stake in them and push them up the hierarchy. Incentives were changed, from rewarding people for what they owned, toward recognizing their contribution to performance. Eleven layers of management were compressed to seven, partly by eliminating "coordinators" who served to link different functions.

Many companies have since followed Scott Paper in hopes of smoothing the hard edges of their command approach and overcoming deep-seated implementation problems. The pattern of moves is now familiar. First, planning is asserted to be a line responsibility, so once-powerful strategic planners are relegated to support positions within the business units. Next, there is much talk of vision, and the need for empowerment of individuals.

On a more practical level, group interactions are structured to encourage functional managers with divergent points of view to offer their ideas during the regular planning process.

These are useful steps on the road to improving the health of the planning process, and especially the quality of information and thinking about the implications of strategic alternatives. These moves do not necessarily result in "true" collective decision making, for senior managers often cannot or will not relinquish their control over the strategy. Their subordinates soon see past the rhetoric and realize they are not true contributors to the strategy dialogue. Not surprisingly, their commitment and enthusiasm for the strategic direction are suspect.

THE BOTTOM-UP INCREMENTAL MODEL

In this approch to planning the strategies emerge from incremental decisions made during the constant tinkering, experimentation, and learning found at the operating level. The strategy is only fully understood after the fact by trying to find the pattern that characterizes these decisions.

Incremental strategies change slowly through a series of small steps that appear as remedies to immediate problems. Supporters of this approach believe it is the only sensible way to cope with complex problems, since managers cannot see very clearly into the future, cannot grasp all the variables encountered in a major decision, and cannot imagine in advance all the possibilities for improvement.

Each increment of change—which might require decisions as big as entering a new market, redesigning the incentive compensation, or exploiting a technological breakthrough—is designed to be acceptable to the organization, so later resistance to change can be avoided. When trade-offs are demanded by a decision, their resolution is guided primarily by shared values and beliefs about what is appropriate. As a result, there is a "company way" of doing things that shapes the strategic thrust. Broad commitment to a major decision is obtained when the probable results fit the prevailing values and beliefs. If it is believed the best way to compete is by entering small, emerging market segments with unique high-value, high-feature products, then an aggressive volume-oriented penetration strategy that emphasizes low costs will be rejected.

Strategic change becomes more difficult when there is no overriding set of beliefs or strategic vision that serves as a touchstone. Then trade-offs require bargaining by all the functional groups involved. The test of a decision is whether it advances the self-interest of each functional group. This means overall values are superseded by the incentives each group is working toward (volume for the sales force, scrap rate or cost for production, and working capital reduction for finance). This is a sure recipe for functional conflict and an unfocused strategy. No one sees the results of the compromises and conflicts more clearly than the customers whose needs are subordinated to organizational imperatives.

The Limits of Incrementalism. Bottom-up planning thrives when the foundation of shared beliefs meshes comfortably with the environment and the organization is prospering. Under these conditions there is little pressure to examine the underlying assumptions, and consider the long-run consequences of competitive moves and environmental trends. The result is that firms tend to stay too long with a winning product, and delay the pursuit of new markets and technologies to take its place. There is little impetus to drive costs down, or impose painful programs to improve productivity in all functions.

When all the initiative is taken by small operating units that are close to markets it becomes very difficult to control and coordinate their actions. This is why Hewlett-Packard has found it difficult to develop an integrated line of computers, peripherals, and communication devices for the office market; each of the discrete products within the company was designed to stand alone and satisfy very distinct customer requirements.

The stresses within incrementing businesses start to build when the strategy drifts out of touch with the market, and performance noticeably deteriorates. Only when the problems are serious and obvious will there be pressure for change—but then there is no centralized mechanism for forcing needed changes to come about. In the meantime, the bargaining mechanisms that worked so well when times were good and resources abundant can't cope with scarcity and retrenchment. Incrementalism, with its gradualist horse trading is not well suited to periods of turbulence, with multiplying sources of competition and pervasive uncertainty. Seldom are the limitations of incrementalism more clearly revealed than in the plight of Avon Products described in the following boxed insert.

BOXES VERSUS BUBBLES

The differences between the incremental and command planning approaches are striking, but not surprising in light of current thinking about organizational change. The command model clearly fits the box metaphor[8] used by Hurst. *Boxes* are the hard-edged, rigid structures that give rational meaning to strategy. By contrast, *bubbles* have flexible, transparent boundaries that can easily expand and join with other bubbles. "In the hard box the leadership model is that of the general who gives crisp, precise instruc-

AVON PRODUCTS: WHEN THE MAGIC FAILED[7]

For 94 years Avon Products single-mindedly focused on the Avon lady as the fulcrum of growth. She was the representative of one of the most efficient distribution systems in the world. Her job was to turn a home or office into a showroom for a diverse product line that ranged from beauty and health-care items to accessories, novelties, and confectionery. Every two weeks all the representatives were sent a new catalog to show their prospects; only one catalog served all the United States. Manufacturing was activated and scheduled according to the catalog, to keep inventories to a minimum. Representatives delivered and collected payment every two weeks and the robust cash flow was not diluted by granting credit.

Growth was determined by additions to the number of representatives. By 1979 there were a record 401,000 reps theoretically covering one half the 80 million households in the United States. That same year the growth magic failed for the first time; as only one-third the planned increase in representatives was achieved. With redoubled efforts the revenues grew, but profits sank sharply. By 1983 Avon stock lost two-thirds of its value. Clearly bottom-up incremental efforts were not going to stem a tide running strongly against the strategy.

The new management team arrived in late 1983 to find the inability to add representatives was only a symptom of other deep-seated problems.

First, the firm had lost sight of its ultimate customers, and had not focused on such trends as: changes in discretionary buying patterns, working wives, inner city crime, shrinking household size, growth in competition, and the emergence of novel distribution patterns.

Second, the strategy of one product line, at one price, with one catalog was out of touch with the proliferating segmentation of regions, ethnic groups, and life-style groups. As a result suntan preparations were withdrawn in August; so Avon was out of the Sun Belt market for more than half a year. The products themselves were often poorly received—consumers felt the makeup line was shoddy, and the packaging was below par.

Third, turnover among representatives was swelling, because pay had lagged behind the competition of Mary Kay and Amway. Among those that remained, productivity was low. Twenty percent of the reps accounted for fifty percent of sales.

Finally, the strategic thrust was shot through with conflicts and confusion. The most obvious split was between a strategy of merchandising anything that would sell, and marketing branded products with distinct images to well-defined markets. Merchandising managers responsible for preparing the bi-weekly catalog would cut prices set by a marketing manager, in order to generate interest among the representatives, and the profit goals for the product would be missed. There was further confusion as to whether the competition was other direct sellers like Amway and Tupperware or cosmetics firms like Revlon and Estée Lauder.

In the next chapter we will see how top-down leadership, exercised within an adaptive planning framework, was able to resolve the internal schisms and inconsistencies while coping with a changing environment.

tions as to who is to do what and when." In the soft bubble a high degree of mutual trust and understanding allows groups to develop a shared vision, that can be translated into a common purpose.

The differences between the two models are highlighted in Figure 3–1.[9] They are better viewed as the extremes of a continuum of approaches. The propositions about the differences owe more to anecdotal evidence than empirical testing. Nonetheless, the weight of insight into the implications of market strategy by the "masses" versus strategy devised by the few is compelling. The differences go beyond those aspects we have already isolated to also influence organization structures, controls, systems, and other means of implementation.

Of special importance to the choice of market strategies is the prevailing "mind-set" toward competitive markets. The top-down view is more attuned to broad generalizations about the industry, with special emphasis on the actions of competitors, prospects for new technologies, and alternatives to the channels through which the market is reached. Judgments about competitive advantage are competitor-centered, made on the basis of direct comparisons of cost and performance with closest rivals. The view from the bottom-up is more customer-oriented. Strategies are formed by those in closest contact with the customers, who are sensitive to their shifting needs and responsive to requests for better performance or new features. While closeness to the fine-grained realities of the market is admirable, it is not a good idea to get too close and lose sight of the broad patterns of change. A balanced view invariably gives a clearer picture.

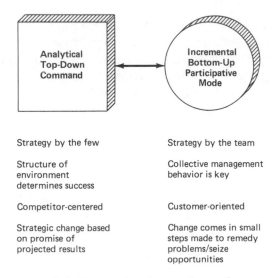

Strategy by the few	Strategy by the team
Structure of environment determines success	Collective management behavior is key
Competitor-centered	Customer-oriented
Strategic change based on promise of projected results	Change comes in small steps made to remedy problems/seize opportunities

FIGURE 3–1 Contrasting Approaches to Strategy

THE (MIS) BEHAVIOR OF PLANNING SYSTEMS

Despite incessant complaints from managers that their planning systems stifle the creativity that is the essence of strategy, they persist in using excessively routinized systems that are burdensome, time-consuming, and geared to short-run budget preparation.

In this bureaucratic approach to planning the responsibility for designing and coordinating the process is assigned to the corporate planning staff. They prepare a set of open-ended forms that ask each business to describe its strategy, environment, competitive position, and past performance. Another detailed form asks for financial projections for the next three to five years. This form gets more serious attention, for this is clearly a prelude to the detailed budgeting for next year. This belief is reinforced by setting the usual date for the forms to be completed at some time in the early fall, just before annual budgeting is due to start.

The planners often don't spend a lot of time on the answers to the strategic questions, for they are not in a good position to challenge the answers. Unless the business is clearly in trouble the staff will accept what the business had prepared. One consequence is that the businesses feel they can get away with a perfunctory update of last year's submission.

The planners can do much more with the financial projections. They consolidate the earnings numbers and then add corporate charges and financing costs to generate an overall company forecast. The inevitable shortfall in profits below what corporate managers need to meet their short-term targets, and keep the stock buoyant, causes distress. After a series of hurried negotiations between top management, planners, and operating managers, a compromise is reached. Finally a consolidated strategic plan is assembled. These are better called "confederation" plans, for they are no more than a pile of individual business plans.

The most obvious weakness is the reliance on operating management for the raw financial data. But these managers are advocates of their own position, and can't make informed judgments about investment opportunities outside their business. Since everyone knows the corporate financial standards, even the weakest business units feel compelled to submit projections showing they will eventually reach satisfactory returns.

Compromises are hard to make in this system. Since business unit managers have to stake out their position first, they commit early to a plan and spend their time buttressing their arguments as advocates of that plan. Compromise means giving up projects that are now important to them; and causes resentment and disruption. Since most companies have a separate capital budgeting system to screen individual projects, the advocates of the projects make sure they exceed the hurdle rate. As one manager commented, "No matter how high the hurdle rate is set, any good manager will be able to get the numbers to come out right." He went on to say that the problem was premature focus on the project rather than whether the project makes strategic sense.[10]

The net result for many companies is that their weak units are allocated too much capital while the best opportunities are underfunded, because the financial forecasts don't discriminate their relative attractiveness. A further flaw is the loss of cohesion and integrated vision for the entire company. The strategy for the company is simply the sum of the parts, because the raw data and proposals are originated by the business units.

ADAPTIVE PLANNING: INTEGRATING THE APPROACHES

Neither the top-down command mode nor the bottom-up incremental mode satisfies the need for a business to continually adapt to changing and ambiguous markets. One mode is too remote from the operations realities and can't provide for functional management involvement that yields strategies that can be readily implemented. The alternative lacks sufficient capacity for major changes before it is too late. In order to cope, firms with a tendency toward one of these extremes try to borrow features of the other.

But usually these are "quick fix" efforts to solve an obvious problem, without a broader concept of how they should be combined. A fully adaptive planning approach seeks to integrate the best features of both approaches. When they converge to achieve maximum planning effectiveness one is embedded within the other, as in Figure 3–2.

Adaptive planning has four distinguishing features:

- top-down guidance that offers a motivating *vision* that realistically challenges the management team, and ensures that adequate financial *resources* are allocated to realize the promise of the chosen strategy. This support is dependent on persuasive evidence the strategy will enhance shareholders' value.

- bottom-up inputs on the *opportunities* and *threats* facing the business, based on thorough understanding of the customer's requirements, channel behavior, technological realities, and competitive setting. These inputs are incorporated into the roster of *issues* the business team is managing on a real-time basis.

- an *integrating theme* around which the analysis and dialogue between levels is structured. To avoid having operating managers limiting their concerns to tactical, operational decisions, and the corporate management dwelling on global concerns, to the point where the two levels are talking past each other, both must keep their focus on the

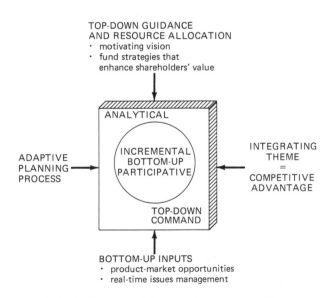

FIGURE 3–2 An Integrated Approach to Strategy Development

competitive position of the business and the sustainability of the *competitive advantage.*

- a flexible and adaptable *planning process* to manage the interactive learning.

The big question is: how should an effective strategy develpment process be designed and managed? The trick is to balance the overall responsibility of the CEO and general maanger of the business to provide strategic direction with the need to give up control to encourage strategic opportunism and commitment.

The best planning processes are initiated by a challenge from corporate management that is designed to have the business team think broadly about the current situation and prospects for improvement. Without this stage-setting the planning activities may simply be viewed as another step on the way to developing next year's budget.

The responsibility for developing the initial strategy proposal is left to the multifunctional business teams. The line managers, who will have to accept and carry out changes in direction and new programs, meet under the leadership of their general manager to debate and resolve their strategic issues and decide which options for strategic action they want to propose. This is followed by a tough-minded corporate review of the assumptions and options identified by the planning team, as a prelude to making re-source commitments. This is not the "show and tell" strategy review found in many companies, with elaborate presentations of a strategy advocated by the business team followed by perfunctory questioning. Instead, these reviews occur during the shaping of the strategy and concentrate on defining mutual expectations and flagging potential problems so later surprises are minimized.

Adaptive planning often forces changes in managerial roles. If strategy development is to be the province of line managers, then corporate staff planners should become facilitators and integrators rather than doers. In this type of role the most effective planners are senior line executives on rotation. They bring expertise and credibility no professional planner or consultant can match and they also learn to be better general managers. Such a shift in responsibility works only when the line managers are properly prepared. But many companies have not provided the right support and training.[11] As a result, strategic planning is seen as just another burden imposed from above. Some line managers have lost the responsibility for planning by doing a perfunctory job, which meant staff planners had to step back in and fill the void. What managers need is process facilitation, and coaching in the skills necessary to guide strategy debates. They want to know why it is important, what questions will be asked, and what challenges they should anticipate when their plans and options are reviewed.

THE BENEFITS OF ADAPTIVE PLANNING

Given the disenchantment with strategic planning, why should companies consider adaptive planning? What are the benefits from integrating top-down guidance and vision with bottom-up opportunity sensing, through the means of a flexible, issues-oriented process that encourages sound strategic thinking? Granted, these features are derived from the experience of successful companies who have learned the hard way how to make planning work for them. A skeptical manager is still justified in saying "show me" this isn't another fad sweeping briefly through management practice with little lasting value. Does an adaptive approach to planning demonstrably improve performance?

One answer comes from Waterman's[12] conclusions about planning in companies that have an ability to renew themselves, and outperform their peers:

> Planning includes communication, elements of control, ways to keep organizations and the people in them from doing dumb things, ways of embracing opportunity on the fly, techniques for generating data, schemes for asking "What if?" and getting sensible answers, means for reinforcing cultural values and a whole lot more. The last thing planning seems to do is cough out a plan that anyone takes seriously.

Some of these planning purposes are best served with bottom-up thinking, others by top-down guidance and vision, which means they may work at cross-purposes. An emphasis on top-down control constrains opportunity seeking, but too much undirected opportunity exploitation leads to random corporate direction. In the next chapter we look at how better balance among potentially conflicting planning purposes can be achieved. The balance is unlikely to ever be quite right, but the closer one gets the better the quality of strategic decision making and execution.

More concrete evidence of the payoff from adaptive planning comes from a recent study of 16 large diversified British companies. Three successful styles of managing through the planning approach were identified:

1. The "strategic planning" style is closest in spirit to a top-down mode. Within companies like BOC and Cadbury strategic objectives come from the top, and usually stretch the business unit managers to formulate more ambitious strategies than they would have considered on their own. Headquarters still reserves the right to have the final

say. This style is judged to be the most effective with organizations that are searching for a broad, integrated strategy across business units, where the focus is on developing a long-term competitive advantage. Thus BP has made large investments in minerals, coal, nutrition, and electronics that yield low immediate returns. The most noticeable drawback is the effect on line management motivation of having so many people involved in planning that the process becomes cumbersome and frustrating and they lack ownership of the final decision.

2. The "financial control" style is like the bottom-up incremental mode in that strategy development rests squarely with the business unit managers. Headquarters may not even review the resulting plans. Instead, they exercise influence through short-run budgetary controls. Specific targets for performance are designed to motivate managers to improve their financial returns immediately. Any deviations from target are watched carefully and negative variances provoke sharp questioning. This strategy is best suited to companies such as Hansen Trust whose portfolios are so widely diversified that corporate management can't be intimate with the details of the market. There are several shortcomings, including a bias against strategies with long lead times and paybacks. Because adherence to budget targets is so important, some flexibility is probably lost when operating managers feel constrained to stick to their plan and not pursue advantageous moves that open up unexpectedly.

3. The "strategic control" style shares many features of the adaptive planning approach we have been advocating as a way of gaining the advantages of the other two approaches while avoiding their weaknesses. Responsibility for strategy rests with the business managers. Corporate management uses far-ranging strategy reviews to test the logic of the strategy and encourage the business to raise the quality of the thinking behind the strategy. In a separate budgeting process they manage the resource allocations to maintain a balance between short-term financial results and long-term business building projects.

Courtaulds, Vickers, Plessey, and ICI have used this adaptive approach to clean up and restructure companies that once were in serious trouble. They all report it is difficult to manage the inevitable tensions between the need for central control and the desire to give the businesses responsibility for their decisions. Strategic objectives can be ambiguous, and managers may be confused about the targets on which they are being evaluated.

Table 3-1 The Payoff from the Planning Approach[13]
(Study of 16 diversified British companies)

	1981–1985 Performance	
	Growth in Assets/Year*	Increase in Return on Capital/Year
Top-down strategic planning	10%	−4%
Bottom-up incremental with tight financial controls	3.5%	−6%
Balanced or adaptive planning	5.0%	+20%

*Established business only (excludes acquisitions)

Although the integrated, adaptive approach is the toughest to manage, companies using it reported the most improved financial results—at least during the 1981 to 1985 period of the study (see Table 3-1). To some extent long-term growth and development were traded for these short-term financial gains.

SUMMARY: PLANS THAT CAN BE IMPLEMENTED

Strategic planning practice has come far since the formula-driven, top-down excesses of the seventies. These efforts were well-intentioned, and often helped top management regain financial control over unwieldy corporations suffering the shocks of the "Age of Discontinuity." However, the eighties brought new competitive challenges that soon exposed the inherent flaws of these systems. These challenges will continue to intensify through the nineties, and force firms to become more flexible and alert, to a degree once thought impossible.

Many approaches to strategy decision making have been tried during the past decade of dissatisfaction. From this trial-and-error learning have come broadly accepted guidelines for the proper conduct of planning. These have been collected here under the rubric of adaptive planning—an evocative term that describes organizations where:

- planning is accepted as a line responsibility, and planners are facilitators, coordinators, and knowledgeable resources.
- top-down guidance and leadership is exercised through the articula-

tion of an aggressive vision of what the business stands for, and how it intends to win in the future.

- there is informed participation of multifunctional teams responsible for setting priorities and managing projects to ensure committed and coordinated implementation.

- resource allocations are based on credible forecasts of the ability of the business to maintain and sustain a competitive advantage. The payoff is the creation of shareholder value.

The most distinctive feature of firms that know how to plan adaptively is their innate ability to learn from experience and seize opportunities ahead of competitors. A superior ability to apply sophisticated market knowledge and deep insights into the capabilities of the organization to make ongoing strategic choices is a competitive advantage. The next chapter deals with the management of strategy development processes with these attributes.

FOUR

Adaptive Planning

Once destiny was an honest game of cards which followed certain conventions, with a limited number of cards and values. Now the player realizes in amazement that the hand of his future contains cards never seen before and that the rules of the game are modified by each play.

—PAUL VALÉRY

It's difficult to look further than you can see.

—WINSTON CHURCHILL

The heart of adaptive planning is a process framework for organizing the myriad of information flows, analyses, issues, and opinions that coalesce into decisions. The framework also serves as a common reference point and shared vocabulary for the members of the planning team. This helps to integrate diverse functional viewpoints within a business, for managers who have participated in all the necessary judgments will have a clearer understanding of why a course of action was chosen. They are more committed to making the decision work, rather than obstructing its implementation because they neither understand nor accept the need to follow the chosen path.

An adaptive process is highly iterative, a reality imperfectly captured in the tidy, closed planning sequence in Figure 4–1. There are four essential stages in this process.

Situation Assessment. This stage begins with a look back to past performance compared to objectives. Substantial deviations from objectives—either positive or negative—by product type, market segment, or channel member, raise early flags of problems and opportunities. To understand

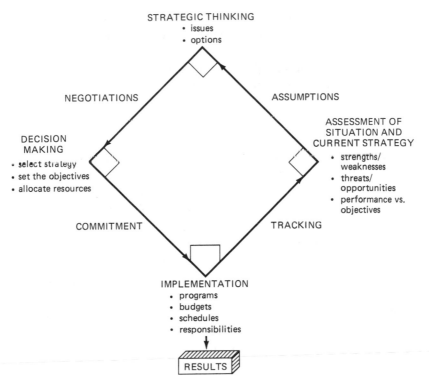

FIGURE 4-1 The Strategy Development Process

why the deviations occurred it is necessary to specify the realized strategy—based on the decisions the business actually took during the past year or so—rather than the planned strategy that may not have unfolded as hoped.

An essential ingredient is an explicit business definition that puts boundaries around the planning process. Within this context, the situation assessment identifies the external (threats and opportunities) and internal (strengths and weaknesses) factors that will influence performance in the future. The link to the next step is a set of assumptions, about the environment and prospects for the business, that have been tested for validity.

Strategic Thinking. Here the information from the situation assessment is put to work. This step requires a concentration of the energies of the business team on the few pivotal issues that absolutely have to be dealt with because they will have a major impact on future performance. The resolution of these issues begins with the generation of creative options for dealing with each issue, followed by analysis and choice decisions. This is an ongoing real-time activity, for the emergence of issues follows no fixed calendar and their eventual resolution may be quite protracted or highly compressed.

Adaptability requires keeping a balance between the continuity of effort needed to resolve a big issue versus the need to be open and flexible in sensing when new issues are demanding attention. Too much flexibility in dealing with new issues will diffuse the scarce energies of the management team, confuse implementation planning, and blur the strategic thrust. Yet it is impossible to anticipate all the major and minor shocks that will influence the choice of strategic options.

Decision Making. The strategic options for dealing with each issue are the raw material for an ongoing negotiation of objectives and resource requirements with corporate management. From these negotiations come the main *strategic decisions:* shifts in strategic thrust, choices of options, and allocations of resources in light of mutually acceptable objectives. Because performance objectives are negotiated in view of what is feasible (rather than being imposed from the top down), they are understood and accepted by the business team. The payoff is a broad-base commitment to decisions and performance expectations that can quickly be translated into action.

Implementation. These are the on-going activities that translate strategic decisions into programs, projects and near-term functional plans. Sweating the details of these action plans is important for good execution: time frames, allocations of responsibilities, resource needs and utilization (human and financial), and performance levels have to be specified while organizational obstacles are overcome. Such planning in detail not only fleshes out a strategy or project but gives a further test of feasibility.

The last step is budgeting, where dollar figures are attached to each revenue and expense-related activity. This is essential if the activities are to fit within the tight envelope of available resources. Budgets also set standards and provide benchmarks for comparing actual against expected performance. The tracking of deviations completes the process and begins the next round of planning activities.

Distinctive Features of Adaptive Planning. The skeleton of this planning process can be used to describe even the most rudimentary of planning systems,[1] whether driven from the top down or the bottom up. However, the surface similarities are deceptive, for there are many features that set an adaptive process apart from the prevailing mechanical versions that follow a fixed calendar as a prelude to an annual budget-setting rite in October and November. The emphasis here is on creative thinking and flexibility, informed by superior insights into the market, and a commitment to change. For this process to work properly it needs to be participative, involving all those with the responsibility to implement the decisions. Other features we will develop further in this chapter are:

- an emphasis on identifying and testing key assumptions in the situation assessment
- real-time issues management
- objectives as both a starting point and a negotiated outcome

SITUATION ASSESSMENT

Know the enemy and know yourself; in a hundred battles you will not be in peril.
 —SUN TZU *(circa 500 B.C.)*

If a principle of competitive strategy is to focus our strength against a rival's weakness, we should follow Sun Tzu and know our capabilities relative to the competition and how well they fit with the present and prospective environment. The scope of this situational enquiry embraces all the trends, forces, and conditions with the potential to influence the performance of the business. The outcome is a set of (hopefully) valid assumptions about the environment, competition, and internal skills and resources.

A standard structure for organizing the situation assessment is shown in Figure 4–2. The key distinctions are between the *external* factors beyond our direct control that present either threats or opportunities and *internal* factors that reflect our skills and resources. Whether these are strengths we can exploit, or weaknesses to overcome depends primarily on how we compare to competition: these are our competitive advantages or disadvantages. For this reason, direct competitors are placed in center stage in Figure 4–2 to provide both a threat and a reference point for strengths and weaknesses.

DIMENSIONS OF THE ENVIRONMENT

Each business unit confronts a unique blend of environmental forces, differing in intensity and meaning along many dimensions. The most pressing environmental realities come from the actions of customers, channels, and competitors within the served market. While most of this book is about these three dimensions, we can't ever lose sight of the broader macroenvironment in which markets flourish and decay. The dimensions of this

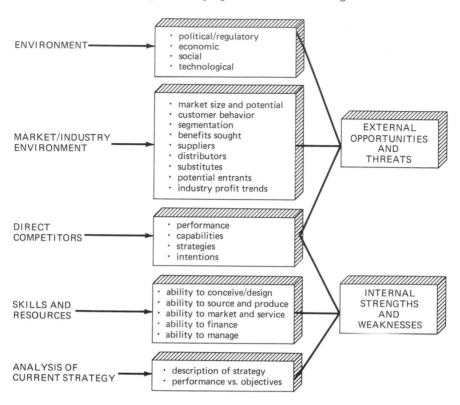

FIGURE 4–2 Overview of the Situation Assessment

macro-environment are known commonly by the acronym PEST: political, economic, social, and technological.

Political. This is the domain of regulatory oversight, legislative decisions, and administrative judgments such as interpretations of the tax code and legal opinions. The addition or removal of regulatory and legislative constraints can create new markets—as we have seen with the deregulation of trucking, communications, financial services, and air travel—or eliminate market opportunities with shifts in defense spending or trade policy. Global firms have a large stake in the political stability of the countries they source from or market to, and so invest heavily in political risk analyses to avoid surprises.

Economic. These forces range from the health of the general economy, in terms of GNP growth and unemployment, to the level of inflation. In a world of interconnected economies it is seldom possible to look only at a regional or national economy, so it quickly becomes necessary to understand the balance of payments and other influences on currency values.

Social. This dimension captures both cultural trends and demographic shifts. Culture is loosely used here to mean the values and beliefs of society that determine the life-styles, concerns, and habits of customers and employees. Demography includes age, income, education, work force participation, and geographic location. Demography often influences cultural values, and vice versa. For example, the shift of the U.S. population to the southwest has seen a parallel trend to political conservatism.

Technological. A business utilizes numerous technologies in all stages of its value-creating system. Some of these may be core technologies, on which the manufacturing process or product performance depends, while others are supporting technologies that facilitate information flows, while some are pacing technologies that may displace existing core technologies or promise new features. Technologies have limitations—that are constantly being overcome by research—and life cycles as they are displaced by new technologies. For example, in the computer-printer business, the pacing technology is ion-deposition, which threatens the still-growing fiber-optic and ink jet technologies, and may entirely displace the declining impact methods.

There are no formulas to guide the choice of environmental factors to consider. Instead, the specifics of the business will determine what is relevant. A consumer packaged foods company will give close attention to consumer trends, while being much less sensitive to the health of the economy than a capital goods producer. It is not always obvious in advance which trends will be influential in a market such as consumer goods. The main influences during the 1980s were:

- demographic shifts, including a record number of aging adults that are relatively more affluent and active;
- rapid changes in the structure of the nuclear family, as a result of delays in first marriages, an increase of 96 percent in the divorce rate within ten years of marriage, and the growing number of working women;
- shifts in values as consumers become preoccupied with maintaining their own economic and emotional stability and with finding personal, not social fulfillment.

General Mills[2] concluded these broad trends meant there would be increased concerns about the quality of food, nutrition value, physical fitness, and "naturalness." These trends held little promise for their traditional flour, cake mix, and frosting categories. On the other hand, shifts in food consumption patterns toward "grazing" or snacking, and away-from-home eating were good news for restaurants and snack foods responsive to these trends. Thus the company entered the market for "healthy," "eat-on-the-run" products such as granola bars. The lesson here is that the test of relevance for a trend lies in the consequences for future business performance—either positive or negative.

OPPORTUNITIES AND THREATS

Opportunities. These are anticipated events or trends *outside* the business that open up the possibility of improved performance if exploited.

The event or trend may suggest a new basis for competitive advantage: new features, new production processes, or new delivery systems. Otis Elevator exploited developments in information technology to tie their customers closer. Other changes may disable competitors. Competitors that have just undergone a leveraged buyout or mounted an expensive defense against a takeover are likely to suffer cash flow problems as they struggle to pay the interest on the debts they have amassed. Other opportunities are created as new market segments emerge. Avon Products saw and exploited a trend to the purchase of beauty products at the workplace, and by 1988 were getting 25 percent of sales from buyers at business locations. They gained access not only to customers but also to potential sales people, as many of their representatives are women who hold other jobs. Their prospective customers sit at the desks around them.

Threats. This is the dark side of the external world. A threat may impede the implementation of a strategy, often increases the risks and the resources required, and by eroding the sustainability of the present advantages will sooner or later reduce performance. When Avon undertook their situation assessment in 1984, they saw many *potential* threats: a decline in home direct selling, a maturing domestic market for cosmetics, fragrances, and toiletries, fewer representatives willing to sell door-to-door, and the emergence of direct mail competition.

Focusing the Environmental Assessment. Management teams find it easy to enumerate the threats and opportunities their business is likely to face. The result is a long laundry-list of environmental topics, trends, and possible events each marked by considerable uncertainty about timing and magnitude. Regrettably they are prone to dwell too long on the possible threats, and often reserve their most creative efforts for speculating on the myriad things that could go wrong, rather than on business-building opportunities. This is not a new phenomena. The English historian Edward Gibbon once observed, "There exists in nature a strong propensity to depreciate the advantages and magnify the evils of the present time."

What is needed is a procedure for sorting all the possibilities into a few that have real strategic significance, and directing scarce planning time to their consideration.

Step One: For each significant environmental trend make *assumptions* that are specific and have action implications. Examples:

- energy prices will remain soft and fluctuate between $16 and $21 per barrel for the next 3 years,
- there will be 30 percent excess auto production capacity in North America by 1992.
- video-conferencing will not noticeably reduce business air travel,
- a shakeout will continue among facsimile machine manufacturers, and only the top seven will survive.

If an assumption doesn't pose an obvious threat or opportunity, it probably lacks pertinence and can safely be put aside.

Step Two: Test the *validity* of each key assumption. What evidence is there to support the judgment about timing and magnitude of the trend? Speculation and surmise will not serve here; a push must be made to find corroborating evidence as to what the competitor is really doing, or whether a new segment is big enough to matter. This effort will likely surface disagreements about the probability of the event or trend actually occurring.

Step Three: Assess the potential short-run and long-run *impact* of each opportunity or threat, and isolate the few that are especially critical to the business. Watch carefully for those trends that can be a two-edged sword, such as new technologies that may threaten the base product but create opportunities to lower costs and expand the market.

Scenarios. When there are a few trends that are highly uncertain, and likely to have significant impact on performance, a valuable next step is to construct a few reasonable scenarios. These are alternative, theoretically possible futures, that differ in critical ways. Within each scenario the trends are considered together in an internally consistent package, rather than being treated separately.

Scenario construction is a well-developed art among large corporations coping with turbulent environments. Airlines had to resort to scenarios when the end of federal regulation had unpredictable effects on profitability. Traditionally their long-haul routes were the most lucrative; and new equipment provided an advantage. After deregulation shorter "monopoly" routes became the most profitable, and new equipment became an expensive capital burden for companies unprotected by fare and route regulation. This pattern only became clear after much turmoil and restructuring.

Scenarios are also useful for business units facing uncertain changes along key dimensions of their competitive and market environment. A classic example is the situation faced by the gasoline-powered chain-saw market in the 1970s.[3] At that time most buyers were professional woodcutters or farmers. These buyers sought durability and quality, and usually bought their chain saws from servicing dealers.

Three market trends were especially uncertain, each having the potential to reshape the competitive structure. These trends were: casual-user demand, the shape of casual demand over time, and the future mix of distribution channels. For example, casual-user demand (the extent to which nonprofessionals would buy and use chain saws) depended both on demographics, such as the number of households formed, and rising energy costs, which had already resulted in increased use of home fireplaces and wood stoves.

Scenarios were constructed from various combinations of three levels of casual chain-saw demand (in units); two possible shapes of the casual-user penetration curve (steady rise versus peaked); and dealer versus branded sales. Only mutually consistent combinations were chosen to construct three possible scenarios: two represented "polar" extremes and the third was an intermediate possibility. In one "polar" scenario the casual market didn't happen, and consequently the competitive situation was stable. The opposite "pole" foresaw high casual-user demand, and significant market penetration by private-label saws sold through nondealer channels. In this scenario success depended on acquiring a share of the casual-user segment and put a premium on low-cost design, marketing, and production. There might be a chance to concentrate solely on the professional market, but this strategy would run the risk of vulnerability to low-cost spillovers from the casual market.

Eventually a strategy has to be chosen in the face of uncertainty about the future. Because the optimal strategy varies with each scenario, one would like to find a robust strategy that minimizes adverse effects over the broadest range of scenarios. Alternatively, the mangers could elect the most probable scenario, try to remain flexible until the picture becomes clearer, or go with the scenario that best utilizes their competitive advantage.

STRENGTHS AND WEAKNESSES

Strengths are derived from superior skills and resources, that taken together give the business the ability to do more or do it better than the competitors. These are the "distinctive competencies" that can be used to exploit opportunities and parry threats.

At the time Avon's turnaround was being plotted, the new management team identified significant strengths they could utilize:

- an unmatched ability to manage direct selling systems
- a strong and identifiable consumer franchise
- a strong balance sheet, with a debt-to-capitalization ratio under 30 percent
- a research and development capability that routinely turned out 600 new or reformulated products each year.

Weaknesses are deficiencies or constraints that inhibit the ability of a business to outperform or even match competitors. Avon management identified their weaknesses as a heavy dependency on direct selling to the home, as well as an eroding beauty image and an inability to meet the needs of emerging segments.

A comprehensive strengths-weaknesses analysis should embrace all facets[4] of the business, including the following functional *abilities* to:

1. *conceive and design,* including marketing and technological research capabilities, patents, and design and funding available to support innovation.
2. *source,* in terms of assured access to raw materials, ability to manage a supply network, and achieve low input costs.
3. *produce* with respect to costs, quality, productivity, capacity and readiness to serve, and flexibility of manufacturing.
4. *market,* including coverage of the served market, knowledge of customers, breadth of product line, response to customers, ability to promote and advertise effectively, provide service and finance customers.
5. *finance,* which considers both sources and amounts of funding, the ability of the business to generate income, and the willingness of the parent to finance growth.

6. *manage,* including leadership; depth of experience in the business, planning capability, loyalty and turnover, ability to work as a team, and effectiveness of systems and controls.

A frequent shortcoming of these internal analyses is that often they yield an indiscriminate listing of possibilities that fails to isolate the few that are going to be important in the future. At its worst it is a vacuous back-patting exercise with little insight and few challenges to the status quo.

Why are these analyses so often unsatisfactory? First the judgments are often made without an explicit reference point, leaving one to speculate whether the so-called distinctive competencies are relative to the competition or to the other lesser competencies of the business. Second, there is often no distinction between what the business does well that is valued by the customer and skills and resources the customer does not value. Finally, the criteria for judging superiority often shift in midstream. One analysis[5] found that strengths were often justified on historical grounds, and seemingly reflected past successes. But when managers thought about weaknesses they took a different tack, and based their opinions on the kind of performance they should have been getting.

Judgments about strengths and weaknesses should be informed but not confirmed by history or "what should be." The proper standard is their influence on competitive advantages or disadvantages and the prospects for sustainability. Having a modern processing facility with abundant capacity is only an advantage when the competitors don't have something equally modern and can't match the costs. This notion is so important we will devote Chapters 6, 7 and 8 to the assessement and creation of competitive advantages.

OVERCOMING PITFALLS IN THE SITUATION ASSESSMENT

Let's dispense with one myth of strategic planning, that it requires a superior crystal ball. Better forecasts would be nice, but in a turbulent and uncertain environment they are hard to obtain. A better view of strategic planning—and especially of the situation assessment stage—is that it enhances self-insight and the ability to act on emerging trends and issues before the competitors can sense and react. Thus, information is a strategic advantage. It is also a very difficult advantage to secure. The relevant information is usually obscured by data of uncertain quality and vintage, that come in the form of raw, unprocessed bits of fact, opinion, and informed speculation. Furthermore, even the raw data are so widely dispersed throughout the organization that patterns and linkages are hard to discern.

A sales manager may have heard that a major off-shore competitor has acquired land for a new plant, and a manufacturing engineer may have seen their new equipment being built in a supplier's plant, but the two data points may not be connected until a response is too late. The likelihood of a comprehensive picture is further compromised by two shortcomings in the ability of managers to make sense of a complex environment.

Internal Orientation. In many businesses less than 15 percent of effective management time is directed to customers, while no more than 5 percent is devoted to thinking about competitors. The other 80 percent is spent on internal matters that only indirectly deal with customers or competitors. These estimates[6] are based on reviews of planning documents, agendas of meetings, logs of time spent in meetings, as well as on whether incentives were based on competitive performance results or internal factors like the scrap rate this year versus last year. The unavoidable conclusion is that most businesses don't focus enough on the two key elements that will determine success: customers and competitors. Most situation assessments can be faulted for the same reason. So many of the critical issues deal with the "internalities" of reorganization, production scheduling and capacity, cost containment, management development and compensation, and so on. The point is not that these aren't extremely important, but that the balance of emphasis is usually wrong.

What does an external orientation require? Three basic elements are: (1) a focus on the way customer needs are changing; (2) paranoia about competitors, which means "You don't just analyze them. You see a threat in everything they do. You must overestimate their strengths and you must overreact to their challenges"; and (3) staying ahead of customer needs. Another revealing test of an external orientation is a willingness to obsolete a successful and profitable product—before the competitor does it. By ignoring these basics Xerox missed the emergence of the small copier market segment in the early eighties. They also ignored the Japanese competitors when they first attacked, and hung onto the 660 model, which was their only low-end entrant, for two years after it was obsolete. By then it was less reliable than competitive products and twice the price. Xerox has since learned their lessons, with a resurgence in the copier market that earned them the title of *American Samurai.*[7]

The main weapon for overturning an internal orientation is a broad base of information from many different sources. This means directing the scanning outside the accepted scope of the business: what is happening with foreign suppliers and markets that might be precursors, what are the trends in the base technology, what are other businesses who sell to the same customer doing to adjust to their changing needs? The president of one Fortune 500 company routinely visits the top accounts and asks, "Who is your best supplier of all the firms you deal with? Why are they so good and what do we have to do to be like them." Unfortunately, he has learned that his firm is usually seen as big, arrogant, and inflexible relative to the best suppliers—who are usually smaller and committed to one line of products. These are deep-seated disabilities to overcome.

To gain real advantage with external information it may be necessary to go outside the usual sources that every competitor will see, to tap unconventional and protected sources. These might include on-site personnel to screen relevant Japanese technology, boards of advisers from other industries, competitor analyses by each functional manager, and so forth. There are limits as to how far to scan, that force a trade-off between the breadth and detail of information. Gluck[8] offers an apt metaphor, "It's a bit like an eagle hunting for a rabbit. He has to be high enough to scan a wide area in order to enlarge his chances of seeing prey, but he has to be low enough to see the detail—the movement and the features—that will allow him to recognize his target. Continually making this trade-off is the job of the general manager—it simply can't be delegated."

Unspoken or Unwarranted Assumptions. "It wasn't our plan that went wrong, it was our underlying assumptions." This is a common plaint of managers when they realize, yet again, that their carefully crafted strategies and forecasts have been undermined by dubious assumptions, or that major environment factors were overlooked.[9] The variations on this theme are endless. "We were assured that oil would remain at $28 a barrel and then prices plummeted." "We planned to have production from the new plant to solve our capacity limitations, and the contractors missed their schedule." "How could we know that its product would be banned by the EPA?"

No planning process can cope with the completely unexpected, but neither should it be susceptible to inadvertent omission or myopia. Matters of omission are best dealt with by ensuring the situation assessment is wide-ranging and comprehensive, and ideally guided by an outsider without a history of immersion in the conventional wisdom of the industry.

Myopia can be tackled by ensuring the environmental scan is externally oriented. But this will not prevent a tendency toward unquestioned optimism about the path of each environmental assumption. A bias toward optimism is inherent in the way managers' cope with ambiguity.[10]

- *Anchoring.* Decision makers tend to "anchor" on a particular outcome they believe will occur. This outcome dominates their thinking and suppresses consideration of uncertainties. As a result, downside risks are understated.
- *Selective perception.* There are several biasing elements here: People

tend to structure problems in light of their past experience (marketing people will interpret a general management problem as a marketing problem), their anticipation of what they expect to see will influence what they actually see, and as a consequence conflicting evidence will be disregarded.

- *Illusion of control.* Planning activities may give decision makers the illusion they can master and control their environment. At the same time, decision makers have a tendency to attribute success to their own efforts and failures to external events and "bad luck."
- *Availability.* Emphasis is usually given to facts and opinions that are easy to retrieve. Often these are hard data about past successes, which are given greater weight than soft assessments of future adversity. As a result, the ability of new competitors to gain market acceptance and penetrate previously secure markets is often underestimated.

Unwarranted assumptions are best tackled by bringing evidence against each stated assumption. Such a validity test was described in Chapter 2 for testing strategies, and can easily be applied to testing environmental assumptions for their impact and likelihood of occurrence even before the strategy is formulated.

A continuing problem is knowing which assumptions deserve attention, and which can be ignored. Managerial time constraints make it impractical to identify and test too many, which means most assumptions receive only a superficial glance without time for reflection on the action implications. The sorting of the critical from the merely interesting is best undertaken in the context of an issues management process when priorities for action are decided.

STRATEGIC THINKING:
REAL-TIME ISSUES MANAGEMENT

For every complex problem there is a simple solution that is wrong.
—GEORGE BERNARD SHAW

Issues are the main currency of the strategy dialogue, and a major impetus to deep strategic thinking. They are also the vehicle for mobilizing the concerns of individual contributors. When an individual's issue is accepted as an issue for the whole organization, that person has a better chance of achieving his or her own agenda for change.[11]

Businesses benefit in several ways by focusing on issues. Issues help concentrate the plethora of forces, problems, and uncertainties into manageable chunks. In this form they become focal points for decision making, and specify the needs for information collection and interpretation. Once all the issues have been properly framed, the full array can be compared in terms of their relative immediacy and impact. Then priorities can be set so only those few problems and challenges with a significant impact on future performance will be addressed. The focusing of scarce management time and energy on high payoff issues is probably the most compelling reason for adopting an issue orientation. No wonder management teams trying to spread their limited time across many issues, and seeing little from their dispersed efforts beyond frustration and unremitting fire-fighting, are quick to embrace a tool that better harnesses the collective energy of a management team.

Planning Cycles Are Not Budget Cycles. An important consequence of real-time issues management is the unhooking of strategic thinking from the rigidities of the budget cycle. Issues arrive and are resolved on a schedule that is dictated by the pace of events, not by the annual calendar.

The trigger for a scan of issues and sorting for potential impact may be the arrival of a new general manager or CEO, a serious downturn in performance, or a restructuring of the industry under pressure of deregulation, technological change, or new customer demands. In periods of turbulence, the identification and sorting of issues may have to be done once or twice a year. When the environment is stable and the strategy is on course, there may be no need to do this more often than every three years.

Experience suggests that when the issues resolution activities are distinct from the formalities of budgeting, the quality of strategic thinking improves. Conversely, when the planning process is obviously a precursor to the preparation of an annual budget, management attention is narrowed to short-run implementation concerns, rather than possibilities for strategic moves that play out over a longer time frame. Insightful strategic thinking is then made a prisoner of short-run pressures. We shouldn't encourage more myopia by designing systems that encourage bad habits.

IDENTIFYING AND FRAMING ISSUES

A strategic issue is a condition or pressure on the business, created by internal or external developments, that involves:

1. *possible outcomes* that will have a high impact on future performance;
2. *controversy,* in that reasonable people can take and defend different positions on how to deal with the issue; and
3. *strategic consequences,* since the resolution may mean implementing a change in strategy.[12]

Issues with these characteristics should be posed as questions, to make it obvious that a response is needed. "Inflation" is not an issue, while "the effect of inflation on our relative cost position" is an issue that demands analysis and action.

It is hard to overstate the importance of formulating the issue questions correctly, to facilitate the discovery of a solution. Suppose, for example, a business is persistently unable to satisfy its delivery promises. If we frame the question as: "What should be done to reduce late deliveries?" many answers will suggest themselves; work overtime, promise realistic schedules, build buffer stocks, and so on. But these are not solutions, they are remedies to symptoms. None of these responses will tackle the underlying strategic issue.

Digging deeper might reveal that the critical issue should be framed in the following way: "Should the business expand production capacity?" Different questions might be suggested by probing into other reasons for the late delivery problem. Whatever emerges should be in the form of a question ideally answerable with either a yes or no answer. If analysis suggests the answer is no, there isn't enough capacity, then a number of solution options can be explored. Big issues, such as, "How can we become more market-oriented?" need to be broken down to more manageable issues, under this broad issue umbrella.

RESOLVING ISSUES

A thorough situation assessment and review of past performance against objectives of a business unit in a complex, fast-moving market may uncover as many as 50 issues for the management team to consider. The richness of the array of issues can be seen from a sampling of the 43 issues surfaced in a strategy review for a major building materials manufacturer. Their product was used in a variety of new construction and renovation markets, by installers who purchased both materials and components from warehouse suppliers.

- Should we undertake more component manufacturing in company-owned warehouses?
- Should we seek off-shore sources of low-cost products? If so, should we buy from someone else or manufacture?
- Will the recent leveraged buyouts of competitors X and Y affect their strategy, by forcing an emphasis on short-run earnings? What opportunities does this present us for gaining share at their expense?
- What is the right number and mix of company-owned versus independent warehouses?

As a rule, no more than five to seven issues require the value-added time of the full management team. Trying to handle too many more will dilute time and energy, so priorities are essential. This means getting a consensus within the team on the immediacy and impact of each issue, using a grid such as Figure 4–3 to sort the possibilities. Obviously, the high-impact and immediate issues will get the bulk of attention. If there are too many priority issues it may be necessary to rank order them by importance. This can be a tense exercise if the members of the management team don't share the same assumptions about the business, or adopt a parochial functional perspective as to what is important. Logjams will require the exercise of both leadership and diplomacy by the general manager.

The most troublesome category of issues is the high-impact event or condition with a low likelihood of happening very soon. Changes in government regulation or decisions by major customers to back integrate often fall into this category. These are ignored at the peril of the business, for they may boil up quickly and demand immediate attention. The indicated action is to assign someone to monitor and report regularly. If the issue poses a threat then steps must be taken to reduce the potential impact or the likelihood of occurrence.

Generating and Evaluating Strategic Options. Each priority issue can be handled in many possible ways. However, the effectiveness of the action taken depends on having a wide array of options to consider. Seldom will

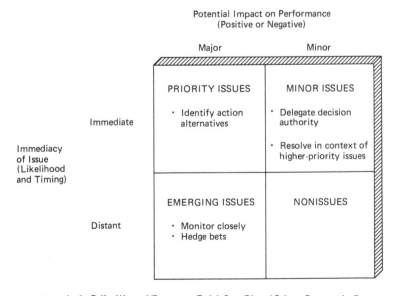

FIGURE 4–3 Likelihood/Impact Grid for Classifying Strategic Issues

"more of the same" be an acceptable option, but, without adventurous thinking about new possibilities, such a pedestrian outcome is likely.

A defining feature of adaptive planning is the separation of the creative act of generating options from their detailed evaluation. If critical questions and comments aren't deferred until all the possibilities have been identified, the atmosphere of the meeting soon resembles a "day in court." This will quickly suppress adventurous thinking and novel solutions. What is needed is a supportive and open setting for stretch thinking, that encourages half-baked ideas with potential for elaboration. The flow of ideas may lead down blind alleys, but also may trigger new options that combine the best features of several different options.

Invariably when issues resolution is treated as a creative activity, the process leads management out of the trap of narrow, unquestioning variations on current themes. There are many procedures available to achieve this end.[13] A manufacturing division used a creative strategy session to address their top 10 issues. The participants were first loosened up with creativity exercises, and then put into five groups and given three hours to address the issues. The groups were told to concentrate on the quantity, not quality, of ideas; to defer judgment; not to argue; and to focus on "what's" not "why's." Over 150 ideas/solutions/options were generated. Next, the participants were reshuffled into five new groups. The task of these groups was to rank all the earlier ideas by their attractiveness. However, maverick ideas were not necessarily killed. Then the leaders of the new groups were asked to report their conclusions. Eventually, five strategic programs emerged.

When all members of a planning team participate in the full discussion of all the options for dealing with an issue, and understand the reasons why one was selected (or their proposal was rejected) they are much more committed to implementing the options. But besides these process advantages, it is essential to have meaningful strategic options to enter into the dialogue with corporate management on the feasible resources and objectives for the business.

DECISION MAKING:
NEGOTIATING OBJECTIVES AND RESOURCES

Sound objectives are needed to mobilize and stretch an organization, and establish the benchmarks against which actual performance can be judged. Unfortunately, the objective-setting process is too often a charade that yields flawed or meaningless objectives. In one firm, a new CEO found that objectives were usually written and then ignored; lists of as many as 20 objectives had been formulated by some businesses but not challenged; other businesses didn't write any objectives, while others delayed presenting their annual objectives until the year was almost ended. This is a recipe for confusion, not clarity of purpose.

Sound objectives satisfy several criteria: they are few in number, clear in direction, and amenable to measurement. Otherwise, they can't be communicated down and through the organization or tested for internal consistency. These are important but not sufficient conditions, for they do not assure the agreed-on objectives will offer challenging targets for performance that are realistically within the reach of the business.

Unrealistic objectives are self-defeating if they pressure the operating managers to make commitments beyond their grasp. Some of Texas Instruments' problems in the early eighties can be traced to the tendency of senior management to dictate nearly impossible targets. Planning meetings were designed to create a "We'll make it happen" attitude rather than figure out where TI could or should be going. Once senior management got the commitment to the objectives they wanted, the managers of the business were left to figure out how to get there. In the words of one participant, "the planning sessions generated false hope, not business plans."

Stretch objectives are laudable—and even essential—so long as they are grounded in reality and supported with adequate resources. Without ambitious objectives TI would not have achieved its breakthrough development of a seismographic system for oil exploration that reveals underground formations in three dimensions.

Which Performance Variables? It is both customary and misguided to set objectives only for the hard, quantitative variables that guide resource allocation decisions: return on investment, growth in profitability and market share. These numbers mean a lot to senior management, but very little to the lower levels of the organization where only fragments of the big picture can be seen. Consequently, these variables can't be broadly shared, and an opportunity is lost to focus the energy of the organization. The solution is to complement the necessary financial variables with objectives such as quality and order responsiveness that are more broadly visible and meaningful. These variables should relate to enduring key success factors, to avoid episodic objectives ("last year's emphasis was on quality but this year we want productivity improvement") which may send contradictory signals and will certainly diffuse commitment.

How Should Objectives Be Set? There is a deep-seated but erroneous belief among managers that strategies should be tailored to fit the desired objectives. This is reinforced in many planning models, on the grounds that managers must know their objectives before deciding how to go about attaining them. This model also implies that the choice of strategic thrust should precede the assembling of resources. Two problems result. First, the objectives may be unrealizable. The opposite problem arises when the objective is eminently achievable, but too short-term or too easy. Hayes[14] argues that strategic objectives that can be achieved within five years are usually either too easy or based on buying and selling something. The resulting advantages are likely to be short-lived, for anything a company can readily buy or sell is probably available to its competitors as well. Short-term objectives also tend to be extrapolations of forecasts (What do we think is going to happen?) rather than visions based on changing the competitive game (What do you want to happen?).

An effective objectives-setting process recognizes that while objectives shape strategies they also have to be cut to fit the resources and long-run possibilities for the business. In an adaptive planning process, the negotiation of these objectives is part of the ongoing strategy dialogue between corporate and business management.

THE NEGOTIATION PROCESS

The steps in this process are sequenced together in Figure 4–4. Essentially the outcome is a reconciliation of what the stakeholders want versus what is feasible for the business to achieve with its resources.

Preliminary Objectives and Guidelines. At the kick-off to the planning process corporate management spells out what they hope to see from each business. These performance expectations are influenced by: (1) the performance requirements of the stakeholders, notably the kind of profit performance sought by investors in light of the capital structure of the firm (other stakeholders, including unions, governments, and employees at all levels will also play a role); (2) the role the business unit is expected to play to support the corporate portfolio—is it a build, harvest, or hold business? How will it support the strategies of other business in the company through shared programs? (3) the resources available, given the financial structure and competing demands for capital from other businesses; and (4) the past growth and profit performance of the business, and reasonable prospects for continuation.

Along with preliminary performance objectives, corporate managers will likely also raise specific concerns that they want the business to address. Some may be specific to that business, stemming from shifts in customer requirements, raw materials availability, or competitive moves that the corporate environmental scan has revealed. Others will be company-wide concerns and priorities, such as quality enhancement,

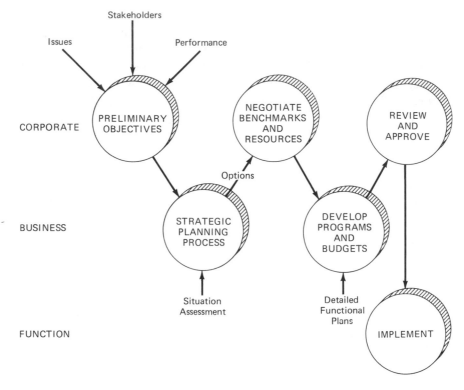

FIGURE 4–4 Negotiating Objectives

working capital conservation, or productivity, to which each business will be expected to respond with a focused program.

Gap Analysis. The preliminary objectives and issues serve to trigger the strategy development process outlined earlier in this chapter. However, the process can only be pushed as far as the strategic thinking stage before discussions resume with corporate management. By this point the business team has identified their major issues, and the options for action. These options are combined into discrete strategy alternatives that are internally consistent packages of strategies, objectives, and resource requirements. For example, the building materials business we looked at earlier in this chapter had one strategic alternative that foresaw incremental strategic growth with modest capital expenditures. This was dubbed the "momentum" strategy because all the pieces were in place to carry it out, and no shift in resource priorities or direction was required. The management team was more excited about several other options that grew the business very rapidly by investing in company-owned warehouses at double the previous rate, and moving aggressively into component manufacturing in these warehouses, rather than simply using them to stock materials.

At this point, the preliminary objectives proposed by corporate management were compared with the likely performance if the "momentum" strategy was followed. The results showed a growing gap, along all performance dimensions, as illustrated in Figure 4–5.

Negotiating the Gap. The parties to the negotiation of the gap closing are corporate management—who know the resource needs for all the business, but don't know the details of the opportunities for each business—and the business unit management team—who have the intimate knowledge of the business. There are two ways to close the gap: either change the objectives in light of what can be achieved, or adopt a strategy with different objectives. Generally the gap is sizable and so a negotiated solution is needed to close it to each party's satisfaction.

Negotiating a Decision. The dialogue during the negotiation is about the feasible strategic alternatives that imply different resource requirements and objectives. To be sure there will be a lot of pushing and pulling during this stage, especially as corporate management explores and challenges the assumptions behind the alternatives, and perhaps demands even more ambitious alternatives. The favorite question of some CEOs at this stage is "What could this business do if it had twice as much cash in the next two years?" As the dialogue proceeds, the management team is learning more about their alternatives and clarifying the implementation requirements. The process is undeniably messy, but it does lead to a two-way commit-

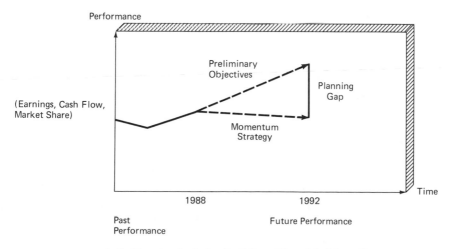

FIGURE 4–5 Gap Analysis for Building Materials Manufacturer

ment to support and implement a strategy option that is internally consistent, realistic, and supported with the right amount of resources.

Compare this negotiated outcome—where the broad strategic direction is shaped jointly at an early stage in the planning process—to the "challenge" reviews of many companies that occur late in the planning cycle. During these sessions the corporate staff seemingly tries to shoot holes in the business unit plans, while corporate management presides as combination referee and judge. In self-defense the operating managers become committed advocates of their preferred alternative, which they endeavor to sell to corporate management in advance of the strategy review. The early commitment to one alternative means that other possibilities for the business are given short shrift or not even considered, while top management has no hand in shaping the possibilities to better suit their needs and expectations. Because top management is isolated from the ongoing dialogue about strategies and objectives it has real difficulty giving a meaningful response.

Reviewing and Approving. The contribution of top management should not be limited to the early negotiation over strategies, objectives, and resources. While they may have agreed in principle to the strategic direction, they want to keep their hand firmly on the process by reviewing the detailed forecasts, functional programs, and budgets and continuing to ask the "tough questions" posed in Chapter 1. This doesn't have to be done every year, but only when the press of issues and events causes the strategy to be rethought and redirected. So this detailed review may or may not coincide with the annual budget activities needed for detailed control and resource allocation.

During the review stage top management has to be especially alert to the dangers of unrealistic forecasts. For example, in Monsanto Chemicals:[15]

> The long-range plans had always asked the operating units for a "most probable" forecast of earnings, a term that meant there was a 50 percent chance of their being lower that the forecasted number. Because long-range plans were widely circulated and often used as motivational tools, as the numbers moved upward from lower levels in the organization they tended to become highly optimistic, almost unattainable. Much of the unreality of the forecasts had evolved in response to the perceptions that optimism was desirable behavior.

Their solution to this distorting behavior was deceptively simple. The operating units were asked to provide a "nearly certain" number, one that had a 90 percent probability of being achieved. The strategic plans were to provide a bridge between the "most probable" and "nearly certain" numbers. As soon as the operating management had to explain why there was a difference, the underlying assumptions were thrown into sharp relief. External issues such as the relative strength of the dollar and changes in GNP rate assumed greater importance. The result was that senior management got more realistic forecasts, and operating management took more ownership of the results they promised.

COMPLETING THE PLANNING PROCESS

Planning is a living, adapting, and continuous process. Thus, the end of one cycle, including the iterative steps from situation assessment through strategic thinking about issues, to decisions about performance objectives and courses of action that culminate in implementation activities, signals the beginning of another cycle of the cycle.

The bridge to the next cycle is provided by a monitoring and control system that tracks whether the strategy is on course to achieve the promised objectives and whether the underlying assumptions remain valid. The heart of this system is performance criteria and related measures that are derived from the objectives and key success requirements. For a strategy requiring new distribution methods an inventory control system would be a high priority. The main purpose would be to ensure that inventory levels at various stages were not excessive and likely to back up in the system, or if they started to balloon in size there would be ample warning so corrective action could be taken. Of course, if too many serious departures from the expected are flagged by the control system, it may be necessary to initiate a complete strategy review or pull together a project team to deal with the specific issue causing the problem.

PART

THREE

Assessing the Competitive Position

FIVE

Understanding Competitive Markets:
Their Structure and Attractiveness

We've treated the car market as a mass one, but now I'm convinced that concept is dead. We now believe in target marketing: specific products and ads aimed at selected groups.
—LLOYD REUSS,
General Motors

With few exceptions, when a manager with a reputation for brilliance tackles a business with a reputation for poor fundamental economics, it is the reputation of the business that remains intact.
—WARREN BUFFETT

These quotations neatly capture the contemporary realities of competitive markets; they are populated by customers with increasingly diverse requirements, and crowded with competitive suppliers whose intensifying rivalry inevitably depresses the overall prospects for profitability. An understanding of these forces is critical to the informed choice of market arenas and target segments that begins the process of strategy development.

The world automobile market has become such a fragmented battleground that even General Motors has adopted target marketing. A glut of more than 350 different models of cars and trucks has weakened the advantage that any one producer holds in styling or technical features. To survive, automakers are focusing tightly on the needs of distinct customer segments. But these are often difficult to identify. Take four-wheel drive vehicles. Many customers want them for the obvious reason: off-road recreational driving. But many suburban families also buy them for their carrying capacity and foul-weather safety features. These important distinctions are obliterated by traditional approaches to segmenting along obvious demographic lines—young, first-time buyers, families, more affluent drivers, and so on. Instead, carmakers have to learn why different customer segments buy.

The experience of Warren Buffett is a sobering reminder that all markets are not created equal in their prospects for profitability. Although he is one of the world's most astute investors,[1] he wrote the quotation above as a requiem for his experience with a textile company he was compelled to close in 1985. For 20 years he had nursed this manufacturer of such mundane products as suit linings, in markets where his company was one of many commodity operators with no discernible advantage. The lesson was extraordinarily costly; the opportunity cost over the time he held an equity stake in the business was estimated as being around $500 million.

What Buffett learned about poor economic fundamentals was that the overall market was unattractive because the intensity of competition was so severe the customers captured most of the economic value created, leaving little for suppliers' profits. The problem was compounded by an absence within the overall market of protected segments or niches where the prospects were any better.

Clearly the choice of market arena and target customer segments where the business elects to compete is fundamental to the long-run profit prospects for the business. This chapter addresses the principal questions to be answered to ensure these are sound choices:

1. How is the market defined? That is, which customers and products should be included within the broad scope?
2. Are there strategic segments that can be protected from the profit-sapping competitive threats in the overall market?
3. Does the market have attractive immediate profit prospects? How long is it likely to remain attractive?

Once the market has been properly defined the identities of the leading competitors will then be established, market shares can be measured, product life cycles can be tracked, and there is a context for assessing one's advantages. Only then can management decide how much of the market they should serve. These are essential conditions for clear-headed stratetic thinking.

DEFINING THE MARKET

A market is an arena where customers with similar needs or problems meet with sellers of reasonably substitutable products or services who are competing to satisfy these needs. At a minimum a market is defined jointly along a customer dimension that describes the collection of possible customers, and a product or service dimension that arrays the competing choice alternatives. When markets are globalizing then regional distinctions become important. This creates the cube of possibilities shown in Figure 5–1 that describes the market for the delivery of documents and small parcels.

Which products, customers, and geographic regions should be included within the market definition? There will usually be many answers, depending on the decision that is involved and the vantage point used—that is, whether we view the market from the customer's viewpoint or adopt an industry perspective and define the market in terms of the competing suppliers.

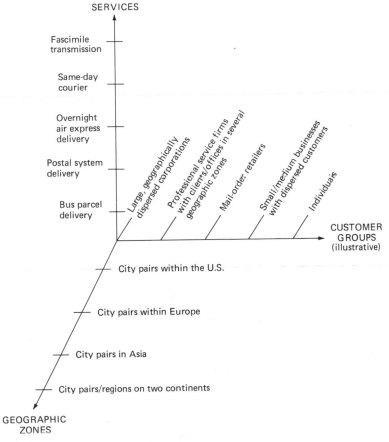

FIGURE 5–1 Boundaries of the Market for the Delivery of Documents and Small Packages

Decision Context. Seldom can one market definition be used for all purposes. Tactical decisions, such as short-run budgeting and performance evaluation, use narrow definitions, to correspond with the short-run concerns of product and sales managers who regard their market as "a chunk of demand to be filled with whatever resources [they] can command." Here the definition of customers is limited to those who are currently served, while competing products are those that look alike, perform the same functions, and are sold through the same channels.

Strategic decisions require broader market definitions to embrace: (1) presently unserved market opportunities, (2) changes in technology, price levels, and supply conditions that broaden the array of perceived substitutes, and (3) potential competitive entrants from adjacent markets. Sticking with a narrow definition for too long can make a firm vulnerable. For example, American firms are still prone to restrict themselves almost entirely to their domestic market. After all, it is a large, known entity. This provincialism has given their foreign competitors breathing room to develop a global capability and superiority from a protected home base. Many markets such as ceramics and pharmaceuticals are inherently global and market position depends on share of worldwide sales. It is no longer possible to participate in only one part of this market.

CUSTOMER-DEFINED MARKETS:
DEMAND-SIDE PERSPECTIVES

From this perspective a market consists of shifting patterns of customer requirements and needs that can be served in many ways. Although this view tends to direct our attention to the fine-grained structure of customer groups, it can also tell us about the array of competitive offerings to be included in the market. This array goes beyond *substitutes-in-kind*—all those products that look alike and represent the same application of a distinct technology to the provision of a distinct set of customer functions—to encompass *substitutes-in-use.* This broadened concept of substitutability depends on shared functionality and the constraints of economic feasiblity.

Testing for Shared Functionality. This test uses the customer's perceptions of all the ways their needs can be satisfied in a given usage or application situation. In some social entertainment situations wine coolers may compete more with certain beers and wines than with other beverages. Seldom however is a substitute a straightforward replacement:

- the substitute may perform a wider range of functions. Thus a word processor is much more than a typewriter, by virtue of being able to store and manipulate text.

- substitution may result if the buyer decides to perform the function, rather than buy it. The alternative to a gourmet frozen dinner is one from scratch. In the property and casualty insurance market, buyers are increasingly turning to self-insurance or setting up captive insurance subsidiaries.
- another type of substitute is the used, recycled, or reconditioned product. For some applications a recycled thermoplastic is acceptable. Rebuilt automobile and aircraft engine parts are a major threat to the sale of new spare parts. One of the advantages of the so-called mini steel mills is the ability to use low-cost scrap steel.

The difficulty with the shared functionality test of substitution is knowing when to stop. At some level of generic need every product is a contender for the consumer's scarce resources. The purchase of a new compact disc player comes from discretionary income that is no longer available to buy a motorcycle, take golf lessons, or travel to the Caribbean. While it is important to not lose sight of this broad context, to avoid being blindsided by a substitute, a tighter market boundary is usually needed to focus on the strategic issues.

One characteristic of customer-defined markets is sharp discontinuities between markets in both customer needs or benefits sought and the degree of substitutability of the product or service alternatives for satisfying these needs. According to this rule, a multiple function material such as nylon competes in several different end-use markets such as tire cord, carpeting, and hosiery, since the customer needs in each application are very different. Thus, there is a distinct market for synthetic carpet fibers, but not a single nylon market. Substitutability implies that the purpose or application, rather than product features as such, becomes the organizing theme for considering competitive alternatives. The customers for whom these purposes are relevant comprise the market demand.

While shared functionality is a necessary condition for including a product within a market, it doesn't give a complete picture. Two further constraints are imposed by economic inducements and the awareness customers have of the possible substitutes. Because these constraints can loosen or tighten over time, market boundaries are constantly shifting.

Economics of Substitution.[2] A potential functional substitute for an existing product becomes an immediate threat when the economic incentive to switch is large enough to overcome the resistance to switching. In some markets this calculation is governed strictly by relative prices. Fructose is viewed by bulk users of sweeteners, such as soft drink companies, as essentially a functional substitute to refined cane sugar. The cost of switching from cane sugar to fructose and back is minor, since only a known change in formulation is required. However, fructose can only capture a significant volume of the sweetener market when cane sugar prices rise above 12 cents a pound, and the cost saving becomes meaningful.

The analysis of substitution is seldom so straightforward and predictable. Normally, different customers will have different perceptions of the incentive to switch, depending on their circumstances, and how they estimate the following factors:

Incentive to switch = Cost savings from switching to the substitute
(after switching costs are accounted for)
+ Value of additional benefits perceived by customer

where:
Cost savings = Life cycle cost of present product
— price of substitute
— switching costs
— present value of postpurchase costs of the substitute

The life cycle cost of the present product includes the purchase price (after taking into account financing charges, tax savings, and so forth), and all postpurchase costs over the useful life of the product. These costs include operating labor charges, maintenance, fuel and other consumables, spare capacity, and insurance. These costs are often difficult to attribute to a specific product because of the vagaries of the accounting system, and require a detailed knowledge of the customer's usage behavior. A further complication is the time value of money. A cost three years from now has to be discounted back to present value with the customer's discount rate. If the customer places little weight on future cost savings rather than the immediate price, then the implied discount rate will be very high.

The attractiveness of the substitute product depends on (1) its initial price, which may be declining over time relative to the present product, (2) switching costs, that are the result of a need to redesign or reformulate a product, retrain employees, or invest in ancillary products (a sizable imputed cost will be added if there is a perceived risk of failure or side-effects of the substitute), and (3) postpurchase costs of operation, when they are appropriately discounted. The opportunity to save costs here often determines whether a substitute will replace an established product. For example, radial truck tires initially cost 40 to 60 percent more than bias ply tires, but this is more than offset by the savings in life cycle costs. Not only do radials last 20 to 30 percent more miles, they have a lower downtime from punctures and can be retreaded more often.

A substitute product will also prevail if it offers additional benefits the customer perceives and values, such as:

- performance benefits, from saving time, improving output, or providing new functions. Electronic cash registers cost more than the mechanical forerunner, but provide extensive on-line transactions data that can be used to control inventory costs and improve purchasing.
- security benefits, that result in improved safety, resistance to burglary, or invulnerability to fire damage.
- availability benefits, gained from the assurance of immediate, reliable delivery, that permit lower inventory levels.
- flexibility benefits that mean the product can be used in a wider variety of situations, use several different types of fuel and so on.

The incentive to switch will be different for different customers, depending on how they use and derive value from their present products. The economic value of a new super minicomputer will depend on whether it is substituting for a mini or microcomputer, and on whether it is used for a production line control, distributed processing, or energy-saving application. Thus, whether or not a substitute product is included in a market is a question that can only be resolved within a distinct segment of customers who have similar needs or requirements.

COMPETITOR-DEFINED MARKETS: SUPPLY-SIDE PERSPECTIVES

Customer-defined markets reveal patterns of substitutes that are perceived to offer similar or closely related functions. Thus there is a market for financial instruments that provide short-term credit to retail customers, including credit cards, NOW accounts, overdrafts, and so forth.

The contrasting supply-side approach to defining markets starts with all the competitors who could possibly serve the needs of a group of customers. This may give a different picture because it explicitly considers technological similarity, relative production costs, and distribution coverage. Questions to be asked include: Which competitors are serving related product classes with the same technology, manufacturing process, material sources, sales force, and distribution channels? What is the geographic scope of the market—is it regional, national or global? Which competitors should be included—only those presently serving the market or potential entrants with a capacity to compete? These questions are vital to an understanding of the relative cost standing of a business, and degree of transferability of experience into related markets. In this supply-side view, a market is an arena of competition where company resources can profitably be employed.

The supply-side approach looks for significant discontinuities in the pattern of costs, capital requirements, and margins along the product and customer dimensions. These are barriers that insulate prices and profits within the market from the activities of competitors outside the market. They also discourage easy entry by potential competitors. When boundaries are properly defined the relative profitability of competitors within a market can meaningfully be compared.

Boundaries are encountered when participation in an adjacent category—whether a different technology, customer group, or function—is impeded by the need to enter with a large-scale operation to avoid a cost disadvantage, or to invest substantial financial resources for fixed facilities or working capital, or to employ a different marketing strategy. These barriers are lessened if some of the company's experience base can be transferred to the new market.

When the market is defined as broadly as an industry, to include competitors who have achieved viable levels of experience and cost economies for major cost factors, it may encompass product classes that are only loosely related on other criteria such as customer needs satisfied, similarity of functions provided, or production methods. Thus the helicopter industry includes both military and commercial helicopters, even though the respective customers don't see them as interchangeable. The cost position of many consumer packaged goods firms is dictated by their experience in sales and distribution through grocery outlets, and advertising and sales promotion to mass markets, for these activities are a significant proportion of total cost. This industry perspective on the market is often too broad for most competitive strategy purposes, but is essential when considering acquisitions and new products, or anticipating the entry of new competitors.

The two approaches to defining markets are closely entwined, as we see in the appliance example in Figure 5–2. From the customer's perspective coffee makers have nothing to do with food mixers, because they serve totally different functions. Their consideration set may include all coffee

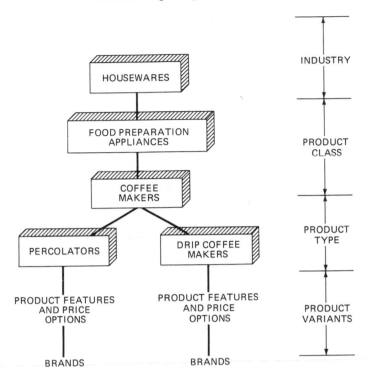

FIGURE 5–2 Product–Industry Hierarchy

makers, whether percolator or drip varieties, because these are perceived to be functional substitutes. The suppliers to this market have to take a broader view, since the present and prospective competitors include all those with the capacity to design, produce, and distribute coffee makers and all related food preparation appliances within a geographic market. Here the question is the extent of sharing of manufacturing facilities, R&D capabilities, and sales forces.

In Summary: What Is a Market? Several answers have been suggested, depending on the perspective used, and the reason for wanting to define the market. There is no single answer, for a market is not an observable reality. It is a very handy abstraction that gives useful insights into customers' requirements, the behavior of competitors, and strategic issues. For most purposes we will be trying to understand a *core market* that includes products offering similar or related functions to groups of customers with distinct needs. Sometimes we will be looking into the segment structure of this core market for market niches a firm can protect from competitive incursions. For other purposes, we need an *extended mar-*

ket definition to encompass all competitive possibilities for satisfying customer needs, including substitutes and potential entrants. This latter perspective is especially needed to help understand why some markets are attractive and others are not.

FINDING ATTRACTIVE SEGMENTS

Not all parts of a market have equal allure. Instead of homogeneity there are diverse submarkets within the market that vary widely in profitability prospects because customer groups have different needs and behavior, and product groups will vary in costs, capital requirements, and margins. The immediate payoff from successful segmentation of a market into sub-markets is the identification and nurturing of product groups and customer groups where competition is less direct and profitability prospects are superior. In the household cooking appliance market there is an attractive and protected segment for high-priced, built-in cook tops with special features such as indoor barbecue grills, sold primarily as replacement units in existing homes, or custom installations in high-priced new homes. This market segment is more profitable on a unit basis than the moderate-price gas or electric stand-alone cook-top and oven combinations sold to builders of tract homes.

There are other benefits to imaginative dissection of a market into segments. Early identification of an emerging or neglected segment can offer an easy gateway for entry into a market. Toshiba entered the CAT diagnostic medical scanner market in North America and Europe by seeking customers that didn't want the fully-featured scanners offered by GE and Siemens. These customers had simple needs, limited to standard diagnoses at low power, that could be readily satisfied with a lower-performance unit. There was little immediate reaction from competition who didn't believe there was such a segment. Similarly, Federal Express preempted the market for overnight delivery of small packages, by designing a strategy that could serve this segment better than competitors who were trying to serve it as part of a broader-scope strategy.

A segmentation mind-set in an organization also sharpens the understanding of customers and encourages firms to find strategies that serve different segments with different products and strategies. Some years ago Marriott Corp. became concerned that the market for traditional first class hotels, defined as all those offering a complete bundle of food, meeting, and banquet services, was being picked apart by competitors with specialized facilities. They now divide their offerings into nine categories to serve distinct segments of the business traveler market. Each category is a combination of location—airport, downtown, suburban, convention, resort, or international—configuration, such as the time-share and all-suite hotels that appeal to long-stay guests, and price level—quality, upper-moderate, and budget—with the last two categories offering only minimal lobbies and public spaces. Each category serves customers with different needs, and most are managed as separate businesses.

The benefits of segmentation can be elusive, especially because the best segmentation scheme is often obscured by the myriad of possible ways to divide up and group the products and customers in a market. The challenge is to find the smallest possible set of groups, where the groups are:

1. Sufficiently *distinctive* in cost and capital requirements, and customer purchase criteria and behavior, that a meaningful difference in strategies to serve the segment groups can be justified. This also presumes that barriers to competitive entry to each segment can be erected.
2. *Substantial* enough to justify the incremental costs of a tailored strategy, including differentiated products, programs, and services.
3. *Measurable* as to size of present sales volume and rate of growth.
4. *Durable* enough that the differences used to justify a distinct strategy will not evaporate before the profit potential is realized.
5. *Identifiable* so each distinct group of customers can be efficiently reached with a targeted sales and communications effort.

If these conditions are satisfied the resulting segments will also differ in intrinsic profit prospects. Unfortunately the conditions are often not met, and the market is divided into either too many or too few segments. In the first case the result is confusion while the second leads to failure to achieve a meaningful competitive advantage. A typical complaint from management is,

> Now that they've identified the 90 core product/market and geographic segments, my marketing people tell me they can't develop the necessary facts to develop winning niche strategies because the data just aren't available. Maybe we were taking too broad an approach to the market in the old days, but we're certainly no better off now. If this is market segmentation, you can have it.[3]

The Process of Strategic Segmentation. Finding the best segmentation structure is a creative activity that demands a disciplined step-by-step process to guide it:

Step One: Identify Possible Segment Groups. Start with a feasible set of segmentation variables that could be used to identify discrete groups of buyers and products within the overall market.

Step Two: Select Segment Groups: Screen the identification variables by their ability to distinguish groups that have different response profiles: their buying criteria, geographic location, and purchase behavior are such that they have very different requirements and costs to serve. Further distillation of the set can be achieved by combining and collapsing any variables that are correlated.

Step Three: Test for Relevance. Probe the segmentation matrix that portrays creative combinations of product and customer groups for strategic implications. Segment by segment, do competitors' strengths, weaknesses, and market shares fall logically into place? Are the resulting segments substantial and durable? Are the growth rates different?

Once a relevant segmentation structure has been found, the business then has to decide which ones to choose as target segments where it can effectively compete. This issue will preoccupy us in Chapter 8.

IDENTIFYING POSSIBLE PRODUCT AND CUSTOMER GROUPS: STEP ONE

The choice of segmentation approach—how segments are identified—is often so ingrained in the fabric of the organization that it is hard to conceive of better approaches. When asked why customer groups are identified by a variable such as industry type, size, or demographics, the response is apt to be:

1. "We've always done it this way" (which means that's how my predecessor did it, and furthermore "if it ain't broke don't fix it")
2. "That's the way we're organized"
3. "That's the way our competitors do it," or
4. "That's the way the data are organized" (we just take our market data from the industry trade association or census bureau).

Following conventional wisdom is more likely to lead to imitative strategies, and obscure emerging segment opportunities. Creative thinking requires testing a broad array of ways of segmenting markets.

Product Groups. These are customarily identified by physical similarity (including size and features), technology (e.g., analog versus digital, or lithium versus alkaline batteries), price level, or performance rating. The most useful groupings are those that translate into noticeable cost differences. This lesson was important to a components manufacturer who was barely breaking even, despite operating at full capacity. What management found was that profit contribution per machine hour depended more on pounds produced per hour than price realized per pound—which was totally contrary to conventional wisdom. Furthermore, pounds produced per hour was directly related to the size and simplicity of the parts. Armed with this insight, management resegmented the market according to size and complexity, and drastically shifted the pricing and customer focus. Instead of pricing bids for a fixed 30 percent gross profit, the prices were raised for small, complex parts and the company began to emphasize simple, large parts. The change in strategy was well rewarded with a 20 percent aftertax return on investment (ROI).[4]

Customer Groups. The possible ways of identifying and grouping customers are almost unending, and include their characteristics, geographic location, and channel position.

The customer characteristics of interest are classified according to whether they identify customers or describe how they behave toward a product or service. *Identifiers* are the relatively enduring and generic descriptions of individual customers or organizational buying units that can be used to reach them with a marketing strategy. These descriptions are usually based on demographics or distinctive aspects of their life-styles, approach to doing business, or decision-making process. The *response profile* is unique to the product or service, since it is based on attributes and behavior toward the product category or specific brands and vendors in the category. This distinction between identifiers and responses is amplified in Exhibit 5–1.

Geographic location can simultaneously affect customer needs, and the cost to serve the buyers. The segments may be defined by boundaries between countries, or by regional differences within them. The country differences are usually the most influential since they dictate the size of tariff and nontariff barriers, the role of government regulation, and the channel and logistics structures which determine the extent of competition and the cost to reach the market.

A recurring problem in devising segmentation strategies is deciding who is the real customer. Distribution channels can vary from passive conduits (such as construction supply houses) to active purchasing agents working on behalf of their customers (such as specialized electronics or hydraulics distributors who can configure systems from the products they carry). The latter group, as well as big retailers, can control access to a large part of the market, so they have a great deal of bargaining power.

SELECTING CUSTOMER SEGMENTS: STEP TWO

The essence of segmentation is catering to the differences in benefits sought or applications requirements of distinct customer groups, by creat-

Exhibit 5-1 Customer Characteristics Commonly Used to Describe and Distinguish Segments

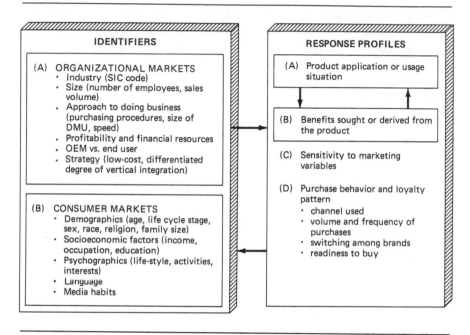

SIC = Standard Industrial Classification of goods and services
DMU = Decision Making Unit (all the decision makers and influentials in an organization that are involved in the purchase)
OEM = Original Equipment Manufacturer

ing distinct products and adjusting the strategy to be more appealing to these groups than the competition. This logic can also be applied to guide the selection of the best segment identifiers from among the myriad of possibilities.[5] This can be done either by:

- Starting with the identifiers of customers and seeing if the resulting customer groups have distinct response profiles,

or

- Starting with groups of customers that have distinct response profiles and working backward to find whether the groups can be described according to differences in their identifying characteristics.

The notion of a customer response profile is pivotal in this analysis, for it describes the specific reactions of customers to the product or service as

Identifiers of Customer Groups	⇄	Customer Response Profiles

a consequence of the requirements or needs they are trying to satisfy. Customers can respond in four related ways; by how they use the product, by the benefits they are seeking, by their sensitivity to marketing variables such as price, or by their purchase and usage behavior.

Application or Usage Situation. This is a hybrid variable, for it can be used as either an identifier or to describe the response profile. Consider the business market for personal computers. Organizations buy PCs for combinations of applications, including word processing, desk-top publishing, accounting, financial analysis, computer-aided design, data base management, or information retrieval. Each application implies a different pattern of benefits sought—such as portability, memory, connectivity to a network, or service support—that suppliers such as Compaq, Apple, and IBM have varying abilities to meet.

Benefits Sought or Derived. For strategic relevance there is no other variable that is as revealing as the benefits the customers are seeking from the product or service. Benefits are defined by the relative emphasis placed on an attribute or characteristic of the product. A good segment identifier will reveal groups that are similar in the benefits sought. Trucking firms find that customers selling perishables emphasize speed of delivery and refrigeration capability. Size of firm may also be related to differences in benefits sought, for small shippers are more concerned with willingness to ship less-than-truckload lots.

The hitch with benefit segmentation is the need to collect special data rather than rely on readily available industry data. When distinct segments that are homogeneous with respect to desired benefits are found in the data, they may be hard to identify. A study of buyers of "dumb" or "nonintelligent" data terminals found four benefit segments by using ratings of the importance of 33 selection criteria, and the perceived differences among suppliers on each criterion.[6] One benefit segment was one-stop shoppers (who emphasized breadth of line and price flexibility), another was hardware buyers, and a third was brand buyers. While the segments were distinct and behaved differently, there was no relationship between benefit segment membership and type of industry or size of company.

Sensitivity to Marketing and Product Variables. This aspect of the response profile takes the benefits sought idea, and pushes it down one level to ask how the segment will react to changes in price, quality level, and performance. Buyers of semiconductors can be grouped by those that are exceedingly quality-conscious (notably, military applications) versus those that are highly price-sensitive and need only minimal functionality for low-end audio equipment.

Purchase Behavior and Loyalty Variables. These describe the:

- past behavior—historical patterns of switching between suppliers, fluctuations in size of purchases, and purchase frequency
- present behavior—size of purchase (number of units, transactions, etc.) and channel used (direct versus brokers versus supply houses)
- future behavior—awareness of the product and intentions to buy.

These purchase behaviors may cut across common geographic areas, product groups, and customer identifiers, but yield important insights. For example, a heavy capital goods manufacturer, serving 50 end-use segments, concluded that for strategic purposes only two segment groupings really counted. One was "entrenched" customers who rarely changed suppliers after they had standardized on maintenance and parts inventories. The other was "open" customers who tended to buy on price and machine availability and demonstrated no loyalty. These groupings dictated three different strategies for the company: one for its own entrenched customers, a second for those entrenched with a competitor, and a third for the open segment.

Costs to Serve. When two segments differ in their requirements and response profiles, the costs to serve them will likely differ as well. Unfortunately for sound decision making, these cost differences are usually obscured in broad-brush cost allocation procedures. This means that the best most firms can do is to compare the profitability of segments according to their relative contribution margins after direct costs and factory overheads have been assigned. Just how limited and misleading a cost picture this gives is illustrated by the recent experience of a components manufacturer shown in Exhibit 5–2. According to their contribution margin yardstick, their small customers, who paid full list price, were more attractive than the large customers who continually bargained for quantity discounts and extracted deferred payment and delivery concessions. Imagine the consternation when activity costs were properly assigned to the customers who required the activity. Almost all the costs to serve the small accounts were dramatically higher, to the point that the company was losing money on this segment. This insight led to a round of price increases and a shift to lower-cost distribution arrangements. Some small accounts that were especially costly to serve were dropped.

Exhibit 5-2 Segment Differences in Cost to Serve

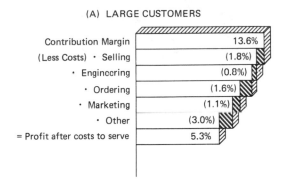

(A) LARGE CUSTOMERS

Contribution Margin	13.6%
(Less Costs) · Selling	(1.8%)
· Engineering	(0.8%)
· Ordering	(1.6%)
· Marketing	(1.1%)
· Other	(3.0%)
= Profit after costs to serve	5.3%

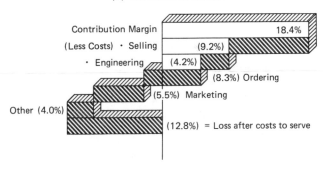

(B) SMALL CUSTOMERS

Contribution Margin	18.4%
(Less Costs) · Selling	(9.2%)
· Engineering	(4.2%)
	(8.3%) Ordering
	(5.5%) Marketing
Other (4.0%)	
	(12.8%) = Loss after costs to serve

TESTING SEGMENTS FOR STRATEGIC RELEVANCE: STEP THREE

The strategic segments of a market are formed from distinct groups of products sold to distinct groups of buyers, and described by those few segmentation variables that account for large differences in buyer behavior and costs to serve. The results can be displayed in a two-dimensional matrix such as Figure 5–3, to facilitate strategic thinking. This matrix shows how a Japanese ship-building company dissected its market by product type and the different customers for each type.[7] Note that product types are defined by various combinations of cargo type and value of the cargo (since high-grade cargo ships can be sold for twice as much per ton as low-grade

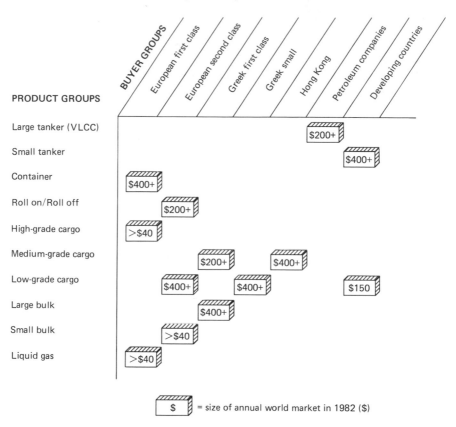

FIGURE 5-3 Segmentation of the Global Ship-Building Market

vessels). Similarly, buyer groups are described by both geography and class, to capture important differences in behavior and ordering patterns. The resulting display helped identify strategically important size segments that required distinct strategies.

It is not always possible to display all segments in one matrix, but it is certainly desirable to avoid too many matrices that obscure rather than reveal. Simplification can sometimes be achieved by combining groups defined by correlated segment variables. Watch for situations where a group of buyers is served by a single channel, or cluster in a single geographic area.

Strategic relevance means the market segments that have been discovered satisfy the conditions of strategic distinctiveness, substantiality, measurability, and durability. Only then can they be used for resource allocation, opportunity identification, and competitive position decisions. Satisfaction of these conditions will be revealed as significant differences between segments in terms of: (1) buyer behavior and their responsiveness to marketing variables, (2) the fixed and variable costs to serve the different segments, (3) the rate of growth, and (4) the performance of different competitors. We would certainly not expect to find exactly the same competitors with the same market share in two strategically different segments. Similarly there should be significant differences in profitability. If there are no meaningful differences to be found it is fair to conclude that a segment boundary is not worth management attention, and the two segments should be collapsed into one.

Strategic segments are like mini-markets, each with their own competitive structure and profit prospects. To understand why one segment is more attractive than another we have to delve more deeply into the operation of competitive forces within markets.

MARKET ATTRACTIVENESS

Attractive markets promise average returns on investment well above the cost of capital for the firms serving the market. Between 1982 and 1987, the pharmaceutical industry passed this test with flying colors, while the tire industry flunked. Conditions were so bad within the building and mining industry that virtually no one reported profits during this period (Exhibit 5–3).

Because market attractiveness has such an important influence on a firm's profitability,[8] strategists must be prepared to answer two fundamental questions: (1) what factors account for the present level of profitability of this market? and (2) will profit prospects be better or worse in the future given the trends in the market and our strategic moves? The answer to the first question depends on the collective strength of five competitive forces:[9] (1) direct rivalry among the competitors serving the core market, the bargaining power of (2) suppliers and (3) customers, (4) the threat posed by substitutes, and (5) prospects for entry by new competitors from related industries or other geographic markets. These forces will be modified—either abated or accentuated—by three additional influences: government intervention, technological change, and market growth. The rest of this section explains how these forces influence profitability.

ECONOMIC VALUE CREATION:
THE SOURCE OF PROFITABILITY

Whether the prospects for profitability of the firms serving a market are wretched or appealing depends on how the economic value that is created

Exhibit 5–3 Exceptional and Unexceptional Performance (5 year average return on equity: 1982–1987)

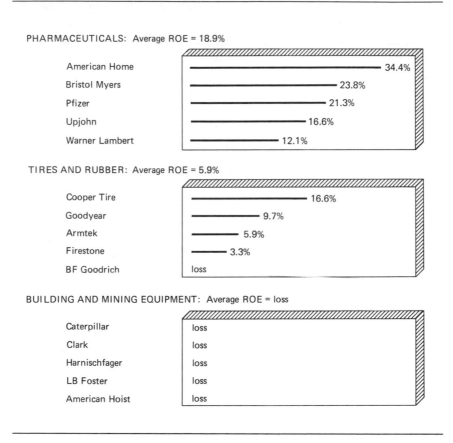

PHARMACEUTICALS: Average ROE = 18.9%

American Home	34.4%
Bristol Myers	23.8%
Pfizer	21.3%
Upjohn	16.6%
Warner Lambert	12.1%

TIRES AND RUBBER: Average ROE = 5.9%

Cooper Tire	16.6%
Goodyear	9.7%
Armtek	5.9%
Firestone	3.3%
BF Goodrich	loss

BUILDING AND MINING EQUIPMENT: Average ROE = loss

Caterpillar	loss
Clark	loss
Harnischfager	loss
LB Foster	loss
American Hoist	loss

for customers is shared among the players in the market. The identity of these players depends on where we are in the business system: the chain of activities that obtains and transforms inputs and then sells, distributes, and services the output to the end customer. This notion is equally applicable to gourmet canned soup, semiconductor test equipment, or foreign exchange services for large corporations. The nature and importance of the specific activities within the chain will be very different for each product and service.

Each activity in this chain of events adds value to the product or service. The cumulative value of the activities is whatever the customer is willing to pay for the stream of benefits that has been created. Realized price is not always a reliable guide to the amount of value created, if the customer was able to exercise bargaining power and force the price down. They might have been willing to pay more to get the benefits but were able to exploit weaknesses among their suppliers.

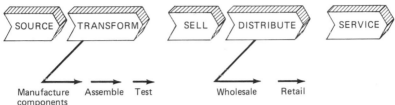

Several stages of value-creating activities may be combined within one firm, with different firms choosing different combinations depending on their capabilities and served markets. For example, some personal computer manufacturers are strictly assemblers of standard components, and adhere to IBM industry standards to ensure access to software. Other PC makers design and source their own components and have a proprietary operating system. Some reach their customers with a direct sales force, while others rely on mass retailing channels or specialized computer retailers. Few of the firms will have identical business systems.

Sharing Value. Who gets the value created for the end customer? This depends on the relative influence on prices and costs of the players in each of the five competitive roles. The bargaining power of the customers, and any threats of substitution will directly influence the price charged by the firms in the market. Powerful customers are usually more costly to serve. The costs of input materials and services depend on the bargaining power of suppliers. The intensity of competition among direct rivals influences both prices and the costs of meeting competition with new products, enhanced service coverage, advertising, and sales coverage (see Figure 5–4).

As a general rule competitive roles with only a few big players exercise more power than roles with many players. The adage, "Those that have the gold make the rules" can never be ignored. Of course, there are many other factors that determine the strength of each competitive force. These are a consequence of the economic and technological characteristics of the different groups of players.

DIRECT RIVALRY AMONG COMPETITORS

In some markets the direct rivals coexist comfortably, and appear content with their respective market shares. Other markets are constantly on a war footing, as the competitors look for a temporary edge with price cuts,

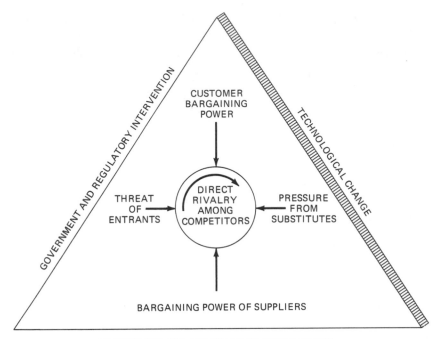

FIGURE 5–4 Forces Influencing the Attractiveness of a Market

promotional deals, ad blitzes, and aggressive new product spending. Others in the market have to match these moves to protect their position, and a wave of fare cutting escalates to the point where everyone suffers damage to their margins. The domestic airline industry, in its eagerness to fill seats to cover fixed costs, has a long history of behaving this way, despite experience that tells them that cut-price market expansion is short-lived and erodes profits while leaving shares unchanged. The following factors determine whether the direct rivals are in a state of war, peace, or perhaps observing an uneasy truce.

Structure of Competition. Rivalry is most heated when numerous small players serve the same market, each making moves they hope the others won't notice, or when there are a few equally balanced competitors. Despite there being only two competitors, Spectra-Physics and Coherent Radiation, in the otherwise attractive market for industrial lasers, neither is profitable. Deep-seated antagonism between the managers of these implacable rivals often leads them to use their resources to attack and retaliate against each other, with price-cutting being a favorite weapon.

When competition is concentrated among a few companies and one competitor clearly dominates, by virtue of a share at least 50 percent larger than the second, rivalry is quite subdued. The followers coexist under the leader's umbrella, and seldom challenge the price structure for fear of retaliation. This is especially likely when differences in cumulated experience mean the leader has much lower costs than anyone else.

Structure of Costs. When fixed costs are high, the emphasis is on capacity utilization. Whenever there is excess capacity, competition reverts to a "volume-grubbing" contest, with price as the main weapon. As often happens in the pulp and paper market, these price cuts are quickly matched by other competitors also striving to maintain their capacity utilization.

Extent of Differentiation. An absence of perceived differences among competing products means the conversation with customers soon turns to prices, terms, and sales conditions, and rivalry intensifies. This rivalry is muted when there are large perceived differences, for customers then develop strong preferences and loyalties that make them more resistant to competing offerings. The long-run attractiveness of such a market is further enhanced when the differences are difficult to imitate. The odds of this happening go up when the information about the process or system is tacit, rather than in the public domain, and employee mobility is low so that critical knowledge stays within the firm.

Customer Switching Costs. These costs tend to tie buyers to one supplier who is then protected from raids by others. These costs are high when the product is durable or specialized, when the customer has invested a lot of time and energy in learning how to use the product, or has made special-purpose investments that are useless elsewhere. A commitment to a computer operating system makes it very difficult for a customer to switch from DEC to IBM, or vice versa, without expensive software development, retraining, and general disruption.

Diversity of Strategies and Objectives. When all competitors adopt similar strategies, have similar cost structures, place equal emphasis on short-run profitability versus market share, and are managed by people from the same backgrounds, they naturally understand one anothers' intentions and can accurately anticipate their reactions to strategic moves. When the players come from diverse backgrounds (where some are foreign-based, some are closely held, and others are state-owned), and vary in size and objectives (some are low-overhead local producers, while others are global players), and thus have different ideas about acceptable profits, they will follow conflicting strategies that eventually depress average profits.

Exit Barriers. These hurdles keep companies trapped as participants in a market even when profitability is miserable. Excess capacity remains as a drag in everyone's profits, but no one is willing to shut down unneeded plants. This happened in the early eighties in the market for float glass, because the large U.S. firms that controlled the capacity were unwilling to either write off the fixed assets and suffer the impact on earnings, or to sell to foreign manufacturers who wanted to establish a position in the United States because this would be a new threat to the profitable parts of their glass markets.

THREAT OF POTENTIAL COMPETITORS

Easy-to-enter markets soon become overcrowded to the detriment of future profit prospects. One reason is the increased power handed to customers who can wring concessions from existing suppliers by threatening to go to an off-shore competitor or help a company from an adjacent market to enter. Once the new entrants have established a beachhead they frequently go on to assault the entire market, and intensify the level of competition.

The seriousness of the threat of entry depends on the height of entry barriers that impose disadvantages on prospective entrants and depress their expectations of profitability. These barriers are created by:

1. *Factor cost advantages.* Such advantages of incumbents are created by lower labor or capital costs, preferred access to raw materials, favorable locations, or proprietary technology.
2. *Economies of scale.* These are a deterrent if they force the prospective entrant to spend heavily on facilities, advertising, sales force coverage, distribution, and so forth to achieve cost parity with incumbents, to come in at a smaller scale, and suffer a cost disadvantage. The aircraft engine business has very high scale thresholds in all functions, that severely limit the number of possible players.
3. *Differentiation and switching costs.* Not only do these factors abate direct rivalry, they also deter new entrants.
4. *Channel crowding.* Most distribution channels have limited capacity, and restrict the number of product lines they will handle. Computer retailers have space for about five manufacturers at a time. Each new line of computers imposes fixed costs, ranging from training, to allocation of shelf space, spare parts management, and so forth. New entrants must either chase niche segments or pay substantially larger margins to offset the retailers' extra costs. Sometimes the incumbents have preempted the existing channels, with long-run or exclusive arrangements, leaving the prospective entrant with the cost of establishing a completely new channel.

Expected Reactions of Incumbents. Barriers to entry will be raised or lowered depending on how aggressively the incumbents have defended their position in the past. If they have ignored previous entrants or been unwilling to take a short-run profit hit to protect their position, then further entrants will be encouraged. When they have retaliated hard in the past, regularly signal their deep commitment to the market, and have deep pockets to back up their threats, then a prospective entrant would be foolish to make a frontal attack. A flank attack on a small, unprotected segment may be the only way to enter.

Turning Barriers into Gateways.[10] The height of the perceived barriers depends on who is looking at them; a well-endowed entrant from an adjacent market may be able to nullify them if they have a strong brand name, a ready-made distribution and services network, or lower costs because they source off-shore. Incumbents may be restrained from retaliating if the entrant has deep pockets or signals a willingness to spend heavily to gain a position. Airbus Industries entered the U.S. market by offering financing provided by European governments that even Boeing was unwilling to match. Late entrants may actually gain an advantage from being late. They can employ the latest technologies, while copying the best practices of the incumbent, and improving in areas where customers appear to be dissatisfied.

CUSTOMER POWER

Relations between customers and sellers range from tight, just-in-time manufacturing systems, where suppliers of auto parts become extensions of the auto assemblers, to mass market encounters of proprietary drug makers with seekers of branded cold remedies in super-combo drugstores. The ability of auto-makers to force down prices by playing suppliers against each other is legendary—to the detriment of the suppliers' profitability. Cold remedy makers are not as vulnerable to bargaining pressure because their end customers are not price-sensitive; but they still face aggressive retailers who control access to the shelves and extract sizable promotional allowances, quantity discounts, and other charges for the privilege. The extent of customer power in these and other situations depends on the credibility of their bargaining leverage and their sensitivity to price—each having a number of dimensions.

Bargaining leverage is enhanced when there are:

- few customers making large-volume puchases. Consequently the supplying firm becomes dependent, and faces considerable excess capacity if the relationship is severed. This is the plight of private label suppliers to large retailers such as Sears.

- few constraints on the customers to making a switch from one supplier to another; either because there is little differentiation, the costs of switching are low, or there is a cost-competitive substitute. If so, loyalty is ephemeral, and the conversation soon turns to price.

- credible threats of backward integration, that can and will be used to wring concessions on prices and terms under the guise of making the "make" alternative more attractive than continuing to "buy." This threat continually overhangs the beverage can market, where more than 25 percent of all cans are made by the beer and soft drink companies. Similarly, large long-distance customers such as banks and governments often contemplate bypassing the public telephone network to build their own system. Some large liability insurance customers are protesting high premiums by self-insuring and spreading the risk among many operating units.

- knowledgeable customers who know their suppliers' costs, or have learned that the supplier badly needs their business to soak up excess capacity.

Price sensitivity is a measure of how important lower prices are to the customer and hence the intensity of their demands for concessions. Sensitivity is heightened when:

- the product or service has little influence on the performance or quality of the end-product.

- the cost of the product is a significant proportion of the customer's total costs.

- the customer is suffering poor profitability, and looks to the supplier for help. When survival is at stake the pressure for concessions can be intense.

When these factors describe buyers who perceive little differentiation among the competing suppliers, the pressure on price is further intensified.

SUPPLIER POWER

The ability of large suppliers to withstand bargaining efforts by their customers and increase their share of the value created depends on:

- their size relative to the customers'. This is especially noticeable in the advantages large textile fiber manufacturers have relative to their small, dispersed customer base.

- the reliance of the customer on the supplier's product, either because he can't get an equivalent quality elsewhere, or he is locked into the supplier to the extent that the cost of switching is much greater than any benefits a new supplier can promise.

- the credibility of their threats to integrate forward in their value chain and sell directly to the end customer. This threat will blunt aggressive attempts to get better prices.

THREAT OF SUBSTITUTES

Air express is a fast-moving example of the restless effects of substitutes on the markets they assault. The story in the following boxed insert[11] describes how the shaky competitive equilibrium among overnight express companies was upset by improvements in the ability of facsimile machines to meet buyers' needs for immediate delivery of documents. The impediments to buyers using these machines are falling fast; initial costs are dropping and there is a growing network of facsimile machines on the receiving end.

THE INTERPLAY OF COMPETITION IN THE AIR EXPRESS MARKET

Although the market for next-day delivery of documents and small parcels was becoming global in 1989, each national market had a distinct competitive structure. Within the U.S market there were seven major rivals, that fell into three groups. Federal Express, Airborne Express, and Purolator concentrated only on this market. Emery Air Freight was a heavy freight handler that had moved into small packages and overnight letters. United Parcel Service and the Postal Service got most of their revenues from other services, but were aggressively pursuing a larger share of the overnight air express market.

Direct rivalry. Although the U.S. market was hardly 14 years old by 1989, and growth was still a heady 20 percent a year, the future was bleak for most players. Emery, Purolator, and Airborne were losing money, and the Postal Service barely broke even. Even the market leader Federal Express, with 37 percent of the market, saw operating profit margins shrink from 16.9% in 1981 to 9.8% in 1988. Meanwhile UPS, with a 15 percent share, was determinedly using its financial resources to gain share. Traditionally UPS avoided price discounts. But in 1989 they introduced volume rate cuts that smaller competitors couldn't match.

While a relentless price war, due to aggressive rivals fighting for share to maximize utilization of their high fixed-cost systems, coupled with overcapacity and impending maturity were mainly blamed for the declining attractiveness, there were other drains on profits.

Customer bargaining power. By 1987 air express services were largely undifferentiated, with customers flocking to the lowest-price courier. While infrequent users of air express paid $14.00 for an overnight letter, big users were getting big price breaks. Federal Express led the way with a 50 percent price cut to AT&T, to encourage heavier usage. Their reasoning was that the more packages a driver could pick up at a location the lower the cost per package. Airborne followed with discounts as much as 84 percent below Federal's rate card, to capture a three-year contract to become IBM's primary U.S. overnight carrier. To the further dismay of the air express companies, some customers were putting tighter controls on usage, and encouraging their employees to use second-day service. The second-day service was 30 percent cheaper, but the packages often got delivered with the overnight mail because workers at the express hubs couldn't easily distinguish one from the other.

Substitutes. The market for overnight delivery of documents had grown mainly at the expense of regular postal services, but also drew from traditional telex and teletype services. All these alternatives were being shouldered aside by the explosive growth of facsimile which offered rapid telephone transmission of an exact rendering of an original, including pictures and signatures.

By 1989 fax had become the preferred delivery medium for short documents and was expected to take as much as 30 percent of the overnight letter delivery market. Not only was fax faster, it was also cheaper. Fax took off in 1987 when equipment sales grew from 180,000 to 465,000 units, and created a critical mass of machines that could communicate. In effect, each unit sold created demand for additional units. The trigger was the 1986 introduction by Sharp and Canon of so-called convenience facsimile machines. By eliminating some features, prices were cut from more than $3,000 to under $1,000 and the machines became affordable.

Facsimile transmission of documents is having a double impact on the profitability of the overnight delivery market: There is a lower ceiling on prices the customers are willing to pay, and the ensuing slowdown in market growth has intensified the direct rivalry among carriers looking for incremental capacity to fill their high fixed-cost airplanes and sorting and delivery facilities.

Substitutes depress the profit prospects of the firms in a market when there is a significant economic incentive for customers to switch and the costs of switching are low. This threat to profitability is worsened if the rivalry among the firms offering the substitute is intense, and leads to rapid declines in the price of the substitute or improvements in relative performance. The picture can change very rapidly, as we see with the incursion of facsimile into air express.

COMBINING THE FORCES TO ASSESS ATTRACTIVENESS

Each competitive force works in combination with the other forces to determine the overall attractiveness of the market. A rough indication of their joint effect on attractiveness can be found in Exhibit 5–4. If the level of the factors that shape each competitive force is found mainly in the left-hand column, the average profitability is almost certain to be below average. Future profit prospects will remain depressed if the conditions on each factor remain the same or worsen.

However, Exhibit 5–4 can only give a directionally correct idea of whether—and why—a particular market offers appealing or repelling prospects for long-run profits for the average player. Precise estimates are elusive for several reasons: Firstly, the relative importance of each of the 25 factors enumerated in Exhibit 5–4 is unknown and variable across markets. Some guidance as to which factors are likely to be generally important can be extracted from the PIMS (Profit Impact of Market Strategies) data, on the performance of 2,200 businesses. These findings are summarized in the following boxed insert. Second, the factors seldom all point clearly in one direction. It is more likely that some will be favorable, but their positive effects on profits will be negated by other factors that are unfavorable. Even when two factors do point in the same direction, their effects are not always additive. Sometimes they multiply, as when strong buyers amass even greater-than-expected bargaining power by playing off two warring suppliers—each desperately bidding for their patronage.

A further complication is the impact of trends in the macro-environment that can accentuate or dampen the impact of the five forces. The influences

Exhibit 5-4 Factors Influencing Market Attractiveness

	Will Lower Profitability	*Will Raise Profitability*
1. *Rivalry among Competitors*		
—structure	numerous or equally balanced	one dominant
—fixed costs	high	low
—differentiation	negligible	substantial
—buyer switching costs	low	high
—diversity of strategies and objectives	significant	limited
—exit barriers	low	high
2. *Entry Barriers*		
—factor costs	entrant has advantage	incumbent has advantage
—scale thresholds	low	high
—differentiation	negligible	substantial
—channel crowding	easy access	difficult access
—incumbent reactions in past	passive	aggressive
3. *Customer Power*		
Bargaining Leverage		
—number of buyers	few	many
—purchase volume	large	small
—ability to switch to substitute or other suppliers	easy	difficult
—threat of back integration	highly credible	impossible
—knowledge of supplier	thorough	negligible
Price Sensitivity		
—Influence on end-product performance	modest	major
—cost of product as % of total costs	high	low
—profitability	poor	healthy
—perceived product differentiation	negligible	significant

continued

Exhibit 5-4 Continued

	Will Lower Profitability	Will Raise Profitability
4. *Supplier Power*		
—size relative to customer	large	small
—dependence on supplier	high	low
—credibility of threats to forward integrate	high	low
5. *Threat of Substitutes*		
—economic incentive to switch	high	low
—resistance to switching	low and declining	high and increasing

of government intervention, technological change and market growth operate indirectly so their impact is harder to predict. But they can't ever be overlooked, for they sometimes emerge to become the dominant influence on attractiveness.

Government and Regulatory Intervention. This influence is pervasive, and especially strong when the intervention defines the rules of competition to the extent of deciding who competes. Regulatory requirements often restrict entry, usually because there is a scarce resource such as a radio or television broadcast frequency to be allocated. Performance or safety standards are more subtle barriers, especially when they favor the incumbents in the market. Testing of drugs to satisfy FDA safety requirements can take five to seven years. Pollution standards may determine whether there is even a market. If acid emissions standards for power plants burning coal are loose, then there is little or no demand for scrubbers of the stack gases. As standards tighten the market suddenly becomes much larger.

Regulatory rulings have had a powerful influence on industries such as telecommunications. AT&T was prevented by law from meeting MCI's prices on long-distance service for seven years after deregulation to give this entrant time to get established.

Governments are also powerful buyers. The purchasing policies of the Department of Defense determine how much profit contractors will make, as they shift from cost-plus to fixed price contracts. Government foreign policy may even determine whether a buyer, such as a COMECON state agency, can even be served.

Technological Change. No competitive force is immune from the restless

THE IMPACT OF MARKET FACTORS ON PROFITABILITY: EVIDENCE FROM PIMS[12]
(Profit Impact of Market Strategies)

W ithin the PIMS data base on the environment, strategies and performance of more than 2,200 business are variables that correspond to most of the factors that influence market attractiveness. The data allow us to compare rates of return (ROI) for hypothetical businesses that operate within attractive markets (specifically they are rated in the top 20 percent of each factor) with other businesses that are in markets at the bottom fifth on each factor. These two businesses are otherwise assumed to be the same on the other strategic factors known to influence profitability, such as quality, market share, and investment intensity. Thus the differences in their performance are solely due to the varying intensity of the competitive forces.

Factor	Unattractive Market		Attractive Market	
	Level	Impact On ROI	Level	Impact On ROI
Market growth rate	−4%	−1.2	+11%	+1.1
% purchases from top three suppliers	17%	−0.8	70%	+0.8
Purchase importance (% of customers total purchases)	5%	−3.0	<1%	+1.8
Purchase amount (average size of purchase)	$10K+	−4.0	<$1K	+5.2
TOTAL IMPACT (variation from average pre-tax ROI of the 2200 businesses of 22.4%)		−9.0%		+8.9%

To put these results into perspective, the prototype business operating in an unattractive market would have an ROI of 13.4% (that is, 9.0% less than the average ROI of 22.4%). The business fortunate enough to serve an attractive market would have an ROI of 31.3% (when all other factors are held constant).

effect of technology. Substitutes are creations of technology, and become increasingly threatening as price-performance improvements are made. While this displacement effect is obvious, other consequences are more subtle: information technology may help to open a gateway for new entrants by eliminating the need for large-scale distribution, and rivalry may increase if new manufacturing technology makes short production runs feasible and accelerates product design cycles. The balance of power with customers or suppliers may also shift, depending on where the technology is developed. Otis Elevator reduced the bargaining power of service customers by tying them into a computer monitoring system that anticipated breakdowns. Big customers can also assert power by flexing their technological prowess as General Motors is attempting to do with a standardized language that will permit all their manufacturing equipment to communicate.

Growth and Volatility of Market Demand. Vigorous growth generally enhances market attractiveness, because demand may exceed supply and diminish the pressure on prices. Meanwhile, the rivals in the market are preoccupied with building capacity to meet demand and are less likely to react to losses in their share.

Unfortunately, high-growth markets lose their luster if a surplus of competitors is attracted, and each brings unrealistic market-share expectations. This is a volatile situation that eventually leads to a wrenching shake-out.[13] The odds of a surplus of competitors go up when (a) the market and its growth rate have high visibility, and firms in related markets are anxious that they not miss an inviting opportunity, (b) there are few apparent limits to growth to dampen the enthusiasm of prospective entrants, (c) barriers to entry are low, (d) products employ an existing technology rather than a risky or protected technology, and (e) some potential entrants have low visibility, and surprise everyone when they emerge.

When growth slows there is a noticeable shift to share competition, where gains by one firm are resisted by other firms trying to avoid reductions in their capacity utilization. Meanwhile, customers are becoming more knowledgeable about the product, and less willing to pay a price premium. At the same time, slowing growth reduces the threat to new entrants who are likely to be deterred by the overcrowded conditions.

Using the Competitive Forces Framework to Improve Decisions. What is the value of this framework for organizing the competitive forces if precise forecasts are so elusive? It's greatest virtue is that it demands thinking about the future of the market, as a consequence of the changes and evolution in the underlying factors. The payoff comes when the management team understands the forces they have been coping with, and begins to think about how changes in strategy might alter the attractiveness of their market to their advantage. These are "change the game" strategies that dampen the competitive forces, perhaps by dramatically increasing differentiation, raising switching costs, or using capital investments to raise the minimum scale of operations to deter potential entrants. Markets do not unfold inexorably, with the firms on the sidelines as interested observers. Their strategic responses also determine the future of the market. Even when prospects in the overall market are poor, there are usually protected segments that offer superior profitability. The trick is to find them early, and exploit them forcefully.

SUMMARY: CHOOSING THE MARKET ARENA AND TARGET SEGMENT

Markets are complex, moving targets for strategists. Their structures are continually shifting in response to changes in the environment, customer requirements, and competitive behavior. Thus, the first challenge is to define which products, services, and customers to include in the market definition.

As markets fragment into finer-grained segments it becomes increasingly difficult to serve an entire market with a common strategy. Instead, businesses are having to focus on distinct segments or use different strategies for different segments. But which segments should be the focus? At a minimum a target segment should be different from other segments in requirements and responsiveness to marketing efforts. Attractive segments will also have superior growth and profit prospects as a consequence of a favorable competitive structure.

Market segments are like mini-markets in which each of the five forces of competition has been subdued. However, there are some important differences between the market and the segment level of analysis. Potential segment entrants include both those outside the market, as well as those serving adjacent product or customer groups within the market. Barriers to segment entry are correspondingly lower. Direct rivalry will include all firms serving only that segment with a tailored product, plus those serving all segments. On the other hand, properly chosen buyer segments will result in sharp differences in buyer power, and the cost to serve those buyers. Supplier power may also be fragmented if the different product types require different inputs.

Just because a segment is attractive on structural grounds doesn't mean it is a suitable target for a particular firm. Before this can be known we have to know more about the capabilities of the firm. Only when there is a good match of the skills and resources a firm possesses or can acquire, with the requirements of the segment, should the segment be chosen as a target. The reward for finding a good fit is a competitive advantage. This is what the next three chapters are about.

Assessing Advantages

*The first sustaining edge of excellence, "Take exceptional care
of customers via superior service and superior quality."*
—TOM PETERS and NANCY AUSTIN

The true nature of marketing is not serving *the customer—it is
outwitting, outflanking and outfighting your competitors.*
—AL RIES and JACK TROUT

Competitive strategy is about seeking new edges in a market while slowing the erosion of present advantages. These advantages result from some combination of low delivered cost and differentiation that offers superior customer value. The promised payoff is market share dominance and above-average profitability.

The less attractive the profit prospects of a market, the more pressing the search for profitable advantages.[1] Even when market demand is sliding, it is possible to be highly profitable with the advantage of a strongly differentiated product. A sample of 800 businesses, all with declining unit sales, drawn from the PIMS (Profit Impact of Market Strategies) data base, found that roughly 150 were highly successful, with operating profits averaging at least 15 percent of sales over the past four years. In judgments of product and service quality they scored high, in the seventieth percentile on average. Another 150 businesses from this same group lost money; their grades on product quality averaged in the forty-third percentile.

The development of an effective competitive strategy begins with a tough-minded understanding of the advantages and deficiencies of a business, and the vulnerability of the current position to copying or leapfrogging by competitors. Otherwise, there is no basis for choosing the best moves to defend or enhance this position. This chapter is about the ways a management team can make a thorough assessment of their businesses' competitive advantages as a prelude to identifying the specific competitive strategies. This assessment will be guided with a framework that distinguishes the *sources* of advantage—the superior skills, resources and controls that describe the "distinctive competencies" of a business—from their consequences for *positional* superiority in cost or customer value, and the resulting market share and profit *performance*.

PERSPECTIVES ON COMPETITIVE STRATEGIES[2]

The two quotations at the beginning of the chapter offer contrasting ideas on how to gain advantage. Trout and Ries are captivated by military metaphors for competition. They argue that success comes from looking for weak points in the position of competitors, and launching attacks against these vulnerabilities. In their view this is what Pepsi was doing when they took advantage of a sweeter taste to challenge Coke in the cola wars. Similarly, Savin exploited Xerox's weaknesses in small, inexpensive copiers to establish themselves.[3]

Seemingly in opposition, Peters and Austin[4] observe there are only two ways to create and sustain superior performance—what they call sustaining edges of excellence—superior care of customers and constant innovation, and these in turn are built on turned-on people and inspired leadership. In their view grand strategic moves count far less than managing every aspect of the business just a bit better than the norm the customer expects. The customer is the arbiter of whether an advantage has been achieved.

These two contrasting views on how to compete also shape how managers decide what advantages distinguish their business, and how those advantages were gained. Are they inclined to take the vantage point of customers or competitors? Not all businesses will tilt toward one dominant perspective or the other; some will combine the best aspects of both and be truly market-driven, while others march to their own drummer with a self-centered or internal perspective (see Figure 6–1).

Competitor-Centered Assessments of Advantage. These are based on direct management comparisons with a few target competitors. This mindset is most often found in concentrated, capital-intensive industries, that have been stalemated because slow growth and technological maturity have reduced competition to a zero-sum game. In this setting the players are constantly looking for an edge, so the emphasis is on "beat the competition." These businesses watch their relative cost position very closely, quickly match the marketing initiatives of their competitors, and look for sustainable advantages in technology. With high fixed costs comes a fixation on capacity utilization, so there are periodic bursts of price cutting to

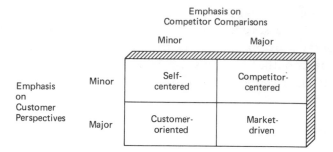

FIGURE 6–1 Perspectives on Advantage

protect market share and volume. Managers keep a close watch on overall market share and contracts won or lost to detect shifts in their competitive position. At all times they are sensitive to the relative sizes of capabilities, especially distribution and sales coverage, and plant capacity. Customers are not ignored, for they are the prizes gained by prevailing over the competitors.

Customer-Oriented Assessments. These rely on customers to make the comparisons of the business with its competitors, rather than using the collective judgments of the management team. This perspective relies on detailed analyses of customer benefits and relative satisfaction within end-use segments, and works backward from the customer to the firm to identify the actions needed to secure new advantages. This "market back" orientation is most evident in fragmented industries where there are numerous competitors, each trying to stake out a distinct position in a highly segmented market such as magazines. It is also found in service-intensive industries such as investment banking where new services are easily imitated, all the players have the same cost of funds, and entry appears easy. Relatively little time is spent watching competitors and making comparisons with their capabilities and performance—the emphasis is on the quality of customer relations. Evidence of continuing customer satisfaction and loyalty is more meaningful than market share.

Self-Centered Businesses. These look to year-to-year improvements in key operating ratios, such as inventory turns, scrap rates, and sales per employee, to assess their performance. There is usually a strong sales volume orientation, so sales growth is a key indicator of competitive performance. The absence of a direct comparison with other competitors means this is an inward perspective. This is why general merchandise retailers have so often been undermined by specialty retailers; an acceptable sales volume increase in products such as towels will mask losses in share to bath boutiques. A business can only afford or survive this perspective if it has no direct competitors, by virtue of a commanding technology lead or a well-protected market position, or all the other competitors behave the same way and coexist comfortably.

Giving Meaning to Markets. Why should it matter how managers view their competitive position? The reason is that markets are complex, ambiguous, and fast-changing abstractions, that are given meaning in the minds of managers by processes of selective attention and simplification.[5] Otherwise they couldn't cope with the welter of trends and events that must be organized, analyzed for patterns, and acted upon. A customer-oriented or competitor-centered perspective helps simplify this unruly part of the environment, by guiding the choice of information to be selected and how it is screened and interpreted.

Simplification comes at a cost, which is the risk that only a partial and biased picture of reality is created. A competitor-centered perspective leads to a preoccupation with costs and controllable activities that can be compared directly with the corresponding activities of close rivals. Customer-focused approaches have the advantage of examining the full range of competitive choices in light of the customers' needs and perceptions of superiority, but lack an obvious connection to activities and variables that are controlled by management.

A truly *market-driven management* works to avoid costly oversimplification by balancing openness to customer inputs with direct competitor comparisons. This is tough to do—for the prevailing perspective is so much a part of the mind-set of the organization that the absence of balance seems entirely natural. Only when problems arise are the negative consequences appreciated and confronted. This is what John Akers of IBM concluded in early 1987, when he blamed the revenue and profit problems of the previous two years on getting out of touch with customers. The company persisted in trying to sell them products, when what they wanted was solutions to network connectivity problems and help in using their information technology for gains in productivity and competitive advantage. The dual culprits were sales force complacency, born in the previous era of very strong demand, and the distraction of aggressive competitors such as DEC with an easy "networking" capability and niche players such as Tandem with a highly regarded line of fault-tolerant machines. These competitive incursions demanded response, and subtly changed the mind-set from customer-oriented to competitor-centered. This is what Akers was trying to redress.

THE CONCEPT OF COMPETITIVE ADVANTAGE

The picture of the competitive advantages or deficiencies of a business is not complete when we know that a business has a strong position based on superior customer value or the lowest delivered cost. If the information is to be of practical value we need answers to three more questions: How were these advantages gained? How valuable (profitable) are they? Can they be sustained?

Positional and performance superiority are derived from relative superiority in the skills and resources a business has to deploy. In turn these skills and resources are the result of past investments made to enhance the competitive position. The future sustainability of the positional advantage—and continuing profitability—depends on the impediments the business can put in the way of competitors' efforts to imitate or leapfrog. Because these barriers to imitation are continually being chipped away, the business has to keep investing to refurbish the advantage or find new ones. Thus the creation and sustenance of a competitive advantage is a long-run iterative process with continuing feedbacks of information and investment dollars (see Figure 6–2).

SOURCES OF ADVANTAGE

If positional superiority is the "what" dimension of competitive advantage, then superior skills, resources, and controls are the "how" dimension. Taken together, these three sources of advantage represent the ability of a business to do more (or do better) than competition.

Superior resources are the tangible requirements for competition we can readily see and count because they have a physical presence or can be found

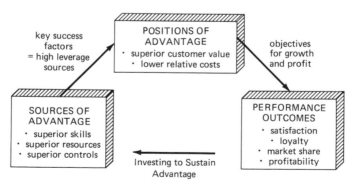

FIGURE 6–2 The Elements of Competitive Advantage

in financial and activity reports. Much competitor analysis is directed at understanding the relative size of resources because it is possible to make direct comparisons and rankings of competitors on such key inputs as:

- distribution coverage (number of dealers or retailers who carry and display the product)
- number of service and sales people by territory, region, and market
- scale of manufacturing facilities and capacity utilization, right down to the details of the size and throughput of specific machines
- total investment in dedicated computer systems and software support
- expenditures on advertising and promotion support
- financial capacity and cost of capital—both debt and equity—as a result of the financial structure
- cost of raw materials and purchased inputs such as energy as a result of ownership of raw materials sources or supply agreements

Brand names are also a resource with a value based on goodwill built up from the residue of past successful efforts to compete. However, the financial value of solid and respected names such as Band-Aid, Tide, or Jello is usually obscured from view until someone agrees to pay a premium over the appraised values of tangible assets, such as land, equipment, and inventory. When Philip Morris acquired General Foods for $5.8 billion, the tobacco giant added $2.8 billion worth of goodwill to its own balance sheet.

Superior skills are the distinctive capabilities of key personnel—"what we do better than anyone else"—that transform the passive resources into competitive weapons. A superior resource only offers an opportunity to gain advantage—it is given meaning and impact by the mobilization of the following skills:

- specialized knowledge of the needs and requirements of a distinct segment. The capillaries of the software market are filled with specialists who have an in-depth understanding of, say, the problems that dentists have with accounting systems.
- strong relationships with customers—an historic strength of J. P. Morgan in serving the investment banking needs of their major corporate accounts—or with retailers. This is a skill Compaq Computers nurtured, when they realized that computer retailers were key and that their shelf space would become very scarce. Instead of competing with them by selling direct they offered their dealers exclusive franchises and attractive margins.

- design and applications expertise (worth a boxed insert because its importance is so often overlooked).
- a fast and flexible response capability. A German maker of custom paving machines swept the market with an ability to use CAD/CAM (computer-aided design/computer-aided manufacturing) and a flexible organization to respond to requests for proposals in seven days rather than the 35 days of their competitors.
- ability to manage information systems and networks to deliver information and services to remote locations.
- close attention to operating detail and organizational arrangements that reward continuing efforts to control costs.
- experience in identifying, negotiating, and managing alliances such as joint ventures and technology licensing agreements.

In short, it is not enough to know the scale of resources a competitor has to deploy. The fact that Merck, Johnson and Johnson, and 3M are heavy spenders on R&D is interesting—but becomes significant when unleashed by the superior climate for innovation in these decentralized firms.

Skill sets are often underestimated because they are so elusive. Most firms have trouble knowing how customer-oriented they are. This happens, despite the long-term superiority of an organization committed to listening to and responding aggressively to customer needs, with superior service, knowledge, and courtesy. This mind-set pervades companies like Marriott and Ryder, and sets them apart in the eyes of their customers.

THE RESURGENCE OF DESIGN SKILLS

For most U.S companies design is a low-level—and often last-minute—cosmetics function. This is definitely not the case with leading foreign competitors such as Braun and Honda. These firms have long recognized that good design not only appeals to the eye, but is reliable and economical to manufacture and service. The old ways in the United States are changing in the wake of the design success of the Ford Taurus-Sable cars. Here was an old-line company that invested heavily in a new organization centered around design teams with a high corporate profile and a mandate to be involved in all facets from specification to manufacturing. This is a package of skills on which long-run success is built.

This issue is so central to the theme of effectively competing that we will return to it in the final chapter and ask how it can best be achieved.

Superior controls provide the information glue that tells managers the current state of health of their business and how well the resources are being combined with skills to deliver superior performance. If they are working properly they will deliver the kind of information we're going to describe shortly that will tell us how well we are competing.

Unfortunately "controls" have both a negative and a narrow connotation to most managers, who see them as intrusive, inflexible, and irrelevant to running the business. But properly configured, cost controls, quality tracking, customer satisfaction monitoring, inventory management systems, cash flow reports, and the like, will improve the business in three ways.[6] First, they will provide accurate information on which to base decisions. There is no substitute for knowing where profits are being made, by product line, market segment, or individual customer. Citicorp is far ahead of most banks on this score, with a tight system of credit checks combined with financial controls. But to know profits, one must know costs: McDonald's knows their business in infinite detail, down to the number of washes before a plastic tray loses its luster and has to be discarded.

The second contribution of controls is to communicate management expectations through the standards of performance that provide the reference point for the system. This is especially true in service businesses, and customer-contact functions in general. Finally, good controls will quickly and graphically compare what is expected with what is actually being tracked. Are we achieving the satisfaction levels we wanted in the emerging segment we have targeted? Is the segment growing as fast as forecast? And so on. Without this information there is no basis for learning, correcting mistakes, and adjusting assumptions to better fit reality.

POSITIONS OF ADVANTAGE

What we see in the market—from the vantage point of customers or competitors—is the positional superiority of a business. This can be achieved by providing superior customer value or reaching the lowest delivered cost. To succeed with a value strategy the price premium the customer is willing to pay must exceed the costs of providing the extra value. Similarly, a cost strategy must offer acceptable value to customers so prices are close to the average of the competitors. When the low-cost position is achieved by sacrificing too much quality or eliminating worthwhile features, the price discount demanded by customers will more than offset the cost advantage.

The distinction between antecedent *sources* of advantage and the *positional* advantage gained when they are deployed adroitly is clearly seen in the turnaround of Foremost-McKesson in the drug distribution business. In the late 1970s volumes were stagnating at $1 billion, and their 12,000 independent pharmacies were struggling to compete with chains in price and availability. Management recognized that their skills—derived from an in-depth knowledge of their suppliers' and customers' businesses and the myriad of products they handled—could be parlayed into something more than a delivery and billing service.

A renamed McKesson Corporation enhanced the existing skills with a $125 million investment in computer hardware and systems that sharply reduced the costs of the many activities between the suppliers' finished goods and the pharmacy shelf. With this system orders can be placed at any time via a hand-held programmable computer that hooks up to a regular phone line. Deliveries are made daily and the rarest drugs can be readily obtained. These actions made the firm so efficient that its suppliers could not possibly do so well on their own.[7]

Beyond price and availability, McKesson used the flow of information about transactions to design unique value-added services. They can now help their suppliers manage inventories, analyze market data, and plan new products. Retailers are linked more closely through leases of electronic ordering equipment, shelf management plans, and even the provision of price labels. The performance rewards have been handsome—sales have grown more than fourfold and return on assets is a solid 20 percent.

Value Superiority.   Customers are seldom persuaded to choose moderate performance and quality at an average price. If the benefits of superior performance or quality are not important they will simply opt for the lowest price. Otherwise they go with the alternative that is noticeably better—in ways that are important to them—so long as the extra price they pay doesn't exceed the extra benefits (or their budget). The alternative offering the best value has the largest spread between perceived benefits and perceived costs. There are many ways to deliver value superiority as we see in the value map shown in Figure 6–3.

Most businesses position their offerings on the diagonal from the economy to the premium end and thus price their products to capture the customer value they have created. However, some of the competitors will be off the diagonal, by accident or design. Those charging average prices for lower benefits are offering inferior value—not a secure position for the long run.

A winning value position for customers is superior benefits for an average price. This is how the Acura Legend Coupé was positioned to pene-

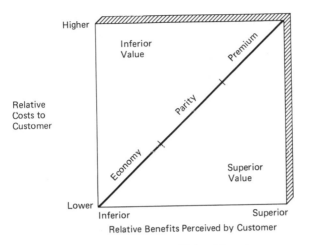

FIGURE 6–3 Value Mapping

trate the U.S. market. This car was acclaimed on many dimensions . . .
"sumptuously smooth and very quick . . . great seats . . . stable at 120 mph
. . . its viscously smooth V6 and excellent ergonomics place it in good company." Indeed it was judged to offer the same level of benefits as luxury
coupés from BMW and Mercedes-Benz, yet the price was $20,000 less.
This superior value was designed to capture attention and market share for
a new car line to be sold independently of Honda. Subsequently the Acura
price did rise and the car moved closer to the diagonal.

The most profitable position, according to the PIMS data base, is to be
on the diagonal of the value map at the premium end of the market. Surprisingly, superior value businesses offering a premium quality product
with no price premium are almost as profitable. According to Buzzell and
Gale,[8] what is lost in price is made up in lower costs that stem from their
ability to gain share while incurring lower marketing costs because of the
attraction of superior value.

There are many ways to differentiate products and service that create
meaningful benefits for customers:

- providing superior quality that cuts customer costs or improves their
  performance. Kodak leads the photographic film market with consistent high quality, because the consequences of poor quality are immediately evident
- providing a superior service or technical assistance capability through
  speed, responsiveness to difficult orders, or ability to solve customer
  problems

- utilizing a strong brand name that connotes the appropriate image of style (Gucci or Lancôme) or luxury and prestige (Mercedes-Benz)
- offering a full line of products in a market where one-stop shopping is important, or modularity of systems components is desirable
- attaining wide distribution coverage
- being first to offer innovative features employing new technologies.

Cost Leadership. The lowest delivered cost position—not simply the lowest factory cost—is usually achieved by firms that offer standard or economy products. This cost advantage is gained with large-scale operations that permit spreading of overheads, low factor costs by operating in low wage areas such as Taiwan and Thailand, dedicated cost control, limited product lines, and a willingness to invest in cost-reducing plant and equipment.

The most direct approach to a low-cost position is to simply remove all the frills and extras from the product offering. This is how discount audio stores, legal services clinics, and grocery stores selling bulk goods from crates in out-of-the-way locations operate. A cost leader must offer products that are comparable to those of the average competitor and acceptable to buyers. This is easier when there are well-known product standards for design size and performance, as is the case with industrial products such as electric motors. Then a company like Emerson Electric can excel with its combination of automated facilities, efficient plant scale, and nonunion work force. However, in terms of product features, service coverage, or other attributes Emerson is no more than average.

The lowest delivered cost position pays when price discounting is not necessary, so the cost advantage can be translated directly into above-average profits.

PERFORMANCE OUTCOMES

The most popular indicators of a successful competitive strategy are market share and profitability. They are closely related at any given point in time, although the reasons for the correlation have been hotly disputed. Seldom are other performance indicators such as customer satisfaction used, even though they directly reflect customer responses to the positional advantages of a business.

Market Share. The premise is that we can distinguish winners from losers by the proportion of transactions or volume they have gained, just as the outcome of a horse race is shown by the final standings. The analogy can be quite misleading, for competition is played out over many time periods, while the rules of the game keep changing. Thus it may be dangerous to extend the interpretation of market share from an indication of past performance to a predictor of future advantages.

This doesn't mean current market share won't be a good predictor of future market share in many markets. We will be more confident of maintaining a large share when the positional advantages are hard for competitors to match, and the market boundaries are stable. Dominance of a market in which competitive forces are evolving rapidly is no guarantee of future advantage. Since most positional advantages decay over time, we are likely to find the share of large firms slipping (or converging toward the mean), while small firms typically gain share.

Profitability. Current profitability is the reward from past advantages after the current outlays needed to sustain or enhance future advantages have been made. Because profitability is influenced by actions taken in many previous time frames, it is unlikely to be a complete reflection of current advantages. When the environment is turbulent it may be a misleading indication. The objectives of the business may also distort the signals that current profitability sends about the strength of the competitive position. Above-average reported profits may be extracted by harvesting the business, and cutting investments in the sources of future advantage. Conversely, the business may decide to not take profits now but exchange them for increased market share with a penetration price.

Market Share and Profitability. There is no denying these two variables are strongly related; on average for each 10 percent difference in share there is a corresponding 4.7 percent difference in return on investment for the businesses in the PIMS data base. However, this seemingly innocuous fact has been widely misinterpreted and misused, to the detriment of sound strategic thinking. At one time market share was viewed as the cause of profitability, due to economies of scale and experience differences. On sober reflection and reanalysis, a number of other reasons for the relationship have emerged, that give different strategic messages.

There is a competing possibility that profits cause market share. In this scenario, businesses that are lucky or especially insightful stake out strong and defensible positions early in the product life cycle. With the initial profit rewards, plus their superior skills gained from early learning about the market, they make astute continuing investments that enable them to grow faster than their less fortunate rivals.

Most likely—as Figure 6–4 suggests—both mechanisms are operating concurrently; although the relative importance may vary as the market matures. In the early stages, first mover advantages are most influential. With maturation, the challenge is to adapt the strategy to new requirements for

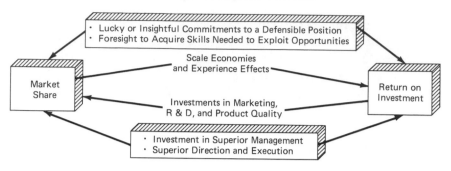

FIGURE 6–4 Market Share Profitability

success while capitalizing on the initial advantages. Some first movers can't shift their strategy quickly enough to cope with the fragmentation of markets, technology changes, and other shocks that offer gateways for new entrants.

In summary, market share is best viewed as an outcome of strategic moves, and a measure of success, and not an intrinsically valuable asset to be bought or sold. What counts are the fundamentals, as reflected in the relative position of the business on the key sources and positions of advantage.

KEY SUCCESS FACTORS

Knowing a business has gained an advantage in sources, positions, and performance is only a means to an end. What managers really want to know is how to get the greatest improvement in performance for the least effort. For this purpose we want to find the handful of skills and resources that will exert the most leverage on positional advantage and performance outcomes. These are the key success factors (KSFs) that must be managed obsessively to ensure success. Poor performance on these factors will almost certainly mean failure.

While a brief section on key success factors is obligatory in most strategic plans, the so called "factors" are usually too superficial and too numerous to be actionable. There will be a long listing of "things" such as customer service and access to distribution, rather than input-output relationships that can be managed.

For a KSF to be useful it should persuasively identify a source of advantage where a change could have a large impact on positional advantage, and where differences among competitors are sizable. If these conditions aren't satisfied then the factor is a low priority for management attention (see Figure 6–5).

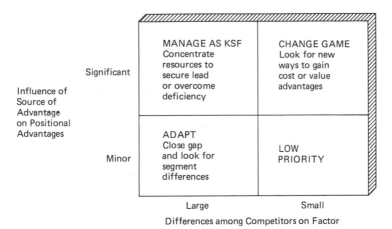

FIGURE 6–5 Strategic Implications of Key Success Factors (KSFs)

What we are looking for is relationships like the following that identify significant differences among competitors A, B, and C.

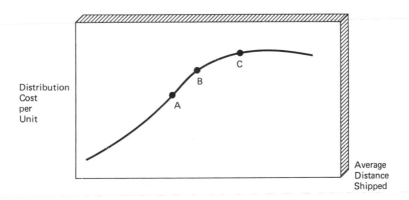

Each KSF will be unique to the market (or market segment). In the elevator market, service coverage is a major determinant of speed of service response. But in the deregulating transportation and communications markets it is ownership of a large facilities network—whether a long-distance telephone network or a railroad track network—that counts. Those with large networks gain economies of flow or density that yield large cost advantages.

It is not enough to know the KSFs; they must be aggressively nurtured. This is how the Pepperidge Farm division of Campbell Soup Company regained share and profits in the ready-to-eat cookie market.[9] In 1986 the firm increased its share from 3.5 to 4.5 percent, which is very respectable in a $3 billion, fragmented category. To compete with other cookie companies, such as Nabisco, Keebler, and P&G's Duncan Hines, and cookie stores, the key success factor was identified as freshness. Generally, national cookie makers deliver products to stores from inventories that are five to ten days old. Pepperidge was able to trim these times to less than five days on average, with a goal of 72 hours from ovens to stores. This required setting new production standards and moving information much faster. Previously, orders from drivers were assembled manually at regional offices and mailed to the bakeries. A new information network permitted drivers to record the inventory at each stop with a hand-held computer and periodically phone the information directly to production managers. Supporting actions such as more flexible production equipment were all directed at making major improvements to an important positional attribute.

For a response curve to deserve attention as a KSF there must be some degree of stability in shape. But that doesn't mean they can be counted on to endure; shifts in competitive forces will eventually neutralize old KSFs while creating new ones. The one-time advantages of large-scale or highly specialized manufacturing operations are being blunted by the advent of flexible automation and CAD/CAM. Alert managers will position their firms to capitalize on these new sources of advantage. But first they must be fully knowledgeable about the current sources and positions of advantage.

CUSTOMER-ORIENTED ASSESSMENTS

A proper "market back" assessment relies on the judgments of customers for advice on whether and where an advantage has been achieved. Their feedback comes in various forms: specific value judgments, reports of satisfaction or unhappiness with their purchases and relationships, or the results of their choice decisions. Although customer purchase behavior is the least ambiguous type of information it is also the least revealing, for it doesn't tell us the customer's reasons. This is why firms rely on direct questioning with formal and informal surveys as their main feedback channel. A revealing variant of the customer survey is the positioning map that graphically displays the relationships among competitors.

Customer Value Analysis. The guiding premise for all customer-oriented approaches is that perceived differences between competitors are not meaningful unless they can be converted into:

- benefits—by lowering customer costs or improving their performance,

- that are perceived by a sizable customer segment,
- which these customers value and are willing to pay for, and
- cannot readily obtain elsewhere.

Competitive differences as seen by management don't always pass the benefit test. For example, a manufacturer of hydraulic components, for farm and construction equipment and heavy-duty machinery, was comfortable with their superiority in quality. To this manufacturer it was readily apparent their product line was the broadest in the market and had the widest distribution. These beliefs had been unchallenged until an outsider asked whether the differences really offered benefits. A subsequent survey found that higher quality did mean greater reliability and reduced downtime to customers, and they valued the wide product line because it lessened their system integration problems to have all the parts available from one source. To management's surprise, however, wide distribution was not seen as a benefit—customers didn't believe they were getting noticeably more responsive service. So long as the parts arrived reliably within four hours they were happy. It didn't matter that a distributor was around the corner and could deliver within two hours. This was a clear signal to the manufacturer that their costly, widespread network of stocking distributors could be pruned substantially, with an eventual saving of 5 percent of sales. The customers didn't notice any change in service—and if anything were better served, because the chosen distributors were bigger and more knowledgeable than some of the smaller ones they displaced.

How does a business learn from its customers about their advantages? The following four questions dictate the main steps in the learning process:

- Who is the customer?
- What values are they seeking?
- How well do we perform compared to our competitors?
- What are the sources of the perceived differences?

IDENTIFYING THE CUSTOMER: STEP ONE

A major complication is deciding whose judgments and values deserve attention. Sometimes, as with prescription drugs, the person who pays for the drug is not the specifier—since this is the doctor's decision (unless government requirements limit the options to a generic drug). A channel member, such as BusinessLand Computers will make its own decision about whether to carry a new line of personal computers, based on a different set of values from those used by the end customer.

For complex purchases such as when a major corporation chooses an investment banker or an airline chooses jet engines for a new fleet of planes—there will be layers of decision makers with separate values that have to be considered by the suppliers. At least three roles can be identified within most decision-making units (DMUs) that will influence the final choices:

- *owners* (in the sense of owning the decision) are those with overall responsibility. They tend to be most concerned with economic value and long-term implications.

- *evaluators* either take or are given responsibility to ascertain the technical features and suitability. In an airline, the funding arrangements for a jet engine purchase would be reviewed by the Finance Director, the product performance would be the responsibility of the Director of Engineering, and the Director of Fleet Planning would assess guarantees and service support.

- *implementers* either use the product or are involved in implementation planning. This is the role that the airline pilots assume.

The mix and importance of these roles varies with the decision, but each member of the DMU does make an evaluation, and can make a "yes" or "veto" decision that will be binding unless their concerns are looked after. The final choice eventually emerges from the interplay of the individuals in all roles.

DETERMINING CUSTOMER VALUES: STEP TWO

There are two questions at this stage: What are the attributes of the product or service that create value for the customer? And which attributes are most important?

The attributes of value go well beyond physical characteristics, to encompass all the support activities and systems for delivery and service that make up the augmented product. In the lodging market, the key attributes are honoring reservations on time, good value for money, and the quality and amenities of the guest rooms. Each market has unique attributes that customers employ to judge the competitive offerings. These can be understood only through careful analysis of usage patterns, and decision processes within that market. This knowledge comes from informed sources and in-depth surveys of customers. Not only are these efforts essential to taking the customers point of view, they also help specify the attributes precisely so they can be acted on. Does better service mean repair capability, response time, or delivery time? The following boxed insert describes how one firm gained by using this approach.

In the course of dozens of studies of customer values, such as the one discussed above, DuPont managers have acquired some interesting insights. They invariably find that the managers of most of their businesses feel they already have a good understanding of the values of their customers—especially because DuPont usually has a highly qualified direct sales force talking to them regularly. To counteract this belief each member of the business team is asked to list and make their own rank ordering of the attributes the customers are likely to use before the survey is made. Seldom is the internal list as detailed as the subsequent customer responses reveal. Normally, about 15 attributes are found—whereas the management list is only 8 to 12 attributes deep. There is also a wide variation in the rank orderings of attributes within the business team. The sales force has one view, internal marketing people another, and manufacturing and R&D managers very different opinions.[11]

Dissecting the Value Equation. Another way of understanding the attributes that create value for customers is to specify their value equation; that

---

UNDERSTANDING A SPECIALIZED INDUSTRIAL MARKET

A chemical manufacturer in southern Europe began integrating forward into speciality chemicals in 1981. Its first move was almost abortive, for it entered the complex market for tactifiers, a key component of adhesives, with little idea of customers' requirements and no clear positioning. Belatedly it undertook a major study of about 120 European adhesives manufacturers.[10] Exploratory interviews with the buyer and major specifier in some of these prospects identified six product-specific attributes affecting choice: softening point, viscosity, color stability, starting color, tack, and price. Beyond these quantifiable variables they found that the supplier's product range, service support, geographical coverage, and overall reputation for reliability determined which supplier to choose.

The research also found that adhesive makers had to buy from several sources of tactifiers because none could satisfy the diversity of applications from packaging and woodworking to nonwoven goods. Eventually they found nine end-use segments, each with different profiles of values (attributes) being sought. Then the size, growth, strength of competition, and their relative ability to compete was judged for each segment, as a prelude to choosing a target market.

is, how do they decide that the perceived benefits exceed the identifiable total costs? We've already seen this model in action in the analysis of the economics of substitution in the previous chapter. It is just as applicable in other settings when put in the following form:

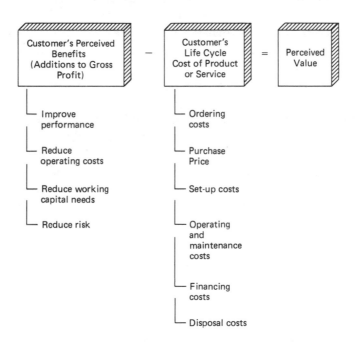

The basic idea of the value equation can be seen in the results of a study undertaken by Texas Instruments. They found that the total cost of an integrated circuit might be as much as five times the purchase price, when it is a component part of an assembled product like a test instrument. Cost adders included the following for a single 40¢ integrated circuit:

1. Inspection—uncertain quality requires
   100% check of incoming ICs $0.10
2. Inventory—undependable deliveries require back-up stocks $0.12
3. Manufacturing—high IC failure rate requires system rework $0.24
4. OEM warranty—poor IC reliability raises warranty cost $0.53
5. Maintenance—end-user cost incurred to keep systems working $1.06

                                          Extra costs per IC $2.05

How can this value equation help identify the attributes that are important to the customer? In the case of ICs we can see that customers will benefit when quality is high and consistent and deliveries are dependable. If however, the customers don't perceive the impact on their operating costs of poor IC quality to be as high as TI found, then they will put more emphasis on the purchase price. In general we want to know how the product can improve customer performance by improving end-product quality, enhancing end-product flexibility, or increasing speed of response. This suggests that for ICs customers will value technical assistance, and flexible designs that allow them to add new features to their product. Other customers may put the emphasis on vendor attributes that help to reduce their operating cost, including the cost of related activities, the rate of consumption, and the risk of failure. By taking the customers' perspective in constructing their value equation, we gain new insights into what they are looking for. This is invaluable both for understanding our competitive position in serving their needs, and looking for ways to improve that position.

CUSTOMER COMPARISONS OF COMPETITORS: STEP THREE

This is the critical step. Here we learn how our offerings are judged by customers on each value attribute using the toughest standard—the best of the target competitors. This requires a rating of each competitor on each attribute.

The immediate outcome is an overall competitive standing, usually obtained by adding up the attribute scores for each competitor (after the attributes have been weighted to reflect their importance). The assumption when this is done is that good performance on one attribute can offset or compensate for poor performance on another attribute. While this is usually a safe assumption, it is always helpful to validate it by comparing the resulting competitive standings with market share. DuPont has found that overall ratings correlate well with share data, and this gives managers confidence in the approach.

The diagnostic insights come from attribute-by-attribute comparisons with competitor ratings, as illustrated in Figure 6–6. When each of 10 or 15 attributes of value is plotted in the competitive comparison matrix it becomes apparent where remedial efforts are most needed. If an attribute is important to target customers, yet we are rated as inferior, it usually takes good performance on several other attributes to offset this disadvantage. More controversial are attributes where we are seen as superior, yet customers don't value that performance. This happens with attributes such as customer service when markets mature. The customer is more knowledgeable and less in need of applications counseling and product support. Do we then cut back our commitment to this competitive advantage? The answer is yes, if the delivery of the advantage costs more than the

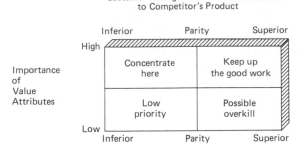

FIGURE 6–6 Competitive Comparison Matrix (for each value attribute)

customer is willing to pay as a premium. Then the resources could be better used elsewhere.

Segment Differences. A major caveat: insights into advantage will be lost if all customers are lumped together. The competitive comparison matrix is most revealing when it is done for each benefit segment. These are groups of customers that have similar patterns of values they are seeking—that is, they give roughly the same weight to the same attributes.

Businesses do best in benefit segments where there is a good match between their offerings and the values the customers are seeking. This insight was slow in coming to a maker of electric motors who spent months searching for a niche within the 47 different industry categories in the market.[12] This approach to breaking up the market was both unproductive and confusing; no useful differences were found and the task of sorting through such a large number of groups overwhelmed the management. Only when the market was divided into benefit segments did management see what was happening. They found four segments. At one extreme was a highly price-sensitive segment that bought only standard items in large lots. Customers in this segment placed no value on engineering support and product service, where the company excelled. Not surprisingly the firm had only an 11 percent market share, and lost money in the smaller orders it was getting. At the other end of the spectrum were two segments that bought nonstandard or modified motors for special applications. They bought in smaller lots and valued quality, features, and service support. Here the company had shares between 22 and 28 percent, and made attractive margins because price was not the overriding concern. This was the portion of the market where they focused their strategy.

Positioning Maps. The message from customer value analysis is simple—and profound. If a business wants to succeed it must distinguish itself favorably on attributes that are important to a target segment. This is the *position,* or place the product occupies in the market, that is the reason for being, and the reason customers keep buying.

Positions are revealed with two-dimensional maps that compress customers' judgments about a wide array of attributes into a few composite dimensions. Automakers, faced with narrowing design and performance options, are big users of positioning maps. Chrysler draws up a series of maps, three times a year, using surveys that ask owners of different makes to rank their autos on a scale of 1 to 10 on attributes such as "luxury," "practicality," and "youthfulness." There are many ways available to convert this information to reveal where to plot each make of auto on the basic dimensions. A typical result from a 1984 survey[13] is shown in Figure 6–7.

From this map Chrysler would conclude that cars with the Plymouth name are saddled with a practical, though somewhat stodgy image. This map also points out the problem of lack of differentiation that plagued General Motors in the eighties. The market was unable to see a difference between Buick and Oldsmobile, which meant they were mostly fighting each other, while confusing their customers. It also shows that Pontiac had been successful in staking out a clear position with a youthful, high-performance image. In 1981 this division broke ranks with the tendency of other GM divisions to be all things to all people, and limited their focus to 25 to 44-year-olds. They avoided the velour seats, white walls, wire wheel covers, vinyl tops, and mushy suspension that turned off this target segment. Instead they offered sporty styling, bright colors, stiffer seat backs, leather

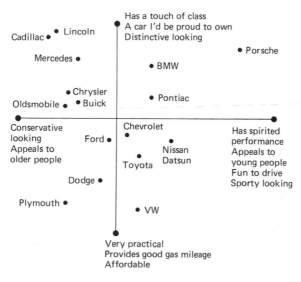

FIGURE 6–7 Automobile Positioning Map

wrapped steering wheels, aluminum wheels, and stiffer sport suspensions. The results were impressive. Pontiac was the only GM Division to gain share between 1982 and 1985, at a time when the company overall lost 1.6 share points.

Maps serve as civilian analogs of the "war boards" used by military strategists to understand the geographic location and type of enemy emplacements, as well as targets of opportunity. When the amount of customer demand is plotted on a map, a firm can see whether it is on target in meeting the needs of a large potential group of prospects.

DIAGNOSING CUSTOMER COMPARISONS: WHAT ARE THE SOURCES OF ADVANTAGE?: STEP FOUR

Most customer-oriented assessments stop short of explaining why one firm is seen by customers as superior to another. Only by understanding how differences in skills and resources between competitors result in differences in customer judgments can we tell how to sustain the current advantages or overcome disadvantages. This is hard to do because it involves linking the capabilities of the firm to the customer's purchase and using environment. The first step is to account for differences that arise because the firm is unable or unwilling to compete in portions of the total market—using market coverage analysis. Then the determinants or drivers of differentiation are identified by looking for differences in skills or resources that explain why customers see one competitor as having superior service, quality, and so forth.

Market Coverage Analysis.[14] Customers may be leaked away—not seriously pursued—for three reasons:

- *gaps in price range, features or functions.* Some customers will be lost because the firm has made the decision to not offer sizes, ranges, options, or delivery capabilities that competitors provide.
- gaps in *coverage* that arise when the business elects not to serve all geographic areas or outlets in an area, such as independent wholesalers that are expensive to cover.
- *merchandise or customer contact gaps.* The product may be in the channel outlet but be poorly represented because of poor shelf positions, limited stock on hand, or reluctant dealer cooperation. Problems may arise because key decision makers are not being reached or the calls are too infrequent.

Coverage of large parts of a market may also be lost because a one-time customer has back integrated and produces all their requirements. This part of the market is essentially lost. Captive markets can't be ignored, however, for the producers can still muddy the waters of the open market by dumping excess output at prices that barely cover marginal costs. This is a serious seasonal problem in the market for two-part cans, where brewers of beer have integrated production lines that are fully used only in summer months.

Drivers of Differentiation. Porter[15] has proposed a number of drivers as possible underlying reasons for the ability of one firm to outperform another on attributes that are important to customers. A high-leverage driver relates to differences in skills and resources among competitors that account for differences in customer judgments. The principal drivers are: (1) *policy choices* about what activities to perform and how intensely to perform them, including the features, performance, and service to offer, level of advertising spending, special capabilities of the technology employed, and skill and experience of the personnel; (2) *linkages* among key activities, such as coordination between sales and service to improve the speed of order handling; and (3) *timing* of entry that gains first mover advantages. Other drivers include *location, synergy* from sharing a sales force or other activity with a sister division, *learning* and experience, and *scale* that permits broader market coverage or faster service through a larger number of locations.

These drivers are helpful in thinking about how one business has outperformed another. They don't always dig deep enough to reveal the fundamental differences in management capability or organizational orientation that permit the policy choices to be made. This list of drivers also understates the contribution of reputation, consumer awareness, and past investments that tie customers close by creating switching costs, that are a legacy of past management moves. Current positional advantages are rooted in both the past and the present, and these sources need constant refurbishing to keep ahead of changes in markets and competitors.

COMPETITOR-CENTERED ASSESSMENTS

The essence of these methods is the side-by-side comparison of the business against the best of the target competitors, who are similar in served market and competitive stance. The comparative judgments are made by the management team after sifting through their array of formal and informal sources of competitor intelligence. The emphasis is clearly on the relative standings, with particular emphasis on the relative cost position of the business.

The most common competitor-centered method of assessment is the search for distinctive competencies—usually in the broader setting of the strengths and weaknesses analysis described in Chapter 4. This is a useful starting point, for it helps focus on the sources of advantage to remind the maagement team that each functional skill and resource has a role to play. While the conclusion may be insightful, the results usually fall far short of a clear picture. The basis of comparison is seldom explicit, so it is easy to fall into the trap of judging a skill as a distinctive competence just because it is better than other, lesser capabilities of the business. There is a tendency to compile long and indiscriminate lists, with little or no evidence to back up the presumed strength or weakness. Most business teams, when asked by an outsider about their strengths, will point to the experience and quality of management. This may shore up the self-esteem and confidence of the group, but is simply delusive unless there is compelling supporting evidence.

Direct comparisons of resource commitments and capabilities help to reduce the subjectivity of the usual strengths and weakness questions. They often err in the other direction, by giving disproportionate weight to "hard" data about competitors that are accessible and in a format that is amenable to direct comparisons with similar data on hand within the firm. Tangible and visible aspects of competitors, like size of sales force, number of dealers, plant capacity, and cost of capital come to dominate thinking about the capabilities of rivals. This narrow perspective understates the importance of:

- the flexibility and responsiveness of the competitor's organization that could be revealed by such measures as the number of successful new products, speed of response to service calls, the flexibility of processing equipment, or the rigidity of the union contract,
- the competitor's capability to exploit opportunities as a consequence of uncommitted cash reserves, excess plant capacity, and new products on the shelf, and
- future strategic intentions and objectives, based on forecasts of the competitor's investment priorities and patterns of spending.

Not long ago a manufacturer of electrical components—that we'll call Alpha—was struggling to understand why it was only half as profitable as its major competitor, Beta. Both firms had the same share of market, and roughly equal sales forces, plant capacities, and numbers of employees. Both faced the same powerful buyers in a maturing market with market-dedicated sales forces. On the surface the strategies looked the same. If anything Beta should have been at a cost disadvantage with five domestic plants, compared to Alpha's two off-shore plants located in low-wage countries.

Further digging into the differences showed that Beta was following a different strategy, that was superior on dimensions that were important to the customers—with greater emphasis on less price-sensitive residential customers. The details of the differences are given in the boxed insert.

COMPARING COMPETITORS

	Alpha	Beta
Segment Sales		
% Residential	40%	60%
% Commercial	60%	40%
Market Share	25%	25%
Distribution Channels		
% Direct	20%	0%
% Independent	80%	100%
Manufacturing	Off-Shore	Domestic
	2 Sites	5 Sites
Sales Training/	2 Weeks—Classroom	24 Weeks-Classroom
Product Application	4 Weeks—Teams	24 Weeks-Teams
Warehouse Shortage	25%–35%	5%
Finished Goods Inventory	Y	1.4 Y
Promises Kept	60%-80%	95%–98%
Annual Sales Force		
Turnover	40%	10%–20%
New Hires	60% Technical	100% Technical
(Sales/Product)		
Measurements	Nonintegrated	Integrated
Advertising	Product	Market
Income	$ X	$2 X

When the full profiles of the two strategies were put side-by-side it was painfully apparent that:

- Beta was using a high service level to pull product sales from attractive segments. This thrust was supported with integrated inventory, distribution, training, staffing, and manufacturing strategies and appropriate measurements of key result areas such as inventory availability.

* Alpha had evolved toward a minimum cost and minimum acceptable level of service strategy—but didn't have the low overheads needed to achieve satisfactory profitability.

When managers at Alpha were confronted with the cost of their service disadvantage, a major rethink of their service strategy became urgent. Should we close the gap? Can we close the gap? Are there other positions that will deliver satisfactory profitability? These issues became management's overriding concern.

IDENTIFYING THE VALUE CHAIN

The value chain[16] is a useful tool for sorting out the myriad of possible comparative judgments about competitors. Instead of looking at the business as a whole it starts with the strategically relevant and distinct activities that are performed to convert inputs into outputs that customers will value. These include purchasing, manufacturing, design, sales, distribution, and services. In theory, the value chain requires a comparison of all the skills and resources the firm uses to perform each activity. In practice, it is most useful for comparing relative cost positions.

Each business has its own value chain—uniquely configured to reflect the strategic choices, history, happenstance, and competitive forces in the served market. What is appropriate for a transaction-based business, like a bank or insurance company, is not suitable for a chemical manufacturer producing many products from a continuous processing facility, or an airline or hotel company. In a life insurance company, the key activities are the following:

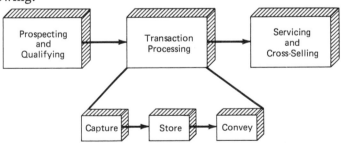

While each business has to think hard about which discrete activities do the most to add value, it is useful to have a generic framework as a departure point. The best articulated generic value chain has been developed by Porter, and has some very useful features that should be included in any analysis: (1) the separation of the *primary* activities involved in the physical creation, sale, and transfer to the customers, from the *support* activities that provide technology, personnel, and purchased inputs and coordinate the primary activities, (2) the focus on *total value* versus simply the value-added portions, on the grounds that the cost and quality of inputs will have a major impact on subsequent activities, (3) the recognition that the way each activity is performed is influenced by *drivers,* or structural determinants such as policy choices, and the position of the business on each driver influences both relative cost and customer value, and (4) the careful attention to *linkages* between activities within each value chain, as well as with activities of suppliers, distributors, and customers.

The basic idea of a series of linked value chains (see Figure 6–8) also reminds strategists that no activity is sacrosanct; if something can be done better or cheaper by an outside supplier, distributor—or even the customer—without compromising the firm's advantages, then it should be eliminated. There may be great advantage to be gained by not doing something.[17] Some of Compaq's success in the personal computer market is attributable to a decision by IBM that they would compete with retailers by selling their machines directly to large customers. Instead, Compaq offered exclusive franchises and attractive margins to key dealers and won the distribution battle. Similarly Liz Claiborne—a leader in selling fashions to professional women—benefited by bucking the conventional wisdom of the industry and deciding not to have its own manufacturing plants or direct sales force. The lack of factories increased costs, but gave the company more production flexibility. Without a sales force, the company had to focus on winning orders from the large department stores and specialty retailers whose buyers routinely came to New York. With little overhead the company took off.

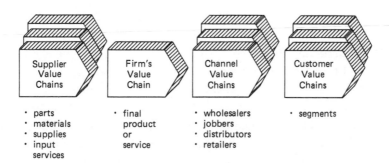

FIGURE 6–8 A System of Value Chains

A Marketing-Driven Value Chain. The value chain or business system described in Figure 6–9 owes much to the Porter framework, but differs in one important respect: marketing is highlighted as an integrating general management function that ensures an external orientation to all value-creating activities. While marketing is especially concerned with the sum total of customer-impinging activities that provide meaningful differentiation, it also has a responsibility for identifying cost-reduction possibilities that will not compromise the competitive position. But marketing should also be pervasive in thinking about the relations among primary activities. Most activities have internal customers—which are the downstream activities—with their own requirements that have to be satisfied if the whole system is going to prosper. Thus the sales group is the customer for operations, which in turn is a customer for purchased materials. Too often activities and functions that should be related in a common purpose behave like adversaries because of differences in backgrounds, objectives, and training. A customer mind-set can go far in eliminating this corrosive conflict.

Primary value activities are the distinctly identifiable steps necessary to acquire materials, components, and other inputs, create the product or service, persuade the market to buy it, deliver it to the customer, and follow up with service support. These activities are best revealed by flow-charting the progress of a product and the associated paperwork through the organization, but will include most of the following:

- *Sourcing.* This refers to the organization's function of purchasing materials and supply inputs and may go well beyond the traditional role of its purchasing department. It is usually not a big function in terms of cost, but can have a big role in shaping subsequent costs.
- *Inbound logistics activities.* These include material receiving and handling, warehousing, inspection, and inventory control.
- *Design activities.* These comprise both the design of the product (or service) for ease of processing, aesthetics, and functionality, and the design of the manufacturing facility and process. This is another area that is often ignored but has a big impact on subsequent activities.
- *Operations.* This area includes all activities necessary to fabricate and assemble the elements of the product, test the result, and package for transfer to inventory.
- *Communication and persuasion.* These are associated with the activities of the sales force, as well as media advertising and promotions to build awareness, change attitudes, and secure orders from customers.

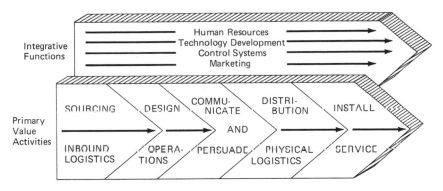

FIGURE 6–9 A Marketing-Driven Value Chain

- *Distribution.* This involves the managing of physical goods, inventories, order processing and handling, and scheduling.
- *Physical logistics activities.* These are the linkages from the firm to the customer via the shipping mode, and may include fleet operations, as well as traffic and freight expediting.
- *Installation and service.* These activities include initial setup, adjusting, and training, as well as ongoing monitoring and repair services needed to ensure the product continues to function.

All businesses carry on with these activities in one way or another, although some may be very unimportant. The general rule is that an activity is worth isolating if it has (1) a distinct relationship to the skills and resources of the business, so that cost-cutting moves or changes in procedure will have different consequences, (2) a high potential impact on the value a customer gets from the product, as is the case with design activities, and (3) represents a substantial and growing proportion of total costs and assets. It is not always obvious where an activity belongs. Is credit screening and granting a part of operations or is it a selling tool that should be assigned to marketing?

Integrative functions provide the glue that coordinates and integrates the primary value activities. In theory they can be deployed to impact on any single function, but their value comes from the integration of multiple activities to achieve a clear-cut objective or strategic outcome. The role of marketing—as a general management function—is to ensure that all primary activities are organized to deliver superior customer value. The management control system monitors costs and outputs against preset standards. A good control system will help identify opportunities for cost savings that span multiple activities, as well as serious departures from cost targets that demand remedial action.

Technology development is frequently integrative, for efforts to improve products or processes often impact several related activities. This is especially true of information technologies, which may tie together the design, inventory control, and production activities with a combination of CAD/CAM and telecommunication links with suppliers to speed the adjustment to a new mix of products. Office automation may simultaneously affect the purchasing and accounting departments and help link sourcing and control activities. The possible linkages are only limited by the imagination and energy of the developers. Thus, technology goes well beyond product features design and performance to influence every activity.

Human resource management embraces all the recruiting, hiring, training, selection, and compensation activities, and can go far in achieving integration through common policies. Ultimately this function is responsible for nurturing the core skills, and ensuring there are no bottlenecks because of a lack of trained machinists, salespeople, or designers. The function and associated costs of benefit plans, salary negotiations, and training are often dispersed through the business and seldom separated as a distinct cost element. This can be very revealing, as Chrysler discovered when they estimated their second-largest cost item was the medical coverage provided their employees.

Assigning Costs to Activities. This step is seemingly straightforward, but may be daunting if the accounting system is organized on some other basis than strategically relevant activities. One major impediment is the habit of allocating overheads—themselves an aggregate that swallows everything from the security guard to the quality assurance group—according to estimates of labor costs. This may have made sense when direct labor was the largest cost element, but for many firms it is now less than 5 percent of production costs. Other problems are encountered when a major activity is shared by several business units. For strategy analysis it is better to be vaguely right than precisely wrong, so a good deal of judgment must be exercised to override the rigidities imposed by the accounting system.

COMPETITIVE COMPARISONS OF COSTS

A cost advantage is gained when the cumulative cost of performing all the activities is lower than the competitors' total costs. The first step toward determining the relative cost position is the identification of each competitor's value chain. Ideally, costs and assets then should be assigned to each of these activities. In practice this step is extremely difficult because the business does not have direct information on the costs of the competitors' value activities. Some costs can be estimated from public data or interviews with suppliers and distributors, whereas others can be derived by reverse engineering and similar techniques. For example, it is usually possible to determine the size of a competitor's sales force and its expense and compensation arrangements. The result is a partial picture based on accurate data that can be fleshed out with informed judgments.

There are several reasons for differences in relative cost positions. The first place to look is how the competitors have configured their value chains. At one time Xerox was at a serious cost disadvantage in small copiers because it was a fully integrated manufacturer. It did everything from the dedicated manufacturing of specially designed parts to serving the market with its own direct sales and service force. By contrast, Savin was simply an assembler of standard, off-the-shelf parts (that were very economical) and relied on exclusive dealers to take care of service and distribution. The Savin copier was designed to be repaired with quick-change modules that could either be disposed of or repaired later. This meant sophisticated and costly repair skills were not required—at great cost savings.

Drivers of Cost Differences. Even when a business has the same value chain configuration as a competitor it may have a cost edge or suffer a penalty in performing each activity because of different standings on the sources of advantage. These are the drivers or structural determinants of the cost differences between competitors. The principal driver identified by Porter is *economies of scale,* arising mainly from increased efficiency due to size, coupled with an ability to spread fixed costs across a larger base. Seldom does an increase in throughput require a matching increase in capital investment or salespeople in the field. Scale also creates the potential for volume discounts, and the division of labor. Not every activity is equally scale-sensitive, and sometimes increasing the scale of operations can be dysfunctional. Professional service firms periodically discover the negatives of scale as they grow beyond the ability of the parties to manage the organization. Some manufacturing firms argue that the largest plant should have no more than 400 employees, as otherwise working relations and control are diluted.

Closely following scale as a driver of costs is *learning* as the result of practice and the exercise of ingenuity, skill, and enhanced dexterity in repetitive activities. The performance of production equipment typically improves as personnel learn the idiosyncrasies of the process and experiment with ways to unstop bottlenecks. Improvements in cost from learning reflect the accretion of small improvements, and thus are often related to cumulative volume in the activity. Comparing the degree of learning between

two or more competitors is complicated by the leaky nature of the phenomenon—a follower can learn a lot from the leading firm by a "tear down"
analysis of their product, or by hiring their key personnel. All competitors
may benefit equally from cost reductions achieved by outside suppliers,
and a later entrant may actually have access to more advanced technology.

The third important cost driver is the extent of *linkages* of activities
within a value chain. The cost of one activity may depend on how another
activity is performed. For example, high-quality inputs such as castings
may save a great deal of subsequent machine time and produce a superior
quality end product with lower service and warranty costs: Better coordination of purchasing and operations may reduce the cost of carrying inventory.

Other drivers of cost that may be significant are the sharing of activities
across several business units, the degree of vertical integration, the rate of
utilization of capacity, and access to low-cost sources of energy, labor, or
raw materials as a result of location or government subsidies.

Seldom will it be possible to reveal all the reasons for an observed cost
difference, but for strategy purposes it is often sufficient to know only the
direction of the difference. This insight can be combined with informed
judgments of the relative size of each value activity to arrive at a general
picture of the competitor's cost position. Once this baseline comparison of
costs has been completed, the value chain offers a useful framework for directing the search for better information or simply making sense of the
fragmentary bits of data, gossip, and speculation about competitors that
routinely flow into a business.

BENCHMARKING

Competitor comparisons can't stop when differences in capabilities and
costs are uncovered. The best firms are constantly probing to learn what
activities their competitors are able to do better. This is built into the IBM
culture with their "best of breed" analysis, coupled with a pervasive anxiety that their competitors are about to catch up and pass them. Managers at
all levels are asked which competitor is best in the world at what they do—
whether quality assurance, distribution, software, or R&D. Planning sessions are dominated by questions about the reasons for their success. The
key questions are "why can't we do that?" and "what are we going to do
next?" to keep IBM equal or superior to worldwide competition. This is a
constantly changing game, for the top three or four competitors will shift
their position on specific dimensions of competition as new models are
shipped or distribution initiatives are undertaken. Not surprisingly there is

little complacency within IBM with the status quo, and considerable respect for the prowess of their competitors. This keeps the entire organization externally oriented and provides a healthy stimulus for continuous improvement in all activities.

Small competitors cannot be overlooked in benchmarking exercises for they provide stimulating ideas for change. According to Andrall Pearson,[8] when he was president of PepsiCo, "The majority of our strategic successes were ideas we borrowed from the market-place, usually from a small regional or local competitor. These include Doritos, Tostitos and Sobritos, with combined sales of over a billion dollars. Each was developed by a different West Coast snack company. Pepsi Free . . . we borrowed from Royal Crown . . . . In each case what we did was spot a promising new idea, improve on it, and then outexecute our competitor."

INTEGRATED ASSESSMENTS OF COMPETITIVE ADVANTAGE

Whether a business is competitor-centered or customer-focused dictates the ways the managers come to understand their competitive position and arrive at answers for the central strategic questions: Where are we superior to our competition? How were these advantages gained? How durable are the advantages? Only when these questions are answered can a new strategy be designed.

The two perspectives differ fundamentally in whether the management team relies on customer judgments about the relative merits of competitive alternatives, or uses its own judgments to make side-by-side comparisons with the resources, costs, and competencies of the competitors (see Figure 6–10).

Although one perspective usually prevails within most businesses, it is seldom taken to the complete exclusion of the other perspective. The real question is which one delivers the information that managers best understand and pay attention to when deciding what to do next. This choice is often made by default, in a passive response to whatever information is widely available and customarily used in the industry. Whether this is the right choice depends on the limitations of these two prevailing perspectives and the insights lost by not broadening the perspective.

Risks of Competitor-Centering. When market demand is predictable, the competitive structure is concentrated and stable, and there are a few powerful customers, the emphasis has to be on competitors. Even in this setting, solely competitor-centered measures have drawbacks. The preoccupation

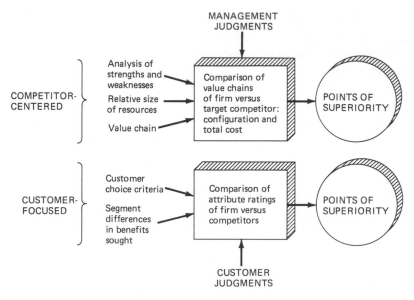

FIGURE 6–10 Comparing Competitors

with comparative costs and internal activities may obscure opportunities for differentiation through creative linkages of seller, distributor, and buyer value chains. This perspective also deflects attention from changes in market segment structures or customer requirements that might change the perceived importance of attributes or introduce new attributes.

In the machine tool industry U.S. manufacturers had emphasized ruggedness, durability, and long life. By 1980 Japanese entrants were prospering by emphasizing price, delivery, and adaptability of their more standardized machines. This allowed them to deliver machines in 7 months, while U.S. firms were taking 18 months. The Japanese had effectively reset the evaluation criteria used by the customers.[19]

Centering on competitors sometimes leads to an overestimate of their capabilities, and an untested assumption that they are doing a proper marketing job. When managers begin to envy what their competitors are doing they are likely to try and imitate them and then fail because they didn't fully understand how the strategy was executed. Imitation without reflection also reduces the likelihood of experiments with innovative strategies that might alter the basis of competition. This is unfortunate, for strategies that "change the game" with new types of service, new delivery systems, or new production methods are the surest way to gain a sustainable edge.

Fixating on competitors may even be unhealthy if it produces a threat mentality and an obsession with military metaphors. Seldom are markets like zero-sum games where one competitor wins only at the expense of another. Instead, there are many markets where rivals can be mutually beneficial at one level, even when behaving like fierce rivals at a tactical level. A credible competitor, like IBM in the personal computer market, may actually increase primary demand by making personal computers a serious business tool. Competitors may share the cost of market development for new products or technologies—and become essential when the costs of development are prohibitive because of extensive needs for education, service, or technological improvements. RCA licensed competitors to make color TV sets, so they would have some help in opening up the market. They were happy with a smaller share of a large market rather than a large share of a small market. When markets mature, "good" competitors enhance the structure of the industry by stressing attributes such as quality, design, and services that reduce customer price sensitivity and reduce price cutting.[20] These benefits will be lost if the emphasis is on gaining market share at all costs, by "repulsing" the "enemy" with marketing "weapons" and pricing "wars" using the sales force as "shock troops."

Risks of a Customer Focus. In dynamic markets with shifting mobility barriers, many competitors, and highly segmented end-user markets, a tilt toward customers is mandatory. Unfortunately, most customer-oriented measures are remote from the activities of the business. It is seldom apparent how attributes that are important to customers are influenced by activities in the value chain. A perception of superior service gained by faster delivery of orders could come from changes in manufacturing processes, the choice of technology, shipping methods, or order-handling activities. These relationships are not available from customer-oriented measures. There is always a nagging doubt when using these measures as to their validity—especially when the choice process is obscured in complex decision-making units.

Just as a competitor-centered business may be blinded to evolving customer needs, so can a customer-focused business pay too little attention to competitors (until it is too late). Even P&G has been susceptible to this competitive myopia; notably when Encaparin, a coated aspirin launched in 1984, was overwhelmed with new, nonaspirin painkillers.

SUMMARY: TOWARD MARKET-DRIVEN ASSESSMENTS

Peter Schutz, one time CEO of Porsche AG, sounded an important warning when he said "God help the companies that begin to believe their press notices." His point was that there can never be enough grounding in external observation and data. Yet few companies do a thorough job of watching their competitors and listening to customers. Worse, they may believe they are listening openly and carefully, when they are mostly confirming past assumptions. Even leading-edge companies like IBM and P&G have suffered for their myopia.

This chapter has offered an antidote to myopia about competitive advantage, by proposing that sound evidence should satisfy the following requirements:

1. Illuminate the sources of advantage, as well as their manifestations of superior customer value or lowest delivered cost and superior performance.

2. Reflect a balance of customer-oriented and competitor-centered methods to minimize the risk of selective attention and simplification. Too much reliance on one perspective at the expense of another is often traced to an unquestioning reliance on whatever information is readily available.

3. Produce results that have credibility while being more than a simple confirmation of prior prejudice and industry conventional wisdom. The tendency toward conformity in assumptions, data, and interpretation is a recurrent explanation for the ability of new entrants to change the rules of competition even when they were acting on widely available information.

The last point reminds us that proprietary insight into key success factors, and early information about the emergence of new market segments or changes in customer needs, is itself a competitive advantage for the first mover able to capitalize on the information.

FOUR

Choosing Arenas and Advantages

SEVEN

Deciding How to Compete

*The race isn't always to the swift, nor the battle to the strong,
but that's the way to bet.*
— DAMON RUNYON

"If you knew Time as well as I do," said the Mad Hatter, *"you
wouldn't talk about wasting it."*
— LEWIS CARROLL, *Alice in Wonderland*

The leader has an advantage in a competitive market—the rewards are market share dominance and superior profitability. But how is this position of leadership achieved and sustained? The most generic routes are: differentiation (through superior quality and service, closer relationships with customers, or faster responsiveness) and low-cost leadership. But regardless of which of these routes is emphasized, the effort will fail unless significant customer value is created.

Even after leadership has been achieved, there is no room for complacency. No position of dominance lasts indefinitely. Every business that succeeds at differentiation serves as a model for new competitor behavior. Some competitors will strive to catch up by matching any edge in performance or process, while others will try to leapfrog the leaders the way Japanese auto manufacturers did to GM, Ford, and Chrysler.

Both the leaders, and the followers that aspire to match or depose them, have to address the same strategic question: Where do we want to position our business in the future, and how do we get there? The answer lies in a robust planning process that establishes the need for change, generates meaningful alternatives, and then builds a consensus within the management team on the best positioning for the business.

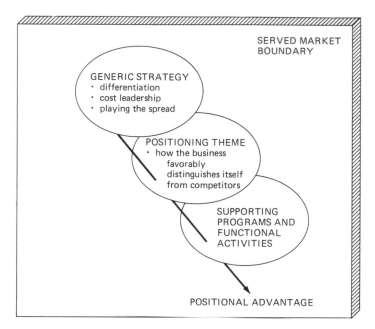

FIGURE 7-1 Describing the Competitive Strategy

STRATEGIES FOR COMPETING

The diversity of ways a business can achieve a competitive advantage quickly defeats any generalizations or facile prescriptions. Instead, the answer depends on thoughtful decisions concerning the generic strategy, positioning theme, and functional supports (see Figure 7-1). The final outcome of decisions on the generic strategic thrust and the overall positioning theme must set clear guidelines for the supporting programs that structure and orient the day-to-day business activities of a firm.

First and foremost, a business must set itself apart from its competition. To be successful, it must identify and promote itself as the best provider of attributes that are important to target customers. For example, Maytag is known for durability of laundry equipment; Jaguar for sophisticated styling and superior quality in the luxury auto market; and Federal Express is inextricably associated in customers' minds as the courier to use if your package "absolutely, positively has to get there by tomorrow." These leadership positions have been earned across years of effective execution, but they currently succeed because they give customers a sound reason for buying. The price for this loyalty must be very carefully gauged. Too large a price premium, and customers will defect—although grudgingly because they know they haven't been able to afford the best for their needs. Too small a premium, and income that could be invested in creating entry barriers to competition (R&D, information systems, or low-cost production processes) will be left on the table.

GENERIC STRATEGIES

In many businesses there is an internal strategy debate over choosing differentiation that offers superior customer value versus striving for the lowest delivered cost. These are usually viewed as mutually exclusive choices. Two arguments are made to support this distinction. The main rationale is that higher quality usually requires the use of more expensive components and less standardized production processes. Additional service people, higher inventories, and more sophisticated systems that enhance value also raise costs and are incompatible with managing for lowest delivered costs. It is further argued that the two generic strategies require different skills and resources, and imply different organizational arrangements, systems, and controls. Certainly, a lot of firms have come to grief trying to make and sell both a low-end utility product and a premium, full-service product using the same organization.

Playing the Spread. Like many generalizations about strategy, the notion there are only two distinct generic strategies soon unravels under closer scrutiny. Champion firms like Kellogg pose especially awkward questions.[1] Despite unexciting growth prospects in the cereal market, this company gained five share points between 1982 and 1988, and recorded an average 36 percent return on common equity, while cementing their dominance. This was done with a combination of innovative products responsive to health-oriented adult customers, more new products than anyone else (47 in 1987 alone), heavy ad spending devoted to building the brand ($865 million in 1988), and equally heavy spending on plant and equipment (including the most expensive food-processing plant ever built). The manufacturing cost efficiencies have helped improve gross margins from 41 percent to 49 percent. At the same time, new, highly automated plants helped Kellogg improve cereal quality—with products that were 20 percent to 25 percent more consistent in quality than cereal from older plants.

Firms like Kellogg are not alone in prospering by simultaneously lowering costs and gaining price premiums with superior customer value. Growing empirical evidence suggests that these strategies often go together. One reason is that product quality can indirectly lower costs.[2] Higher quality leads to higher market shares, and this in turn reduces total costs due to experience effects and scale economies. Quality may also have a direct effect on total costs. The slogan "quality is free" is supported with persuasive evidence that the costs of higher quality are more than offset by lower reject rates, lower costs of make-good and field repairs, and higher customer satisfaction.

Choosing the Scope. Another major factor that determines generic strategy is the choice of market coverage. The three basic possibilities are:

- broad market coverage, with a common strategy for all segments. The products and programs are designed to have the broadest possible appeal.
- broad market coverage, with tailored strategies and programs for each segment. The degree of tailoring will depend on the size of the differences between segments. At the extreme a retailer of fashion goods may operate one chain that serves shoppers wanting very high style, and another chain that caters to budget shoppers. These chains will have different names, products, and locations to accentuate their market differences, while operating with a common organization structure.
- focused coverage of a single segment (or group of segments) within a market, to the exclusion of all others. This dedication to the needs and requirements of a discrete group of buyers works best when broad-scope competitors are unable to serve these buyers at the same time as they are serving others, or the costs to serve the segment are very different.

The three dimensions of a competitive strategy—emphasis on customer value, emphasis on costs, and scope of market coverage yield a rich array of generic strategies, (see Figure 7–2). The dimensions are not independent, and often interact in complex ways. One rule that is seldom broken, however, is that it is not possible to be all things to all people. So even if a business elects to serve all segments, with equal emphasis on cost and customer value, it must also follow the Kellogg approach and offer distinct products supported with distinct messages to each segment.

While there are many routes to advantage, some may not be feasible. Businesses that can't exceed parity on at least one dimension in at least one market segment are in a very exposed position. Because their very survival is so doubtful we should look for unusual reasons such as special relationships, dispensations or protection behind trade barriers to explain their existence.

DEVELOPING THE POSITIONING THEME

Whether a business chooses to compete with superior customer value or the lowest delivered cost, it still must find a way to favorably distinguish itself from competition. Otherwise the customer will have no reason for buy-

ing, and will turn to the alternative with the lowest price for adequate performance or pay a premium for meaningful benefits.

The purpose of the positioning theme is to translate the generalities of
the generic strategy choices into meaningful distinctions for customers.
The most obvious positions make direct comparisons with competitors.
This is what Savin did when it entered the low-end copier market with the
claim it was the same as Xerox, only cheaper. In the same spirit, Avis prospered with a theme that took the customers into its confidence. "Avis is
only No. 2 in rent-a-cars. So why go with us? We try harder." Alternatively,[3] the business can:

- position to an attribute, feature or benefit. BMW is known as the
  "ultimate driving machine" because the car connotes superior handling and drivability. This theme succeeded because it appealed to
  younger drivers, and distinguished the firm from Mercedes-Benz.
  While both are expensive German cars, Mercedes had arrived first
  and preempted the "superior engineering" theme in the minds of
  buyers.

- position for a particular usage situation, or problem solution. Pitney-

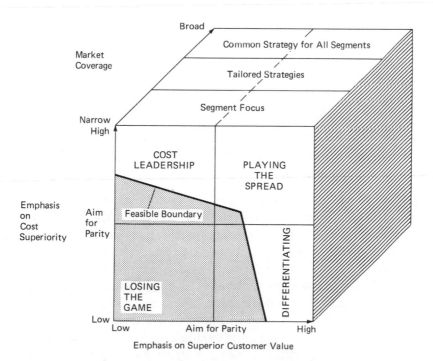

FIGURE 7–2 Generic Competitive Strategies

Bowes now has a secure position as the company that can solve difficult mail-handling problems. Domino's Pizza owns the home delivery position by emphasizing its 30-minute delivery time.

- position to a particular customer segment. This is often done in conjunction with positioning to attributes, benefits, or solutions to the needs of distinct segments.

Eventually every business has to reassess the positioning theme that gives it an identity in the market. The trigger might be a recognition that the current position is eroding under competitive pressure, the position is no longer meaningful to customers, or the performance results are unsatisfactory. The search for a new positioning theme around which the next generation of strategic moves can coalesce is a four-step process:

Step One: Identify alternative positioning themes.

Step Two: Screen each alternative according to whether it is:

1. Meaningful to customers.
2. Feasible given the firm's competencies and customer perceptions of what the firm is capable of achieving.
3. Competitive—superior or unique relative to competition and difficult for them to match or exceed.
4. Helps meet long-term performance objectives.

Step Three: Choose the position that best satisfies the criteria, and generates the most enthusiasm and commitment within the organization.

Step Four: Design the programs needed to implement the position. Compare costs of these programs with likely benefits, such as price premiums and customer loyalty.

While this process may be embedded within the overall planning process it is best undertaken by a special task force drawn from all parts of the business. This is not a job to be delegated to staff or outside consultants, although they may play a strong supportive role. When all functions are intimately involved, there is a shared understanding of why a change is needed, how the positioning theme was chosen, and how each function needs to support the shift in direction. These are key ingredients in building enthusiasm and overcoming the inevitable implementation problems.

Recently a major food ingredient manufacturer undertook this process, when it learned its dominant share position was being threatened (see boxed insert for details). Since most big customers had a policy of dual

BREAKING A STALEMATE

The Calumet Corporation supplied food ingredients to grocery chains (where they were sold under the company's label) and to food manufacturers (as a raw material for processed foods). By 1988 the company had gained a 52-percent share of its served market with a series of acquisitions of regional competitors having long-term supply contracts. The next-largest competitor, with 38 percent of the market, had elected to diversify into other product categories.

For several years the energies of the management team had been consumed by the problems of integrating the acquisitions. This deflected their attention from the ongoing management of the existing operations. This began to take its toll in an apparent decline in customer relations, and threats that some long-run contracts would not be renewed. These were not the only signs that the company had become very self-centered, or internally oriented:

- there was a strong emphasis by the sales force on maintaining volume, and little or no emphasis on profitability or innovative marketing programs.
- the management team couldn't agree on the advantages they had in the eyes of their customers.
- surprisingly little was known about the chief competitor's capabilities, cost structure, and intentions.
- quality was treated as a matter of adherence to standards for physical product quality, and not of superior performance on attributes that customers value.

To determine the seriousness of these problems a survey was undertaken with 17 customers accounting for 55 percent of total sales. The objective was to learn how these customers perceived the company, and gain ideas on how to better serve them.

The results were gratifying in one respect. The customers generally agreed that the company was performing very well on the five key attributes of delivery dependability, price, product quality, sales representation, and delivery flexibility. A serious problem was highlighted when customers were asked to compare the two main suppliers. Virtually no difference was seen.

| | Number of Customers Who Rated Calumet vs. Competitor as: | | | | |
| | Slightly | | | Slightly | |
Attributes	Worse	Worse	Same	Better	Better
1. Delivery dependability	0	0	17	0	0
2. Price	0	1	13	1	0
3. Product Quality	1	0	15	0	0
4. Sales Representation	0	0	14	0	1
5. Delivery flexibility	0	0	14	1	1

sourcing (splitting orders between two suppliers to ensure supply) it was feared that contract volumes would eventually equalize and their present 52-percent share would decline until it was the same as the next-largest supplier who currently held a 38-percent share. This was very serious in a slow-growth market with a very high fixed-cost manufacturing facility. Worse, it appeared that the market had reached a stalemate, with few present or potential differentiation advantages, and where each advantage was likely to be small. This describes many large, standardized materials markets such as newsprint and electric motors. Competitive success in such markets usually lies in the durability of customer relationships, service quality, and cost leadership.

Evaluating Alternative Positioning Themes. An internal company task force was quickly formed to find ways of reestablishing a meaningful position in the minds of customers that would give them an edge over an extremely capable competitor. Their work lead to the identification of 22 possible positioning themes, a list that was then narrowed to the six best candidates. Each of these themes was thoroughly discussed by the task force members, using the screening criteria to focus the judgments. The results—summarized in the following table which graded each them on an A, B, C scale—were given to senior management for resolution. They found no suprises here, for they had been well briefed on the progress of the task force. Now they had to make the decision on whether to proceed with the positioning theme preferred by the task force. On the next page is a summary of what they had to work with.

Before management agreed to proceed with the partnering theme they asked for external validation—let's get some customer reactions to this theme—and for detailed programs of implementation. The most conclusive argument for this theme was evidence that the competitor could not re-

	Criteria for Screening		
	Alternative Positioning Themes		
Positioning Theme	*Meaningful to Customers*	*Feasible*	*Competive Superiority*
1. Provide superior delivery responsiveness	A/B	A	B
2. Act as partners in the effective management of your requirements	A	A	A
3. Help you buy better	A+	B	B
4. Technical expertise to help you solve product and process problems	B	B	B
5. Provide the most secure source of supply	B	B	C

spond quickly and neutralize the advantage. The apparent enthusiasm throughout the organization for this theme was another plus. The firm did implement a thorough repositioning program, but is still waiting for clear evidence of marketplace success that will be revealed when major contracts come up for negotiation.

SUPPORTING PROGRAMS AND ACTIVITIES

There are no quick and easy formulas for devising strategic programs to support a positioning theme. Winning programs feature bold moves that take a long time to put in place, and must be continually refurbished to ensure they keep delivering significant customer value. Because these programs involve the commitment of the organization—to ensure attention to the myriad of details that make the program work—they are very hard for competitors to fully understand and imitate. As Jan Carlzon of SAS put it, "Good service depends on a million moments of truth," as ticket agents, boarding agents, cabin staff, pilots, and others come in daily contact with passengers.

To see how a theme shapes the design of all elements of a strategy, let's

Exhibit 7-1 Establishing a Positioning Theme for a Commercial Airline

Functional Elements	Alternative Themes	
	In-Flight Comfort	*On-time Reliability*
Fleet Policy	• fleet configured to meet route-specific customer profiles	• maintain lowest fleet age
Cabin Configuration	• provide best legroom • more cabin storage • two seats abreast	• competitive parity
Flight Service	• latest design in seating • superior meals • best ratio of attendants to passengers • rigorous training and selection of flight attendants	• competitive parity • seek standardization where possible
Ground Service	• provide lounges at all destinations	• build dedicated terminals if possible • state-of-the-art baggage handling
Schedule	• seek to achieve maximum operating efficiencies	• build a greater margin of safety into published schedules • pay airport authorities a premium for priority takeoff slots
Maintenance	• competitive parity	• leader in preventative maintenance • rigorous standards • maintain close links with equipment suppliers
Advertising Message	• "arrive rested and ready to work"	• "we'll get you to your meeting on time"
Incentives	• offer "class of service" upgrades	• offer partial fare rebate if flight is late
Employee Reward System	• bonuses based on annual customer service survey	• bonuses based on on-time arrival results

compare two commercial airlines pursuing differentiated positions based on superior customer value.[4] One airline is emphasizing a theme that appeals to long-haul frequent flyers who want in-flight comfort; while the other airline is highlighting its on-time reliability in every aspect of operations, service features, and organizational incentives (see Exhibit 7-1). Both will be successful, so long as they consistently execute all dimensions of their chosen strategy and don't try to blur their theme. The right theme can galvanize the organization and provide the rationale for difficult trade-offs. The airline that emphasizes on-time reliability will resist pressure to spend more than necessary to meet competition on the basic cabin configuration and service level. While more legroom would certainly be appreciated by their passengers in all probability they wouldn't be willing to pay extra for it and this feature won't determine their choice of airline next time around.

STRATEGIES FOR ENHANCING CUSTOMER VALUE

Successful differentiation strategies like Amex in travel-related services, Perdue in quality chickens, General Electric in medical diagnostic systems, and Federal Express in overnight courier services draw on some combination of three possible positioning themes:

Better—through the provision of superior quality and service.

Faster—by being able to sense and meet shifting customer requirements quicker than competitors.

Closer—with the creation of durable linkages, relationships, and even partnerships with channel members and customers.

Our interest here is in gleaning lessons from these successful themes that can be applied generally. Because the possibilities for enhancing customer value by drawing the customers closer can't be separated from the overall role of the distribution channel, we'll develop this route to advantage in Chapter 9 where channel issues will be covered in depth.

SUPERIOR QUALITY AND SERVICE

Boosting quality is now seen as the surest route to creating superior customer value. This has long been recognized by European and Japanese firms who generally lead the world in quality. The Japanese have an especially fortuitous culture that reveres economy of design and ease of operation—creating the marriage of form and function that customers value. In the United States, quality leadership has been lost by all but a handful of firms; the rest are struggling to catch up to increasingly tough standards for performance reliability and durability set by off-shore competitors. These laggards are now progressing through the unproductive stages of *rhetoric* (where quality is proclaimed by the CEO as a priority but the message is mixed as research budgets are cut and schedules speeded up to boost productivity), and *quick fixes* like the 1970s fad of quality circles that weren't backed up with a commitment to invest in new systems, standards, and training. Those who survive and go on to prevail will have taken to heart three enduring principles of quality superiority:

1. Superior quality is profitable.
2. Quality is more than conformance—it is achieved only to the extent a product or service meets or exceeds the customer's requirements.
3. Superior quality is achieved with a total system of quality that reaches every aspect of the business.

How Quality Drives Profitability. Evidence from the PIMS data base supports the conclusion that "quality is the most important single factor affecting a business unit's long-term performance."[5] The quality measures used in this study are based on customers' views of the quality of competing offerings, and include all the nonprice attributes that influence the choice decision. (Quality scores are expressed as percentiles of the companies in the data base.) On average, businesses with quality scores in the top third outearn those in the bottom third by a 2 to 1 margin—regardless of their relative market share (see Figure 7–3).

Other PIMS analyses have dug behind these basic relationships to find that: (1) quality affects relative price, but (2) when quality is held constant there is only a modest relationship between market share and price, and (3) market share affects relative direct costs, but (4) perceived quality has little effect on cost. This is an important—and encouraging—result, for it says that, as quality improves, the extra costs of improving performance on key attributes are offset by the savings in costs from scrap and rework reductions. The premium that customers are willing to pay for superior quality then goes straight to the bottom line. The size of the premium is a strategic choice, with the alternative being to charge the same as competitors and offer superior value that can be converted into share gains and/or enhanced customer loyalty that helps keep marketing costs down. It is a truism in marketing that it is a lot cheaper to keep an existing customer than steal one away from a competitor.

Understanding Quality. Many efforts to improve quality have been misguided because of mistaken beliefs that quality is a matter of ensuring that the factory or the service provider sticks to standards. Squadrons of inspec-

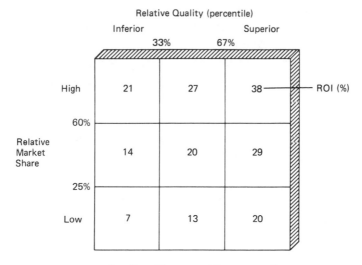

FIGURE 7–3 Quality, Share, and Return on Investment

Adapted with permission of The Free Press, a Division of Macmillan, Inc. from *The PIMS Principles: Linking Strategy to Performance* by Robert D. Buzzell and Bradley T. Gale. Copyright © 1987 by The Free Press.

tors are placed at the end of the line to find the mistakes. This is enormously wasteful, for it still requires the typical factory to invest 20 to 25 percent of its operating budget to find and repair mistakes. This doesn't include the expense of field repairs or replacement of flawed goods that slip through the screen.

Conformance to standards is only one of three components of quality, and is now seen as less important than *design quality,* or the intended degree of excellence, and *fitness for use,* which is the match between the product or service and the customer's needs. Growing attention is given to design quality in the wake of findings by quality experts that no more than 20 percent of quality defects can be traced to the production line. The other 80 percent are traceable to faulty design or purchasing policies that value low price over quality of purchased inputs.[6]

Design quality includes both simplicity of style, to match the product to the way the customer uses the product, and simplicity of assembly. "Design for assembly" leads to trimming the number of assembled parts, which also pares inventories and shortens assembly time. It pays off because assembly often accounts for two-thirds of total manufacturing costs. The possibilities for savings are suggested by IBM's experience with their Proprinter. Previously the company purchased dot-matrix printers from Epson, then the world's lowest-cost producer. By analyzing and simplifying parts, IBM developed a better printer with 65 percent fewer parts, and cut assembly time by 90 percent. This made it possible to keep production of the printer in North America.

When quality is viewed from the customer's perspective—as degree of fitness for use—a number of dimensions have to be considered before the quality of a product or service can be judged:[7]

- performance—how well do the primary operating characteristics meet customer expectations—of speed or absence of waiting time for fast foods or airlines and clarity of picture for television sets, for example.
- features—does it have the enhancements that customers want, such as automatic tuners on TV sets, that augment the primary characteristics.
- reliability—which reflects the likelihood of malfunctioning or failure within a specified period of use.
- durability—measures the total product life, before being replaced.
- serviceability—such as speed, courtesy, competence of the service encounter, and ease of repairs (when necessary). This dimension extends to handling of complaints and resolution of problems such as mishandling accounts.
- aesthetics—how the product looks, feels, sounds, tastes, or smells.
- perceived quality—when quality cannot be judged accurately before the fact, customers rely on cues from the image, advertising, and brand name.

The variety of dimensions offers a multitude of ways to differentiate products or services in ways that add value to customers—and with variety comes strategic choices. It is seldom possible to pursue superiority on all the dimensions at one time, for trade-offs are soon encountered: motor manufacturers will trade off speed and specialty features against fuel economy, and paper towels can be either tough or soft, but not both. The choice is made on the basis of the dimensions of quality that are most important to the target segment—and supports the positioning theme that defines the basic identity of the business.

PROGRAMS FOR ACHIEVING SUPERIOR QUALITY

This is not a treatise on organizational change—but a discussion of quality can't proceed without first recognizing that managers have to be committed—even obsessed, about getting better—and willing to support that committment with specific deeds and resources, and secondly, that quality

---

REPOSITIONING MIDWAY AIRLINES

Midway Airlines[8] began as a no-frills airline providing a simple service at cut-rate fares that appealed to price-sensitive customers. This strategy worked well only during periods of heavy traffic, when the major airlines didn't need to cut fares. As soon as traffic volume fell the majors offered low fares and Midway's traffic switched. Without a competitive advantage the airline faced prospects of meager earnings at best, followed by large losses as soon as traffic dropped.

To break out of this pattern the management undertook to reposition the airline to serve the frequent traveler. The move was based on significant research that showed these frequent travelers were unhappy with the service on all airlines. What they wanted was reliability, timeliness, and comfort. Reliable, on-time departures and arrivals were deemed vital.

A number of improvements were made in response to the research findings—seats were removed, carry-on luggage facilities were provided, gate areas were redesigned, and food quality was improved. At all stages the employees were involved. These product design changes were a signal that changes were coming, but these didn't address the top-priority issue of timely departure.

---

won't happen without multifunctional teamwork. The beginning of enlightenment comes with the recognition that customer satisfaction is the objective, and that each person and activity in the business is a customer of the preceding activity. Each person's goal should be to make sure the quality of his or her output meets the expectations of the next person in the chain of activities. When this happens, the satisfaction of the end customer is also assured. But how should the energies of these committed and energized teams be focused on strategically relevant changes? One way is to concentrate on key success factors; the high leverage skills and resources that determine customer value. Then progress at improving quality has to be measured and rewarded. The story of how Midway Airlines overcame the service quality problems that were impending a repositioning (see boxed insert) illustrates how these two program steps work together.

Managing the KSFs of Quality. Earlier we defined key success factors as sources of advantage, embodied in superior skills and resources, that have the greatest leverage on improving positional advantages—in this case, the perception and reality that Midway had the best on-time departure record.

A tool of statistical process control called "fishbone analysis" was used for this purpose. In this analysis an effect—namely, delayed flight departures—is defined. Then the major causes of delay are listed on the "spine" of Figure 7–4. Midway employees had no trouble suggesting possible causes. The actual causes were then tallied for each location for a month.

The biggest single cause of delay was accommodating late passengers. These weren't passengers who had connection problems, they were simply casual about being at the gate on time. Individual gate agents were making their own decisions to delay the plane, so Midway wouldn't lose the fare,

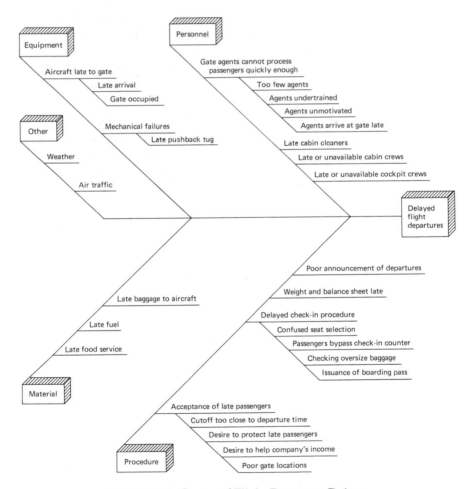

FIGURE 7–4 Causes of Flight Departure Delays

Source: Daryl Wyckhoff, "New Tools for Achieving Service Quality," *Cornell Hotel and Restaurant Administration Quarterly* (November 1984), 78–91.

but also out of sympathy. Midway then established a policy that it would operate strictly on time—a discipline appreciated by the majority of passengers. The second cause of delays was at the time of "pushback" because the motorized pusher tugs weren't available. This was solved with better scheduling and the addition of more tugs.

This systematic program of attending to the details worked for Midway. It is equally applicable to other businesses—so long as they are ready to: (1) listen to the customers—and design the quality program around their requirements, (2) involve the employees and keep them fully informed, (3) identify the root causes of poor performance, and (4) invest the time and money to minimize or eliminate these reasons. While this was mostly skill building for Midway, it also involves upgrading resources until they are also superior to competition.

A final step is critical if the quality improvement program is to endure: the performance has to be recorded and monitored so that everyone can see whether there is progress, and quality performance is rewarded. For Midway a simple control chart showing percentage of on-time flights sufficed. These charts were filled in by the employees, who saw the results as an opportunity to learn. Employees were rewarded for an improvement from 65 percent on-time departures in January 1982 to 95 percent by the end of 1983.

SUPERIOR RESPONSIVENESS

Time may become as important as quality as a strategic weapon in the battle to offer superior customer value. Customers are becoming increasingly impatient, and unwilling to wait for their specialized or urgent requirements to be satisfied. They have learned they don't have to wait, and can point to good experiences with fast response firms such as Federal Express, Toyota, The Limited, Wilson Art, Domino's Pizza, and Benetton for proof. When all competitors were equally fast—or leisurely—about responding to orders or changes in customer requirements, time was not an issue. But few firms can now ignore the possibility that response time will be the next basis of competitive advantage in their market.

Response time has always been important in service industries; this is what "fast foods" promise! The Midway Airlines turnaround shows that timeliness of departure is so important to customers that it is part of the service quality definition. Rapid response has only been a latent customer value in most other markets, with the possibilities usually unrealized because of high costs. In fashion-oriented markets there have always been some customers willing to pay a sizable premium for a broad choice among

the latest fashions. Few retailers have been able to respond because the traditional eight-month order cycles mean carrying large and expensive inventories if all fashion possibilities are to be carried, and bad guesses are
further penalized by large markdowns at the end of the season. Similarly,
in produce-to-order markets, like custom motors or furniture where there
is an infinite variety of possible designs, customers have long been frus-
trated by leisurely delivery cycles, but seldom had an alternative. Now
these and other markets are being transformed by rapid response systems,
with just-in-time (JIT) production systems leading the way.

The goal of JIT is zero inventory with 100 percent quality. As practiced
by auto, office equipment, and electronics companies it means component
parts arriving at the customer's factory exactly when they are needed. Ideally neither the customer nor the supplier carry inventory; instead there is
such a close synchronization between supplier and customer production
schedules that buffer stocks are not necessary. Actually, JIT systems are
the joint result of quality programs—because only perfect quality parts or
materials can be used if the customer's production process is to continue to
run uninterrupted—and rapid-response logistics based on frequent and reliable delivery of small orders.

Achieving a Rapid Response Advantage.[9] The formula is well known and
deceptively simple: make only what the customer buys, and then don't lose
any time filling orders or responding to new requirements. The ingredients of the formula are:

- a market *positioning theme* that unifies the fast response strategy with
  the other elements of the strategy. Often the responsiveness is in
  terms of rapid changes in the product line. Thus Stouffer's offers a
  constantly changing collection of frozen entrées, but the logic of the
  fast introduction and withdrawals is dictated by the overall theme of
  high-quality, contemporary favorites with lots of variety and choice.

- *rapid feedback from the market,* that tracks changes in customer needs
  precisely, and translates any changes in requirements into real-time
  production orders (or if necessary into the design of new features,
  variants, and styles that are then quickly put into production). JIT
  systems exploit new communications technologies to hook customers' computers to suppliers' computers, with a capability for
  just-in-time ordering as stocks change. But electronic links are not
  sufficient; the sales force must be able to provide quick feedback and
  expect to have it acted on as well.

- *flexibility in manufacturing* to accommodate quick shifts in requirements and small lot sizes so there is more frequent production within

the range of products. This requires such major modifications to factory layout, scheduling methods, and worker autonomy that most established factories can't make the adjustment.

- *compressed order cycles*, achieved by slicing time needed for each order-handling step: processing orders, forwarding them to manufacturing, putting orders into inventory, preparing paperwork, and arranging delivery. Each step may be done quickly, but the cumulative effect over many steps is excruciating delays and uncompetitive slowness. The solutions usually require direct links from salespeople to production scheduling. But this won't work unless the factory has enough flexibility to handle small runs.

The integration of these elements can be seen in the strategy of Atlas Doors. This firm makes industrial doors in every conceivable combination of width, height, and material. This variety means doors are mostly made to order. This takes most manufacturers almost four months—but Atlas can do it in just a quarter of the usual time. The first obvious difference is with order-entry, engineering, pricing, and scheduling. By automating this entire process, Atlas can price and schedule 95 percent of incoming orders while callers are still on the phone. The competitors may take a week to get an estimate of price and delivery. The doors are built in a JIT factory that employs extra tooling and machinery to reduce changeover time and a scheduling system that ensures all parts are finished at the same time. Logistics are also on a JIT basis that ensures that only fully completed orders are shipped to construction sites. Tremendous time losses can result when some parts miss a shipment, and may even delay the whole project. By minimizing this aggravation and offering fast delivery, Atlas slowly built a satisfied customer base. After only ten years in the business, the firm had replaced the leading door suppliers in 80 percent of the distributors in the country, and with a pretax 20 percent return on sales it was five times as profitable as the industry average. Despite this success the competitors had not responded aggressively, possibly because they failed to appreciate the value of time as a source of competitve advantage.

PROGRAMS FOR ACCELERATING RESPONSIVENESS

Rapid response strategies take hold first in markets that value variety and have diverse requirements, with their life cycles being compressed by a continuous parade of new features, designs, and enhancements. The fast tempo market profile is being seen in an increasing number of markets—

partly because new players like Atlas see opportunities for advantage by shaking up the old rules of the game that once conferred an aura of stability. Successful programs for transforming a business to "competing in time" have five mutually reinforcing components:

1. *Setting ambitious objectives for improvements.* Real breakthroughs in speed of response don't come from incremental improvements. The motivation that forces all members of the organization to work together to rethink everything they do is usually a simple top-down announcement of an objective that is clearly out of reach of the existing approach. It was in this spirit that John Young, the CEO of Hewlett-Packard, declared that the break-even time, or the interval between a new product's conception and profitability, must be cut in half across the entire corporation.

2. *Challenging the causes of delays.* To speed up doesn't mean doing things faster. Real gains come from eliminating or compressing delays. This is what General Electric did to meet an objective of cutting the time between receipt of an order for circuit breaker boxes for a building, and their delivery from three weeks to three days.[10] The analysis that gave them confidence this objective was reasonable had uncovered three primary sources of delay. First, it took considerable time for salespeople to write up and transmit their orders to the factory. Then an engineer spent a week to custom design each box from 28,000 unique parts. When the design was released for production a decision had to be made as to which of six plants would do the assembly. Once in the plant a myriad of supervisors and quality inspectors had to approve each step of the process, causing further delay.

3. *Rethinking organizational designs and processes.* New arrangements designed with speed uppermost have several features in common. First, they sharply reduce the number of approvals required to move a product ahead in a manufacturing organization, or to process loan requests in banks. As a rule of thumb, manufacturing takes between 5 and 10 percent of the total time between order and delivery, the rest is administrative. One of the quickest ways to cut down approval steps is to reduce organizational layers. This is why General Electric got rid of all line supervisors and quality inspectors in their circuit breaker operations, reducing organizational levels between worker and plant manager from three to one.

4. *Designing for manufacturability.* Many delays are traceable to excessively complicated designs, that use unique, hard-to-find parts, and uncoordinated product lines that evolved one model at a time in response to unique customer requests. GE was able to build a new circuit breaker series that had only 1,275 interchangeable parts, rather than 28,000 unique

parts, while still offering customers an array of 40,000 different sizes and configurations.

5. *Investing in information technologies.* Enhanced computer power and superior communications links have made it feasible to use computer-aided design/manufacturing and computer-integrated manufacturing systems to link all components together. In some systems the salesman can enter product specifications and customer order data directly into a computer that automatically programs the factory machines.

The speeding of production, distribution, and service handling requires a basic shift in attention from cost reduction to time savings. Paradoxically this may be the best way to cut costs. Trying to cut costs in one function at a time, such as accounting, may leave the department understaffed and lead to small delays that cascade through the organization, causing much bigger and more expensive delays. Conversely, spending a little on speed cuts these delays and also boosts morale which further improves productivity.

The benefits of "competing in time" will only be realized in the long run if interruptions and errors in the short run are avoided.[11] But one consequence of compressed cycles is the loss of traditional comfort zones, buffers, and other components of slack that help cover delays and correct errors. The damage from such delays and breakdowns can be minimized by simulations of new procedures, pilot tests, and holding temporary buffers of resources and information.

IMPLEMENTATION PITFALLS

Failures of strategies designed to differentiate firms by offering superior customer value can be traced to one or more of the following pitfalls:

1. **Meaningless differentiation.** This happens when the points of superiority are unimportant to customers. There are no benefits to the customer—either in improved performance or lower costs. This is particularly a problem when the value of the difference is not obvious or measurable. Considerable software has been written with memory-consuming features that users have no need for, but appealed to the designers.

2. **Uneconomic differentiation.** When a business sets out to enhance customer value, it usually works from the market back, and seldom isolates all the costs it has incurred. Adding features or product line extensions can burden products with extra costs that far exceed the price premium that can be achieved. Other forms of differentiation, such as improving quality or enhancing order responsiveness, may not be very costly. This is usually a difficult judgment to make as the benefits are often realized in the future

via increased customer loyalty and reduced price sensitivity, while the costs are immediate.

3. **Invisible differentiation.** The firm may be superior to the competition on important values, but if the customer is not aware there is a difference or doesn't see any value from such a difference then the strategy has failed. This is a consequence of communication problems (the amount of advertising and sales force activity) or insufficient cues for the customer to use. When the products are hard to evaluate and purchased infrequently, customers need help in comparing alternatives, and turn to cues such as design, packaging, price, the reputation of the firm for superiority or exclusiveness, warranty coverage, the expertise of the sales representative, the decor of the offices, and so on. In short, as Levitt reminds us,[12] people use appearances and external impressions to make judgments about realities. And when performance is hard to evaluate, customers need to be reminded about why they bought the product or service to ensure they keep coming back.

COST COMPETITIVE STRATEGIES

Cost-based strategies conjure dreary images of penny-pinching managers doing everything possible to drive down costs: cutting layers from the organization, moving production to low-cost countries, building efficient new facilities to get scale economies, and perhaps focusing the business on a subset of key activities. The product is either a strict no-frills offering with no extra services, such as offered by the discount airlines and warehouse furniture outlets, or a standard but limited range of acceptable quality. Such strategies have worked well in "volume" markets where there are few bases of differentiation.

The dedicated pursuit of the lowest delivered cost position will be rewarded by superior profits so long as the prices are average for the market. These profits won't be realized if the perceived quality is noticeably lower than average and customers demand discounts that are greater than the cost advantage. Striving for overall cost leadership can also be a risky strategy, especially when there are several firms with the same scale and intentions and each realizes that every point of market share is crucial to maintaining capacity utilization. The risks are further increased if cost leadership is achieved with single-purpose, inflexible facilities and systems that resist adaptation to changing requirements. This exposes the business to attack by competitors who play a different game. Many of GM's current difficulties can be traced to a volume orientation using a middle-of-the-road appeal. This worked well until the mid-eighties when it was undone by the trend in the U.S. market toward a collection of niches where customers could personalize their needs with a specific model. No longer was tailoring limited to modifying a basic car type with a variety of options. Meanwhile, GM was trying to down-size and cut costs to match Japanese competitors. Their solution was to share parts across models to get greater volume advantages in high-speed assembly lines. In retrospect this was exactly the wrong way to go: commonality of parts led to a confusing similarity of styling and engineering across the entire GM line, and the assembly plants designed for high-volumes of a single car type lacked flexibility for mixed assembly. This left most GM lines susceptible to specific customer targeting by other manufacturers. GM didn't lose share to any single competitor; instead it was "nibbled to death" by focused attacks on its exposed flanks.[13]

Outright cost leadership that subordinates all other strategic priorities to cost cutting is a restricted option in most markets. But every market requires strategies of relentless *cost improvement,* to achieve competitive costs in the context of the level of customer value being offered. Few markets are so protected that they permit sloppy cost management for long. How each firm proceeds depends on its competitive position and the cost improvement opportunities in its market. Successful cost improvers do appear to follow a well-defined process that is explained in the next section.

A PROCESS FOR IMPROVING COSTS

Successful cost cutting—that takes out unnecessary costs but doesn't jeopardize the value to the customer—begins with an enduring commitment by the organization. The best practitioners, such as H. J. Heinz, have a "chip, chip, chip" culture that works on cost problems continually. There are no limits to the details they will pursue, including getting rid of the back label from large bottles of ketchup. Most firms can cut costs under duress, with one-shot reductions in personnel or the advertising or training budgets. Seldom will the results last, as costs are likely to bounce right back when the immediate pressure is released. It takes leadership and persistence, supported by the culture, to keep them down.

The second element of a successful cost-improvement strategy is a competitor-orientation, using what Xerox calls benchmarking. This goes beyond tearing down competitors' machines and estimating the cost of making each part, to estimating all costs. Thus to find Kodak's distribution and handling costs, a number of Kodak copiers were ordered, then their shipping path was traced. In short, nothing in the firm's value chain is off-limits to the critical questions: "Who has the best costs for this activity? Why are we doing it this way? How can we do better? And should we be doing it at all? The value chain provides a framework for guiding these questions through the following steps:

Step One: Assess the current relative cost position by:
- estimating costs of activities in the value chain
- comparing costs to competiors
- diagnosing drivers.

Step Two: Assign functional groups the responsibility for cutting costs from the activities under their immediate control.

Step Three: Form multifunctional teams to examine linkages between activities and opportunities to reconfigure the whole system.

Step Four: Monitor progress against agreed-on cost reduction targets and begin the process anew.

The well-known declines in real costs documented in hundreds of experience curves reflect a combination of (1) continuous small improvements in activities as a result of *learning* through the practice of discrete activities and the exercise of ingenuity and skill, (2) *technological improvements,* such as new production processes, and (3) *economies of scale* from the greater efficiency due to increasing size.[14] Each of these sources has to be carefully managed so the business can avoid being left behind the competition.

IMPROVING THE COSTS OF SPECIFIC ACTIVITIES

The first rule is to focus attention on high-yield activities—those with a poor relative cost position that are worth fixing because they account for a large proportion of total costs or impact other activities. Once all the activities in the firm's value chain have been classified within the cost-improvement matrix in Figure 7–5, those that fall into the high priority category can be assigned to the appropriate functional groups. The mandate for each of these groups should embrace any and all the following alternatives:

- restructuring to reduce overheads
- low-cost sourcing of labor, services, or materials
- reduced labor intensity from automation
- changes in product mix and range, level of performance, and service
- low-cost product designs for ease of assembly
- developing low-cost processes

Cost of Activity Relative to Competition	Significance of Activity →	High	Low
	Higher	Highest priority for action	Monitor cost position
	Lower	Manage for continuous improvement	No action needed

FIGURE 7–5 Setting Cost Improvement Priorities

- changes in marketing practices: including channels used, and level of advertising spending.

With attention comes action, and the cost improvement matrix helps focus the attention of the organization. The results can be seen in the experience of H. J. Heinz which has become the low-cost producer in each of their six biggest product markets (see the following boxed insert).

HOW HEINZ IMPROVES COSTS AND PLAYS THE SPREAD

The basic Heinz strategy[15] is to obtain a premium price for mature staples such as ketchup and vinegar, using strong brand name support and superior quality. Heavy advertising spending is needed to persuade and remind customers there is a difference worth the premium. Low-cost operations are crucial to ensuring a high gross margin that will support large marketing budgets.

Traditionally, Heinz's approach to managing costs concentrated on procuring cheap raw materials. After all, these materials accounted for half the costs. To attack the other half management adopted a zero-budget approach, by constantly asking "If you were going to start a ketchup business today, how would you do it? What would your costs be?" This line of thinking has lead a number of task forces that identify and assign priorities to projects with major cost-saving potential. The division producing frozen French fries developed new processes for peeling potatoes and reusing water from one processing area in another.

When one particularly cost-competitive product, canned tuna, came under attack from imports they used a Hershey solution—so-called when Hershey downsized its chocolate bars when cocoa prices soared. They were able to save $7 million by reducing the height of a can by 2 percent and still met government standards.

Heinz has spent heavily to automate plants. At the largest soup plant in the United Kingdom, product-line speeds were doubled to 800 cans per minute and more bulk processing was done, in order to eliminate 1,200 jobs.

A major attack was mounted on marketing expenses—despite success in using heavy media outlays to build shares. Anthony O'Reilly publicly attacked what he saw as an "unconscious conspiracy" between brand groups and ad agencies to spend ever more on advertising to hold share and increase it. In one move the company switched to 15-second TV spots after learning that shorter spots reached 75 or 80 percent as many people as the 30-second versions.

Each of these moves was supported with a delayering, that saw one layer of management removed, combined with incentive compensation geared to profitability.

MANAGING LINKAGES FOR COST SAVINGS

When a multifunctional team recognizes how the cost of one activity depends on the way another activity is performed, it can begin to take concerted action.[16] This may mean spending more on one activity to save money overall. Typical of such cost linkages are:

- improvements in the quality of inputs such as castings or the precision of machined parts will reduce downstream inspection, reject and warranty costs
- better coordination of purchasing and assembly can reduce costly work-in-process inventories.
- investing in CAD/CAM systems that take the output of computer-aided design systems and feed them directly as instructions to machining centers.

The notion of the "cost of quality" rests on an understanding of cost linkages—specifically, how the cost of doing something wrong early in the value chain can impose extra costs on subsequent activities. The costs of sending back materials that aren't up to standard, pulling defective parts out of an assembly for rework, employing quality checkers to catch oversights, and making warranty repairs can all be reduced by getting each activity right the first time.

Channel and supplier linkages are also sources of cost savings. These may be realized when an activity is shifted from one value chain to another, or the coordinating mechanisms such as order-entry systems are redesigned to draw the supplier or channel member closer. A revealing example is the chocolate bar maker that used to have to melt solid blocks of cocoa from their suppliers before adding ingredients and molding individual bars. They were able to eliminate this activity by having their supplier deliver molten chocolate in tank cars. Not only did they save the costs of handling and processing, but so did the supplier who no longer needed to mold the raw chocolate into blocks for shipping.

Increasingly, firms are working closely with their suppliers to achieve joint management of costs. This might mean training the employees of suppliers, such as Xerox has done to ensure a full understanding of new quality control procedures. Motorola goes even further by training its suppliers' suppliers' work force. Among the closest links are those managed by IKEA, the Swedish retailer of casual, non-lifetime furniture in kit form. They reason that no single supplier is likely to be excellent at making everything from leather couches to shelves. Their suppliers are specialists, making large volumes of a few, similar standard parts to be assembled by customers. The linkages with IKEA are very close, with IKEA handling all the product design work, establishing quality standards, and investing heavily to improve manufacturing systems of their suppliers. This ensures consistency of design, because the IKEA signature is obvious in the attractive shapes and colors; but above all it yields low-cost production, packaging, shipping, and display.

SCALE AND SCOPE AS COST WEAPONS

There is still truth to the old adage that being big is an enormous advantage.[17] We don't mean big as in overall size, which was a mistake that conglomerate firms have often made when they acquired unrelated businesses in search of ephemeral synergies. Think rather of "focused mass" or the ability to dominate a sector or activity with better resources and deeper skill bases than anyone else. As markets fragment it becomes increasingly difficult to focus the mass effectively. Thus economies of scale usually have the greatest leverage on overall relative costs in volume markets where there are few ways to differentiate. Economies of scope, which behave like economies of scale in that average costs decline as traffic in a network increases, are the key success factor in the deregulating communications and transportation markets. Comparisons of firms that have succeeded in those markets versus their weaker rivals show that ownership of a large facilities network—whether it is miles of fiber-optic cable, miles of railroad track, or numbers of airports served—yields larger-than-expected cost advantages.

Scale or scope influences relative costs in four ways:

1. *Cost spreading.* Seldom does increasing size require a corresponding increase in advertising expenditures, sales force size, product development costs, or general overhead. Boeing is a fine example of the benefits of a large base on which to spread costs. Each new model of an aircraft demands enormous start-up costs. So far Boeing has been able to amortize the costs of the 747 over 13 different versions. Each new version is costly to develop, but not nearly as expensive as designing a new aircraft. This is a business with high break-even points—usually about 500 planes—requiring the ability to manage a complex procurement system with 1,500 subcontractors and 4.5 million parts.[16]

2. *Operating efficiency.* High throughput means the facilities are more likely to be at an efficient size (doubling capacity doesn't mean doubling the investment) and ensures continuity of operation. Borden grew from a 6 percent share of the pasta market in 1980 to a 31 percent share in 1988 by exploiting national economies of scale. They have 17 regional brands (such as Prince and Gioia) and a national brand (Creamette) to cater to special tastes. Their pasta products are made in 14 plants in the United States. Huge volume lets Borden eliminate the delays and costs of shutting down production lines to convert to specialty pasta shapes. Instead, three or four of the plants are devoted full-time to these shapes.

3. *Purchasing power.* The ability to bargain for special services and advantageous delivery and payment terms while also extracting the maximum quantity discounts is directly related to size.

4. *Increased profits to plow back.* If large scale or scope can be converted into lower costs, the resulting high profit margins, when multiplied by the largest sales base, mean the biggest-scale competitor also has the most profit dollars to reinvest into advertising, R&D, new market development, information systems, or global expansion. Anthony O'Reilly of Heinz describes the cycle (for their major brands such as Heinz Ketchup and Weight Watchers foods): "where greater marketing expenditures result in additional growth and future margin expansion, which in turn permit increased marketing expenditures." A virtuous cycle indeed!

Disadvantages of Scale. The pursuit of scale advantages can follow one of two paths: large runs of standard units in purpose-built plants, or increasing the breadth of the product range in search of incremental volume from previously unserved segments. There are potential problems lurking on both these paths.

The standard volume approach can introduce a great deal of rigidity and inflexibility. These plants are designed to make one or two products very well. When a changeover is required to assemble or process a new product or part, a great deal of time may be lost and money spent on new equipment, jigs, and so on. Other rigidities come from the increased likelihood of unionization in large plants and the impediments to clear communication down large hierarchies. These all become disincentives to change and make it difficult to pursue smaller specialty opportunities. Some useful indicators of a plant or business that is too big are declining profit margins, employees devoting most of their time to turf battles and coordination activities, and cumbersome processes that involve many steps.

If volume is gained with increased variety the cost advantage of superior scale may quickly be negated by increased costs of complexity and coordination of setups, materials handling, and inventory. As a rule of thumb, costs will increase by 20 to 35 percent each time variety doubles. For example, a study of the European auto industry found that the third-largest firm in 1983 had the lowest cost per engine produced. How? It only made two different engines while the largest firm made five engines and had costs per engine that were 5 percent higher despite 40 percent bigger sales volume.[18]

Compensating for Small Scale. As a rule it is unwise to directly confront a large competitor who has a scale advantage. With large plants and high fixed costs they can ill afford to see their capacity utilization drop, so they will retaliate fiercely to protect their share. Thus, increasing volume is normally not suggested for improving a weak relative cost position. Effective cost strategies for small players will instead hinge on (1) differences between activities in their sensitivity to scale, (2) differences between segments in price sensitivity, and (3) the costs of variety in the market.

The key is to properly estimate the relationship between scale and relative cost for each activity. It is important to know also what the best measure of scale is for each activity: it could be a global or national scale for R&D, whereas transportation and servicing costs probably depend on local or regional scale since this is usually an indicator of density of customers to serve. Once this relationship is known the small-scale firm has a number of possibilities to consider:

- narrow the product line, to increase the volume per product
- share volume-sensitive activities with outside suppliers or distributors, or even with competitors. The auto industry is a vast web of

joint manufacturing agreements such as between Peugeot and Fiat to produce engines, or

- employ flexible manufacturing systems to overcome the costs of variety.

The best advice for a small-scale competitor is to find a niche, where either the large-scale competitor is at a disadvantage in serving the customers, or a small scale of operations hurts least. These could be regional markets in which high importance is attached to local service, customer groups who demand extensive customization, or fast-changing markets that value flexibility and innovation.

SUMMARY: CHANGING THE COMPETITIVE STRATEGY

Major strategic moves are usually triggered by market turbulence, changes in the rules of competition, or a crisis associated with poor performance and/or the threat of a takeover. Then, previously comfortable operating styles, cultures, and implicit assumptions have to be challenged.

The lone strategist or the management team has the choice of making changes at any or all levels of strategy. Fundamental change in response to wrenching discontinuities starts at the generic strategy level. This may mean a shift in the relative emphasis on cost leadership, or a search for new ways to offer superior customer value with improved quality or enhanced responsiveness to customer requirements. Generic strategy change often leads to a simultaneous shift in the scope of market coverage. The considerations behind alternative scope strategies are the main topic of the next chapter.

Short of a major redirection, the firm can stay within the present generic strategy and look for a new positioning theme to give the target customers a more compelling reason to deal with it. Finally, there are possibilities for improvement of supporting programs and functional activities within the positioning theme. Most firms will continually tinker with supporting programs, to sharpen their existing edges and keep ahead of competition, and only contemplate fundamental shifts in their generic strategy and positioning theme under duress. To be effective, however, these program improvements have to support the overall thrust of the competitive strategy. Consistency and congruity of functional activities, based on a shared understanding of the overall strategy, are essential to superior performance.

EIGHT

Deciding Where to Compete:
Focusing and Sustaining the Advantage

M idsize high-growth companies succeed by identifying and meeting the needs of certain kinds of customers, not all customers, for special kinds of products and services. . . . Business academics call this market segmentation. Entrepreneurs call it common sense.

—CLIFFORD AND CAVANAGH[1]

There is an axiom in economics . . . that there is no such thing as a free lunch. Everything costs. There is also a law in economics that derives from this axiom, namely, that every situation bears the seed of its own reversal. This is the law of nemesis: Nothing good lasts indefinitely, because others will want to share it.

—LANDES[2]

Two themes increasingly cross-cut contemporary strategy dialogue. One is that fragmenting markets and technology change are creating new opportunities in secure niches. The other, gloomier, message is that no competitive advantage or niche position is ever secure in the long run—and the definition of the long run is shortening under the pressure of the same forces of change.

This chapter brings these two themes together. The departure point is the array of alternative strategies implied by the questions: Where will we compete—now and in the future . . . ? Do we cover the entire market, or just a segment? Can we use the same strategy in all segments, or will different strategies have to be tailored to each segment? A major consideration in the choice of market coverage is the answer to the further question, How long are our advantages likely to last? Here we need to consider the likelihood of competitors in the served or neighboring markets meeting or exceeding our advantages. Armed with this insight, we can judge the urgency of the search for new advantages and the need for defensive moves to discourage challenges. This never-ending process is the essence of strategy development.

The interplay of the choice of market coverage and the rate of erosion of competitive advantages is well illustrated in the box below, which tells the

---

COPING WITH A FOCUSED COMPETITOR

SKF competed in the bearing market with factories scattered throughout Europe, each producing a broad product line for a local market.[3] This made them a big target for focused Japanese competitors with product lines that offered only half or a quarter the variety. The Japanese focused on high-volume segments, such as automobile transmissions, and used the low costs of their highly productive factories to sharply undercut SKF prices.

The SKF response to the Japanese threat was to avoid direct price competition by adding high-margin specialty products. They did not drop any low-margin products, which complicated plant operations and increased costs. The resulting high prices opened a price umbrella under which the Japanese could slowly expand their range.

Had SKF continued to retreat toward specialties, its costs would have risen, low-margin items could no longer have been carried, and the competitors would have moved into the vacated position. As the revenue base began to decline, the margins and volume would no longer support the fixed costs—triggering further retrenchment. SKF was able to avoid this fate, and beat back the Japanese, by focusing each factory on the products it was best suited to make. If a product didn't fit a factory it was dropped.

The Japanese competitors then faced the classic dilemma of a focused strategy which is running out of room to grow. They could either reduce product variety to regain the cost edge, or accept the higher costs of a broader product line.

---

story of a Swedish ball-bearing manufacturer dealing with focused Japanese competitors. This story shows the two faces of a sharply focused strategy: on one side it is hard to defend against, on the other side it eventually limits a firm's ability to grow because it covers only part of the market.

ALTERNATIVE COVERAGE STRATEGIES

A broad coverage strategy that covers the entire market is feasible and profitable only as long as (1) the product or service attributes are broadly desired by most customers—for example, superior service is essential to almost all buyers of heavy construction equipment, and (2) cost positions are largely determined by economies of scale in the primary value-creating activities. Companies like Heinz and Kellogg's win by investing in large-scale facilities, building strong brand names with heavy advertising expenditures, and maintaining broad distribution networks. Their broad coverage strategies do not inhibit the offering of many product variants under a broad family brand umbrella, because the same organization is responsible. Cost advantages are secured because a common plant, sales force, and R&D facility can be used.

As markets fragment, customers seek and find a diversity of offerings, and new manufacturing technology permits economical variety production, these broad coverage strategies giving way to *tailored strategies* that adapt to segment differences. The intent is still to cover the whole market—but now the diversity is explicitly recognized. IBM's response to these trends in the computer market is illuminating. At one time IBM wouldn't bother entering a market that didn't promise at least $100 million in long-run volume. That criterion is now obsolete. They have also reorganized into five autonomous groups so decisions can be made closer to customers.

The position of firms covering the whole market with a common strategy is being further eroded by focused-niche competitors who cover only one or two distinct segments, with no intention of serving the whole market. These focused competitors find segments where broad-scope firms are uncompetitive; either because they overperform in meeting the needs of the segment and incur high and unnecessary costs, or underperform by not catering to the distinct needs of the segment. Clear evidence of a supportive environment for focused players is an increase in the share taken by "other" brands, at the expense of well-established "big" brands[4] sold by broad-coverage firms:

- Twenty years ago there were 100 semiconductor firms. Now there are over 300.

- The frozen orange juice concentrate market has three well-known brands—Tropicana, Minute Maid, and Citrus Hill—that now have only 46 percent of the market. The rest belongs to hundreds of mostly small private or local brands.
- The personal computer market in 1986 had more than 300 IBM clone makers who collectively took 36 percent of the market compared to IBM's 26 percent share.
- Contrary to forecasts in the eighties that soon there would be 5 to 8 world-class auto makers, each offering only a few types, an auto buyer at the end of the eighties could choose from 300 different types of cars and light trucks from domestic and imported sources.

SEGMENTATION FOCUS STRATEGIES

Focused competitors dominate their target segments—by fending off broad-coverage competitors who have to compromise to serve the segment, and outperforming any rivals with the same focus. They do this with the strategy ingredients discussed in Chapter 7, reflecting an appropriate balance of emphasis on cost and superior customer value, and a positioning theme that favorably distinguishes them in the minds of their target customers. Focused strategies also gain meaning from the differences between the segments being covered and the rest of the market. They are successful because no compromises need be made in order to cover other segments, and dilute the advantage of meeting needs precisely.

PATTERNS OF FOCUSED MARKET COVERAGE

A firm can focus along any—or all—three dimensions of a market (see Figure 8–1). There are three possible types of focus on product markets,[5] and each can be pursued in a variety of geographic settings.

- *Niche specialist.* Snap-On Tools sells only hand tools and only to professional mechanics. They have a unique method of direct distribution and sales to the work location.
- *Product specialization.* Only one product is sold to all market segments. In the scientific equipment market some firms specialize in single products such as microscopes but cover all types of customers.
- *Market specialization,* as practiced by manufacturers of integrated production systems that meet all the equipment needs of semiconductor companies.

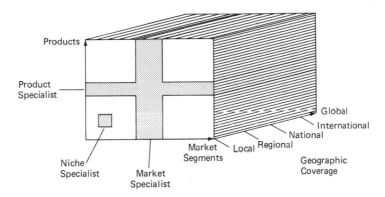

FIGURE 8–1 Focus Strategies

Since each of these focus strategies implies heavy reliance on a specific customer segment and/or product type, they increase the risk exposure of the firm and limit the growth potential. Thus most successful specialists begin to edge out to closely related areas where they can build their strengths. Analog Devices had prospered by only offering products that process real-world signals so computers can understand and use them. Their original offering was a device that amplified and processed analog signals. Then they progressed to converting analog signals to digital form. Their core competency—processing real-world signals—took them into diverse segments with related needs, including lab automation, industrial automation, avionics, and telecommunications.

Sequential Market Entry. When a business has aspirations to be a broad-coverage player but is short of resources, or doesn't want to invite retaliation from the established players, it will plot a course of entry through a sequence of low-visibility niches. This route is often followed by foreign firms seeking beachheads in markets dominated by domestic companies. Japanese companies have done this to enter the U.S. market for refrigerators, and are now employing the same approach with food and cosmetics.[6] Their general approach is instructive, for both these industries are highly competitive, and the entrenched domestic companies have powerful brand and channel franchises.

When Sanyo decided to enter the major appliance market in the United States, they began by focusing on a narrow product niche—under-the-counter refrigerators for hotels, wet bars, and recreational vehicles. This entry point had three advantages:

- major domestic manufacturers like General Electric and Whirlpool had decided the market was too small to be profitable, so they didn't have to be confronted.

- the product was sold in large lots to a few purchasers like hotel chains. This meant a small sales team could easily cover the major accounts. When a sale was made the order could be economically shipped in one bulk shipment.

- manufacturing of small refrigerators was an area where Sanyo had extensive experience, and low costs, since refrigerators made for the Japanese were generally smaller than those sold in the United States. Their superior quality meant that breakdowns could be fixed with a replacement refrigerator—thus reducing service costs.

Sanyo next moved to a related niche, for less-than-normal-width refrigerators. Again, they faced little direct competition from domestic manufacturers. However, segment demand was growing fast as it rode the trend to smaller homes and renovated buildings with limited kitchen space.

Unlike the under-the-counter refrigerators, this product required a presence in mass distribution outlets like appliance stores, discount stores, and department stores. These outlets were willing to take this line since it meant incremental sales that would not simply cannibalize sales of their existing lines. This toehold helped paved the way for future lines of Sanyo appliances, using the relationships with the retailers that had been established.

POSITIONING IN A SEGMENT

Focus strategies succeed by exploiting the differences between a segment and the rest of the market. They do this by achieving a close identity with their customers, and avoiding the extraneous costs of serving other segments.

Close to Customers. The closer the business is to their customers, the more likely the product is unique to the point of being customized to meet highly specific needs.[7] The payoff is that customers are willing to pay a sizable premium to have their needs so precisely satisfied. A. Schulman has followed this recipe to become the largest independent plastics compounder in the United States. They buy basic resins from oil and chemical companies, and then precisely blend colors and other additives to produce specialty resins for every conceivable application, from skateboard wheels to lobster pots.

Customers buy solutions to problems—not specific products. Often the core product is standardized, but with unique enhancements that add value to the customer. This is particularly evident in "vertical marketing" of computers, which means selling systems tailored to the requirements of particular industries. Triad Systems, for example, has positioned itself to solve the complex inventory problems of automotive parts wholesalers. A typical parts wholesaler stocks 20,000 items and finances this inventory with supplier credit. The key to profits is paring this inventory. Triad uses standard computer hardware with special software that enables wholesalers to record every sale and continuously analyze inventory movement (slow movers versus fast movers). Another feature permits them to project the financial results of changing the inventory mix and prices. With this system the average wholesaler can cut inventories 10 percent, turn them over twice as often, and add two percentage points to its net profit margin.

Even in mature markets like bus transportation it is possible to be highly profitable by focusing on a distinct segment. Laidlaw Transportation has become the largest operator of school buses and special education vehicles in North America, with more than 13,000 vehicles in service. Because they know the needs of school boards, and how their decisions are made, they can develop customized packages to meet the specific needs of a particular board.

The downside of being very close to one group of customers is vulnerability to economic conditions in that market. During the 1982–83 recession, Triad suffered when parts jobbers went bankrupt in record numbers. Furthermore, little of what a niche specialist knows about the intricacies of its customers' businesses can be effectively applied to other markets.

Avoiding Extraneous Costs. Focused competitors often start with a significant cost disadvantage. With low volumes they can't realize the economies of scale achieved by broad-coverage competitors. They can overcome this disadvantage to achieve competitive, if not superior, costs in a number of ways:

- specialized sales coverage. Instead of relying on direct sales forces to reach dispersed specialty markets the firm may cut costs by using trade publications, trade shows, direct marketing methods and spreading word of mouth.
- specialized manufacturing processes, that produce products or accept very short runs without excessive changeover penalties.
- locational superiority, to minimize their transportation costs and increase responsiveness.

By carefully adapting their activities and processes to the requirements of the segments being served, focused competitors are usually able to achieve price premiums that more than offset their cost disadvantages. Furthermore, if they are not part of a multidivision corporate structure they avoid many corporate overhead charges. To them the corporate fashions of delayering and restructuring to cut staff are foreign ideas—they have always operated with lean, purpose-built organizations.

Positioning and Identity. A study of winning, medium-sized companies found that their success was achieved with market segment leadership, often in markets they had created through innovation. This success also shaped the culture and values of these firms:[8]

> They have an unusually clear vision of the markets in which they will and will not compete, the kinds of products and services they will and will not offer, the level of quality they expect, and the basis of their competitive advantage. In parallel, they work hard to maintain a common set of company values that spell out their commitment to serving customers, the way people are to behave and be treated, and the way the high level of financial performance they expect is to be achieved.

When this kind of an integrating strategic vision pervades the organization from top to bottom, the organization is very resilient. With clear priorities all functions can work together to quickly adapt to opportunities and changes as they emerge. A sense of common purpose is in itself an advantage over competitors who are less clear about their identity or can't reach a consensus within their management.

CHOOSING THE SCOPE OF MARKET COVERAGE

A broad-coverage competitor has to decide whether or not to retrench—and, if so, where? If they don't retrench, should they tailor strategies for each segment? Meanwhile, *focused* competitors are deciding whether to stay where they are, broaden their market coverage from the present base, or find entirely new segments. Both types of competitors will ask roughly the same series of questions before they reach their decision:

Step One: How is the market segmented? Which segments have the most attractive competitive structures?

Step Two: What segment coverage best fits our competencies?

Step Three: How vulnerable is the position to attack?

The steps in this process overlap with step one in the search for distinct and strategically relevant segments that was discussed in Chapter 5. To get this process under way we'll assume we know how the market is segmented and concentrate on how to use the information.

FINDING STRUCTURALLY ATTRACTIVE SEGMENTS: STEP ONE

Although attractiveness is ultimately in the eye of the beholder—what appeals to a big multinational will not necessarily be attractive to a modestly capitalized regional firm—both will be looking for segments with above-average profitability and growth prospects. Overall attractiveness will depend on their ability to exploit these characteristics better than others.

Relative profitability will be jointly determined by the size of the price premium that can be achieved—which is a reflection of the intensity of competition—and the cost to serve that segment. Segments of small buyers are usually not price-sensitive or strongly contested by other firms, which means high prices can be achieved. They can be very costly to serve if they have to be reached through distributors, and still provided with typical levels of technical assistance.

Often, however, the profit potential of a segment is obscured—either because the firm isn't presently serving the segment or does serve it, but uses inappropriate cost allocation rules that obscure important cost differences. The usual culprit is the practice of allocating corporate and marketing overheads on the basis of labor costs or sales volume.[9] One firm was considering dropping its OEM (original equipment manufacturer) business because it had a 27 percent gross margin, and 2 percent operating margin, compared with a 12 percent overall operating margin. What they failed to recognize was that OEM customers used virtually no selling resources: advertising, catalog, sales promotion, and warranty. When a proper allocation of activity costs was made the operating margin was actually 9 percent. The OEM segment looked even better when capital was properly allocated, for it required far less working capital in the form of accounts receivable and inventories.

Growth prospects for each segment depend on untapped opportunities. Even mature markets may have segments with significant growth potential that may have gone unnoticed. One company went from nothing to $400 million in revenue within the seemingly stagnant athletic footwear market, by meeting unsatisfied needs for better engineering and sharper styling. The incumbents had ignored the signals, either because they were complacent or distracted by other problems. Seldom, however, are data readily available to reveal the rate of growth of emerging segments. It takes careful marketing research, guided by the segmentation process described in Chapter 5, to uncover these segments before others see the same opportunity.

MATCHING SEGMENT COVERAGE TO COMPETENCIES: STEP TWO

Why should a business focus its efforts on only one segment? The simplest answer is that it lacks the resources or staying power to compete in the broader market. This is a good answer only if what the niche competitor can do with these limited resources is highly valued by the target segment—and larger competitors are put at a disadvantage.

When Broad-Coverage Strategies Pay. If a niche competitor could always win because it specialized in satisfying the requirements of a distinct segment there would be no place for broad coverage firms serving many adjacent segments. Of course, this is not the case, and breadth often confers advantages. There are many markets where programs and activities can be beneficially shared across segments. When one sales force can be used to reach customers in a number of segments, one plant can economically produce all the product varieties, and advertising can be done under a single wide umbrella, the resulting economies of scale yield a large cost edge. A broad-coverage business may also offer superior customer value—especially in activities like service support where density of coverage means speedy response. The shakeout in the medical diagnostic equipment market, that forced out specialists like EMI who only made CAT scanners, was precipitated by their inability to field enough service people without incurring crippling costs. Bigger firms, such as GE, selling wide product ranges (including modalities such as X-ray and ultrasound) to all customers could support bigger and better-trained service groups with much faster response times. This was a compelling edge in a market where customers were heavily penalized for equipment downtime. The leadership of broad-coverage firms was reinforced by their ability to invest more heavily in R&D to continually improve product performance.

Constraints to Breadth. Eventually the broad-coverage competitor will be constrained as (1) the costs of diversity and compromise overtake the cost savings from scale, (2) the positioning theme loses meaning because it embraces too many disparate segment needs, and (3) the inherent disadvantages of size start to hurt. Operating in multiple segments with shared activities imposes costs of compromise,[10] where the strategy and activities appropriate for one segment are not optimal in another segment, and attempting to serve both dilutes the positioning theme. A pooled sales force that carries several products can't be as knowledgeable about each one as a specialist (although they may have an advantage in selling integrated systems). Often brand names and images are only suitable for a single market segment—prestige lines like Ralph Lauren or Nino Cerrutti would destroy their brand equity if they tried to pursue a middle-market fashion position.

Broad-coverage strategies sometimes risk alienating customers (or dealers and distributors) in one segment because of participation in other segments. Retailers, such as specialty bicycle dealers, won't take kindly to a bicycle supplier who offers essentially the same machine to discount department stores. They know these high volume stores can undersell them by 35 percent, with a combination of quantity purchase discounts, savings on shipping, and lower markups. The margin for a specialty dealer might be 40 percent, compared to the 25 percent margin for the discounter. Since they have other brands they can carry they will simply drop the offending supplier.[11] Toro almost lost its dealer network when it tried to solve an excess inventory problem by flooding discount chains with premium snowblowers. The penalty was a close brush with bankruptcy in 1980.

Tailored Strategies. One way for a firm to cover most of a market, and perhaps avoid the constraints to breadth, is with tailored strategies—and even a different organization—for each segment or set of related segments. This can be costly, with no guarantee that some customers will not be antagonized. If there are few shared activities between the different organizations the cost-spreading benefits of wide coverage will be lost. These problems are especially severe within companies trying to serve global markets while maintaining autonomous country organizations—each with a distinct strategy. The need for global strategies and the challenges of managing market diversity are the subject of Chapter 10.

DETERMINING THE VULNERABILITY OF A SEGMENT POSITION: STEP THREE

The final consideration in the assessment of a market coverage strategy is the durability of the favorable conditions within each target segment. This is an especially compelling issue for niche competitors whose target segment is both attractive—because of a lack of direct competition—and well-suited to their specific capabilities. They must constantly look over their shoulders for two threats. One comes from focused followers who either imitate their strategy in the segment or perhaps leapfrog with a new strategy even better suited to the segment. The other threat is from broad-coverage competitors who decide the segment can no longer be ignored and warrants a tailored strategy. Both these threats will be aggravated by changes in the needs of the customer segment that either makes them more like other segments or more difficult to serve.

Threat of Imitation. Eventually a firm that has found an attractive segment is going to attract focused imitators—whether start-ups or migrants from adjacent segments that are either overcrowded or don't offer growth potential. The likelihood of direct imitation depends on the size of the segment and the need for unique skills or technology. If the segment is too small to support more than one or two competitors at their minimum efficient scale, then entrants will be deterred. However, rapid growth will attract imitators because the visibility of the segment has been raised and the carrying capacity of the market has increased. Another consequence of segment growth is the emergence of small subsegments with distinct requirements that can be catered to by small start-ups. Many computer software segments have followed this scenario. The burgeoning market for spreadsheet programs attracted droves of competitors, since there were few economies of scale in any activity and many ways to differentiate the product.

Attacks by Broad-Coverage Competitors. Broad-coverage competitors will be relatively ineffective in serving a segment if they consider it too small for special attention and/or their strategy causes them to underperform on attributes that are important to the segment, or they overperform on unimportant attributes at high costs. This is most likely to happen when the needs of the segment are very different from those in the rest of the market.

This combination of circumstances initially allowed Tandem Computers to prosper as the specialist for nonstop computing applications. They offered fail-safe systems for critical jobs where vital data had to be captured second-by-second, such as controlling an airline reservation system or running a network of automatic teller machines. Their success was built on specially designed fault-tolerant minicomputers that operated at far lower costs than could be achieved with standard IBM equipment. Eventually the market grew so big that IBM could no longer afford to ignore it, and so they entered with tailored products. Their entry was also speeded by growing pressure to respond to the need of large computer customers to give more employees, such as financial and marketing analysts, access to the very kinds of "live data" that Tandem computers were collecting. IBM management saw that if they didn't take major steps they ran the risk of seeing Tandem machines used as major hubs in corporate networks that could serve data to mainframes and desktop computers throughout an organization. Now Tandem's once-secure segment has become part of a much larger open systems market, which has forced them to confront their rivals more directly.[12]

SUSTAINING THE ADVANTAGE

The law of nemesis, which introduces this chapter, gloomily reminds us that nothing good lasts indefinitely. Others will want to share the wealth and continually look for ways to narrow or neutralize a leader's advantages. Their efforts are usually encouraged by changes in the technology or market that replace barriers to imitation with gateways to entry.

The unseating of the Swiss from their preeminence in time-keeping demonstrates all the forces at work.[13] For 700 years the Swiss were masters of the intricacies of mechanical watch movements. Their downfall was not taking the quartz watch seriously. After all, what did electronics firms know about time-keeping? Not that they weren't warned. Quartz time-keeping went back to the 1920s, and extraordinarily accurate quartz marine chronometers were displayed in 1961. What they underestimated was the intrinsic superiority—quartz was 10 times as accurate—or the rate of improvement. During the seventies Japanese and American firms were able to reduce energy consumption by 60 percent (so permanent displays were possible), thickness shrank by 80 percent, and retail prices at the end of the decade were perhaps 2 to 3 percent of what they were at the start. Meanwhile, the Swiss were working to make mechanical timepieces better and cheaper. This seems to be the visceral response of a once-dominant technology.

When the Swiss finally took the quartz threat seriously, they were ill-prepared to respond. The small companies that formed the industry had been profit-protected for so long they had little capacity to innovate. The new electronic technologies demanded larger investments than the majority could afford. The competitors in the meantime had amassed substantial economies of scale in related devices (calculators, recording instruments, computers) and the chips that held the necessary integrated circuits. Not surprisingly, the Swiss industry shrank fast—between 1974 and 1981 the export of watches and movements dropped from 87 million to 45 million pieces. Employment dropped by 50 percent, as the remaining firms retreated to high-price points, where they played up the prestige, luxury, and styling prowess of the famous brand names. Even here they were followed by Seiko. Only with the Swatch was the retreat finally reversed. But this breakthrough was achieved by a complete outsider who broke all the rules.

Lest one is tempted to think that only in-bred and traditional firms fall from grace, the PIMS data show that most leaders tend to lose ground over time. They are much more likely to lose share than their smaller competitors—and this erosion gets worse the bigger they are! The following data are based on the share performance of the leading firms in the market over a five-year period.[14]

Leaders' Market Share	Percent of Leaders' Losing Share
Under 20%	16%
20–29	24
30–39	34
40–49	41
Over 50%	46
All leaders	31%

For the rest of this section we will seek to explain why erosion is close to inevitable—although the duration of the advantage can be very long under some circumstances—and use these insights to argue that the most sustainable advantages draw on the "invisible assets" of the firm. Along the way we will also see just why being first in a market confers so many advantages.

WHY ADVANTAGES FADE

Sustainability is a matter of degree, for most advantages are contestable because they can be duplicated.[15] The most contestable are price advantages, for they can be rapidly countered. Most product innovation is quickly contested, as competitors are able to secure detailed information on 70 percent of all new products within a year of introduction. Even process improvements are hard to protect—60 to 90 percent of all learning eventually diffuses to competitors.

Three mechanisms are at work in most markets to undercut the leader:

- technological and environmental changes create gateways to the market, by eroding the protective barriers
- competitors learn how to imitate the sources of the leaders advantage
- the firm itself suffers inertia, and doesn't take strong action to protect its position.

When Gateways Are Created.[16] Among the forces most destructive to an advantage are technological change that is accessible to competitors and permits them to match or leapfrog the leader, and shifts in customer requirements that change the attributes that they value highly. More generally, whenever there is high turbulence in the environment—for reasons such as deregulation, new government policies, as well as customer and technology change—that changes the "rules" of competition, the less secure is the leader. Conversely, this is the time for a new entrant to grab the lead.

Technology change spares few markets. Even the competitive standings in the staid industrial gas market are being reshuffled by a new manufacturing process—see the boxed insert.

IMPERMEABLE MARKETS FOR GAS

For nearly a century the global market for nitrogen, oxygen, and other gases for industrial use has been dominated by five companies.[17] Often these companies achieved local monopolies, which combined with long-term contracts, stable prices and products, high barriers to entry, and negligible technological change to yield high and protected profits.

The business is capital-intensive enough to deter outsiders. It takes 2 dollars in capital spending to generate about one dollar in sales. Geographic markets are protected by the problems of transporting gas. Because transportation costs are some 40 percent of the selling price, it is uneconomical to sell outside a 200-mile radius. Customer switching costs are inordinately high. Heavy users, such as steel companies, have their gas piped "on-site" through dedicated pipelines. This makes it almost impossible to switch to another supplier.

New technologies using artificial membranes have changed this comfortable calculus of competition. These methods offer new ways to produce gas more cheaply—although the results are not as pure as the traditional manufacturing processes. This does limit the market size. On the other hand, the systems are quite portable. As a result, industrial-gas companies are moving more freely into each other's once-protected territories. It appears now that all five major competitors are trying to increase their shares—with adverse consequences for short-run profits.

Advantages can also be pared down by changes in customer needs, experience, and buying habits. DuPont has often observed that as chemicals and plastics products mature, and the customers have less need for supporting technical services and other product augmentations, the size of the price premium achieved by the superior quality competitor begins to decline. The start of this decline signals that maturity is impending and the product category is losing differentiation. Then relative delivered cost position—and the scale economies that are the main drivers of cost—determine profitability. This pattern is summarized in Figure 8–2.[18] This pattern is played out in many other markets, although the market usually fragments at the same time, leaving groups of customers with special requirements or intensive service needs that will still pay a premium price. Even the emergence of these niches can cause a leader's share to shrink if the compromises needed to serve all segments become too great, and some specialty segments have to be ignored.

When Followers Catch Up to Leaders. The sustainability of complex advantages often hinges on imperfect observability by competitors. This is the hidden know-how, embodied in superior skills, that enables a business to consistently respond faster to service requests, achieve superior quality, or maintain close relations with key customers. For example, the sheer size and complexity of IBM make it hard for competitors to learn what is going on.

Yet competitors do copy or leapfrog each other: IBM brags about its efforts to understand the "best of breed" among its competitors. No doubt

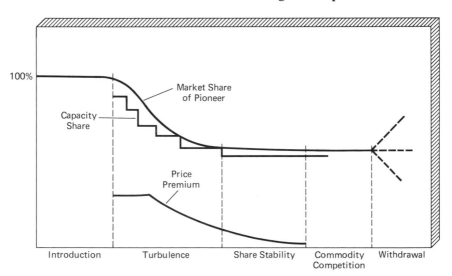

FIGURE 8–2 Pricing in Capital-Intensive Industries

Apple Computer has IBM under similar scrutiny in the PC market. As a result, the office product lines of the two firms are converging. Features that distinguished personal computers in the past—differences in ease of use, microprocessor speed, memory, disc drives, and expendability—are quickly converging. Major software houses are writing their new programs for both machines, so no retraining of users is needed to shift between machines. Meanwhile, clones are proving especially adept at emulating IBM products—although not the organization that created the products.

Followers can catch up to or pass leaders in many ways:

- the follower can learn from the leader's mistakes and experience by hiring key personnel, "tear-down" analysis of the product, and conducting marketing research to identify the unfulfilled expectations of customers and distributors.

- a follower may be able to leapfrog the pioneer by using more current technology or building a plant with a larger current scale of operations.

- there may be cost advantages in certain activities gained by sharing operations or functions with other parts of the company.

- all competitors may benefit from the cost reductions and performance improvements achieved by outside suppliers of components or production equipment. In the spinning and weaving industry most of the advances in technology come from textile machinery manufacturers who share these improvements with all customers. Similarly, construction engineering firms make the latest advances in chemical processes available to all present and prospective customers.

ENDURING SOURCES OF ADVANTAGE

Can the law of nemesis be repealed or at least postponed? The experience of industries like industrial gases is not encouraging, for despite the historic barriers to competitive incursions there are technological and market changes undermining once-secure positions. If the environment is highly turbulent, there are few barriers to entry, few irreversible investments, and low asset intensity, then no competitive position is secure. Yet industry leaders do prevail for long periods, and like Xerox, show they can draw on "invisible" assets to adapt to changing circumstances that attracted competitors. This notion has close kinship to "distinctive competencies," but is more strategically useful.

Invisible assets[19] are mainly embodied in the superior skills of people—the information they have acquired, and their commitment to using the skills to further the strategy of the business. These assets embrace the corporate culture and the prevailing values as well as advanced technical design and production skills and mastery of the dominant technologies. Some invisible assets reside in people outside the firm—including brand name, reputation as a reliable supplier, and sound channel relationships. Among the most powerful of the invisible assets is a pervasive customer-orientation, reinforced by field salespeople who keep the business in close touch with changing requirements.

The distinguishing features of invisible assets are, first, that they are unattainable with money alone. This means they are hard to copy. American auto manufacturers have been able to copy the robotics and sophisticated hardware of their Japanese competitors, but a history of adversarial labor and supplier relations and lukewarm dedication to quality has proven far more difficult to change. Within General Motors layers of middle management in the "frozen" middle have fought the new priorities, although the success of the production joint venture with Toyota has changed many minds. Hence, the second feature—invisible assets are very time-consuming to develop. Businesses don't become market-oriented by edict. Instead, the process of culture change requires years and continuing commitment. Conversely, it is not easily eroded. We will look at both the benefits and costs of a market-orientation in our summary chapter.

Thirdly, invisible assets are capable of multiple uses, and so can be used to speed the firm's adaptation to environmental change. A strong reputation with customers will carry over to related products. Sophisticated technologies can be adapted to related applications. A strong financial control orientation can be used to manage costs in a variety of businesses. Honda has been able to exploit its skill in designing and producing powerful small-displacement engines with a reputation for quality and design integrity, to expand from motorcycles, to lawnmowers, to outboard marine engines, to automobiles. If the invisible assets of the business don't make an obvious connection to the key success factors of a related market that is targeted for expansion, the likelihood of success is poor.

The invisible assets of a market leader are most often traceable to pioneering moves that preempted competitors when the market was embryonic. These assets are further accumulated through experience, continued investment in training, and insightful nurturing of strengths.

THE PAYOFF FROM MARKET PIONEERING

Persuasive evidence of the benefits of early or first entry into a market comes from the PIMS data base. Separate studies have looked at the performance of pioneers in both mature industrial and consumer markets.[20] As one indicator, pioneers have substantially higher market shares than either early followers, or late entrants, as shown in the following table.

Average Market Shares at Maturity

	Consumer Markets	Industrial Markets
Pioneer	29%	29%
Early Followers	17	21
Late Entrants	13	15

Among these pioneers are well-known firms like Campbell Soup, Coca-Cola, Kodak, Hallmark, and Xerox. However, what we see in a mature market (as in the PIMS data) are the pioneers that survived! This obscures a high rate of failure among pioneers who were either bankrupted or were absorbed early in the evolution of the market. They failed either because they entered too early and lost the struggle to overcome the resistance of the market, or got the timing right but were unable to adapt to changing requirements for success.[21]

The benefits of pioneering often make the risks worthwhile—because pioneers get to define the rules of competition to their advantage.

Preemption of Competition. A pioneer can develop and position products for the largest and most lucrative market segments, while leaving less desirable segments to later entrants. The enlarged capacity needed to serve these attractive segments serves as a commitment to maintaining output, with the implied threat of price cuts to make later entrants unprofitable.

Early entrants with a viable product usually have the pick of the best brokers, distributors, and retailers. The followers have the thankless task of persuading the pioneer's distributors to shift or divide their commitment. Failing this, the followers have to find a new channel or settle for less desirable channel members. The problems this creates for followers are acute in the personal computer market where the scarcest resource is the shelf space controlled by the large chains of computer retailers such as Computerland.

Leadership Reputation. The first company in a market naturally has a unique position. This confers a potential leadership image that is not available to followers. Whether this advantageous reputation has more than temporary value depends on the credibility of the firm and its capacity to invest in marketing and continuous innovation. Small firms have often introduced innovations to the industrial battery market, but have not been able to capitalize on them because they are viewed as high-risk suppliers.

Customer Loyalty. A customer may be forced to be loyal to the first supplier in the market because switching costs are high. These are one-time costs the buyer absorbs when switching suppliers, associated with employee training, new ancillary equipment, the need for technical assistance and product redesign, and the time required to test and qualify a new source. For example, hospital management contracts are costly to change, because of the disruption caused by a new administrator, a new computer system, and budgeting and operating procedures.

Proprietary Experience Effects. A pioneer gains an initial cost advantage when learning gained through cumulative experience becomes an important contributor to cost reductions. Whether it is sustainable depends on how difficult the learning is to imitate, and whether it will be nullified by a competing technology. Of course, the best protection against imitation is a strong patent position, but even this advantage must be vigorously policed.

Sustainable Lead in Technology. Such a lead will result if competitors are unable to duplicate the technology, or the firm innovates at a faster rate than the competition so followers are never able to catch up. For example, the first firms to introduce the dominant designs in 10 international semiconductor markets tended to have an advantage in improving the design throughout the product life cycle.[22]

DEFENDING THE ADVANTAGE

The loss of competitive position to challengers—whether they are new entrants or existing competitors hoping to build share—is neither inevitable nor irreversible. The threatening actions of competitors can be managed and their impact minimized through assiduous development of defensive strategies.

Unquestionably, the best defense is a strong offense. Leading firms that continually seek new sources of advantage to enhance their value to customers or reduce their relative costs are difficult to attack. There is no place for complacency in these firms to open a window of opportunity for competitors. Instead, there is a ceaseless search for product enhancements, elimination of defects, and new levels of service, that is epitomized in the Japanese philosophy of *kaizen* or continual improvement involving everyone in the organization.[23]

An explicit defensive strategy complements the offensive strategy by making the business more difficult to attack. The right strategic moves may *deter* some or all of the prospective challengers, by making the profit prospects so unattractive and risky the market share gains are not worth pursuing. Few consumer goods companies dare attack Procter & Gamble head-on in their core markets. With a long history of aggressive retaliation and clear signals as to how they will react in the future, P&G keeps underlining their total commitment to the protection of their share position.

If the challengers cannot be deterred then the purpose of the defense strategy is to *contain* their moves and minimize the damage. Indeed, the costs of complete deterrence are usually so prohibitive that a more measured defense that reduces the extent of attack is usually preferred. The aim is to reduce the challenger's profit expectations, so they adopt less ambitious entry or share-building objectives. Thus, in 1987 American Express was forced to downplay their new Optima card, because of fear of the negative reactions by the banks offering Visa and Mastercard. These banks lost no opportunity to remind American Express that they were very big customers for traveler's checks.

Absence of Defense. Unfortunately the incumbents are more likely to react *passively,* and permit their challengers to flourish without impediment. The reasons for the seeming inertia have to be understood before an appropriate defense can be mounted.

The first reason for a passive reaction is that the threat is not recognized. Competitor-centered firms are especially prone to watching only a few target competitors—who look and behave the way they do—and losing their peripheral vision. In some markets, substitute technologies present the greatest threat. In other markets surprise entrants may include regional competitors from other parts of the country, off-shore companies from similar markets in their home country, or customers who decide to back integrate.

Second, even when a threat is recognized it may be dismissed as unimportant or too diffuse to deal with. When the pioneers of the burgeoning wine cooler market faced over 100 new entrants within a year it was impractical to pay attention to all of them. Only a few entrants with deep pockets could be treated seriously. According to one study using the PIMS data base,[24] the typical entrant doesn't deserve to be taken seriously. They come in at a modest scale (their median scale of entry is only 6%, where scale of entry is the average of manufacturing capacity share and first-year market share), and their offerings are not especially innovative. Only 14 percent report a major product patent or trade secret.

At times, dismissal is delusive. Caterpillar learned at great cost not to underestimate the persistence and ability of Komatsu to take share in segments of the earth-moving equipment market. By the time they responded, Komatsu had gained a secure foothold and couldn't be dislodged. Complacency toward new technologies is also risky, even though it may be hard to take a struggling new technology seriously when it is performing poorly early in its life cycle. What counts is the potential for improvement in performance that comes from further R&D investments and experience in the field.

Finally, the managers of a business may stand aside and watch their competitive position erode because they are unwilling or unable to respond. They may be excessively concerned about cannibalizing sales from existing products with a new product designed to preempt a challenger. This is why Bayer, with the leading brand of aspirin, was slow to respond to the incursions of nonaspirin pain relievers such as Tylenol. Not until 40 percent of the pain reliever market had been taken by nonaspirin products did Bayer try to combat Tylenol directly with a similar product. It wasn't that they couldn't produce a nonaspirin pain reliever, for they had sold these formulations in Europe for some years.

Broad-coverage competitors may be unwilling to respond to flank attacks by niche competitors growing at their expense within segments of the market. The reasons are the same as those we saw earlier in this chapter for establishing the vulnerability of a niche: either the segment is too small, or meeting the particular needs of the segment would seriously compromise the strategy in the rest of the market. This is a continuing problem for the full-service, highly differentiated firm that is being attacked by small, low-cost entrants in price-sensitive segments. A price cut to fend off these nuisances would have to be offered to all customers, with nasty effects on overall profitability.

Eventually, of course, the broad-scope competitor loses so much ground that it has to stop ignoring followers or worrying about protecting the high-profit core business, and seriously retaliate. Xerox was slow to respond to the erosion of its position in the plain paper copying market, because it didn't want to obsolete an enormous rental equipment base. As a result, its share of new placements dropped from nearly 100 percent in 1972 to 14 percent by 1976. Since then Xerox has regained 40 to 50 percent of new placements by matching competitors' prices and product features.

The Defense Dilemma. Aggressive defenses require either a significant front-end investment to preempt competitors, or price cuts and marketing expenditure increases that will reduce the attractiveness of the market. Such moves are costly in the short run, and reduce short-run profitability. But if the moves aren't made, or are half-hearted, because management fears the immediate earnings impact and probable loss of performance bonuses, the present advantage can't be maintained and the long-run share and profits both suffer. Nonetheless, many companies have faced up to this painful trade-off and made the necessary commitments.

MOUNTING THE DEFENSE

Defense begins well before the actual challenge.[25] The purpose of the defensive moves is to persuade prospective challengers that either it is not worth entering or trying to gain more share, or that a more cautious approach should be taken to avoid arousing a costly retaliation. These results can be accomplished by some combination of the following moves:

- signaling intentions to defend
- foreclosing avenues for attack
- raising the stakes
- reducing the attractiveness of the market.

Once the attack is under way the emphasis shifts to retaliatory actions designed to nullify the challengers' attempts to gain advantage, and convince them to settle for modest results.

Signaling Intentions to Defend. We saw earlier that P&G has successfully discouraged frontal attacks on their core detergent and toothpaste markets. Their signals carry a lot of weight, because of a long history of punitive retaliation against aspirants, and frequent public reminders that their first priority is maintaining share. Other ways to amplify these signals include early announcements of new products, building capacity ahead of market growth, and other investment commitments.

Effective signals are credible and clear—to competitors as well as to employees. A signal is futile if it is likely to be missed or misunderstood by the target competitor, who is holding a different set of market assumptions or lacks the means to appraise the impact of a retaliatory action. Signals from some firms are routinely dismissed as mere posturing because there is no evidence of deeper commitment to a long-run, competitively focused intention to win.[26] When the whole organization is focused on beating competitors, this intent pervades all levels and activates and ensures a consistent message will be heard by challengers as well as by distributors and customers.

Foreclosing Avenues for Attack. These moves are designed to thwart challengers and reduce their revenue and profit expectations by building barriers to entry or mobility. Even if the barriers are already high, because of large capital requirements or heavy marketing expenditures, it is wise not to be lulled into a false sense of security. Few challengers are likely to mount a direct attack to go over these barriers. Instead, they will begin with focused probes, seeking niches the market leaders don't currently contest. These might be found in product categories (Japanese firms often start with low-end products, as Sanyo has done with refrigerators), specific activities in the value chain such as components, or particular geographic markets such as Eastern Europe.

Successful defenses begin by anticipating and then blocking these flank attacks by:

1. Broadening the product line to cover most of the possible performance levels and feature configurations, and inserting blocking or fighting brands into feasible positions an attacker could later occupy.
2. Clogging the channels, by entering into exclusive supply agreements, offering attractive stocking terms for new products, or reducing stocking risk by selling some items on consignment.
3. Obsoleting the present breadwinners in the product line with the newest generation of technology or moving to a higher performance level. DuPont's efforts to enter the consumer photographic film market were twice stymied by Kodak product improvements. Each time DuPont caught up to Kodak, and were ready to launch their challenge, they were met with a much superior film. This was so discouraging they eventually gave up.
4. Foreclosing alternative technologies with a web of patents and/or licensing agreements.
5. Preempting the best and cheapest sources of supply, through exclusive contracts, or even ownership of the source. This works well with scarce materials.

Raising the Stakes. Here the emphasis is on increasing the entry costs or investments and depressing the anticipated returns below the cost of capital. One approach is to make it costly for challengers to wrest away customers, by getting them committed to specialized systems for order entry or paying for specialized equipment to use the product or service. Alternatively, the defender can invest in technologies to raise the minimum economies of scale, boost spending in advertising, service, or development, or increase the needs for financing of dealers or customers by extending terms. A challenger with a smaller base of sales to carry these outlays is at a major disadvantage.

Reducing Marketing Attractiveness. Leaders often invite attacks by reporting unsustainably high profit levels. Pioneers who are finally reaping the profit rewards of their earlier risk taking are especially vulnerable. By keeping prices up, while costs are dropping down the experience curve, they open an umbrella of high profits. This attracts challengers and also permits them to prosper even if their costs are higher because of an uneconomic scale of operation.[27] Inevitably the leader loses share.

Early in the formulation of a defense strategy the management has to decide whether the current price and profit level can be maintained. If not, the question is how far and when to drop prices to discourage challengers while still delivering viable profits. Across-the-board cuts are very painful and obvious, while the deterrent benefits are speculative. Not surprisingly there is strong resistance to this preventative action, and so challengers eventually emerge.

Resisting the Attack. If the challenger is not rebuffed, attention shifts to punitive reactions that will contain the attack and limit the damage. When Datril tried to enter the nonaspirin analgesics market in 1975, Tylenol reacted very aggressively with price cuts, heavy advertising spending, and increased sales activity. As a result Datril barely gained a viable position in the market.

Effective resistance requires the defender to correctly diagnose the challengers' assumptions, strategies, and intentions—especially the gaps, deficiencies, and opportunities they hope to exploit, and the share of market they plan to achieve. A helpful precursor to this diagnosis is a role-playing exercise by the defending management team aimed at specifying the strategy they would use to launch an attack, given their inside knowledge of the points of vulnerablity. But timing is everything, and a tardy identification and diagnosis of competitive moves, even if correct, won't help to guide the containment moves. Early detection requires continuous monitoring of the most probable challenging firms, and broad sensitivity at all levels of the organization to the threat of attack. The front-line employees are often first to get early clues from customers, suppliers, or distributors.

To summarize, the law of nemesis reminds us that competitive advantages are never secure for long, and constant surveillance and innovation provide the only antidote for the competitive forces continually gnawing at the leader's position.

LESSONS FOR STRATEGY

The most obvious lesson to draw is that advantages are created by preempting competitors—by moving first to satisfy the needs of an emerging market—or, exploiting market and technological changes and environmental uncertainty to take a piece of an existing market.

These initial advantages are more likely to endure if (1) there are several bases of advantage, rooted in "invisible" assets that make it difficult for the competitor to imitate the strategy, and (2) the ability of the competitors to respond is restrained by inertia, stemming from conflicting commitments or inherent slowness in recognizing and responding.

Since there are no sure things on the road to competitive success, we can't forget that the value of these guidelines is continually undermined by two pervasive forces in all markets:

- it is seldom possible to be all things to all customer segments—increasingly this means focusing on niches, or tailoring strategies to account for segment differences.
- advantages are continually being eroded under the pressure of changes in technology, customer requirements, and input costs, that offer gateways to aspiring competitors. The rate of erosion will accelerate when the environment is turbulent and few invisible assets can be accumulated.

The only certainty is that self-satisfaction with a strong competitive position is dangerous, because it blunts the motivation to continually seek improvements and new sources of advantage. The litmus test of a successful market-driven organization is a willingness to obsolete successful products, processes, or technologies—even when they are delivering handsome profits. This willingness is rooted in the belief that it is better to own customers than to own plants, and to possess a culture that is constantly scanning the external environment for signs of change that can be exploited ahead of the competition.

NINE

Gaining Access to Markets

Making the initial sale is still important but selling by itself is not enough. In today's service- and technology-oriented marketplace, future sales increasingly depend on creating and maintaining a close buyer-seller relationship.

—THEODORE LEVITT[1]

A company with the best distribution system and the best service will win all the marbles—because you can't keep an advantage in other areas for long.

—LEE IACOCCA[2]

The changing competitive environment is pushing firms to reassess the channels used to reach their target markets. No longer can channels be managed passively, with an eye to reducing costs and avoiding conflicts. Now they are at the front line of the battle for competitive advantage.

Traditionally, the access to the market was established early in the history of the business. For reasons of inertia, tradition, industry practice, and an absence of feasible alternatives, management tended to stay with their existing channels. Thus, firms went direct to their markets with their own sales force if they wanted to keep close control over selling, service, and pricing activities or had only a few readily identified customers to reach. Other firms elected to use independent distribution channels because of the superior efficiency of intermediaries in making the products or services available and accessible to the target market. When the market wanted a wide variety of related goods in small quantities, intermediaries offered a real advantage in their breadth of coverage, experience, and specialization that gained them economies of scale.

The old rules and conventional wisdom are being overturned on a number of fronts—each presenting a significant threat or opportunity. First, there is a proliferation of channel alternatives in response to growing fragmentation and complexity of end-user markets. Second, businesses that are restructuring and cost cutting are realizing that sales force and distribution activities are often their single biggest cost element. As they look further they often find a history of rising real costs and poor productivity—a tempting target for a shake-up. Third, the desire to control costs is being tempered by the recognition that the channel is the businesses' main point of contact with customers, who are demanding closer relationships and better service, and willing to make long-term commitments to suppliers who can outperform the rest. With new developments in technology such as telemarketing and computer-to-computer ordering, the channel is demanding significant capital investment if firms are to remain competitive. Finally, the channels are the key to unlocking such closed markets as Japan or competing effectively in the consolidating European market, so any company that pretends to be global has to pay attention to its ability to access these markets. No wonder channels are rising close to the top of the list of strategic issues for the nineties.

The challenge is to find the combination of channels that best supports the business strategy by balancing *customer* responsiveness (to enhance differentiation advantages), with the total *costs* incurred, while retaining adequate *control* to ensure cooperation among all links in the channel network. Fortunately there have been significant advances in our understanding of each of these dimensions of channel performance.

CHANNEL DESIGN DECISIONS

The reassessment of a channel configuration begins with the recognition that a channel exists to perform a number of essential and unavoidable activities in taking a product or service to market. These activities can be an integral part of the firm's value chain or undertaken as a separate link in a system of related value chains. Thus one perspective on channel design is that it is the sequence of decisions on where to undertake the activities outlined in Figure 9–1.

Each of these clusters of activities has the following attributes in common: (1) they absorb costs and capital, (2) they can't be avoided, and (3) done well, they are the basis for a competitive advantage. Furthermore, for most firms these activities can be done better and cheaper by intermediaries, because of their contacts, specialization, and scale of operations.

Communication and negotiation activities include the use of media or salespeople to build awareness and deliver persuasive messages, and follow up with an attempt to reach an agreement on price, and terms and condi-

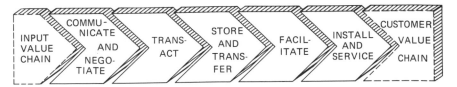

FIGURE 9-1 Channel Activities in the Value Chain

tions of sale. The process of negotiation is vastly easier if significant prior effort has gone into building strong personal relationships and mutual trust.

Transactional activities include the backward communication of the order to the supplier; the provision of credit or financial aid to the purchaser (a step that in big-ticket items may involve negotiating for governmental aid, or using barter arrangements); and absorbing the risks to the buyer of inventory losses and obsolescence.

Storing and transferring are largely logistical processing activities that include intermediate storage in warehouses, transportation to the buyer, and sorting and packaging into saleable forms (sometimes called breaking bulk).

Facilitation activities include processing payments and the associated paperwork needed to transfer title, counseling customers on how to use and maintain the purchase, and providing information about the transaction to the other parties in the value chain sequence.

Installation and service activities are required after the sale to enhance or maintain the value of the product and include start-up assistance, warranty administration, repair, training, parts supply, and product adjustment.

Channel design[3] is about deciding where and how each of these activities is to be done to best support the overall strategy of the business. Four key questions have to answered: How many activities should be performed internally? How many different channels should be used? What density of channel coverage is needed? And how much control should be exercised over resellers? Different firms within the same industry will have very different answers to these questions, depending on their objectives and the competitive advantages they are trying to secure. Thus Rolex sells high-priced watches via selected jewelers and department stores, while Timex sells $15-watches through all possible outlets including food chains and discount and variety stores.

CHANNEL INTEGRATION

All channel decisions are derived from the strategic choice of degree of vertical integration. At one end of the spectrum of choices a business can sell direct with a dedicated sales force, company-owned retail stores, or even direct mail. The other end of the spectrum is complete nonintegration, and reliance on independent agents such as wholesalers, distributors, or manufacturers' representatives to perform all distribution activities. The usual rule is that frequently purchased goods or services sold to widely dispersed markets, offering low gross margins, and requiring minimal adaption at the time of purchase are best sold via independent channels. As each of the conditions is relaxed direct channels look more and more attractive.

Independent agents are often preferred because they are specialists able to offer combinations or families of products that are more appealing to customers, especially the small accounts who would not warrant a sales call for any single item in the line. Another advantage comes from cost savings realized when similar products are sold together. For example, an ice-cream distributor can also handle frozen bakery goods and microwave meals with the same fleet of refrigerated trucks at a much lower unit cost than the manufacturers of the separate products could achieve.

Because independents are painfully aware they can be replaced—by other distributors or the company going direct—they are highly motivated to demonstrate they are performing. Their strongest argument is evidence of effectiveness in generating high sales volume, with efficiency in terms of low selling costs.

Direct, or vertically integrated distribution approachs are most favored with products that are complex, highly differentiated, expensive, and difficult to sell. These conditions usually require the development of supplier-specific capabilities such as: detailed application knowledge (acquired through training), dedicated testing, demonstration, storage or service facilities, and close relationships with customers based on in-depth knowledge of their requirements. When distributors acquire these capabilities their suppliers become highly dependent on them—and less and less able to assess their performance. The resulting immunity to the threat of replacement reduces the independents' motivation to perform. Since excessive dependency on an independent is risky many firms elect to go direct. They are even more likely to go direct if the average order is large and placed infrequently, making it easier to carry the high fixed costs of a direct sales force.

CHANNEL VARIETY

In simpler times it was possible to use a single channel to reach different customers with different products. As customer segments proliferate and new channels become available most companies are creating hybrid arrangements:

- insurance companies are shifting from exclusive agents to nonexclusive outside agents, supported by direct mail and telemarketing, and even using other intermediaries such as banks.

- IBM has moved from sole reliance on a 5,000-person direct sales force by adding more than 16 third-party distributor/dealer programs as well as a sizable direct mail operation. They have even experimented with retail computer outlets.

- General Electric sells major appliances through department stores and discount outlets, as well as directly to large housing contractors.

The arguments for hybrid channels are (1) that each new channel adds incremental volume by reaching new customers, and (2) that reliance on only one channel increases vulnerability to new competition from lower-cost routes. For example, we can see Merrill Lynch's exposure if we array the services they sell through a fairly high value-added, full-service brokerage channel (consisting of local office account executives and home office researchers) on the offering grid shown in Figure 9–2.[4]

As channels multiply, so do problems: loss of control, delivery delays, confusion to buyers, and above all, conflicts that arise when one part of a distribution network competes against another part for the same customers. Computer manufacturers such as Honeywell have been especially beset with these conflicts as they try to supplement a traditional direct sales force with VARs (value-added resellers) who tailor a vendor's hardware and software to the system needs of distinct segments. The difficulty they faced was that large customers with distinct needs were considered by the sales groups to be part of their territory, even if they didn't have the right system, while the VAR was pursuing the same application with a better solution. Equally intense conflicts erupt when manufacturers try to shift from sole emphasis on specialty or exclusive channels to include broader-based outlets. Levi Strauss triggered a backlash when it moved from its traditional reliance on specialty stores for Levi's jeans to selling through department stores such as J. C. Penney and Sears. It actually had little choice because designer jeans had begun to erode their market position by selling through department stores, and targeting the higher price points. Levi's was not only being given an unwelcome low-price, utilitarian image, but was absent from a large and growing source of sales.

Variety may also have to be introduced within a type of channel. For example, one of the difficult choices with a direct field sales force is the mix of generalists, who sell everything to all types of customers, versus specialists who focus on one part of the market. Pitney-Bowes has recently switched its vast 3,500 person sales force from full-line selling to specialized selling.[5] The decision was unavoidable and inevitable, but nonetheless

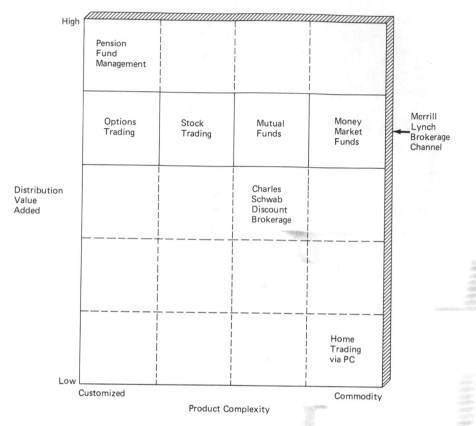

FIGURE 9–2 Offering Grid for Brokerage Services

painful. As the company diversified from mailing products to add shipping, copying, weighing, and inserting products, the salespeople were buried in new products they didn't understand and became increasingly unable to manage their time. Because each salesperson had a geographic territory with a mix of customer sizes, the company was often sending an expert to sell a $13-a-month postage meter and a novice to deal with the most valuable customers. As these problems mounted sales productivity languished. A complex reorganization was needed to first divide customers into tiers; the 200 biggest national accounts were assigned to one person each to manage the account, with help from product specialists, while the next tier of 1,500 multilocation accounts was reached with product sales specialists. The remaining 1,000,000 smaller customers were still reached with product generalists.

DENSITY OF MARKET COVERAGE

The next question is how many middlemen to use at each channel level. A specialty manufacturer like Porsche may choose to appoint only an *exclusive* handful of dealers. While this restricts market coverage it ensures more aggressive and informed selling and enhances the image. Alternatively, an *intensive* network was set up by Bic to sell their pens and lighters through almost every possible outlet in a geographic area. The middle road is *selective* distribution, using a subset of all the intermediaries willing to carry the product. Glidden (with paint), Maytag (with appliances), and Raleigh (with bicycles) all practice selective distribution in order to avoid dissipating effort on marginal outlets in hopes of getting a better selling effort.

As products mature and gain wider acceptance, manufacturers try to increase the density of coverage. This added density creates serious conflicts with the original selective distributors who face more competing resellers carrying the same product just as the product's advantages are dissipating. This is just one of a number of areas where the interests of the manufacturer are at odds with the interests of the intermediaries. If the resellers had their way, channel density would lessen as products mature. Since they don't usually prevail, the inevitable consequence is a dulling of enthusiasm for stocking and supporting the product, coupled with aggressive price cutting.

Channel density decisions are often dictated by channel-variety decisions. When Lego wanted to expand the sales of their plastic construction toys, by getting denser geographic coverage than toy stores could provide, they had to deal with many new and unfamiliar types of retailers.[6]

CHANNEL CONTROL

The final channel strategy issue is the degree of coordination and control to be exercised over the resellers. Tight control comes at a price, because it certainly takes time to supervise and manage the intermediaries' selling, stocking, and service activities, and may require a great deal of investment if there is an ownership stake.

At one extreme of control is a *market linkage*, where a loose coalition of autonomous intermediaries is kept in line by use of the price mechanism. These networks tend to be highly fragmented, with the parties negotiating with each other at arm's length. Tighter control is exercised with *leadership linkages*, where the dominant firm in the channel calls the tune and coordinates the players. Kraft plays this role with other parts of the channel for dairy products, as does Butler, a manufacturer of metal buildings, because of their dominance of their markets. Even more control is exercised with *contractual linkages.* The tightest control comes from *ownership*—at which point it becomes a direct channel. Tire companies, paint companies, and petroleum refiners often rely on company-owned stores. The downside of tight control of intermediaries is a restriction on market coverage and the loss of flexibility that comes with contractual and equity ownership entanglements.

The experience of Harnischfeger Corp., a maker of material-handling equipment like cranes and hoists, illustrates the strategic leverage gained from tightening control.[7] Most of Harnischfeger's products were sold through a network of 250 small distributors; some were industrial supply firms, others were OEMs, and some were crane companies. They were a mixed bag, without much loyalty to Harnischfeger. There was a disturbing tendency for them to build cranes in direct competition—especially at the low-end of the business. The ones that remained were not very professional, often abusing information and privileges, and lacking enough capital for expansion. In short, they couldn't be trusted.

The solution combined a change in strategy with radical surgery that pruned the number of distributors from 250 to 22 larger, more professional master distributors. First the company decided to refocus their strategy on selling parts and machinery and get out of selling steel in the form of girders and supports because of high shipping costs. This meant their distributors had to be able to assemble and ship equipment within a 400-mile radius. In return for exclusive distribution rights in this area they couldn't carry competitive items and had to stock a significant amount of parts and equipment. They also had to be prepared to take on increasing service activities because Harnischfeger had decided that superior service response could only be achieved locally with trained people. To tie these master distributors more closely the company made a risk investment by giving them extra-large credit limits.

With greater control over their channel, Harnischfeger was able to extend their product line so the customer could have one-stop shopping at a material-handling center. Rather than selling only what they made, the company looked for promising third-party products they could put their name on and sell through their distributor network. This not only reduced their need for fixed manufacturing assets, but gave them a significant competitive advantage.

THE TURBULENT CHANNEL ENVIRONMENT

Channel issues don't get much strategic attention when the market environment is stable. The forces favoring inertia are numerous and compelling. It takes enormous effort and investment over many years to build a strong channel; large internal bureaucracies are solidly committed to the day-to-day management of this channel; and competitors have likely locked up the attractive alternative channels. Furthermore, managers who already have plenty of conflicts to resolve in their present arrangements aren't motivated to search for new arrangements that will upset their finely balanced network. These comfortable rationalizations are being challenged, and sometimes swept aside by forces and events in five areas:

- declining productivity
- closer customer relationships
- proliferating channel options
- shifting power balances
- changing corporate priorities.

These trends don't apply equally to all firms and often conflict with each other, greatly complicating the choice of strategy.

DECLINING PRODUCTIVITY

Unremitting pressure on profits is forcing management teams to challenge every activity that absorbs costs. When distribution, and especially selling, costs come under scrutiny companies seldom like what they find. While manufacturing and transaction processing costs have been generally declining as a percent of sales, selling costs have been absorbing a bigger proportion.[8] One sample of large firms found that, on average, their cost of goods sold as a percent of sales declined by three percent from 1978 to 1987, while selling and administrative expenses as a percent of sales increased 31 percent.

A big contributor to the shift in cost structure is the high cost of direct selling. Between 1975 and 1985 the average cost of business-to-business sales calls increased at a 10 percent compounded annual rate, to rise from $71 to $208. Since it may take from four to seven sales calls to win a new industrial account, the total selling cost may exceed $1,500. These costs are prohibitive for small accounts, so new ways have to be found to reach them.

Unfortunately, there is little evidence that companies are getting more results for their increased spending. A 10-year study of 12,000 salespeople across 350 companies and 14 industries found that sales volume per sales representative had increased by only 2 percent per year, while selling time apparently declined by 250 hours per year. No doubt some of this decline in productivity can be traced to the increasing pressure that customers are putting on their suppliers.

CLOSER CUSTOMER RELATIONSHIPS

The changes here are so far-reaching that they have been aptly labeled the "purchasing revolution." They are being triggered by increasingly assertive customers who are driven by their own strategic needs to improve quality and costs, and to integrate their suppliers more closely into their value chain. These customers include the big systems assemblers and integrators such as General Motors and Xerox, as well as powerful retailers such as IKEA and Wal-Mart. They are often emulating the superior purchasing practices of their global competitors such as Matsushita, Toyota, and NEC.

From Arms-Length to Collaborative.[9] The traditional arms-length or adversarial approach to purchasing was designed for bargaining for the lowest prices. The features are familiar to anyone who sold to the Big Three automakers: the buyer relied on a large coterie of suppliers who can be played off against each other to gain price concessions and ensure continuity of supply. Only short-term contracts were given, so there were numerous occasions to reopen negotiations. Orders were allocated to multiple suppliers to keep them firmly in line, and reduce dependence on a single supplier. Indeed one justification for having multiple suppliers is to reduce the risk that supply lines will be cut by labor disputes or other disruptions.

When business was good, and all competitors played by the same rules, there was little incentive to challenge the conventional wisdom of arms-length contracting. Now there is a lot of incentive, as the hidden costs of adversarial relationships are becoming intolerable.

A major cost of traditional arms-length approaches stems from the assumption that there is no meaningful difference in the ability of suppliers to provide value-added services, technology gains, or process innovations that can be turned to the customer's advantage. When all suppliers are viewed as substitutes there is no mechanism for rewarding those best able to support the strategy. Now firms are shifting their criteria away from cost and price factors, as we see in the boxed insert.

A further cost of traditional arms-length relationships is due to poor communications. There is little in these arrangements that encourages suppliers to be open with buyers or vice versa. The buyer is unlikely to know a supplier's costs and capabilities, and there is little incentive for the supplier to develop superior capabilities since they can easily lose their contract next year to a lowball price. Suppliers are usually in the dark about the overall needs of their customers since they will only get to bid on a part that has already been designed. When they win a bid they only attract attention when they miss a performance target on delivery, volume, or quality. This emphasis on the "negatives" does little to engender trust or cooperation.

Just as the costs of arms-length relations are better appreciated, so are the benefits of *collaboration.* In these closer relationships, partners adopt a high level of purposeful cooperation with the intention of maintaining a long-term trading relationship. Such intense relationships are only possible with a few suppliers, which sometimes means single sourcing. This is why Xerox cut its supplier base from about 5,000 in 1981 to just over 300 in

---

THE GENERAL ELECTRIC SUPPLIER
EXCELLENCE PROGRAM

Suppliers of fabricated and machined jet engine parts purchased by the Aircraft Engine Business Group are given a score based on four factors:

30 points for *quality,* based on verified supplier-caused faults, adoption of approved systems, and management surveillance of operations.

20 points for *manufacturing engineering,* including technical depth of personnel, age of equipment, process planning, and history of cost improvements.

30 points for *delivery,* including shipping parts ahead of schedule, maintaining inventories of finished products, and showing a capability to respond positively to changes in schedule.

20 points for *cost/price,* reflecting the soundness of the financial status and promptness of requests for information and quotations.

Supplier scores usually range between 70 and 90. This is converted into a bid factor with the following formula

Bid factor = 1 + ([100-Supplier Excellence Score]/100)

If the supplier score is 70 the bid factor is 1.30, but if it is 90, the bid factor drops to 1.10. This makes a big difference because the bid factor is multiplied by the negotiated unit price to arrive at a weighted price that is the basis for a decision. This means the supplier with the high score (90) is given an 18 percent advantage over the supplier with the low score (70). GE is intending to use this approach to reduce the number of suppliers by almost 65 percent.

1986. Chrysler relies on 500 suppliers for 80 percent of purchased parts, and most of them have multiyear contracts.

The benefits of single-sourcing are sizable, especially when a just-in-time (JIT) manufacturing system is also installed. In the ideal JIT system a supplier ships the exact quantities of parts or materials only when they are needed in the production process. Since the parts are supposed to be of perfect quality, the customer can run this process without interruption. This means big cost savings. But other benefits of single-sourcing are just as compelling:

- supplier participation in design—the arms-length approach cuts the supplier out of the design process, even if the supplier understands it better than the customer. Now suppliers are being given the responsibility for delivering a component that meets performance specifications and motivated to use the best available technology to produce it cheaply. This taps a much broader base of knowledge.
- fragmentation versus focus—when there are many suppliers for each item it is difficult to find, let alone solve, quality problems. Any engineering changes are much harder to coordinate with a fragmented supplier base.
- scale economies—these can be realized by a single supplier, who may have enough volume to justify a special-purpose facility. With the security of a multiyear contract they are also more motivated to make these investments.

Collaborative arrangements require more than band-aids to existing relationships before a mutual commitment is ensured. The main ingredient is the balancing of power, for if the buyer tries to rule with an iron hand and dictate performance, collaboration cannot happen. Even when power is balanced there is likely to be disagreement and conflict, so mechanisms for managing conflict have to be provided at the outset. Among the mechanisms for minimizing the destructive potential of conflict are: (1) open communications that encourage joint problem solving rather than negotiation, (2) supplier participation in the predesign stage of product development, so there is a better mutual understanding of capabilities, (3) the adoption of performance standards for components within which a supplier can experiment rather than be constrained by rigid design specifications, and (4) sharing long-range plans for products, volume expectations, and other strategic information. All these moves will reinforce the atmosphere of mutual trust that a full-fledged collaboration must have to flourish.

The trend to narrower and closer sourcing arrangements appears irreversible. Some firms will be content to stop here and concentrate on managing their existing suppliers. But others are taking their new purchasing skills and more centralized influence to a higher level and reversing the customary buyer-supplier influence process. This is literally "reverse marketing." For a comparison of the different types of supplier relationships, see Figure 9-3.

Reverse Marketing.[10] These are collaborative arrangements with two major twists. The first is that the customer takes the initiative and seeks out the suppliers. At times this means setting firms up in business. Second, the customer is willing to absorb part of the risk of failure in order to demonstrate a commitment to a long-run relationship. This is a very proactive approach to purchasing that can only flourish when purchasing plays a major role in supporting the strategy.

Few firms have gained more advantages from reverse marketing then IKEA,[11] a multinational furniture retailer based in Sweden. IKEA's business is durable, stylish, and affordable "knockdown" furniture. This is an especially appealing concept to young families and singles on tight budgets looking for well-designed and functional items that could have a major impact on their house furnishing problems.

IKEA began with several furniture warehouse showrooms on the outskirts of Swedish cities. Its prices were far below those of traditional furniture retailers, because it didn't provide credit, delivery, or catalog services

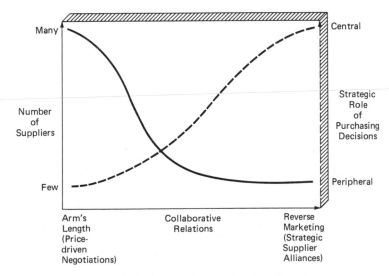

FIGURE 9-3 Progression of Supplier Relations

and had customers assemble their purchases at home. The traditional retailers quickly retaliated by boycotting IKEA suppliers. This left IKEA with no choice but to find its own small suppliers who would be immune from this pressure. Because many were nontraditional suppliers, such as saw mills, and lacked know-how and resources, IKEA had to assist with purchasing, engineering, specialized equipment, storage, and packing, and create, as well as test, its own designs. By 1987 there were over 100 production engineers working as purchasers and a 50-person workshop that built prototypes. However, the company steadfastly resisted doing its own manufacturing. It also avoided purchasing more than 50 percent of any supplier's capacity to ensure flexibility.

The payoff to the close and actively managed linkage with suppliers was the elimination of one stage of the product flow to the customer (see Figure 9–4).

The activities usually performed by independent furniture companies in the traditional flow have either been taken over by IKEA or engineered away. This means higher costs of procurement, since IKEA has to deal with a large number of component suppliers rather than a smaller number of manufacturers who put the components together. These costs are more than offset because the manufacturers' operating costs and profits have been eliminated. Suppliers are also happier to be working with a customer

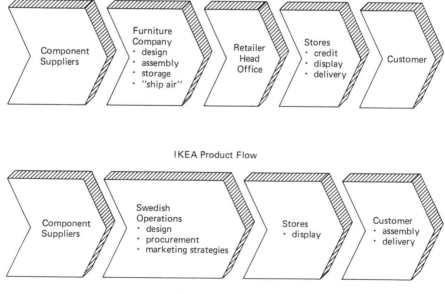

FIGURE 9–4 Reconfiguring the Product Flow

that is financially secure and technologically advanced. Even better, they know what an integral role they have in IKEA's operations and often become part of the "IKEA family."

PROLIFERATING CHANNELS

Tidy distinctions between direct and indirect channels are being swamped by a complicated clutter of competing modes. Each new channel is a distinct response to the fragmentation of end-user markets, or the possibilities presented by new computer and telecommunications technologies. Previously homogenous categories of channels are splitting amoeba-like into more and more specialized subchannels.

Consider a fairly recent arrival: the computer store. At one time these were specialized outlets for PC hobbyists—technically oriented suppliers selling to other technical people. Then came productivity stores selling spread-sheet packages, and accounting systems for small businesses. Now there are specialists by market segment, symbolized by Fortune 1,000 stores and government stores, or by vertical applications such as CAD/CAM. Some dealers are beginning to specialize in networking and multiuser systems as opposed to stand-alone systems. Each may appeal to the same customer, but for different needs in different parts of his or her organization.

The growing complexity and diversity of channels is directly traceable to a series of developments in retailing, and the impact of new information technologies on buyer-seller relations. Both areas present major opportunities to the astute and pitfalls to the unwary.

Structural Developments. Two trends overshadow the rest. The first is the "polarization" of retail stores into two types. One type is the niche store that concentrates on specialized merchandise—say, high-fashion apparel for career women. The merchandise is expensive, and makes a distinct life-style statement. The second type of store may appeal to the same buyers, but they go for commodities such as food, basic apparel, and housewares where low prices are the main selling point. In this category, bigger is better and so hypermarkets may have 60 checkouts while K-Marts have doubled in size in the past few years. In this environment the traditional general merchandise store is less and less viable.

The second trend that cannot be ignored is franchising,[12] a means of reaching markets that already accounts for one-third of retail sales in the United States, and may approach one-half by the year 2000. In this system, a franchisor (in return for fees and royalties) contracts to provide different forms of business assistance to a franchisee, who is usually an independent investor and operator. While franchises have long been familiar in service markets like fast foods, real estate, automobiles, and gasoline, the recent growth has come from the recognition that most lines of activity are franchisable. The new breed includes accounting and legal assistance, dentistry, lawn care, and skin care services. Indeed, whenever there is a consumer concept with recognizable individuality and staying power that can be readily replicated, there is a franchise possibility. But a franchisee is not an employee; the relationship is a partnership that cannot be tightly coordinated simply by exercising power. Most flare-ups in franchising relationships have their genesis in imbalances that have built up over time as the market environment changed. When Holiday Inn found quality was slipping and their independent-minded franchisees were resisting national marketing programs that were a necessary defense against similar programs by Marriott, Hilton, and Hyatt, they had to buy back some of these franchises to regain control over the channel. Despite the undeniable control problems, franchising will continue to be an attractive way to reach many diffuse markets.

Impact of Information Technologies.[13] These changes are not solely due to the proliferation of computers and availability of high-density telecommunications networks. With these new capabilities firms have an incentive to reconfigure their activities from the ground up. For channels designers, the most interesting possibilities are telemarketing and computer-integrated channel systems. Some visionaries don't stop at simply enhancing an existing channel concept, but conceive a completely new business. Federal Express, for example, could not function in the overnight parcel market without computer-equipped trucks and facilities.

Telemarketing uses telephone links to support, or substitute for, a direct sales force. Some systems are designed only to handle in-bound calls to place orders generated by a promotional campaign or catalog. Out-bound systems serve two purposes. One is a sales medium for prospecting for customers, qualifying leads, taking orders, and following up for repeat business. Here telemarketing offers considerable possibilities for enhancing the productivity of the sales force by permitting more specialization by type of account and better focus on high-yield accounts while reducing travel time. Meanwhile, the customers are seeing benefits because they receive better service. A second purpose is for sales support: scheduling sales calls and deliveries, conducting surveys, checking on order status, and handling order problems.

The most compelling reason to adopt telemarketing is the cost savings.[14] As direct sales costs mount, it is hopelessly uneconomic to make direct calls on small accounts. 3M found that the average cost of a face-to-face call was

$200, and that 4.3 calls were needed to make a sale. With these costs the medical and surgical products division could not afford to call on about half of the 6,000-plus hospitals in the United States. But a telephone sales representative could reach the small hospitals for $25 per call.

Computer-integrated channel systems help businesses to gain and sustain a competitive advantage. The initial advantage is gained through serving customers better, by furnishing them with dedicated terminals that give direct access to computers so they can place orders instantly, monitor their inventories and shipment status closely, and electronically seek advice. The customer benefit from this close linkage is big savings in the costs of ordering and carrying inventories. Inland Steel claims that use of its system improves the reliability of steel deliveries to the point that inventory savings by customers can offset the 10-percent cost advantage of an off-shore supplier who is slower to deliver made-to-order steel because it spends a month in transit.

These advantages of closer linkages are readily sustainable because the system often preempts competitors. Many competitors lack the scale of operations to spread out the high initial costs, or don't have the financial resources. Once the system is in place, it is very difficult to displace. Additionally, the costs of switching to a new system are sizable because of the disruption and training required.

Only a few of these channel systems try to tie customers to a single supplier. American Hospital Supply is an exception in this regard—employing what is called heavy tilt—by blocking out the competition. Most use a light tilt; they let customers do business with others and employ subtler means to incline the customer toward the supplier of the system. American Airlines does this with its Sabre airline reservation system, which ties in 8,000 travel agents. Their system is tilted so the apparently neutral schedule and fare information that appears on the travel agents' screen favors American flights by listing them first. Regardless of tilt, these channel systems are only preliminary steps toward the full-fledged conduct of business electronically when integrated computer networks are commonplace. When this occurs the advantages of the pioneers will erode, but traditional channels for reaching markets will be transformed.

SHIFTING BALANCE OF POWER

Few businesses that reach their markets indirectly are exempt from the seemingly inexorable gains in power and control by the intermediaries in the channel. This trend is especially noticeable in all forms of retailing, where manufacturers' brands and power have been seriously diminished.

GAINING ADVANTAGE WITH CHANNEL SYSTEMS

The competitive clout of dedicated channel systems was first demonstrated by American Hospital Supply, which still sets a standard of success that few applications have matched. This firm distributes products from 8,500 suppliers to more than 100,000 health-care providers. In 1974 AHS installed the first order-taking terminals in the stockrooms of large hospitals. Originally the hospitals intended to use the system only when fast response was needed. However, stock clerks preferred the terminals to salesmen and began using them to place routine orders for items like tongue depressors and blood analyzers. Then hospitals found that orders could be placed and filled more frequently, so it was no longer necessary to keep sizable inventories on hand. This so aggravated rival distributors that they filed an antitrust suit—subsequently lost on appeal—to keep AHS from establishing supply agreements with major hospitals. Competitors have had to follow, but AHS stays ahead by using the order information it collects to spot trends and emerging needs more quickly.

Some of this shift in the balance of power is perhaps an inevitable consequence of the retailer's closeness to the customer. Whether inevitable or not, its coming has been hastened by the growth of high-volume chain retailers, consolidation among retailers that reduces the number of direct competitors, and access to superior information.

There are many manifestations of the concentrating power of intermediaries. Here are some illustrative outcroppings:

- one retailer, Toys R Us, controls 25 percent of the toy market in the United States.
- the do-it-yourself market is dominated by mom-and-pop hardware stores that have banded together into alliances to improve buying power.
- automotive superdealers that can handle a dozen different makes may account for 30 percent of automobile sales by the mid-1990s.

Information technologies have also helped to magnify retailer power. Most retailers now have the capability to capture full sales data, sometimes in real time, with point-of-sale scanning devices. This often gives them more information about a particular item than the manufacturer. Some observes wonder whether retailers will continue to sell this data to outside vendors as they do now, or keep it to gain even more leverage.

The consequences for suppliers' profitability of this enhanced bargaining power are predictable. All the elements described in Chapter 5 work in the intermediaries' favor: (1) only a few buyers make large purchases, (2) there are few constraints to switching, (3) the buyers are very knowledgeable, and (4) they can and will back integrate into own-label manufacturing and organize their own in-bound logistics and storage. Each of these elements becomes a major weapon in the struggle to get a higher share of the value that is created.

Retailers exercise their power in many ways—including demands for "slotting allowances." These are payments manufacturers are required to make to secure supermarket shelf space. They have only been in evidence for the past ten years, but have grown to the extent that a major supermarket retailer in Los Angeles may charge as much as $56,000 for distribution of a single brand of yogurt. Slotting allowances are just one of the reasons that spending on trade promotions by consumer product manufacturers has overtaken spending on advertising and other brand franchise-building activities.

The only encouraging news for manufacturers[15] is fragmentary evidence that discounts vary by degree of differentiation. Where there is excess capacity in a commodity such as bread, and capital intensity is high, the discounts may exceed 20 percent. When seller concentration is high, brand loyalty strong, and excess capacity low, then discounts to major retailers are low.

CHANGING CORPORATE PRIORITIES

Many businesses are being pressured to cast aside cherished beliefs about how best to reach their markets in the wake of a broader turmoil about how to structure the entire corporation. Under the impetus of global competition, and corporate raiders trying to extract hidden value, companies are cost cutting, delayering, and restructuring to improve the yield from their assets. One of the first casualties of these pressures is the belief that everything has to be done under one roof. Now businesses are more willing to contract out—by having independent firms carry out activities previously done by employees—or share activities within an alliance or cooperative agreement. Commitments to channels are a logical target for this kind of revisionist thinking because they are generally expensive, consume lots of capital, and are widely suspected to be unproductive.[16]

Disaggregation. In the mid-eighties it was fashionable to talk about the "hollow corporation,"[17] mainly to decry the trend to off-shore sourcing, but also to anticipate a new kind of company that performs most profit-making activities but lacks its own manufacturing base. More recently there has been a recognition that this is one stage in an evolution to a new form of network organization. These are small central units that rely on other companies and suppliers to perform manufacturing, new product development, distribution, and other crucial activities on a contract basis. This frees up capital for companies like Nike Shoes to focus on what they do best, and leave the other activities to lower-cost specialists. Meanwhile, advances in communications technologies make it easier to coordinate suppliers and customers in a network. As a result, more firms are willing to consider substituting sales agents or manufacturers' reps for company salespeople or using independent wholesalers rather than a company distribution division, and providing facilitating functions like credit and logistics through independent firms. This decision requires a careful balancing of cost impacts and gains from flexibility against the problems of conflict and lack of cooperation that result from differences in goals, procedures, and capabilities between suppliers and channel members.

Sharing and Partnering. An increasingly attractive response to cost pressures and global competitors is a strategic alliance. These are interfirm relationships where there is a pooling of complementary skills and resources to achieve common goals—and may take any form from a long-term contract to a joint venture. They are alliances because they fall short of a full merger or acquisition. The broader implications of this trend are so important that we will return to them in depth in the following chapter on managing global markets. However, they also have a very specific role in gaining access to otherwise inaccessible markets[18] by "piggybacking" on the sales and distribution network of another firm.

A precursor of the use of alliances for market access was Glaxo's 1982 entry into the United States market for ulcer treatment. At that time the market was controlled by Smith Kline Beckman's Tagamet, the largest-selling prescription drug in the world. The Glaxo contender, Zantac, used a different compound to achieve the same results. When introduced in Europe in 1981, it had gained shares of 33 percent in Britain and 40 percent in Germany. Glaxo's major problem in the United States was the lack of sales coverage. In an industry where products were promoted (detailed) directly to thousands of doctors, the Glaxo sales force was badly outnumbered by Smith Kline's. Big sales forces are also very costly, at $50,000 to $80,000 for each sales representative. Both these problems were ovecome by an innovative joint sales agreement with Hoffman-LaRoche. For a percentage of sales they agreed to sell Zantac under the Glaxo name rather than the

Hoffman name as was the normal industry practice. This gave Glaxo immediate access to a sales force of 700, and they were able to establish their own name.

Most joint marketing alliances are motivated by the same objective—to gain market coverage and minimize exposure to the risks of an open market, while reducing the costs and capital requirements of vertical integration. These are especially compelling arguments for small firms with limited product lines that need the assurance of an OEM customer base and participation in a full product line offered to end users. The larger firm will have a distribution system in place that is more precisely tailored to the target market than any alternative system that could be assembled. The larger firm sees a profit opportunity from adding a complementary, high-value item to its line and reducing excess capacity in its distribution system. For these reasons, alliances are an increasingly popular option for managers rethinking their channels or trying to reach new markets.

DEVELOPING A CHANNEL STRATEGY

Every business is eventually compelled to rethink how it should be reaching its markets. This is never done lightly. Past commitments, long-time loyalties and relationships, and hard-earned insights into the intricacies of the present channel are at stake. But without such a reappraisal the channel strategy is likely to drift out of alignment with the overall strategy and miss the opportunities presented by the changing distribution environment. Worse, a "laissez-faire" attitude is an open invitation for competitors to exploit the opportunities and become entrenched.

The biggest barriers to an open reappraisal are past history and conventional wisdom about existing channel modes. These barriers can be combatted with a robust process that is zero-based, and initially ignores the present arrangements by working from the market back to find the optimal way to reach and serve the market. Once this customer ideal is specified then the problems of getting there can be addressed.

The steps in this channel design process[19] have a close affinity to the steps followed in developing a competitive advantage. The difference is that the channel has to support the overall strategic thrust while still satisfying the necessary efficiency requirements (reasonable expense-to-return ratios) and ensuring long-run flexibility.

Step One: Analyze the current channel situation—competitive position, key trends, and profitability

Step Two: Obtain customer judgments about the ability of channel alternatives to meet their service needs

Step Three: Compare the relative costs and profitability of channel alternatives

Step Four: Test alternatives for strategic fit and feasibility

Step Five: Design and implement programs for gaining maximum advantage while minimizing conflicts with intermediaries

The remainder of this chapter expands on each of the first four design steps in turn. If these steps are done properly many of the subsequent implementation steps will be resolved.

CHANNEL SITUATION ANALYSIS: STEP ONE

Assembling a fact base that illuminates trends in the distribution flows, coverage, and costs for a business relative to its target competitors can be a daunting task. Most marketing or sales managers will know a great deal about the adjacent links in their channels. Between the sales reporting system and the accounting system they have a wealth of detail on prices, terms, deliveries, returns, stock-out rates, and other performance variables. Unhappily, their knowledge about either their competitors or further stages in the value-chain is likely to be fragmentary and impressionistic. Thus it may be very difficult to assemble even the rudimentary data required by the channel share matrix in Table 9–1.

This matrix provides a far more useful picture than one can get from simply measuring shares at either the manufacturer or reseller level. We can readily see how much volume flows through a particular channel.[20] In this matrix the reseller can either be a single distributor or all members of a type of distributor. Among other insights, we can readily see the important dependency relationships, that are significant departures from a balanced situation where each supplier has a share of each reseller's sales that is proportionate to the reseller's total market share. For example, the X-B channel has a much higher share than would be expected in a balanced situation, perhaps because reseller B has built a name carrying X's products. Because manufacturer X has three other resellers, it doesn't seem to be nearly as dependent on B as B is on X. But market shares tell only part of the story, and it may be that reseller B serves a distinct segment that could not be reached in any other way. To fully understand this matrix, one also needs to know:

- relative profitability of each trading channel
- growth rates of channel types
- market coverage (proportion of total market that is actually served).

Table 9-1 Channel Share Matrix

			Resellers Share			
Manufacturer's Share	A	B	C	D	E	
X	20%	20%	5%	0	5%	50%
Y	20%	0%	5%	5%	0	30%
Z	10%	0	0	5%	5%	20%
	50%	20%	10%	10%	10%	100%

There are a number of reasons why the input data are likely to be difficult to secure. There are all the normal impediments to understanding the behavior and peformance of competitors. Only limited outcroppings of competitor data are available, so the picture is both partial and flawed. Seldom is there a ready-made source of information such as the syndicated research services that track the volume of all the competitors from warehouse to retail outlet, and record all purchase transactions at the retail level. At any rate, the desire to collect better information may be stymied by the reluctance of most intermediaries to share sensitive customer data with their suppliers. This problem is rooted in their view of their own self-interest. As McVey[21] put it many years ago, "The middleman is not a hired link in a chain forged by a manufacturer, but rather an independent market . . . [acting] as a purchasing agent for his customers and only secondarily as a selling agent for his suppliers." This perspective is still valid today, which is the reason manufacturers are often compelled to by-pass intermediaries and mount special studies of their end customers. One forest products company had to acquire a retail lumber yard to learn who was buying its plywood and dimension lumber. Even getting this close to the market didn't help the company find out what its competitors were doing or track broad trends in the channel environment.

Strategically relevant trends. A situation assessment should be a movie not a snapshot. The ability to see where channels have been, and are likely to go in the future, is critical to deciding whether a change in channel strategy is needed. Because it takes so long to change direction, a shift made on the basis of today's requirements may not be appropriate three or four years hence. In particular, trends need to be monitored in the following areas:

1. *Predictable changes in buying patterns.* For example, in the early stages of the cellular telephone market (the wireless or mobile telephone service that offers excellent reception via radio waves transmitted between "cell" stations serving specific geographic areas), most customer prospects wanted to buy directly from the cellular phone company. As the market evolved and buyers became more knowledgeable about cellular phones, surveys showed that 65 percent of prospects wanted to buy their phone at a retail outlet.

2. *New entrants into the channel* that are attracted by the profit opportunity or see it as strategically important for them to participate can offer new ways to reach the market. By 1992 it is expected that auto manufacturers will become one of the biggest channels when they offer cellular phones as new car options.

3. *Growth in the use of new technologies for reaching markets,* such as telemarketing and direct order-entry systems. It is advisable to track customer trials of these technologies and major programs by direct competitors, as well as to watch precursor markets. These are markets that share many characteristics but have a history of adopting new practices earlier than the market being monitored.

4. *Downward pressure on the margins obtainable from the channel.* This may be due to the exercise of bargaining power that we saw in the previous section, or substantial increases in the costs of using the channel.

Each of these trends will significantly influence the *future* attractiveness of the presently used and available channels. The ability to anticipate channel shifts is one of the secrets of Compaq Computer's success in the personal computer market. This firm can fairly claim to be the fastest-growing company in history. In 1982 it did not exist; in 1987 it reached sales of $1.2 billion. Compaq saw early that, as personal computers became part of office furniture, large companies would increasingly prefer to buy from retailers rather than directly from the manufacturer. However, dealer's shelf space is always limited. So Compaq devised a novel approach to computer dealers. Unlike most computer marketers who sell direct, Compaq refused to compete with their own dealers and completely refrained from selling directly to dealers' customers. The dealers responded by ensuring that Compaq's computers got the needed shelf-space and dealer support.

DESIGNING CHANNELS FROM THE MARKET BACK: STEP TWO

The danger with the first step in the process is that it encourages competitor-centered and historical thinking that deflects management from grappling with the questions of what the end customers really want in the way of service from the channel. The purpose of this next step is to break out of the prevailing pattern of thinking and adopt a customer perspective. This means temporarily ignoring questions of configuration, cost, and fit with the overall business strategy, and addressing the following questions:

- what service attributes do the target customers value?
- how can differences in these attribute preferences be used to group customers into segments with similar needs?
- how well do the available channels meet the needs of these segments?
- what new channel configurations might do a better job of meeting these needs?

Attribute Values and Trade-offs. Here customers are asked to put product features and performance aside and deal only with the channel service attributes they most value. For a personal computer the possible attributes include product demonstration, provision of warranties, availability of financing, training in using the system, installation and repair services, availability of loaners during repairs, and technical advice. The problem here is that customers will ask for everything unless they are forced to assign priority weightings to each attribute or make explicit trade-offs that reflect the costs of providing one attribute versus another attribute.[22] The most prevalent trade-offs among channel service attributes to watch for are:

1. *Lot size.* Do customers want to buy one unit, or multiple units?
2. *Accessibility.* Is around-the-counter convenience and contact essential, or would the customer be willing to deal with a remote sales site via an 800 number?
3. *Speed of response.* Do customers want immediate delivery—such as they get with IKEA furniture outlets—or are they willing to wait for several months to get a choice from a much wider range of furniture styles, colors, and fabrication?
4. *Product variety.* Do customers want one-stop shopping to satisfy all their needs at one time, or do they prefer a specialized outlet? This issue is creating major problems and opportunities for financial service companies that are getting mixed signals about the desirability of offering banking, insurance, and brokerage services at the same place.
5. *Service quality.* How important is friendly, attentive and informed service, as offered by a specialty men's clothing store, versus the anonymous, self-selection process of a discount outlet?
6. *Service backup.* Do customers want immediate, in-house repair and

installation service, or are they willing to find their own local repair services?

Segmenting Customers. Customers will differ in the weights they assign to each channel service attribute depending on their needs and shopping behavior. If these *segment* differences are sufficiently large, than one channel cannot hope to serve all the different needs. The same process we introduced in Chapter 5 can be used here to find homogenous groups of customers, and then identify them so the size of the groups can be measured.

Each segment of customers representing a distinct profile of service attribute weights should be labeled according to the existing channel type that seems to serve it best. For industrial operating and maintenance supplies, one customer segment clearly emphasizes moderate prices, emergency delivery service, extended credit terms, availability of multiple brands, local inventories, and simple ordering procedures. This profile of needs accurately describes an industrial/full-function distributor.

These labels are simply points of reference that should not limit the possibilities. If no existing channel seems to fit the service needs of a segment, then a new channel type should be designed. Special thought should be given to customer segments with needs that can be met with emerging technologies such as telemarketing or interactive television. Had this been done more carefully in the personal computer market, then a number of firms would not have missed the significance of value-added resellers or retail outlets with multiple, but more highly focused, product ranges.

Customer Judgments of Channel Alternatives. Numerous assumptions have been made about the ability of existing channels to meet the needs of customer segments. These assumptions need to be verified by first asking these customers how satisfied they are with the present options. This has to be done for channels they now patronize on each attribute they view as important. Often, overall satisfaction will mask frustration with the performance of their present suppliers on key service attributes. These areas of dissatisfaction may suggest new ways to configure the existing channels to overcome the problem. Perhaps the distributor's salespeople are viewed as good troubleshooters and expediters, but ill-informed about industry trends that might affect availability or are slow to provide detailed quotations. These are flags that suggest opportunities for improvement or new ways to reach the market.

The possibilities for innovative, alternative channels should not be underestimated. There is growing evidence that consumers are less resistant to the use of alternative technology-based channels than is assumed by suppliers. The following results come from a U.K. survey which asked: "For which of these purchases can you imagine yourself 'armchair shopping'?"

	% of Respondents[23]
Banking affairs	36%
Foreign holidays	29
Groceries (other than fresh food)	18
Clothes and shoes	16
Books	16

If customers are being asked what they would like about a new channel possibility, they should also be asked whether there are any barriers to their use of the channel. For example, there are many reasons why private practice optometrists should be enthusiastic about tying into the electronic order-entry network developed by a Dallas eyeglass laboratory. These independent optometrists are being severely squeezed by big chains such as Pearle Health Services which has 1,200 eye-care stores in 45 states that each carry large inventories, offer overnight service, longer hours, and can afford to advertise heavily. The new order-entry network promises to put the independent optometrists on an even footing by assuring overnight service. Yet many are balking; they dislike being tied to one eyeglass laboratory supplier. For years they have argued that chains sacrifice quality for speed, and they are unwilling to pay for the customized computing systems and the training of office staff to use them.

To this point in the process the customer has been sovereign. The aim has been to find what customers want from the channels that serve them to identify areas for innovation and improvement. Now the business has to decide whether to simply improve the existing arrangements, replace them with completely new or hybrid arrangements, or start proliferating its channels by tailoring different channels to the needs of different segments. Before proceeding any farther it is essential to do a reality check on the economic feasibility of the channel alternatives.

THE ECONOMICS OF CHANNEL DECISIONS: STEP THREE

Just as customers have to respect economic constraints when making trade-offs among service attributes—and seldom get everything they want at the price they are willing to pay—so do managers have to juggle different combinations of revenues, costs, and capital requirements when comparing the profitability of channel alternatives. On the one hand, a business can virtually eliminate fixed costs by using only intermediaries such as distributors or reps. Alternatively, a firm can emulate the auto finish maker PPG and commit a substantial advanced investment to plant and inventory to tie themselves as directly as possible to their customers. PPG did this by building six satellite paint and coating plants next to the customer plants to which it is sole supplier. This was done at their initiative, with no assurance of a contract in perpetuity. The customer benefits were considerable, including radical reductions of inventory and superior responsiveness enhanced by tight computer linkages and workers dedicated to a single customer. While PPG has no guarantees, it will be tough to displace.

One way to compare channel alternatives is to first estimate the incremental costs of switching to a new channel. If customers want rapid delivery, then local inventories will have to be maintained, training programs mounted and perhaps a new, fast-response distribution center will be needed. These incremental costs can be used for a break-even analysis of the market share gain needed to offset the additional costs. This analysis may reveal that certain modes of distribution are prohibitively expensive and should be removed from further consideration. If they stay in the set of alternatives, then a detailed estimate of relative revenues, costs, and working and fixed capital is needed.

Revenue Consequences. The sales-generating capacity of a channel alternative relative to other alternatives depends on two factors. The first is the *coverage* that can be obtained by making contact with the decision makers and influencers in the potential market. Many channels leave gaps because they miss geographic areas or can't reach a class of customers. The second is the *effectiveness* of the selling effort once contact is made. This in turn has two components: the selling skills and service orientation of the salesperson, and the congruency of the actual selling behavior with the basis of differentiation the firm is trying to achieve.

The arguments in favor of direct channels are usually made on effectiveness grounds. Company sales representatives should be able to concentrate solely on a company's products without being deflected by the demands of other products. They are better trained to sell the products and are likely to be more aggressive because their career prospects depend on how well they perform. By providing value-added services to customers, by providing information, by expediting, and by complaint resolution they are able to build closer relationships with important customers. All this means they should be more productive. A strong endorsement of these direct sales benefits comes from Signode Corp., that has been able to maintain a dominant share of the steel strapping market despite having a physical product that is literally interchangeable with any of its competitors' products. The secret is the depth of experience the sales force has with their product, plus familiarity with such diverse applications as wrapping cotton bales and rolls of sheet steel. The services they are able to provide and the closeness of the long-run relationships have been built on a foundation of mutual trust.

The big question is whether the business can afford the size of sales force needed to cover a widespread and diversified market. If not, management may be forced into a difficult trade-off.

Scale Economies versus Control. A direct sales force means a big, fixed cost commitment, especially when a salary is the largest part of the compensation in order to ensure an emphasis on long-run customer service and relationship building. If the salesperson is part of a multilevel team serving a complex account, or is primarily responsible for servicing established relationships, it is inappropriate to gear the compensation to a variable proportion of sales. However, such a fixed cost soon becomes uneconomic if the sales yield per transaction doesn't generate enough gross margin dollars to cover the cost. IBM can easily justify a direct sales force to sell large mainframes to complex decision-making units, but simply cannot afford to sell typewriters and supplies the same way.

Although direct sales forces tie up scarce (and sometimes unavailable) capital that can be used elsewhere, they also create a daunting barrier to entry. For example, a successful computer company has average sales of about $1 million per salesperson per year. Each salesperson costs at least $100,000 a year to support, and requires an initial training investment of $50,000. For a new entrant to aspire to $500 million in sales they will have to be prepared to invest $25 million in training, even if there is no turnover which is certainly not the case. Not surprisingly companies are quickly motivated to find cheaper alternatives, and turn to intermediaries for help.

The main argument against indirect channels is the loss of control over independent agents or representatives. This supposedly arises because reps or distributors are short-run–oriented and emphasize their relationship with the customer at the expense of advocating their suppliers' interests. Certainly there are numerous instances where a rep has been unwilling to engage in activities for the benefit of their suppliers, including filling out reports, promoting new products to target markets they don't presently serve, collecting and communicating competitive and market intelligence, and performing routine service and support activities. This would seem to tilt the direct versus indirect argument in favor of the direct approach. But this presumes that the control advantages of a direct channel, whether a company salesforce or dedicated retail outlets, can be gained at minimal costs. There is mounting evidence that these administrative or "transaction" costs can be considerable, to the point that they dominate the choice of channel.

Transaction Costs. Indirect channels are likely to have a cost advantage so long as there is rivalry among the intermediaries. When a firm can choose among several competing reps or distributors to reach their market, there is little chance that one can take advantage of the situation and extract excessive margins for their services. But what happens when there are few, if any, feasible alternatives? To keep an intermediary from taking undue advantage of this monopoly situation, the business incurs heavy "transaction costs" to (1) write and (2) enforce very detailed contracts that specify what the distributor, franchisee, or rep is supposed to do, (3) haggle over these conditions, (4) monitor performance, and so on. Further costs result from uncooperative behavior such as withholding or selectively feeding out information to support arguments for commission increases or price concessions. At some point these costs become so prohibitive, and performance so problematical, that it is advisable to vertically integrate forward into the channel and go direct.[24] Certain conditions make the fixed costs and investments of a direct channel start to look very attractive.

Asset Specificity. Firms are especially motivated to go direct—or vertically integrate in general—when they need special-purpose or dedicated assets to support their strategy. These assets are embedded in: special sales and service training of distributors, specialized transportation and storage facilities such as refrigerated trucks and warehouses, customer requirements, or decision processes. Product differentiation often necessitates specialized capabilities to sell the product, such as the sales force used by Cole National to train operators and service key-making machines in retail outlets.

As firms become increasingly reliant on a distributor (or a salesperson) they lose their bargaining power because these people can't easily be replaced. Worse—the distributors know they are hard to replace, and are constantly tempted to take advantage of their position by skimming the territory or demanding bigger commissions and fatter margins.

High asset specificity alone may not push a firm into vertical integration, but when combined with the following factors[25] it will virtually assure the firm will choose to reach its market directly:

- *inability to monitor* selling performance. The effectiveness of intermediaries falls when it becomes difficult to determine how well they are performing. It may be very hard to know whether a distributor is properly training people, calling on new accounts, or collecting market information.

- *team selling* of products like computer systems to major accounts requires coordination among many specialists, as well as across levels of management. In this setting the contribution of a rep or distributor to the sale is very difficult to ascertain, and fairly compensate.
- *free-riding abuses* are a problem whenever intermediaries don't absorb all the costs of their actions. Branded products are particularly susceptible here, since one retailer can get away with poor after-sales service and repair, but tarnish the brand's reputation and reduce sales for other retailers. Franchisers deal with this problem by writing very tight contracts to prevent franchisees from debasing quality. If this doesn't work, firms like Holiday Inn resort to buying back their franchisees.
- *large sales transactions,* where the average order size is large or the customer orders many related products to be delivered at once make it economic to go direct.

This view of channel intermediaries tends to assume the worst about their behavior, when in reality they may be closely bonded to the firm through long-term relationships of trust and loyalty. These are important "invisible assets" that need to be nurtured. Then the challenge is to devise incentives and mechanisms to coordinate their activities and encourage a partnership. These moves can shift the economics back in favor of indirect channels at considerable savings to the business.

Seldom will a situation have all the characteristics that point to a direct channel—high asset specificity, poor ability to monitor performance, extensive team selling, large transactions, and high free-riding potential[26]—or vice versa. Instead, most situations fall into a gray area between the two extremes where a hybrid channel system is indicated. The next question is which mix of indirect, direct, and cooperative channels will best serve the overall strategy.

STRATEGIC FIT AND FEASIBILITY: STEP FOUR

Strategic decisions about how to reach markets are made in a broader context beyond satisfying customer needs and minimizing costs. The ideal channel that passes these tests must then be implemented within the constraints imposed by past strategic commitments, resource availability, and historical rigidities in available channels. The purpose of this step is to confront the best channel alternatives identified in the previous stages with these realities. Once it is established that a channel alternative fits the current strategy and is feasible, it is still necessary to see whether it can adapt to future strategic requirements and keep competitors at bay.[27] If a channel strategy can be readily matched or bypassed by competitors, then it doesn't offer a sustainable advantage.

Strategic Fit. Management must decide whether the proposed channel strategy will allow the business to achieve its performance objectives by supporting the overall strategic thrust. Unfortunately the answer is often "no," unless trade-offs and strategy changes are made. For example, a cellular telephone company concluded that in order to meet its market penetration and market growth objectives, it would need multiple, competing channels, including independent agents and retailers. Yet these indirect channels gave demonstrably poorer service (as measured by time spent resolving customer problems, ease of handling the transaction, and complaints leading to disconnections) which conflicted with a short-run profitability objective that required premium prices based on superior perceived service. Another dilemma was that the company wasn't well known as a cellular service provider, and couldn't afford to spend enough money on advertising to build awareness and brand preference to the point where they could "pull" their service through the indirect channels. With great reluctance they settled for direct channels to ensure the profitability target could be met, and scaled back their market penetration objective. This was done in full recognition of the long-run consequences of not being aggressively present in the emerging retail and indirect channels that would be the future source of market growth.

It is not always necessary to bend the channel strategy to fit the overall strategy. Instead, the channel opportunity may be so compelling that the product and service strategies are fitted to these requirements. Recently a major North American electromechanical systems builder (mainly electric drives and control systems for markets such as plastics processing and machine tools) confronted a real mismatch between the direction of its product strategy—which was to custom-build very high-performance components for original equipment manufacturers—and the opportunities in Europe for a distributor-focused strategy. Traditionally, Europe was a market where 75 percent of sales were made directly. With the economic integration of European markets (the 1992 event), and technology developments that made adaption to end-user system requirements much easier, it was foreseen that equipment distributors would become increasingly important. Furthermore, a sister components division already had good access and relationships with emerging European distributors who could take on the line. This was a major competitive advantage as none of the competitors was similarly endowed with such easy access. But before this opportunity could be exploited the product and supporting services had to be "distributor friendly." This was very traumatic for a firm that lacked adequate documentation, whose "Ferrari" product required an expert to tune it to a given application, and had no experience in assembling the myriad of standard parts and connectors into a package a distributor could sell. Nonetheless, after specifying what the distributor needed in terms of product elements, promotional support, technical assistance, and responsiveness systems, they set about to change their strategic thrust to position themselves as the best-equipped company to meet these emerging needs.

Feasibility. Beyond the constraints of strategy commitments and objectives there are restrictions imposed by the absence of feasible intermediaries. This problem is particularly vexing for a new entrant trying to hurdle the barriers to entry erected by the incumbents who have locked up or control the available channels. Small personal computer manufacturers are increasingly hampered by the consolidation of computer retailers into large chains that can enhance their buying power by carrying only a restricted range of brands.

Care must be taken at this stage to avoid letting historical practices and rigidities become unchallenged constraints on strategic degrees of channel freedom. The dealer system used by the automobile industry is rife with these constraints. Some have even been translated into laws, such as franchise laws and dealer-day-in-court laws. Others are sanctified by industry conventional wisdom. This system is performing poorly against emerging competition for used automobiles, parts, and service from used car specialists, NAPA stores, Midas, Firestone, and Sears. Meanwhile, the auto companies are facing a shift in channel power to mega-dealers who want to carry multiple and competing makes of cars.[28] So far the constraints have not been confronted, but because they interfere with the customers' responsiveness to the channel, this cannot be postponed indefinitely.

Long-Run Adaptability. However the business elects to reach its markets it has to recognize that it is making long-run and sometimes irreversible commitments that reduce flexibility. Thus, before proceeding a final check must be made to ensure that the channel design has the ability to handle new products and services the firm expects to offer and is compatible with emerging technologies.

The final choice of channel strategy is a series of trade-offs and compromises that seek to match what the business can do with its resources and what it should do to satisfy its customers to gain a competitive advantage. This sets the stage for intensive implementation planning activities that are beyond the scope of this chapter.

But with a full understanding of the critical trade-offs and obstacles to implementation that were identified during the previous stages, the management team will be able to quickly reach a consensus on the necessary program elements, timing factors, and expenditure levels to ensure a successful strategy.

NAVIGATING THE TURBULENT CHANNEL ENVIRONMENT

For too long distribution has been the neglected side of strategy. Increasingly, firms are realizing that benign neglect is both risky and wasteful of opportunities for competitive advantage. Under pressure from powerful market trends, they are scrutinizing past practices, loyalties, relationships, and commitments with unusual vigor.

The search for improved ways to reach complex and fragmenting markets is being propelled by the following forces:

- increasingly assertive customers who see important benefits from collaborative relationships with a shrinking number of suppliers
- the growth potential of specialized subchannels is being matched by the emergence of new technological capabilities for reaching markets to give decision makers a rich array of possibilities
- increasingly powerful intermediaries able to bargain for a greater share of value created
- firms discarding outmoded beliefs they must be self-sufficient and turning to partners in alliances to achieve strategic objectives.

The most versatile recipe for dealing with these forces of change is a market-driven channel review process. The departure point for this process is an understanding of the channel service attributes customers most value. This is essential, for firms seldom invest as much in learning how end users want to obtain and service their products and services as they do in learning what the products and services ought to look like. The ideal or optimal channel from the customers' standpoint then needs to be tested for revenue and cost consequences. The final test is whether the preferred channel alternative will fit the thrust of the strategy, and if not, how it should be adjusted so it can enhance the performance of the business.

TEN

Responding
to Global Markets

*The economic system is more and more like one single
interacting organism.*

—AKIO MORITA
Chairman, Sony Corp.

*The globalization of markets is at hand. With that the
multinational commercial world nears its end, and so does the
multinational corporation.*

*The multinational and global corporation are not the same
thing. The multinational corporation operates in a number of
countries, and adjusts its products and practices in each—at high
relative costs. The global corporation operates with resolute
constancy—at low relative cost—as if the entire world (or major
regions of it) were a single entity; it sells the same things in the
same way everywhere.*

—THEODORE LEVITT[1]

The evolution from a world of distinct and self-contained national markets to linked global markets that Levitt heralded in 1983 has been under
way for several decades. It continues to be fueled by the persistent forces of
homogenization of customer needs, gradual lowering of trade barriers, and
competition that gains unassailable advantages by behaving globally. At
the heart of these trends is technology change that makes it increasingly
easier to coordinate far-flung operations and communicate with customers
across national boundaries.

Although the globalization forces are inexorable they don't impact each
market in the same way. So while a global strategy is not—and should not

be—on every business agenda, the consequences of globalization must be faced. The purpose of this chapter is to adapt the concepts and processes of earlier chapters to the question of how a business can best compete when the market is either globalizing or regionalizing. The challenge will be to find and keep the right balance between thinking globally, while acting locally.

GLOBAL VERSUS MULTIDOMESTIC STRATEGIES

Multinational firms have traditionally managed operations outside their home country with **multidomestic strategies,**[2] that enable individual subsidiaries to compete independently in different domestic markets. The multinational headquarters coordinates financial controls and some marketing policies, including brand naming, and may centralize some R&D and component production. Each subsidiary behaves like a strategic business unit that is expected to contribute earnings and growth proportionate to the market opportunity. The decentralization meets the requirements of host countries for multinational to fly local flags, and satisfies the desire of subsidiary managers for local autonomy from headquarters.

A global strategy, in contrast, seeks competitive advantage with strategic moves that are highly interdependent across countries. These moves include most or all of the following:[3]

- a *standardized core product* that exploits or creates homogeneous tastes or performance requirements. Thus Coca-Cola and McDonald's sell essentially the same product in every market—in defiance of local diversity in food preferences. This standardization is equally evident in pharmaceuticals, banking services, chemicals, semiconductors, and telecommunications, to mention a few of the obvious.

- significant *participation* in all major country markets to build volume. This breadth of participation also keeps the firm attuned to trends in tastes or technology that can be shared across markets.

- a *concentration* of value-creating activities such as R&D and manufacturing in a few countries—or even in one location—in order to maximize economies of scale and take advantage of the special strengths of certain countries. Most toy companies do their fabrication and assembly in the Far East to capitalize on the low labor costs and flexibility of supplier relations.

- a coherent *competitive strategy,* that pits the worldwide capabilities of the business against the competition. The aim is to secure a strong position, while making the competitor's response more expensive and difficult. When Tyrolia, the Austrian maker of ski-bindings and boots, attacked Salomon's stronghold position in North America, Salomon retaliated by moving into Tyrolia's home market. Their intent was to distract Tyrolia and put pressure on its margins so it would be less able to sustain a major effort in Salomon's market.

For these moves to be successful strategy development must be centralized. Top management can't adopt a passive stance and limit their role to reviewing strategy proposals and annual budgets and supplying resources for the strategies of a loose collectivity of subsidiaries. While some integration and sharing of national strategies is possible within this multidomestic system, the extent is likely to be limited by vested interests and conflicts in the objectives of the subsidiaries. Some subsidiaries become so powerful they are virtual fiefdoms, eminently willing and able to challenge the authority of the head office. Their willingness to make sacrifices to support a common thrust that benefits other subsidiaries is doubtful.

DECIDING HOW TO COMPETE GLOBALLY

The rewards from a centralized strategy development process can be dramatic. This was demonstrated by Universal Medical Supplies in the worldwide market for disposable syringes. Before they entered, there was only a series of national markets. That changed when Universal promoted the latest technology in syringes, established teams of specialists to talk to cost-conscious hospital managers, and then produced at world volumes in three plants, each specializing in one key component to make it possible to buy raw materials with huge volume discounts. This strategy was guided by a worldwide business director, who gave local management some latitude to make the necessary modifications in product and service to satisfy local requirements. Universal gained 31 percent of the world syringe market with this strategy, while the pioneer of disposable syringes stayed national and was limited to a 6-percent share.

Not every market lends itself to this kind of globally orchestrated attack, but few businesses can afford not to systematically assess the merits of such a strategy. The process of deciding whether and how to compete globally progresses through four steps, each posing a crucial strategic question:

Step One: Assess the worldwide market situation—what is the present and prospective extent of globalization?

Step Two: Specify the appropriate balance between global standardization and local adaption—in light of the strategic thrust and capabilities of the business, the experience and strategies of sister units in the company, and the suitability of the home country as a platform for launching a global strategy.

Step Three: Determine the appropriate means of participating in each country or region within the global market—should we export, franchise, license, create alliances, or invest in wholly owned subsidiaries?

Step Four: Design and implement the appropriate organization structures, planning processes, and management systems. Keep monitoring performance in each country compared to the objectives that were originally set.

The remainder of this chapter takes each of these steps in turn.

ASSESSING THE EXTENT OF GLOBALIZATION: STEP ONE

A global market is one in which the competitive position of a business in one country is significantly affected by its position in other countries—and vice versa.[4] This description already fits numerous markets such as telecommunications, pharmaceuticals, electronic components, commercial banking, and sometimes retailing as Benetton has demonstrated. Other markets are converging toward this definition, while many remain resolutely national in character. The starting point for global strategy development is an accurate assessment of the present and prospective extent of globalization. This will be determined by the presence and intensity of the following underlying forces and trends:

- increasing homogenization of customer needs and behavior
- competitors that think and behave globally
- opportunities for substantial economies of scale or scope in key value-creating activities
- supportive macroeconomic environments that encourage and even demand a global presence
- technological developments that facilitate the coordination of widespread networks of activities.

INCREASING HOMOGENIZATION OF CUSTOMER REQUIREMENTS

This is the driving force singled out most often as the reason markets are behaving globally. This is especially evident in preferences for up-market consumer goods, that are becoming ever more similar as better education, higher discretionary incomes, more leisure time, and increasing international travel create international social groups with comparable life-styles and behavior patterns. This homogenization of buying is called the Californianization of the world by Kenichi Ohmae, "Fifteen years ago Japanese slept on mats in cotton quilts, shopped daily, grabbed a quick meal at a noodle shop, and drank green tea at breaks . . . . Now they sleep on beds under sheets, shop once a week to fill their freezers, hit McDonald's for fast food, and have coffee and doughnuts at teatime."

Although the similarities of customers across countries may be compelling, that doesn't mean there won't be differences that must be catered to in product designs, advertising themes, and marketing programs. When Mr. Donut opened franchise outlets in Japan they found they had to use smaller cups and donuts.

A further complication of the trend to homogenization across countries is that the same forces may also create more segments within each country, reflecting differences in life-styles, income, and so forth. This opens up two segmentation possibilities. The first is the *universal* segment with essentially the same needs in each country. These are likely to be wealthy, mobile, and broadly informed customers. Buyers of Mercedes-Benz touring sedans in Japan, Zaire, and Argentina have much in common because they are seeking a top-of-the-line, high-performance car. Conversely, the market may be evolving toward *diverse* segments, where a universal product can only be sold if it is positioned differently in each country. The Canon AE-1 camera was targeted toward young replacement buyers in Japan, up-scale, first-time buyers in the United States, and older and more technologically sophisticated buyers in Germany. These segment adaptions were made to recognize the different needs and perceptions of the universal features of the camera across these countries.

Another consequence of segmentation within country markets is that it is often not possible to sell exactly the same product in each country. If this reality is recognized early it may be possible to embody country differences in auxiliary services and features that are augmentations to the core product. This is why Brother designed the replaceable daisy wheels in their electronic typewriter so users in different countries could type in their own language. In short, homogenization of customer needs doesn't always mean a universal product to a universal market segment. The array of possibilities is expanded in Figure 10–1.[5]

This homogenization process also feeds on itself to create multinational customers, who are themselves offering near-universal products to universal end-user segments. Thus, Corning Glass sells TV tubes to set makers

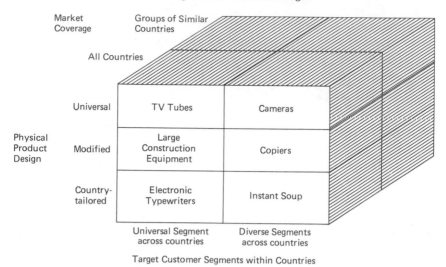

FIGURE 10–1 Global Market Segmentation

like Philips and Sylvania who operate in many countries. These global customers can and will compare prices charged by their various suppliers around the world, demand the same level of service, and make choices using common standards. They may have only one central purchasing point, usually in their home country, that places orders for delivery to plants in different parts of the world. Suppliers have no alternative but to globally coordinate their strategy to serve such customers.

GLOBAL COMPETITORS

Companies with multidomestic strategies are often reluctant to give up their well-established policies of autonomous country operations until a global competitor forces their hand. The trigger is often a belated realization that this competitor is using the financial resources from one part of the world to cross-subsidize a competitive battle in another. The appropriate defense is to pinch off this cash flow by retaliating in the market that is generating the high profits for the competitor. This can only be done if the multidomestic firm adopts a centrally coordinated response that subordinates the wishes of the individual country managers. This evolving pattern of competitive action and retaliation on a global chessboard moves the market another step closer to global status.[6]

The financial advantage of a global competitor can usually be traced to an overall cost advantage plus a high price in its home market. This high price level may be due to dominance in its home market, collusion that limits direct competitive rivalry, government restrictions on entries of new competitors, or differences in the price sensitivity of customers. The resulting cash flow is available to fund product development, global brand development, and global distribution. A purely domestic firm will eventually be at a resource and cost disadvantage. It will be further disadvantaged if it has a dominant market position that allows it to maintain high domestic prices. This price umbrella gives the global competitor freedom to enter without the threat of retaliation because the domestic competitor can't afford to jeopardize the margins on its total sales volume just to meet the low entry prices of an initially small-share competitor. The best defense is an attack on the high margins in the home market of the global predator. Firms such as RCA and Zenith that once dominated the U.S. television receiver market lost out to Sony, Panasonic, and others when they restricted themselves to their home market and were unable to attack the Japanese market. Unfortunately the distribution channels in Japan had been locked up by Japanese companies, and the costs of bypassing them were excessive.

A further impetus to the conversion of a multidomestic to a global competitor is the cost penalties of uncoordinated country strategies. The experience of Black & Decker in the face of Makita's global attack on the power tool market is instructive (see the following box).

Even markets that prize domestic adaption may evolve toward a global visage if one competitor successfully forces the issue. The fragmented major appliance industry has never been an attractive candidate for standardization. Environmental and safety standards, preferences for energy sources (gas versus electricity), sizes of kitchens, and consumer habits vary greatly from one country to another. Nonetheless, by 1989 the competitive structure was rapidly consolidating toward a few global players. The trigger was Sweden's Electrolux, which parlayed a string of acquisitions to become the dominant world firm. Large domestic U.S. firms such as GE, Whirlpool, and Maytag were compelled to form overseas alliances to avoid being left behind. Efforts to integrate these firms will enable faster global acceptance of European-styled appliances designed to fit flush with kitchen cabinets. However the immediate justification centers on the prospects for economies of scale in component making.

COST ADVANTAGES FROM GLOBAL ECONOMIES OF SCALE

The need for huge investments in R&D and production equipment creates a powerful impetus to distribute costs over larger volumes and accelerate progress down the experience curve. This is especially notable with the

---

THE GLOBALIZING OF BLACK & DECKER

By 1984 Black & Decker's dominance of the worldwide power tool market was seriously jeopardized by the onslaught of Makita Electric Works, their first global competitor.[7] During the previous three years Makita had slashed prices and nearly equaled Black & Decker's share of the market for tools for professional builders. The Japanese firm was a lower-cost producer with a superior reputation for quality. Makita didn't care that Germans preferred high-powered, heavy-duty drills, and that the American market wanted everything lighter. The same drill was sold in every market.

The Makita threat was serious because it attacked the high-profit end of the market, and Black & Decker was ill-equipped to respond. The corporate structure was a confederation of nearly sovereign fiefdoms. Each Black & Decker country manager had complete control over operations, under the assumption that he or she knew these countries best and could judge which products would succeed without any regard to global strategy. The resulting overhead wasn't offset by any efficiencies or economies of scale. Worldwide the company made 100 different motors, even though fewer than ten were really needed.

The main attack on bloated costs was a worldwide product strategy that sharply rationalized product lines. Geographical fiefdoms were abolished to concentrate on products that could be sold worldwide. "Just-in-case" local production methods were replaced with "just-in-time" continuous flow methods. This cut costs and sharply improved quality. Best of all, by 1987 the share losses had been reversed.

R&D costs of developing a new drug that may reach $150 million, or a new generation of computers that may cost between $300 million and $2 billion. Even the largest national markets may be too small to amortize these costs. This was the disadvantage faced by three British firms that used to dominate their home markets—British Leyland in automobiles, ICL in computers, and Ferranti in semiconductors. Although they had twice as much share as their American competitors (Ford, IBM, and Texas Instruments), their small world share meant much lower profitability.

Global cost reduction may result from both economies of scale and wider sharing of knowledge. Thus Electrolux estimates that by combining plants and doubling refrigerator compressor production it can save 14 to 16 percent per unit. Electrolux gains further by sharing knowledge of new developments and "best practices" around the world. A new refrigerator plant benefits from prior developments in robotics in other plants without any extra spending on this area of development.

Whether economies of scale are attainable on global production depends first on whether the product design can be standardized. If each country market has distinct requirements or rejects designs from other markets this route to cost saving can't be pursued. With homogenization of customer requirements this impediment is easier to overcome. Witness the similarity of products such as Nike running shoes, Pampers diapers, Band-Aids, Kodak film, Revlon cosmetics, Canon cameras, and Contac in North America, Europe, and Japan. Notice also that these products are small and high in value, with negligible transportation costs. This is why appliances such as microwave ovens and small, under-the-counter refrigerators can be built for worldwide markets, whereas bulky and heavy laundry equipment and refrigerators are too expensive to ship overseas and are only built for national or regional markets.

Further cost advantages are possible if economies of scale can be realized in areas where factor costs such as labor and raw materials are also low. Direct labor costs in South Korea, Taiwan, or Thailand are about one-fourth of those in Europe and North America. This is why many personal computer manufacturers purchase components from Korea, and assemble them in a few low-cost countries around the world. An alternative strategy, followed by Apple and IBM, is to automate the assembly process and centralize in North America to maintain closer control. In either case, the underlying operations strategy is to find the lowest possible worldwide cost of manufacturing and transportation. Since the answer is constantly changing with currency fluctuations and inflation, the need for global coordination becomes even greater.

SUPPORTIVE MACRO-ENVIRONMENTS

Government trade policies, restrictions, and incentives provide conflicting but compelling reasons to think globally.

A positive force is the halting, but nonetheless persistent progress toward liberalization of trade policies, including reductions in customs duties and other nontariff barriers. The harmonization of trade policies in the EEC (European Economic Community) scheduled for the end of 1992, the U.S.-Canada Free Trade Agreement ratified in December 1988, and the emergence of a trading zone on the Pacific Rim are all welcome signs.

If they function as hoped, the results will be a consolidation into three trading zones that have been called the "Triad."[8] While there are few impediments to free movements of goods and services within each leg of the triad, there is a growing risk that the triad countries may build barriers *between* each other. Global players have little choice but to hedge their bets and build a viable presence within each trading zone for their "world marketable" products.

Outside the triad, the negative forces of protectionism are durable and influential, and also demand global coordination. The best way to subvert these trade barriers and satisfy local content regulations is to locate component and assembly plants within each of the protected countries. Thus Peugeot has plants in 26 countries, including Argentina and Zimbabwe, and Caterpillar has assembly plants in each of its major markets. In fact, it wasn't so long ago that the major motivation for foreign investment by U.S. companies was to surmount trade barriers, as shown in the following table:[9]

Reasons for Foreign Investment in 1982
by 108 U.S. Multinationals

Surmount trade barriers	27.6 % of sample
Gain economies of scale	26.7
Take advantage of government incentives	21.0
Follow customers	20.0
Respond to government pressures to produce locally	19.0
Gain access to lower wage rates	13.3

Government incentives can also distort the location decisions made by a global competitor. These may be as subtle as the tax advantages offered by Ireland, or as blunt as the demand by many countries that their purchase of airplanes be linked to substantial offset subcontracting work by local companies.

GLOBAL COMMUNICATION NETWORKS

Global strategies impose daunting coordination burdens on far-flung organizations. These are compounded by the time differences and sheer distance. Fortunately, these impediments are being lowered by telecommunications developments that help firms reduce their reliance on a patchwork of natural telephone systems by building their own private networks.[10]

These are being made possible by the investments of long-distance carriers to upgrade their networks from strictly voice-grade communication to highcapacity digital lines for simultaneously moving voice and data traffic. Also, the infuriating restrictions on equipment and cross-border data flows, imposed by national phone companies in countries such as Germany and Brazil, are being challenged by more responsive competitors in neighboring countries.

These developments encourage global thinking in a number of ways:

- logistics and inventories can be centrally coordinated. Honda is able to manage its inventories by tying regional warehouses to the parent's manufacturing plants. Sea-Land, the shipping company, can track shipments at sea with its satellite network.
- information, such as payroll and sales records, can be centrally analyzed and acted on. This permits accounting functions to be located in a few locations and controls to be exercised by a regional office.
- problem-solving knowledge can be broadly shared. For example, when Digital Equipment's sales engineers encounter an unfamiliar problem they will query their operations in all parts of the world to see if anyone has a solution.
- previously inaccessible locations can be linked together to send and receive coordinating messages, through facsimile transmission or electronic mail. All 400,000 of IBM's employees can retrieve internal "mail" that has been sent over the company's network from anywhere in the world.

These developments are in fact a necessary condition for moves to a global organization. When ICI began a shift from bulk chemicals produced and sold in many local markets, into global products with more value added, the shift from a geographic organization was only attempted when the fragmented telecommunications systems were welded into a cohesive global network run centrally rather than by each division.

IMPEDIMENTS TO GLOBALIZATION

Most products are resistant to a complete globalization approach that seeks to standardize all elements of the strategy. Some local adaption is almost always desirable, even when all the conditions appear propitious. Among the impediments are:

1. Structural variations between economies, due to the differences in in-

come, education, and social norms. A product that is a staple in one country may be a luxury in another.

2. Legal restrictions on pricing practices, trademark protection, performance standards, and promotion practices still vary between countries, and provide a fertile ground for nontariff barriers to trade.

3. Language and culture differences may be felt in laws prohibiting the sale of products not in the local language, growing consumer unwillingness to purchase products in multilanguage formats, and the avoidance of commercials that don't employ local talent in local settings.

4. Media availability varies greatly between countries. In many European countries commercial channels have been either unavailable or restricted.

5. Retail and wholesale distribution channels differ considerably among markets.[11] For example, the ratio of cumulative wholesale to retail sales is 4 to 1 in Japan, compared to 1.6 to 1 in the United States. The Japanese distribution system is not only a less efficient structure, it is much harder to reach because of past custom. These differences in coverage and costs often result in large differences in end-user prices that may lead to "gray market" product movement across country boundaries.

Each of these impediments to globalization is being challenged and sometimes changed by the broader forces encouraging a more global perspective. Thus technology creates new media vehicles, such as direct broadcast television transmission, that can reach entire regions rather than a single country. Most developed countries have evolved efficient distribution systems for consumer packaged goods through large self-service outlets that employ similar approaches to selecting products to sell. The strategist must be aware of these facilitating and inhibiting trends in deciding how to strike the right balance between global standardization and local adaption. The next section reviews the possibilites.

CHOOSING STRATEGIES
FOR COMPETING GLOBALLY: STEP TWO

A business contemplating a market that is globalizing has numerous strategic choices to make. Two of these choices are fundamental to any competitive strategy, whether national, regional, or global. These are firstly the *strategic thrust* that specifies the positional advantages embodied in the core product, such as the enduring sportswear styles of Benetton, the quality and consistency of McDonald's fast-food fare, or the repair service responsiveness of Caterpillar. The process outlined in Chapter 7 applies equally well here. If a completely different thrust is being followed in each country, the prospects for integration are dim. The second strategic choice is the *scope of the target market segment,* whether universal across all countries, or diverse across countries. Beyond these choices global strategies pose several distinctive questions. How much emphasis should be put on global standardizing and centralizing of value-creating activities? Since few if any firms actually standardize everything, how much local adaption should be allowed?

These questions are addressed in the remainder of this section. The answers will depend on a number of factors, such as:

- the balance of facilitating and inhibiting globalization factors discussed in the previous section. Trends in these factors create windows of opportunity to enter new markets or standardize a collection of autonomous local country strategies.

- the speed and strength of any preemptive challenges by other globalizing competitors. There are substantial first mover advantages that may not be available to later entrants.

- the present capabilities of the business in each target market, reflecting past investments in resources and skills that can be deployed in a global context. McDonald's had a great advantage in the management skills it developed in order to marry the advantages of scale in purchasing and marketing with the freewheeling entrepreneurial style of the franchisees that own the stores.

- the suitability of the home country as a platform for launching a global strategy. A good global platform[12] is characterized by: (a) a comparative advantage in the factor endowment of the country, such as availability of skilled research personnel and advanced infrastructure, and (b) a supportive market environment, including demanding buyers, easy conditions for doing business, and a big enough market to provide a base load of demand for products that can be sold off-shore.

- the experience and strategies of sister business units that have already built a global presence. A division of a company such as Kodak, Gillette, or Timex, with many divisions that have global strategies under a strong brand name, has a much easier time, since it already has distribution outlets and a wealth of experience to draw on.

If a business lacks a significant competitive advantage in its home market, that market is a poor platform for a global strategy, global competitors are already well-entrenched, and there are few capabilities that can be transferred to worldwide operations, a global strategy makes little sense. Then it is advisable to retreat into locally specialized niches or find customer groups with extremely high service requirements. For other businesses there are many possible alternatives to consider.

BALANCING GLOBAL REACH AND LOCAL ADAPTABILITY

The generic choices of strategies depend on the competitive advantage to be gained from *global reach* and standardization (achieved by centralizing value-creating activities in one or two countries to maximize economies of scale) versus the advantage of *local adaption.* When we vary the influence of these two factors, four types of strategies emerge,[13] in the strategy grid in Figure 10-2.

Global strategies are highly standardized to exploit all the forces that cause markets to globalize. The airframe, construction equipment, pharmaceutical, and personal computer markets all lend themselves to this kind of strategy. As many activities as possible are concentrated in one or two locations, and even service and selling activities that are close to the buyer are tightly standardized. Thus, Digital Equipment was able to standardize selling practices across 17 European subsidiaries, by incorporating the best practices from each of these countries. This yielded a significant improve-

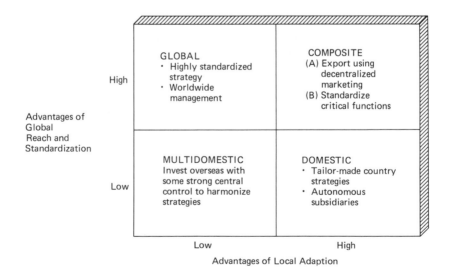

FIGURE 10-2 Generic Strategies for Globalizing Markets

ment in sales productivity, that was only possible because the customers across all the countries had similiar requirements.

Tailor-made domestic strategies are followed in markets like food processing, bulky commodities such as steel and cement, or general merchandise and food retailing, where there are no major arguments for globalizing and strong local adaption is a key success factor. All activities, from R&D and purchasing to marketing, use local resources and fill specific, locally oriented needs.

Multidomestic strategies are indicated when neither a global reach or local adaption is advantageous. A caution here: such markets may be in a state of transition to global status. In the meantime the multinational firm is best served by substantial investments in each country, with central controls to harmonize the overall strategy. There are often benefits to taking a proven positioning theme from one country and implementing it in other countries with similar needs. This may confer some cost-saving rationalization across countries, while enhancing an advantage based on superior customer value.

Composite strategies are favored when a high degree of local adaption is necessary, yet globalization promises significant benefits. Either of two strategies may be appropriate for dealing with this difficult combination of requirements. Some businesses cope by exporting a reasonably standard product, such as a Mercedes-Benz sedan that has various configurations of options for different markets, while using decentralized marketing organizations to adapt to local differences in pricing, dealer programs, service, and so forth. Alternatively, the business can build full-fledged organizations in each country and share only a few critical functions such as R&D. Firms such as Northern Telecom in the telecommunications market employ this latter approach, because their market would be global from a purely economic perspective, but government telephone systems require them to adapt their products and have a local presence.

Applying the Global Strategy Grid. While the grid in Figure 10-2 is helpful for identifying an appropriate strategy for a business operating in international markets, it may give mixed signals. First, the two dimensions are an aggregate of judgments on literally dozens of strategic elements and activities. Some activities, such as R&D and component manufacturing are naturally suited to global coordination. Others, like advertising and promotion, gain little from global scale, and should be carefully adapted to the local scene. Second, it may be difficult to step beyond the current state of globalization to anticipate the advantages of global reach—thus the judgments might only reveal "what is" rather than "what might be." Obviously, this misdiagnosis will be costly if a competitor sees the market differently. Third, it may be difficult for all functions in the organization to agree on where the market is now, and how the forces that facilitate globalization will change the position of the market over time.

A useful step for overcoming these problems is to assess each strategy element for the appropriate degree of global standardization. It soon becomes obvious that few if any firms are in a position to globally standardize every element. To illustrate the varieties of approaches possible we have profiled the strategies of two successful worldwide companies—Nestlé in packaged foods and Corning in electronic products—in Exhibit 10-1. The sharpness of this comparison lies in the difference between Nestlé as a seller of food products that are culture-bound and require local adaption and Corning which markets electronics products such as capacitors and resistors on the basis of performance benefits that are communicated in common terms to all buyers.[14]

The global strategy for Corning Electronics is clearly appropriate to a market for standardized products, where global scale is important for cost competitiveness, the customers are often global, and competitors behave globally. The situation for Nestlé is more complicated, but the need for local adaption generally overshadows the cost benefits of global reach, especially for activities that are close to the customer. Consequently, a multi-domestic strategy, where packaged soups are made in dozens of locally managed plants, instant coffee has a different taste in each country, and the advertising varies to accommodate different positioning themes, is appropriate. Not surprisingly, Nestlé country managers still have more power than head-office product groups, although there is a trend to more central coordination as some multicountry regions begin to converge in taste and marketing requirements. One result is greater sharing of new product ideas and advertising programs across countries, in recognition of the value and scarcity of good ideas in these areas.

Dynamic Strategies. Once the present strategy has been profiled as in Exhibit 10-1, and is tested for suitability within the global strategy grid, the final step is for the management team to assess the future prospects for the strategy. Are the globalizing trends such that there will be increasing scale advantages from global reach, or less need for local adaption? Each of the driving forces that facilitates or inhibits globalization has to be tested for impact on each of the elements of the present strategy, before the need for change can be identified.[15] The answer is usually but not invariably in favor of greater centralization and standardization. The ethical drug market, with its heavy investments in R&D, testing, and quality control, is best managed centrally. Yet the politics of health care in many countries necessitates local production and local clinical testing, and increasingly restricts

Exhibit 10-1 Profiling Global Strategies

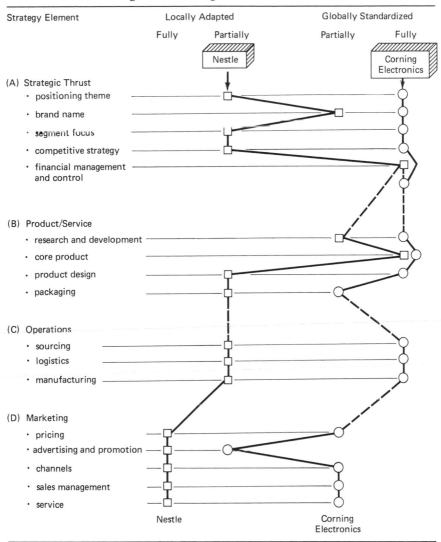

pricing freedom. This is pushing drug firms toward composite strategies. Meanwhile, the automobile finish market, that once required local responsiveness, is rapidly globalizing, as shown on the next page. The main impetus is from the carmakers in Japan and North American who are building "world cars" and want to deal with a set of suppliers able to reliably supply the same quality of finish in all their major markets.

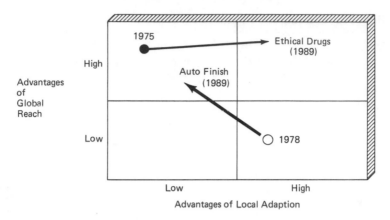

Actions addressing the gap between the present strategy and an optimal strategy for seizing global opportunities can be either reactive or proactive. Typically a *reactive* shift is made reluctantly in the face of abundant evidence that competitors have already gained an edge by globalizing. But catch-up moves are typically too late unless they are made confidently and learn from the mistakes of the pioneers. A *proactive* change is made in expectation of the possibilities of globalization, to gain a first mover advantage. Unfortunately, the rigidities of most multinational firms get in the way of aggressive proactive moves. "[Multinational managers] believe preferences are fixed, not because they are but because of rigid habits of thinking about what actually is. . . . They falsely presume that marketing means giving the customer what he says he wants rather than trying to understand exactly what he'd like. So they persist with high-cost, customized multinational products and practices instead of pressing hard and pressing properly for global standardization."[16]

DECIDING HOW TO PARTICIPATE: STEP THREE

A business has three basic modes it can use to participate in each country or region within a global market: (1) *exporting,* and using independent manufacturers' agents or distributors to make the sales, (2) forming *alliances* with other firms that create long-term relationships falling short of a merger, or (3) setting up or acquiring *wholly owned subsidiaries.* The choice that is made depends on the balance of the following factors:

- past history and investment commitments in each region and country. Most companies are constrained by previous agreements and their successes or failures in attempting to export or operate a subsidiary. This experience provides a knowledge base for evaluating and managing the alternatives, that may signficantly influence the preferred participation mode.

- the thrust of the global strategy as dictated by the balance of advantage of global reach versus local adaption.

- legal and governmental constraints. The mode of participation is often not a matter of free choice. Many governments in developing or centrally planned economies require local participation in any operations that are established within their boundaries. Legal restrictions on direct investment, such as existed in Japan until the 1970s, further limit the choice.

- uncertainty about the political or economic climate, traceable to political unrest or financial instability due to high inflation and/or high external debts, puts a high premium on maintaining long-run flexibility.

- availability of capital to make major investments to acquire or develop an operation.

Increasingly the interplay of these forces is leading firms to form alliances rather than simply opt for the traditional modes of exporting or setting up a wholly owned subsidiary. Most of this section will be devoted to this development, but first it has to be put in the context of the alternative modes.

EXPORTING VERSUS DIRECT INVESTMENT IN A SUBSIDIARY

A firm's first foray overseas usually involves exporting from one or two home plants, with central marketing coordination, while sales are made through distributors or importing agencies in each country. Exporting is advisable when the firm lacks the resources to make a major commitment to the country, is unfamiliar with the market requirements and cultural norms in the country, or wants to minimize exposure to political and economic risk. This mode is best for preserving flexibility, because it enables the business to make subsequent changes in systems and approaches quickly and at low cost, as more is learned about the attractiveness of the market and the requirements for effective competition.

While exporting reduces the downside risk, it also limits the future prospects of the business in the country. The problems of exporting are the same as those encountered in the previous chapter where the merits of direct sales versus distributors or agents were debated. They stem from lack of commitment and lack of control. In many international markets customers are loath to form long-run relationships with a company through its agents because they are unsure whether the business will continue to service the market, or will withdraw at the first sign of adversity. This problem has bedeviled U.S. firms in many countries, and only now are they living down a reputation for opportunistically participating in many countries and then withdrawing abruptly to protect short-run profits.

Exporting also means giving up direct control, which makes it difficult to coordinate actions, carry out strategies, change strategies, or resolve the disputes that inevitably arise when two parties to a contract pursue their separate interests.[17] These problems can be reduced by buying a controlling interest in a local company, or setting up a wholly owned subsidiary in the country. Such a move to integrate forward signals a major commitment to market participation, and increases the likelihood the overall strategy will be implemented. Indeed it is unlikely a global strategy, requiring each subsidiary to suboptimize for the benefit of the overall competitive position, could be implemented without full ownership.

The control advantages of a wholly owned subsidiary come at a high price. At the outset there is a considerable commitment of resources—including management involvement, investment capital, and fixed operating costs. These commitments sharply reduce subsequent flexibility, if the business wants to find a different way to serve the country market. Meanwhile, the exposure to risks of political instability and currency fluctuations are increased.

STRATEGIC ALLIANCES

The formation of alliances or coalitions has been a very prominent feature of global strategies. The main features of global alliances are shared by the alliances for market access described in the previous chapter. There is a formal long-run linkage, funded with direct co-investments by two or more companies, that pools complementary capabilities and resources to achieve jointly agreed objectives.

One indicator of the importance of alliances to global strategies is the following extract from the public statement of General Electric's operating objectives for the nineties:[18]

> Globalization means participating in worldwide markets. To achieve a #1 or #2 global product-market position requires participation in each

major market of the world. This requires several different forms of participation; trading technology for market access; trading market access for technology; and trading market access for market access. This "share to gain" becomes a way of life.

While GE is a major player of the alliance game, with well over 100 such partnerships under way, many other firms are forming alliances for a variety of purposes, from product sourcing, to technology development and market access.

Ford has set up a number of alliances in response to the challenge posed by foreign competitors to their basic strategy of competing with a full line of cars and exploiting global coverage. Their competitors used superior automation and better quality to gain a significant product advantage. In response Ford has set up sourcing agreements with Mazda of Japan and Kia of Korea for small cars. It also participated with Mazda on product development for a new generation of sports touring coupé, the Probe, that combines components from both firms. There is a further agreement with Nissan to jointly make and sell a new minivan designed by Nissan.

Montedison of Italy and Hercules, Inc. pooled their technical and marketing strengths into Himont, Inc., a $900 million polypropylene joint venture that in three years was able to command a dominant share of the U.S. market. Montedison contributed a number of proprietary catalysts and $100 million in cash. Its partner had a large but unprofitable share of world polypropylene capacity, a strong U.S. marketing arm, and wanted to reduce its reliance on commodity channels.[19] The resulting 50-50 joint venture succeeded because the partners had complementary objectives and a long history of working together.

Various computer, communications, and semiconductor companies have been aligning themselves through joint ventures, minority investments, and cooperative arrangements. Companies that have become part of one worldwide coalition are less likely to do business with members of another coalition. It is conceivable these coalitions will begin to behave like the large networks of noncompetitive companies that function under the umbrella of the famous Japanese *sogo shosha*, or general trading firms.

Strategic alliances are not simply a fancy relabeling of the familiar joint venturing and licensing agreements in use for many years. These older arrangements were primarily formed for immediate tactical reasons: to gain access to a third-world market by tying-up with a local firm, or license a technology to markets the business didn't intend to otherwise serve. The new generation of alliances plays an integral role within a global strategy. Also, the strategic benefits are hard to resist—especially when it seems they can be achieved without the cost of an outright acquisition and in less time than either business would require on its own. However, these benefits may entail substantial costs, so the rest of this section looks at the determinants of the cost–benefits ratio.

MOTIVATIONS FOR STRATEGIC ALLIANCES

An alliance is unlikely to be consummated or succeed unless all parties benefit, and these benefits are greater and come faster than internal development, acquisitions, or arm's-length transactions. The biggest hurdles to satisfying this requirement are the inevitable asymmetries between the partners. Each one enters the relationship with different competitive positions, cultures, and strategic priorities, reflecting differences in country of origin, and superiorities and deficiencies in skills and resources. As a result the objectives and the functional areas that participate are likely to differ, as are the benefits[20] each partner is seeking:

1. *Access benefits.* These are realized when one partner has something the other needs, such as:

- local credibility, to the extent that countries such as India and Mexico impose requirements that an entering corporation have a local partner.
- channel coverage. A foreign firm entering the Japanese food and beverage market can hardly escape a joint venture in order to tackle the problems of serving almost a million retail outlets through some 330,000 wholesalers in a country with virtually no street names.
- specialized know-how or technology.
- capital, or access to a borrowing line.

2. *Economies of scale.* Such economies and accelerated learning by experience are gained by combining the manufacturing, development, or marketing activities of the two partners. Ford and Volkswagen have an alliance in Latin America to achieve manufacturing economies by combining production of several models for several countries—none of which is large enough to support economic volumes.

Often one access benefit is traded for another. Thus Komag, a small U.S. firm, brought an advanced technology in manufacturing film for magnetic disks to a 50-50 joint venture with Tokyo-based Asahi Glass, to manufacture high-density magnetic disks in Japan. Asahi's contribution was financial resources (they provided all the equity), and access to a comprehensive Japanese distribution network.

3. *Speed of entry.* At one time new products could be launched in a lei-

surely region-by-region roll-out, following the "cascade" model. The product trickled down from the most to the least sophisticated customers. Ohmae argues that a "sprinkler" model of product diffusion, in which a new product is launched in all markets at once, better meets the needs of globally homogeneous markets.[21] The most effective way to do this is to form alliances that involve the swapping of new products and models among firms that have established strong distribution coverage in each major market. In this way the high front-end costs of new products can be recouped quickly.

4. *Sharing of risk.* Companies in oil and mining exploration and insurance underwriting form their alliances to share the risks and rewards of very large projects, that are beyond the capacity of any one firm to absorb. These alliances are seldom undertaken to improve performance or obtain economies of scale.

Pitfalls in Alliances. Despite the allure of alliances their track record has led some observers to conclude that the successes are the exception. As many as seven of ten joint ventures have been judged to have fallen short of expectations or been disbanded.[22] However, 50-50 joint ventures have the worst record, with 50 percent outright failures found in one study.[23] Although this form is popular because it offers the illusion of "shared responsibility," the result is that difficult decisions about control are often avoided or unclear at the time of negotiation. Why so much disappointment and frustration? Four basic reasons are cited.

The first problem is shifting strategic requirements. An alliance is based on shared power and a sensible division of tasks. If these shared relationships have to be continually modified as conditions change, or the market or technology doesn't materialize as expected, the stress may be intolerable. The problems are especially acute when the venture is formed to develop an uncertain new market. Such uncertainties caused the demise of the partnership of Johnson & Johnson and McDonnell-Douglas Astronautics to manufacture pharmaceuticals in space. Johnson & Johnson was to provide marketing and product expertise. However, when Amgen, a start-up company, later found a way to make the same substances on earth, J & J elected to join with them instead.

The second pitfall is a lack of clear decision-making responsibility, leading to conflicts over who is in control. This is the weakness of 50-50 joint ventures, such as the alliance that married the technological superiority of AT&T in personal computers and the marketing capability of Olivetti in office products. The arrangement called for AT&T to inject capital into Olivetti in exchange for a substantial minority position. Olivetti was the clear short-run winner since their microcomputer gained strong sales in the United States. Unfortunately the AT&T computer offerings did not sell well in Europe. Conflicts then arose over which partner was to develop a new personal computer needed to match IBM's product range. The competing views could only be resolved by the two CEOs which meant long delays, compounding the growing lack of trust between the partners.[24]

A third class of problems stems from conflicts in objectives, cultures, and styles of making decisions. While these should be dealt with early in the negotiations, they are often deferred. This is one reason U. S. companies have trouble teaming with Japanese firms that want to manage for market share and high new product sales, at the expense of the high ROI the Western partner wants.

Finally, there will be problems if long-term interest and commitment wanes on either side. Top managers are often to blame, when they devote all their time to setting up the alliance and then devote little energy to monitoring it to be sure the expected benefits are being realized. In this setting the lower-level executives seconded to the alliance will be less willing to subordinate their long-run career chances with the parent in the name of cooperation and sharing for long-run advantage.

As conflicts build over time and interests diverge, the alliance either disbands, or one partner absorbs the other. This is especially likely when two firms of different sizes and cultures are allied. Consequently, many observers conclude that alliances should be treated as transitional arrangements, analogous to courtship that ultimately results in either marriage and the procreation of an autonomous entity, or breakup. This possibility should be planned for at the outset, and the decision to move to a new relationship made after careful monitoring of performance in light of jointly agreed objectives.

IMPLEMENTING GLOBAL STRATEGIES: STEP FOUR

Global strategies require firm central direction, and standardization of key functional activities. But tighter central direction and harmonization comes at the expense of diminished local autonomy, with the risk of confusion, resistance, and loss of motivation of country managers. The greater the historical autonomy and power of the local subsidiaries, the greater the resistance. If the problems aren't carefully handled, the entire strategy will be compromised.

How Not to Do It.[25] In 1984 Parker Pen launched a global strategy with high hopes. Their position in the premium (over $3.00) pen market was being threatened by a flood of disposable pens from Japan, while Cross was solidifying a strong market position above Parker. About 80 percent of sales came from 150 overseas markets, each managed by highly autonomous country managers who devised their own advertising, channel strategies, pricing tactics, and product lines.

The centerpiece of the global strategy devised by a new management team was the centralizing of key decisions in the U.S. head office. As part of the overhaul, the product line was pruned from 500 to less than 100 items, manufacturing was centralized in a few highly automated plants, all communications were standardized, and the 40 local ad agencies were replaced with one full-service international agency. In a major departure from tradition, the firm entered the fast-growing, low-priced disposable pen segment.

Although the strategy was conceptually audacious, it was doomed from the start. The local managers, who were caught by surprise, resisted fiercely. They objected to the new product line, to the low-end entry, and to the assumption that Parker pens were purchased the same way in all markets. The common advertising theme, "Make your mark with a Parker" was regarded as bland and ineffective and the benefits of "one look, one voice" in all markets were dismissed as trivial. Most of all, they resented being excluded from the decision process. Meanwhile the newly automated plants were not working, and supply problems were acute. The mounting losses led to the demise of the architects of globalization, and a return to decentralized management.

Effective Implementation. The Parker Pen fiasco underlines the need to have management thinking harmonized and supportive, before strategies and activities are standardized and globally directed. This means meshing the intended global strategy with the appropriate organizational structure, and the mechanisms for coordinating actions worldwide. Although organizational changes are the most powerful single tool, they will not work unless local management accepts the assumptions that lead to the change in strategy, and are motivated to support the global competitive advantages and subordinate their local performance.

The remainder of this section describes how to achieve congruency between the two main dimensions of the global implementation program—the degree of coordination and the organizational structure—with the desired strategic balance of global reach and local adaptation that is graphically portrayed in Figure 10–3.

ORGANIZATIONAL SOLUTIONS

Most companies have followed a predictable evolution of their organizational structures to cope with a diversity of country markets. The first stage

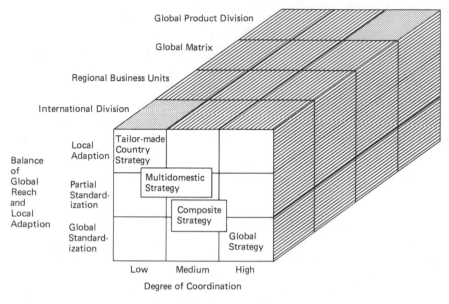

FIGURE 10-3 Implementing Global Strategies

is local manufacturing agents or distributors in each foreign market. These export sales and service activities are considered appendages of the parent, and little effort is made to adapt products or policies to local conditions. As international sales become more important or the market globalizes, this approach becomes less effective. A major exception is franchise arrangements, with ownership of the country operations by local nationals. This is a viable long-term strategy, so long as influence and control are exercised through long-run relationships built on mutual trust. But if franchising isn't appropriate other organizational arrangements have to be designed.

Multidomestic Subsidiaries. The first formal structure companies usually adopt is an international division, with responsibility for the overseas operating subsidiaries. These may have been set up through direct investment, or acquired. These subsidiaries compete autonomously in their separate markets and are subject only to the central financial control and coordination of policies that would apply to any strategic business unit. In this arrangement the primary authority is held by the country manager.

As firms expand in size, diversity, and complexity, the country managers find themselves responsible for a multitude of different businesses with characteristics ranging from national to global. This creates pressure for a more "sophisticated" structure. This opens up the following array of options:

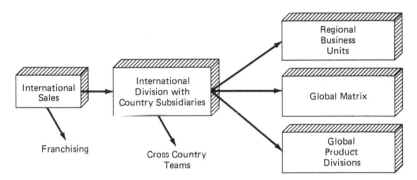

The question is how to maintain and encourage local entrepreneurial spirit while ensuring local activities don't deviate from the long-term strategic thrust of the parent company. In the 1970s the answer for many firms was a global product division. Too often this was done without thinking through the consequences. Now many firms have concluded they don't need to go that far. Indeed, the international division appears to be more flexible than once believed. The key to making it work is to broaden the perspectives of country personnel, and help them learn from each other by setting up *cross-country teams*.[26] These facilitate the transfer of marketing ideas and the coordination of production activities, and encourage the interchange of competitive intelligence and programs for servicing global accounts. But part-time participation in teams will not deliver global strategy coordination in the face of determined global competitors, so other approaches eventually have to be employed.

Global Product Divisions. This structure takes power out of the hands of the international division managers at headquarters and in the foreign subsidiaries and gives it to central product division managers. This means a major shift in authority to headquarters, with greater priority given to rationalizing overseas production activities, and pricing and product decisions become centralized. All these changes are desirable if the market is truly global. To the extent that local conditions and adaption are important, a global product division may be a bad move. One study[27] found the following problems: (1) a significant decline in international commitment, and support for international projects—especially if global product division managers come from the home operation and have never had overseas experience, (2) fragmentation of international expertise, (3) an increase in overhead as the parent duplicates infrastructure and peripheral investments at the country level, and (4) an inability to adapt to fluctuations in local demand because of the constraints of centralized production. At the heart of these problems is the reality that a change in organization structure can signal a change in direction but cannot by itself change the way managers think and behave.

Regional Business Units. As the European Economic Community removes trade obstacles, free trade reduces tariffs between the United States and Canada, and Southeast Asia talks of a free trade zone anchored by Japan, some companies are shifting from a country-by-country to a regional approach. Others are shifting down to regional businesses, having found their global business approach too cumbersome and insensitive to local market requirements. Regionalization requires much the same consolidation and refocusing that a global strategy requires but the geographic areas are now more homogenous. This approach still requires strong efforts to promote teamwork and interchange between regions to develop coordinated approaches to global competitors.

Global Matrix Structures. This format attempts to balance the roles of central product managers, and country-based managers, offering them shared responsibility and authority. These matrices are generally difficult to manage, so most companies let their strategy dictate whether countries or products will be dominant, and use staff people to ensure there is effective advocacy of the other dimension.

PROCESS AND COORDINATION SOLUTIONS

Some firms have sidestepped the multiple traumas of structural changes—open conflict, convoluted and drawn-out decision processes, overlapping responsibilities, miscommunication, and lack of shared understanding of the strategy—by using other levers to respond to global challenges.[28] The possibilities are as numerous as the companies that have been trying to behave globally are varied. Exhibit 10–2 summarizes some of the organizational elements that are involved and how they can be modified to tighten coordination within an existing organizational structure.

Adaptive Planning in a Global Setting. The pivotal role in creating more coordination "glue" across diverse countries is played by an adaptive planning process, similar to that described in Chapter 3, with the following features:

- The process is managed by *teams* with multifunctional, multicountry backgrounds. Procter & Gamble has "Euroteams" organized around key European brands that incorporate managers from the subsidiaries and are chaired by each brand's designated "lead country" general manager. The involvement of the general manager adds credibility to the team.

Exhibit 10-2 Comparing Degrees of Coordination

Organizational Elements	*Limited Coordination*	*Tight Coordination*
Strategic planning process	—Headquarters review of marketing plans and budgets for each country	—Adaptive planning using participative team approaches to resolving issues and developing regional and global strategies
Resource allocation	—Capital budgeting analysis of discrete projects —Country managers have profit responsibility	—Investment decisions distinguish among local projects to develop competitive capability and profitability is measured at corporate level
Management reward systems	—Based on indicators of local performance	—Tied to both local performance and appraisals of cooperative behavior in global setting
Information and control systems	—Financially oriented information (ROI, sales, etc.) only —Each country develops separate systems subject to quarterly performance reporting standards set by the parent.	—Market-oriented information (share) as well as sales and profits —A standard system is used to collect and assemble information on a global basis —Dedicated communication network links all countries
Transfer of know-how	—International information shared among countries on a limited, need-to-know basis —Visits from head office	—Cross-functional and multicountry teams work on common issues —International meetings —Voice-mail systems —Regular publication of ideas —International account management systems oversee relations with global customers

- Time and energy are devoted to *issue resolution,* using project teams or task forces drawn from appropriate subsidiaries with a defined life.
- *Top-down guidance* is provided by means of (1) central staff providing insights on multicountry issues to be resolved, (2) top management using far-ranging strategy reviews to test the logic of the strategy, and (3) a separate objective-setting and budgeting process to manage resource allocations across countries to recognize trade-offs between short-run local profits and growth and long-run global performance.
- *Bottom-up inputs* from local management on opportunities for change and sharing of ideas for other countries. These inputs, guided by participation in the process, help to "pre-sell" the overall global strategy, improve the final decision, and commit the local management to support the programs.

The decisions and commitments flowing from this broad-based participative process stand a good chance of being implemented if they are then supported by the coordination elements detailed in Exhibit 10–2. But this is still not sufficient. For a globally minded business to prevail there must be a *shared theme,* based on an emphasis on competitive advantage, reinforced by *shared values.* Every organizational change, whether it means a new training program, new systems, or a shift in reporting relationships, should be seen as an opportunity to promote and reinforce these shared values and themes to all countries and levels.

MEETING THE GLOBAL CHALLENGE

Globalizing markets are the reality for increasing numbers of firms. The signals are numerous and disruptive:

- customers that accept standardized products that offer superior value in preference to locally customized products
- global sourcing
- competitors willing to cross-subsidize an entry into a new market to broaden their scale advantages, or attack the home market of a powerful competitor
- liberalizing trade policies that diminish national barriers for protecting local firms
- advances in technology that encourage global communication networks.

A globalizing market may not warrant a global strategy, where primary value-creating activities are concentrated in one place, most strategy elements are internationally standardized, and all strategic direction comes from the center. Local adaption and coloration still pay large dividends for activities that are close to the customer. For most firms the proper balance of local adaption versus global reach is in a continual state of tension. There are too many contending and changing forces influencing this balance for it to ever reach equilibrium—so flexibility is paramount.

Strategies that exploit the globalizing forces are enormously stressful for organizations. On the one hand, vigorous central direction is needed to ensure the impact of the strategy is not dissipated by costly, contrary moves at the country level. Yet tight control and harmonization inevitably diminishes cherished local autonomy—with the risk that powerful resistance will be mounted. This tight-rope can be safely walked with organization structures, coordination mechanisms, and strategic planning processes that encourage broad-based participation and reward globally cooperative behavior.

FIVE

Renewing the Strategy

CHAPTER

ELEVEN

Charting New Directions:
Conditions for Successful Renewal

T wo things drive this business—technology and paranoia.

> —*Senior VP for Intel, a leading participant*
> *in the market for micro processors*

"Crisis" or "critical turning point" in Chinese. The upper
character represents "danger" and the lower character means
"hidden opportunity."

> —*An apt metaphor for new ventures*

Successful businesses keep renewing themselves by looking beyond the familiar confines of their present markets and products for new opportunities. They may elect to simply *edge out,* by making natural extensions of their base business. Or they can *reach out,* with further extensions of existing skills and resources, into new markets or technologies. A *break out* move would take the business into areas unrelated to their existing capabilities. Each growth path or "critical turning point" has its own profile of risks and rewards to be recognized and managed, if the business is to continue to prosper.

If firms need to grow in new directions—as well as innovate in the products and services they offer their present markets—how should they proceed? In this chapter we will look to successful innovators and diversifiers for guidance. The essence of their experience can be captured in the following key success factors, which are also the topics to be covered in the following sections.

KEY SUCCESS FACTORS

- The business stays very close to its market, and especially to lead users, to keep focused on delivering superior customer value.
- There is a clear strategic direction that specifies where the business will look for opportunities, what amount of growth is expected, and how it will be achieved.
- The business "sticks to its knitting," by avoiding growth prospects that can't usefully exploit its distinctive competencies.
- There is an overriding sense of urgency in the development process. Winning firms know they have to beat their competitors to market.
- The organization nurtures new products and ventures by supporting committed champions with resources and creating a climate that encourages risk taking.

These key success factors presume the business knows it has to grow, despite the uncertainties and organizational disruption.

WHY PURSUE NEW DIRECTIONS?

What motivates companies to develop new products, invest in new technologies, enter new markets, or acquire businesses outside their current scope? Very simply, renewing companies perceive that resting on the status quo is a sure way to disaster.

Technology threats can range from evolutionary and predictable shifts from one generation of an existing technology to another, to a complete displacement of an old technology by a new one. Usually the major changes come quickly and are a surprise to managers who are enjoying profitable success with the old technology. The root of their failure to respond is the comfortable assumption that the future will be much like the past. They act on this belief by putting their efforts into cost improvements and efficiency enhancements. This is often the wrong move as it makes them vulnerable to competitors who better understand the dynamics of technology.

The technology S-curve describes the relationship of the effort put into improving a product or process and the resulting technical performance. Initially, as funds are invested the progress is slow. When all the key knowledge is put in place improvements come quickly. Finally, a limit is approached and progress becomes increasingly difficult and costly (see Figure 11–1).[1]

As the limits of one technology are reached, new approaches often emerge to displace the old one—such as the shift from bias-belted to radial tires, from audio tapes to compact discs, from electromechanical to electronic typesetting, and perhaps from chemical emulsion processes for taking photographs to electronic cameras that put images on magnetic media.

The new approach often demands skills that have not been needed by the leader in the old technology. The impending attack may even go unnoticed by the leader, who is frequently lulled by strong economic performance and buoyed by faith in evolutionary change until it is too late to respond.

Paranoia about competitors has its origins in technological change or other discontinuities in market requirements and regulation that reduce the structural attractiveness of the present market. These same changes also work to erode existing competitive advantages, as we saw in Chapter 8. Thus businesses may have to pursue new directions in order to defend their present position against leapfrogging moves or flank attacks.

There is mounting sensitivity to flank attacks in the wake of evidence of the success of Japanese firms with this approach.[2] The logic is drawn from *A Book of Five Rings,* in which a leading Samurai of Japan advised, "It is beneficial to strike at the corners of the enemy's force. If the corners are

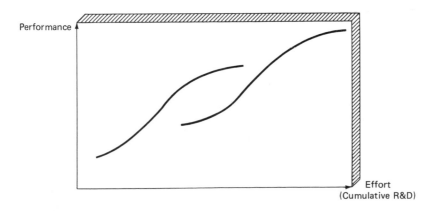

FIGURE 11–1 Technological S-Curves

overthrown, the spirit of the whole body will be overthrown. To defeat the enemy you must follow up the attack when the corners have fallen." Japanese managers view neglected or underserved market segments as corners to attack, and seldom try to compete head-on with established firms. Sometimes they are almost invited. Management of a U.S. tractor firm once viewed Japanese manufacturers as simply filling unprofitable gaps in the firm's product line for small-firm and specialized agricultural operations. Now they can't be dislodged from their beachhead.

Overcoming Slowing Growth. A further impetus to the search for new directions is the need to maintain growth, in the face of the inevitable slowdown or decline in the presently served markets. There are sensible internal reasons for this search: growing businesses are more vibrant, they offer greater opportunities to their people, and the necessary commitment to innovation carries over to all activities and keeps the business renewing. There is no complacency in a fast-growing business! Any lingering complacency is being further shaken by the compression of life cycles. Especially in electronics-related categories, the rate of technological change, plus rapid communications and distribution, means that new products enter the market quickly to soak up demand, but are soon superseded.

Enhancing Shareholder Value. Investors reward firms that promise continuing growth, because they invest heavily in R&D and new products, with high ratios of the market value they are willing to pay for a share of the equity compared to the book value as recorded on the balance sheet. Any suggestion of an unexpected slowing of the growth rate results in a rapid fall in the share price. Thus, managers whose priority is increasing shareholder value through appreciation of the equity value are under continued pressure to pursue growth opportunities.

STAYING CLOSE TO THE MARKET

No matter what direction a business intends to follow to grow and innovate it will not be assured of success unless it delivers superior customer value. This is not simply a restatement of the obvious, for when the idea is applied to growth strategies the implications are both subtle and challenging to common practice.

Successes versus Failures. The most compelling evidence of the need to stay close to the market comes from studies that look for differences between matched pairs of successful and unsuccessful innovations. The earliest of these was Project Sappho,[3] which gave results that anticipated similar findings from later studies. They found that five underlying factors or themes distinguished winners, with the most important being an understanding of customers' needs, problems and benefits. This result was later confirmed and extended by the Stanford Innovation Project and by Project New Prod.[4] The latter study looked at almost 200 new industrial products, half of which were judged successful because their financial return exceeded the company hurdle rate. The distinguishing features of the successes, in order of importance were:

1. Offering a superior product, that met customers' needs better than the competition with some combination of unique features, superior quality, or ability to perform a unique task for the customer. This was a very strong discriminator; the success rate for unique and superior products was 82 percent, while "me too" products succeeded only 26 percent of the time.
2. Strong market orientation, as reflected in extensive market information gathering, and a well-planned and proficiently executed market launch backed by appropriate resources and lots of support from the sales force and channels.
3. Technological fit and proficiency: successful new products demonstrated a good match between the resource base of the business and the technological needs of the project. Again, the message: you win if you "stick to your knitting."

The Role of Lead Users. Another argument for staying close to customers comes from a fascinating stream of research on the sources of innovation.[5] This work neatly challenges the conventional wisdom that manufacturers do the innovating by having autonomous R&D departments bring out products to meet customer needs as identified by marketing research. To be sure, this does happen, but less frequently than expected. It turns out there are many industries where most innovations are developed by lead users or suppliers and only later are they adopted by manufacturers.

Lead users face strong needs that will eventually be widespread in the particular market, but face them months or years before the rest of the market. They are motivated to find their own solution to these needs because they can see how they can gain an advantage and keep it from being quickly copied. In the case of printed circuit board manufacturing equipment, lead users were large electronics firms such as IBM, GE, and AT&T. They were responsible for 67 percent of all innovations, with a further 12 percent a result of joint work with suppliers. But for scientific instruments, the lead users were mostly individual researchers in universities. Typically a scientist with an instrumentation problem built a prototype, and spread information about its capabilities through scientific media. When other scientists asked the instrument companies when a commercial version would be available, a manufacturer would take the idea and eventually launch it as a new product.

The conditions are not always right for lead users to innovate. In markets like construction equipment and plastics additives they play a minor role in product development. But even here the needs and ongoing problems of users offer valuable inputs to the development process. Yet, businesses that are steeped in the belief that innovation starts with the firm are badly equipped to capture these insights.

Service and sales departments should be in the best position to obtain information on promising new ideas or problems, and emerging needs of customers, because they are in regular contact with them. Unfortunately they are more likely to be a major impediment than a clear channel. Service people often react negatively when they encounter a customer modification, no matter how useful it may be. Since service people are evaluated on such measures as time spent on a repair, anything that slows them down or requires a follow-up because parts aren't readily available is a problem, not an opportunity. Similarly, the sales force is usually compensated for its sales of existing products and has no incentive to learn about user developments that might lead to commercial innovations.

Some companies overcome these problems by positioning themselves as problem solvers. Pitney-Bowes gears its entire organization to solving mail and document-handling problems—without requiring customers to take a standard product. One result is that Pitney-Bowes is constantly edging into new markets as customers with unusual problems, who are uncertain whom to call, think of them in that general connection.

SETTING THE STRATEGIC DIRECTION

How do businesses decide where to look for new product-market opportunities, how much to spend, and whether to use internal development or other growth modes such as joint ventures or acquisitions? The basic approaches summarized in Figure 11–2 mirror the modes of strategy development described in Chapter 3.

Bottom-up, Incremental, and Opportunistic. This approach to growth is very organic—new directions literally spread out and evolve from the ongoing processes of reaction, experimentation, and learning found at all levels of an innovative organization. New products or acquisitions are likely to be either (1) *reactive*—triggered by an attractive deal presented to management, or a perceived need to match a competitor's move with superior performance, a new feature, etc., (2) *customer-responsive,* in which the customer comes to the company with a problem, and if the solution is workable

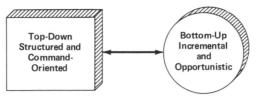

Change comes in big steps taken to match competitors or exploit structural and technological change	Continuous change in small steps in response to opportunities presented, or new technologies developed
Competitor-centered	Close to customers
Senior management vision prevails	Champions prevail by spawning supportive coalitions
Tightly programmed and controlled	Flexible and adaptive

FIGURE 11-2 Contrasting Approaches to Managing Growth

a new product is added to the product range, or (3) *technologically driven—* the lab has developed a new material, process, etc., so let's find a market.

The merits of this approach are that it is very close to the market, and tends to spawn champions who become deeply committed to their new venture or product. This is the kind of environment in which products like Post-It Notes can flourish (see the following box).

The drawback of solely bottom-up growth is that it is reactive to market and technological opportunities as they appear. Each opportunity is evaluated only on its own merits—or even pushed despite a lack of merit—for there is no overriding strategic guidance to help decide whether the opportunity advances the overall strategy.[6] While incrementing organizations tend to be energetic and committed it is not clear that the sum total of the piecemeal, and often small-scale efforts adds up to a cohesive competitive strategy. In the absence of compelling leadership or imminent threats, the organization will not take major moves to jump to a new technology S-curve and embark into a major new market.

Predominantly technology-driven new product strategies are especially vulnerable to the drawbacks of bottom-up approaches. One study of 120 industrial product firms found that 26 percent fit this profile—their programs were technologically aggressive, at the state of the art, and often in high-risk ventures.[7] The results were frequently mediocre, with high failure rates and poor profitability from programs that survived. One reason was that many were "trombone oil projects" (these yield products that may be the best available anywhere, but the entire world needs only about a pint

---

3M'S "POST-IT" NOTES

In the early 1970s a polymer chemist was seeking a super strong latex adhesive. Instead he stumbled on a super weak adhesive with the unusual property of not transferring from one surface to another.

There was mild interest around the company in using the adhesive as a substitute for cork message boards. But when the adhesive coated boards were hung they collected dust, which meant adhesiveness was lost and the messages fell off. Since the market was small to begin with, any enthusiasm soon waned.

In 1974 another chemist, who sang in a church choir, used some of the adhesive on slips of paper to mark pages in his hymnal. It was then he got the idea of selling note pads smeared with the adhesive. However, an early market survey asking people whether they would pay x-amount for the pads found no interest at all. A test market of some pads, to see if they would sell if the customer had a chance to buy them, was an equal failure.

Despite these rebuffs and setbacks the champion persisted. More pads were made up and given away to a wide circle of possible users. That was when the addictive nature of the pads was discovered. Once the pads got into people's hands they found a multitude of uses—and a $150 million business was created.

---

a year). Worse, there was often little synergy between the new and existing markets, which reduced the advantage over competitors.

Top-down, Structured, and Command-Oriented. This approach is often caricatured as a year-long, meticulous study—conducted by central staff along with squadrons of consultants—that scans all possible opportunities and employs complex screening criteria to target a few high-growth areas for serious pursuit. Sometimes this caricature is apt and appropriate, especially when the top managers are contemplating a major shift in *corporate* direction through acquisitions. Such an activity is well outside the confines of the present business scope.

A variant on this command approach occurs when the CEO or president selects a theme area for growth. This choice may be based on conversations within the company, articles, consultants' proposals, gut feelings, or all of the above—but not on a formal strategic planning exercise. The president of one major chemical company decided with little internal discussion that advanced ceramics was a good growth area. He then sent a memo to corporate and business development people to find ways to get into this new area. The acquisition route was chosen to gain rapid market access. Meanwhile he told R&D, "Within one year I want to be in high-tech ceramics. Go out and hire the best people in the field and get started now."

Top-down approaches involve the exercise of vision and leadership to seek major "break-out" moves. They act on a breadth of perspective that is usually not encouraged or required of operating managers at the business level who are close to their customers, processes, and technologies. Big moves may be necessary to reposition a multibusiness company that is mired down in too many unattractive markets. However, it does not serve as well to send the business units themselves in new growth directions. Top-down mandates are by definition remote from the details of the business, and tend to foster a "big move" mentality that stifles individual initiative and spontaneity. Commitment and enthusiasm may be lacking if the operating managers didn't participate in the process of deciding the new growth direction for their business.

Why a Growth Strategy Is Needed! The purpose of a growth strategy is to help a business unit steer a middle course between the opportunistic and unguided results of bottom-up initiatives, and the overly restrictive master plan imposed from the top down. Some discipline must be imposed on the growth direction to ensure it is supportive of the overall business strategy. The growth strategy provides guidance to the choice of new product, new market and diversification programs to pursue, and the magnitude of effort, while at the same time spelling out what the business will not do.

Innovation and growth are highly resistant to formal planning: fortuitous discoveries emerge from the lab, customers propose exciting new products that fit the capabilities of the business, a joint venture is proposed by a supplier who has a new technology but no marketing capability, and an unexpected acquisition candidate materializes when a competitor is forced to restructure. Theses events are unanticipated and need to be encouraged—but not necessarily pursued as new business opportunities. To be useful, a growth strategy must be flexible enough to provide a framework for considering these possibilities, while restricting diversions from what the business is competent to do. The next chapter is all about how to develop such a strategy.

STICKING TO THE KNITTING

The growth dogma of the eighties was "stick to your knitting." This was sound advice in light of the excesses of the seventies when many companies haphazardly diversified away from their core business. The reasons seemed compelling at the time: achieve portfolio balance by participating in new markets that promise higher ROIs, reduce the risk of reliance on a single market, or employ superior management talent to turn around troubled businesses. These diversification moves were often justified by the allure of synergies with the existing skills and resources, such as access to technology, channels, or marketing skills, depth of financial resources, and reputation of brand name. Thus, General Foods bought Burger Chef, a chain of 700 fast-food outlets, because it was a fast-growing market and was "food-related." Quaker Oats bought a clutch of toy companies and restaurants. Sometime later Sears decided to exploit the synergies that beckoned because of their ubiquitous retail store coverage, ownership of Allstate Insurance, and broad base of credit-card ownership by buying a real estate firm and brokerage firm. Even now it is not clear whether enough customers will seek a broad range of financial services from a store chain best known for appliances, tools, and auto parts.

The Cost of Phantom Synergies. So many diversification efforts fell short of their inflated expectations that the whole notion of synergy as multiplicative combinations of businesses was called into question. Indeed, many managers still shun the term because of the negative connotations, while others use less emotive terms such as interdependencies.

The evidence on the performance of wide-ranging diversification moves certainly justified the mounting skepticism. A retrospective analysis of the 10 largest mergers of 1971 found a decade later that half the acquirers would have been better off without their acquisition.[8] Only 3 of the 10 acquisitions had returns on investment exceeding 10 percent, compared with the 13.8 percent median return for the Fortune 500. A broader study of 2,021 acquisitions made in new markets by 33 large, diversified U.S. firms between 1950 and 1980 found that more than half were divested by 1986.[9] The divestment rate largely depended on how closely related the acquisition was to the core skills and resources of the acquirer: 74 percent of the unrelated ones were divested, whereas less than 30 percent of the related acquisitions came to this end.

The high rate of failure of unrelated takeovers reflects the relative inability of management knowledgeable in one market to even know what questions to ask of a potential acquisition in unfamiliar territory, much less to know how to operate it to mutual advantage. These problems are exacerbated when an excessive premium is paid in the excitement of the negotiation. Even good operating performance cannot overcome the drag from a heavy burden of debt. As these lessons have been absorbed, businesses are becoming less venturesome in their acquisitions and diversifications, to concentrate on those that confer strategic advantage on the core business.

Eventually synergy will come back in vogue, with a new meaning derived from the compelling need to build on the existing competencies to assure success.

INNOVATING UNDER TIME PRESSURE

Time is the new battleground in the innovation war.[10] With shortening life cycles and accelerating technological change, the business that gets its new products to market fastest enjoys a big advantage:

- In autos, Japanese companies can develop new products in half the time—and with half as many people—as their counterparts in Europe and the United States. This gives them a lead in new designs, but also means they can freeze their designs closer to the market launch so they respond to up-to-date market information.
- Slowness can be costly. Although Philips introduced the first practical home videocassette recorder in 1972, three years ahead of the Japanese, they didn't bring out the next generation until 1979. Meanwhile the Japanese launched three generations of VCRs between 1975 and 1979. When Philips did launch their V2000 their North American affiliate refused to sell it because it wasn't compatible with VHS or Beta. By 1988 Philips was losing money with only 2 percent of a $16 billion market.
- In custom plastic injection molds Japanese firms are able to develop molds in one-third the time of U.S. competitors and at one-third the cost.

The advantages of speedy development are not limited to preempting the competition; there is evidence that quality is superior and inventories are reduced, with consequent cost savings. Production costs are often lower because the designs tend to be more efficient to produce. Speed pays off even when it means going over budget. One recent study[11] found that high-technology products that come to market six months late but on budget will earn 33 percent less profit over five years. In contrast, coming out on time, but exceeding the budget by 50 percent, will cut profits only 4 percent.

The widely acclaimed resurgence of Xerox in the copier business has many sources, but a major one is its halving of the time to develop and launch a new machine from six years to three years. At the same time development costs were shaved by as much as two-thirds, with a saving of more than $100 million a year. Thus the gains of fast-paced development are not limited to simple products or short-cycle electronics products. Even Boeing was able to shorten its usual 12-year cycle of plane development for the 767 in order to beat the European A310 Airbus to market by eight months.

To accomplish such startling gains in development time companies have to be prepared to change their mind-set and their organizational processes. Doing traditional activities faster won't suffice—breakthrough improvements only come when management is forced to abandon familiar ways and contemplate dramatic changes. Sheer survival offers a compelling reason for change. When competitors can develop new products twice as fast, there is little alternative to keeping up with them. But this is defensive. Rather than waiting to fall behind, top management can create a climate of urgency by challenging the organization. John Young, CEO of Hewlett-Packard did this in 1988 with a company-wide program called BET (for break-even time) in which he challenged all departments to cut by half the interval between a new product's conception and profitability, including covering all development costs.

Incrementing and Learning. A hallmark of successful development processes is a continuing emphasis on small increments of improvement[12]—introduced frequently—to gain experience and learning that is fed back to the next generation of products. This highly adaptive process is guided by an overall sense of strategic direction. Within the Campbell Soup company, a stream of new products has been coming out that appeals to the target market of health-conscious and sophisticated consumers, to reinforce the goal of becoming a well-being company.

Continuous small moves are a big departure from practice for Western companies, like Philips, which in the past preferred to make more significant improvements less often. The view was, "rather than simply copy the new technology, our challenge is to leapfrog." There is a growing recognition of the risks of big leaps: there is a bigger risk the product will fail and the odds of a successful start-up are low, while the cost of failure is large because major projects tend to get launched on a large scale. Meanwhile, the competitor has incorporated a series of smaller improvements, gotten market recognition for them, and moved to new improvements. All this time the competitor is learning from its successes as well as the smaller failures that were killed quickly.

Team Organizations. Many, if not most, Western companies use a sequential organizational approach to managing new product programs. Each function is compartmentalized and takes over the project after a hand-over from another function in a sequence of steps from: concept development ⇨ feasibility testing ⇨ product design ⇨ development ⇨ production design and tooling ⇨ production ⇨ market launch. This is a very time-consuming procedure as functions wait for each other to finish, so project hand-overs are cumulatively late, and the project may have to be passed back for a rerun because of problems such as poor design for manufacturability. Needless to say, relationships between functions are strained, especially if each blames the other for problems.

In the parallel or "rugby" approach, a hand-picked, reasonably autonomous team, representing each key function, works together from start to finish.[13] The approach is highly flexible as team members interact closely while ignoring traditional demarcation lines. Many steps overlap, as for example when tooling development is begun well before the design is frozen, which saves both time and later rework.

What Role for Planning? Paradoxically the looseness of time-sensitive innovation—with its inherent flexibility, rapid adaption to new insights, and willingness to consider and carry along several technology options into development—makes planning more important. At the front end an adaptive growth strategy provides the overall framework, and imposes broad limits on the development activity. From this plan comes the "go-no go" performance criteria that serve as targets for program teams. What the plan does not do is attempt to impose a detailed, step-by-step plan of attack on the interwoven stages of the project.

Later, when the project is moving toward the expensive development, scale-up and commercialization phases formal launch plans are prepared. These are not exercises in pin-point forecasting and detailed anticipation of all feasible steps. Instead they are used to force the business managers or project team members to think their projects through, to provide compelling evidence of the scope of the opportunity and the anticipated payoffs, and to present credible scenarios for retrenchment in case they are wrong.

ENSURING ORGANIZATIONAL SUPPORT

The final ingredient for success is concerted leadership that simultaneously sets the tone and direction for strategic change so people know where they are supposed to be going and provides a climate that supports and encourages those willing to take sizable personal risks to pursue opportunies that fit within this strategic envelope. The need for the discipline of a clear strategic direction has already been established. The question now is, how is leadership to be exercised to get the organization to move in the chosen direction? Winning companies have several answers.

1. *Demonstrate top management commitment.* Few organizations can consistently innovate or enthusiastically seek new ventures in the face of uninvolved, uncertain, and unwilling senior managers who would rather nurture the established businesses than pursue unfamiliar and unproven

possibilities. Just as an unsupportive climate can quickly squelch growth strategies and experimentation, a supportive management team that believes new products and new directions are key to future growth can energize the organization. The perceived impact of this commitment is evident in a survey of senior executives in 179 companies on the factors they thought most contributed to new product success (see Table 11–1).[14]

Top management has to say it believes in innovation, and then behave as though it believes it. No lip service is permitted, for organizations are adept at reading between the lines for the true message. A visible commitment can be demonstrated in many ways: participation in new product review meetings, regular and spontaneous visits to labs and development sites, arranging ceremonies to mark the launch of a new product team, and visibly singling out and rewarding the members of a team.

2. *Ensure access to resources.* New ventures and new products are disruptive because they make unanticipated demands on the organization's resources. These demands go beyond simply providing a reliable and substantial flow of funds to research and development, although that is a necessary condition for success. What winners seem to do especially well is pull the needed skills and insight from various parts of the organization and focus them on well-defined projects. Rather than fight for good people—and frequently lose—the project leader can expect to get them when they are needed. This doesn't mean there won't be loud protests from functional managers, but in the end the need for innovation prevails.

The success of Procter & Gamble's introduction of calcium-enriched Citrus Hill orange juice shows the advantages of access to seemingly diverse resources.[15] Researchers in the health-care unit, in the course of development of drugs to treat bone disease, had learned of the extent of

Table 11-1 Factors Associated with Success in New Product Development
(Proportion of 179 respondents indicating factor was most important)

Top management support	85%
Enthusiastic product manager	78
New business closely related to old	68
Clear lines of authority	45
Decentralized responsibility	39
Specific screening criteria	36
Monetary incentives	18
Tight control of expenses	16
Large and flexible budget	10

calcium deficiency among adults. As a remedy they proposed adding calcium to the orange juice marketed by the beverage division. Neither group knew how to make the mixture palatable. The answer was found in the detergents group, which had years of experience in sequestering or suspending calcium particles in liquid soap products.

When the skills aren't available in the organization they will be sought outside. When Monsanto decided a decade ago to shift its strategic focus to biotechnology, it invested heavily in joint ventures with small start-ups like Genetech to help build experience; similarly, seed money was given to research scientists at leading universities. The payoff has been slow in coming but promises to be sizable, with products such as proteins to stimulate milk production in cows.

3. *Avoid segmentalism.* Studies of successful innovation practices find that even large companies can behave like small ventures by eliminating bureaucracy (including the tight controls and extensive reviews and reporting), allowing fast, unfettered communication, and instilling a high level of group identity and loyalty. A carefully balanced venture team won't work unless the conditions satisfy the old truism about innovation: "Introducing a new product or process to the world is like raising a healthy child—it needs a mother (champion) who loves it, a father (authority figure with resources) to support it, and pediatricians (specialists) to get it through difficult times. It may survive solely in the hand of specialists, but its chances of success are remote."[16]

Innovative firms of all sizes have a distinctive "integrative" approach to problems. There is a "willingness to move beyond received wisdom, to combine ideas from unconnected sources, to embrace change as an opportunity to test limits.... thus challenging established practices."[17] Because there is little position consciousness—people do things despite the box on the organization chart they occupy—it is easy to exchange information and ideas across departmental lines and quickly form teams and task forces to pursue opportunities.

The enemy of fast-paced innovation is "segmentalism," a contrasting style that relies on compartmentalizing activities and keeping organizational units separate and distinct. Segmentalist approaches deal with problems as narrowly as possible, and independently of their broader context. The prevailing belief is that problems are best solved by breaking them into pieces that are assigned to specialists working in isolation. Change is resisted because it threatens the established order and comfortable rhythm.

4. *Syndicate risk.* Champions won't come forward and organizations won't embark on prudent experimentation if they know that their failures will be punished—unless, of course, the punishment was for sheer incom-

petence. Some likelihood of failure is always present: the technology may not work as expected, costs may go out of line when the project is scaled up to commercial volumes, competitors may leapfrog, and customers' needs may change. If the organization is constantly looking over its (collective) shoulder and is unwilling to take calculated risks, little progress is made. The best way to overcome this drag is to syndicate the risks. A derivative of management by consensus, it basically means drawing a wide range of people into any risky decision, including, whenever possible, the senior management. Everyone should feel a shared sense of responsibility for the decision to proceed.

SUMMARY: THE CONDITIONS FOR SUCCESS

Few companies rely exclusively on either a top-down, command-oriented or a bottom-up, incremental approach to managing growth. Instead they try to combine them to get the best features of each. This means that one is embedded within the other, as in Figure 11–3.

When growth comes from the bottom up, a lot of possibilities are generated—largely in response to events in the market. Directions for choosing among them, and channeling the organization, have to come from the top,

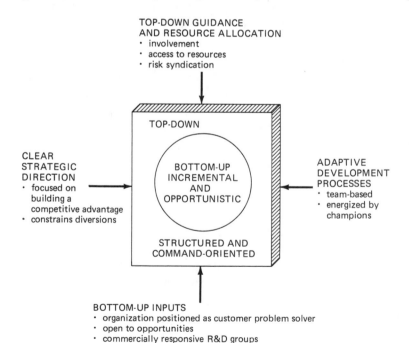

FIGURE 11–3 A Balanced Approach to Managing Growth

without stifling either the initiative of the lower levels, or their openness to new opportunities they can put forward as champions.

What, then, are the responsibilities of senior management? (1) to provide a supportive climate, with sufficient investment in critical resources, (2) to structure the organization so it behaves as though it were small, (3) to instill a sense of urgency, and (4) define a strategy for growth that is clear enough to enable the operating levels to sort opportunity from inanity. Intel's engineers, for example, know the company has to continually replace its own products before competitors render them obsolete, while meeting its customers' demands that succeeding generations of chips retain design continuity. These strategic guidelines are well understood, and almost self-enforcing, since they enable engineers to quickly decide whether an idea fits. This cuts down dramatically on the need for stifling oversight.

Just as superior strategic planning processes rely on informed, multi-functional teams from the business, where operating managers meet under the leadership of a general manager to debate and resolve issues, so does an effective development process rely on teams. Teams have more focused energy, because of the presence of a motivated champion, that permit them to adapt and develop faster. They also mesh with the trend to decentralization, downsizing, and horizontal growth via the addition of small projects and related businesses. Even the very largest companies are reorganizing to focus development work on small teams, amidst a growing recognition that large-scale projects are not always the best way to grow. 3M is a master of turning small projects aimed at small markets into profitable businesses—for no project is too small for consideration. But even 3M, with its unparalleled capacity to spawn dozens of new businesses and products each year, imposes a strategic discipline and direction, of the type we'll spend the next chapter describing and evaluating.

TWELVE

Setting the Growth Direction

"Would you tell me, please, which way I ought to go from here?" asked Alice.

"That depends a good deal on where you want to get to," said the Cat.

"I don't care where," said Alice.

"Then it doesn't matter which way you go," said the Cat.
—LEWIS CARROLL,
Alice's Adventures in Wonderland

Predicting rain doesn't count, building arks does.
—*The Noah Principle*

The purpose of a growth strategy is to define expectations, clarify the general directions to take, and establish the boundaries of effort. At the heart of a useful strategy are the beliefs that no business can be all things to all markets, and that real success comes from leveraging the capabilities of the business to reach seemingly unattainable objectives. Modest ambitions will lead to modest results—especially when the competitors are committed to overtaking the cautious target.

This chapter addresses the key strategic issues that surface as soon as the need for a new growth direction is recognized: What kinds of opportunities should be considered—should the business stay close to home base or go far afield? How should these opportunities be pursued—with internal development or acquisitions? What is the best timing—should we be an early mover or is it better to be a fast follower? And what organizational arrangements will be required to ensure success? The resolution of these issues is a strategy that can direct the energies of the management team toward the areas they are competent to exploit, yet offer a reasonable assurance of gaining a sustainable and profitable advantage. This strategy shapes where the business looks, the risks that will be tolerated, the criteria that new ventures must satisfy, and the method of entry.

For the growth strategy to add value—rather than satisfy a bureaucratic requirement—it must sensibly guide both the search for options and the narrowing of the feasible set. When Brik Pak decided to concentrate its aseptic packaging technology only on liquids, that decision eliminated yogurt, soups, and puddings. This was a deliberate decision to avoid the unproductive dispersion of resources that comes when the business is deflected into too many unattractive markets.

Normally, the growth strategy is embedded in a business plan, and serves to support the objectives and overall thrusts of the strategy of the business. Sometimes it is prepared separately as a means of translating corporate development plans (the statements of intent that chart new directions for the entire firm) into specific development or acquisition responsibilities for the business unit. Some of the possible linkages among the types of strategies are shown in Figure 12-1.

A useful growth strategy acts like a searchlight into the future, by (1) focusing attention on a narrow band of the terrain, (2) illuminating the dark corners of opportunities obscured by uncertainty, and (3) providing a beacon to follow. The direction to follow is set by answers to these questions:

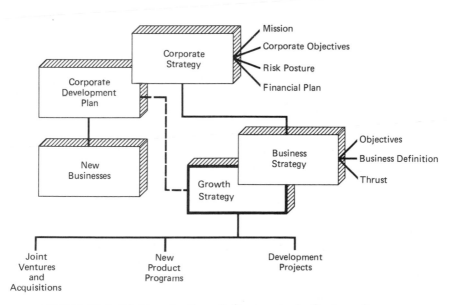

FIGURE 12-1 Linking the Growth Strategy to the Business Strategy

- What are the *growth objectives?* What portion of future growth and profits should come from new products and/or new markets?
- What *purposes* should new products and other growth options play in supporting the business strategy?
- What is the best *growth path?* Where should the business team be looking to find opportunities that satisfy the objectives and purposes of the strategy, without exposing the business to excessive risks?
- Should the business *participate* in the new growth direction by relying on internal development, or external means such as alliances, licenses, or acquisitions?

The notion of an explicit growth strategy to address these issues is relatively recent. Some aspects were addressed as early as Henry Ford's "any color so long as it is black" policy, or the steel industry's early disdain for plastics. The first evidence of widespread use came in the late seventies with a study[1] of "product innovation charters." This term was used to signify a specific directional charge given to a team, that told them where to look for new products, and defined the programs for achieving the goals.

The first evidence of the payoff from explicit growth strategies came from a study by Booz, Allen and Hamilton.[2] This firm had conducted a major study of "best practices" in new product development in 1968, which it replicated with a similar sample of 700 companies in 1981. Three specific results attracted a great deal of attention:

- there was a dramatic reduction in the number of new product ideas considered for every successful new product introduced—from an average of 58 in 1968 to only 7 in 1981.
- the percentage of total spending on new product development allocated to products that were ultimately successful increased from 30 percent in 1968 to 54 percent in 1981—an enormous increase in the efficiency of spending.
- the rate of success of commercialized new products had not changed in the two decades—holding steady at 67 percent. Here success was defined as meeting the specific financial and strategic criteria that were set for the product before it was launched.

Whereas new product development was a highly *reactive* process in the sixties, with little discipline exercised on the source of ideas or the directions to pursue, by the eighties companies were becoming very *proactive.* Successful companies were more likely to have an explicit new product strategy, and avoid too many tempting but resource-sapping diversions from this direction.

The emphasis in the strategies studied by Booz, Allen and Hamilton was mainly on internally developed new products. Now, a decade later, there is much greater interest in achieving growth by other means. Even companies like IBM, Ford, and AT&T that were once proud of their self-sufficiency are turning to joint ventures, acquisitions, marketing agreements, and other devices to achieve their growth objectives. This new generation of explicit statements of growth objectives, directions, and purposes achieved by a variety of means is what we mean by a "growth strategy."

GROWTH OBJECTIVES

Whether the growth objectives—the needed and desired performance results to be reached by means outside the present products and markets—are aggressive or modest, incremental or great leaps, will profoundly shape every part of the growth strategy.

For much of the seventies Time, Inc. pursued very aggressive growth objectives, and was willing to look far afield for the means to achieve these ends.[3] These stretching objectives seemed reasonable because few publishers matched its historic success with major magazines like *Money, People, Fortune,* and *Sports Illustrated.* And the company had made an impressive transition to new communications technologies with Home Box Office. Often these successes were achieved by defying the odds, and absorbing heavy losses for some years before profits were realized. The consequence was an admittedly arrogant organization, where one insider felt, "it was hard to believe we could go wrong." With a high stock price, reflecting investors' beliefs in continued high growth into the eighties, that the company tried to live up to, there was no hesitation in reaching for ambitious objectives and big projects.

But by 1984 Time's three biggest projects had failed at a cost of $180 million. The casualties included the ill-fated acquisition of the *Washington Star,* the closing of a teletext program for two-way interactive TV, and the termination of *TV-Cable Week,* a program guide for cable viewers. In the wake of these reversals, management scaled back their growth plans to fit more modest objectives aimed at steady but slower growth. A humbler but wiser search began for acquisitions within related areas. There was even a willingness to consider acquiring other magazines in a radical departure from past practice.

Types of Objectives. Fundamental direction comes from a direct translation of the business objectives into growth objectives. These can be derived from the gap analysis described in Chapter 4, by separating out the forecasts of growth and profit contribution of the present products and markets from the overall objectives. This residual becomes the contribution of growth strategies to closing the gap by means of:

- the percent of sales that will come from new sources. For example, 3M aims for 25 percent of sales to come from new products introduced within the previous five years.
- the percent of profits to be derived from new products.
- the rate of return required from each project.

Operational objectives are used to guide decision making within the new product or business development organization, by setting targets such as :

- the number of annual new product launches.
- the proportion of sales growth from internally developed new products versus other means.
- the minimum sales volume. For some companies it is not worthwhile to fund projects that promise volumes of less than $10 million, on the grounds that the effect would be too small to have an impact.

Functions of Objectives. When agreement on growth objectives is reached the organization is able to calibrate the size of effort and allocate the appropriate resources. If plans call for rapid growth from internally developed new products, then research programs, testing facilities, organizational structures, and all the rest of the infrastructure have to be sized accordingly. These resources take time to put in place, and that recognition may require a modification in the objectives. If the objectives are not feasible in light of the available resources and cannot be changed, then other approaches to internal development, such as new product subcontractors or licensing arrangements, have to be explored.

Objectives also energize managers—if they are taken seriously. Within 3M the 25 percent new product test is a crucial yardstick at bonus time.[4] So when this percentage dropped below 12 percent in the division making an aging product category—disposable face masks—the managers knew they had to accelerate the stream of new products. Using technology derived from face-mask filters, development teams came up with innovative products such as a sheet that absorbs grease from microwaved bacon, and a super-absorbent packing material that solved the problems of handlers of blood samples.

DEVISING A GROWTH STRATEGY
FOR LIFE SAVERS, INC.

In the mid-eighties growth was lagging at Life Savers because of insufficient new product investment.[6] Their major brands like Life Saver candy, Carefree Sugarless gum, Bubble Yum bubble gum, and Breath Savers were securely positioned in slow-growth categories. To get back on track—and satisfy its new owners, Nabisco Brands—Life Savers opted for a "quick fix" growth strategy. To provide direction for this strategy a thorough analysis of resources and capabilities was undertaken.

What emerged from the internal assessment was a picture of a specialist in front-end merchandising and rack control at the retail level. The company had a sales force of more than 700 people, and an additional direct vendor sales force that was unusual in the industry. Given the other constraints, and concerns about cannibalization of existing products, it was clear the best course was to seek either acquisitions or distribution arrangements.

Life Saver Competencies	Current Position	Implication
1. financial strength	underutilized	acquisition possible
2. specialized facilities for manufacturing candy	limited production capacity available, very hard to adapt	avoid any manufacturing
3. sales force with broad coverage and superior retail merchandising skills	somewhat underutilized	easily leveraged
4. management depth in confectionery and snack products	operating below potential	easily leveraged

When the role of the growth strategy shifted to capitalizing on distribution strengths, a number of possibilities were unearthed. The most attractive was found with the number two brand in the antacid market, TUMS. This brand was marketed by Norcliff Thayer, a subsidiary of Revlon. TUMS's prospects for growth seemed poor because of distribution problems.

> TUMS were sold in single rolls and in three-roll packs. Most of the distribution was through brokers to health and beauty-aid buyers, with little coverage of the confectionery area. This was exactly where Life Savers was strong. After a quick round of negotiations an agreement was reached where Life Savers would be paid to distribute and merchandise single rolls of TUMS in the confectionery area.

STRATEGIC PURPOSE

A growth strategy stands a much better chance of reaching its objectives when the programs and opportunities build on the core competencies of the organization and support the thrust of the overall strategy.[5] While these *purposes* are almost self-evident they are seldom spelled out in a way that gives the management team a clear sense of direction. Yet if they are not articulated it may be difficult to know how the possible growth opportunities are to support the strategy by defending or expanding the existing business or reaching out toward new markets. This is a recipe for confusion, for it gives a license to each player in the team to interpret the growth strategy in his or her own terms.

Feasible purposes fall into two categories: some are *competency-based*, because they are designed to capitalize on core skills and resources or shore up competitive deficiencies, and others are *market-driven* in response to customer or competitive forces. These purposes are stated in fairly general terms and precede the consideration of specific possibilities. A really attractive opportunity is one that promises to achieve a number of purposes.

Competency-Based Purposes. These are mainly derived from the assessment of sources of advantage that permits a business to outperform its competitors. These can range from utilizing superior distribution coverage to capitalizing on a proprietary technology or advanced design skills. Overcoming internal deficiencies is another source of strategic purpose: utilize excess capacity, find a use for by-products or toxic waste materials, offset seasonal fluctuations, or develop a cost-reduced product to fend off foreign entrants.

Market-Driven Purposes: These are based on the need to respond to customer or competitor developments or exploit market opportunities. They can generally be identified from the critical issues that surface during the planning process. Examples of possible purposes are:

- maintain a leadership position in a market category
- preempt competition in an emerging health-oriented segment

- gain entry into a new market to assure access for existing products
- broaden distribution coverage by entering hardware and do-it-yourself outlets
- use the equity of a strong brand name
- expand a modest presence in Pacific Rim countries
- reinforce reputation as an innovator.

A number of actions and programs may be required to satisfy any one of these purposes. For example, Black & Decker, the housewares maker, has been facing intense competition from both European and Japanese companies, who encounter few barriers to entry into the fragmented U.S. market. Often these entrants exploit shifts in consumer life-styles when they make their move. In order to preempt these competitors, a series of line extensions, cost reductions, repositionings, and new-to-the-company products were required. The small-kitchen-appliance line was redesigned to fit under overhead cabinets, a single-cup coffee maker was added to extend the line, and a fire extinguisher was introduced for the first time.

Satisfying the Purposes. Each new product program, acquisition candidate, or joint venture needs to be appraised both on standard technical feasibility, market acceptance, and other criteria, as well as fit with the competency-based and market-driven purposes. Absence of fit is a clear warning the project not only doesn't support the strategy, but is likely to encounter implementation problems. Conversely, the better the fit, and potential to serve several purposes, the greater the odds of winning. Quaker Oats has been celebrating the success of rice cakes because this new product simultaneously: (1) allowed the company to enter the low-calorie segment of the snack-food market and expand the existing snack business into more healthful foods, (2) exploited the equity of the Quaker Oats brand name in grain-based foods, (3) capitalized on the merchandising capabilities of the direct sales force, and (4) increased its total share of shelf space in retail outlets.

Purposes are usually derived from the requirements of the business strategy. There are times when it pays to reverse the process, and take a project designed for a certain purpose and see if it could or should serve other purposes. This is particularly helpful when projects are narrowly conceived to match competitors' moves and protect the current position. When this kind of reactive thinking prevails the results are usually no more than pallid imitations, with no added value to customers. And, as many companies have found, an imitation with such limited aspirations doesn't do much to excite the organization.

Sealed Air Corp. faced this problem in 1983 when several new regional competitors threatened their dominance of the closed-cell cushioning material market.[7] Sealed Air had pioneered the use of "coated" bubbles for packaging applications where bubbles had to hold air for long periods. The new competitors offered uncoated bubbles that didn't hold up as long, but were adequate for light-weight, short-haul applications. This product was quite a bit cheaper, which appealed to emerging price-sensitive segments. Sealed Air's reaction was that uncoated is a "low-quality product," and "not what we do as market and technological leaders." They did eventually launch a "me too" uncoated product, solely to prevent the new competitors from establishing a beachhead. No other strategic purposes were considered, which meant they excluded the possibility of opening up new flexible wrap markets by displacing other materials with the cheaper uncoated product. There was no enthusiasm for the new product, in part because it was considered inferior, but also because it was much less profitable and purely defensive. Not surprisingly the product fared poorly when it was introduced.

STRATEGIC PURPOSE AND RISK POSTURE

The choice of appropriate purposes for the business development or product team to pursue is more than a restatement of the growth objectives in the business plan. Nor is it a lengthy wish list where everyone contributes his or her favorite solution to the problems of the business, without any concern for feasibility or risk. Selectivity is critical if the energies of the organization are not to be diffused. There is no point in spending a lot of time on high-risk projects if senior management will later decide they prefer something surer. But before the fact it is difficult to specify what level of risk is going to be acceptable.

Numerous factors influence the riskiness of a new opportunity, as illustrated below:

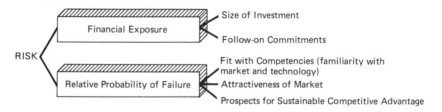

Different purposes can be assigned to different risk categories. A low-risk purpose would be to look for products to utilize excess distribution capacity, since the incremental investment is modest, and the firm that is looking for a distribution channel to reach a new market has already built a successful product. This was the appeal of the arrangement between Life Savers and TUMS. But at the same time one cannot expect high returns if the forecast returns are quite certain.

The riskiest purposes take the business into uncharted markets with "me too" products. Not only is the market unfamiliar, so it becomes difficult to collect valid market information and understand the customer requirements, but the competencies of the business are of little use. Some of the risk factors can be dampened by the choice of entry mechanism—an acquisition or joint venture can provide both a window and the needed competencies. The merits and drawbacks of alternative entry modes will be discussed in the final section of this chapter. But before the entry issues can be properly appreciated we need to look more closely at the importance of fit and the trade-offs between innovation and imitation.

Fit with Core Competencies. The farther a business moves away from its core competencies, the greater the risk. Although this notion is widely understood, it is often not acted on when a growth strategy is being designed. The determination of fit requires both a clear idea of the competencies of the business, and the key success factors demanded by the new opportunities. The strength of the common thread between what the business is presently good at doing, and what has to be done to assure success in the new market, defines risk, as illustrated below:

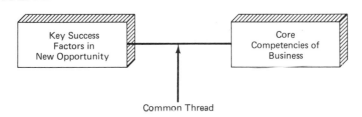

Viewing risk this way poses an interesting dilemma. On the one hand, a strong common thread keeps risk low, but probably contradicts the growth objectives since the business will have to stay close to the slow growth products and markets it knows well. A thin common thread will take the business into new arenas but the risk associated with lack of experience may be unacceptable. One way out of this box is to push the analysis a stage further to ask whether and how the missing competencies can be acquired.

This approach was used by a fabricator of high-precision plastic component parts for computers and communications gear, when it explored a forward integration move into the market for subassemblies using its molded parts. The fabricator soon found very different manufacturing and quality control requirements, because of the need to coordinate the assembly of several hundred different component parts and then test the performance of the completed subassembly. The marketing task was also very different since the most likely competitor was the customer who could (and often did) assemble the purchased parts, and had to be persuaded to contract the job to outsiders. This meant reaching a completely different set of decision makers, who put a lot more emphasis on the economic analysis of the make-versus-buy decision. Fortunately, the firm had a very strong reputation for quality it could draw on to gain access to the key influentials within the customer organization. The problem of building a completely new internal manufacturing organization—with appropriate skills, controls, and coordination—proved insurmountable within a reasonable cost. It was also viewed as a risky move, because late delivery or poor performance of the completed assemblies could jeopardize the firm's present customer relations. With few acquisition candidates available and limited resources to commit, the company decided against this diversification path.

What Role for Imitation? The relative emphasis on innovation versus imitation has major consequences for the risk exposure of the business and the capabilities needed to support the growth strategy.

Innovators that survive usually do well. They prosper by taking relatively large risks to get an emerging technology into the market while demand is still nascent. Their organizations are oriented to basic R&D to generate a flow of technology, while staying in close touch with market needs—often through lead users in narrowly defined market niches. The most successful have a capacity for continuous innovation that allows them to keep in front of each succeeding generation of technology. Among the masters of this strategy is 3M. As one manager put it, "We hit fast, price high (full economic value of the product to the customer) and move on when the 'me too' products pour in." The new niches pioneered by 3M are generally small ones of $10 million to $30 million and may be dominated for only five years or less. Then it is time for them to launch the next generation of abrasives or tape products to supplant the contested products.

Imitators are content to take smaller rewards to keep the risks manageable, by consciously waiting until the market has been established. Most of the uncertainties about technology, performance requirements, and customer acceptance have been dispelled or clarified. The segmentation structure, customer requirements, and usage behavior are known, or a least knowable. It is also clear where the market pioneers are making mistakes or leaving openings for a superior product that better satisfies an underserved segment.

There is a big difference between creative imitation and making copies that are close to duplicates. The meager rewards from "me too" products are well documented, and deserved, because little incentive is given to the customer to switch unless prices are slashed. Conversely, a "creative imitator"[8] probably understands what the innovation means to customers better than those who developed it, and makes meaningful improvements that add customer value. The Japanese are well-known for making continuous technical improvements to the initial borrowed version, to the point where it is almost unrecognizable. New features will be added to make the product even more user-friendly, overcome customer problems, or adapt it slightly to fit different segments. Meanwhile, manufacturing costs are reduced to make the product better value.

Tylenol is a classic creative imitation. It is based on acetaminophen, a compound originally sold as a painkiller by prescription—leaving aspirin to dominate the over-the-counter market. Acetaminophen is as potent as aspirin, and has none of the side effects such as gastric upsets that come from using aspirin in large quantities. When acetaminophen first became available without prescription it was positioned solely as a drug for those suffering side effects from aspirin. What Johnson & Johnson saw was not a specialty painkiller, but a drug that could replace aspirin, with aspirin confined to applications where anti-inflammatory effects were needed. They positioned Tylenol as the safe, universal painkiller and far outsold the pioneering firm. But the pioneer showed the way.

Johnson & Johnson has the skills that a creative imitator needs to be successful:

- insightful market and competitor monitoring to sense unfilled needs, segment gaps, and anticipate changing requirements
- strong developmental R&D,[9] with a definite tilt toward application engineering and process improvements rather than an emphasis on basic advances in technology
- an ability to respond quickly (J & J is known for its ability to create small, entrepreneurial groups that eventually become businesses)
- a willingness to out-invest the pioneers. The myriad subsidiaries—a total of 166 in 1988—ensure managers focus their energy and imagination on a small group of related products while the parent has the deep pockets needed to support good ideas with funding for research and marketing.

Creative imitation is not without risk. There is a temptation to hedge the bets by dispersing the development efforts too broadly. Speed is essential to success, especially if the market is growing fast, and that may force a hurried response or even a misreading of the opportunity. As with all growth strategies a sense of focus is essential, which is the next element of the growth strategy.

GROWTH PATH

Here we return to the question posed earlier, Where should we be look-ing to find opportunities that satisfy the growth objectives and support the overall strategy—without exposing the business to excessive risks? The answer should specify the direction that growth is to proceed and also spell out what should be avoided—either because of a poor fit with the core competencies or market prospects that are inherently unattractive. The need for an explicit growth path goes back to the saying, "If you don't know where you are going all paths will get you there." This is a recipe for unfocused search and diluted efforts that usually deflect the business away from what it is best at doing. But there are also situations where an expansionist growth path needs to be chosen because the core business is being threatened or a new technology can be applied to differ-ent markets. In either case, the organization needs clear signals on which path to follow.

The problem is that there are many possible paths to follow, depending on how far from home base the business wants to proceed along each of the following dimensions:

- customer needs or requirements to be satisfied
- technologies used to provide the capabilities
- customer segments served
- geographic scope
- stage in the value chain (degree of vertical integration, forward or backward).

A recurring mistake in many growth strategies is to emphasize growth along a single dimension: product type (e.g., liquid pumps), technologies employed (e.g., rotary hydraulics), or customer segments (e.g., oil refine-ries). This is both myopic and unfocused, as an emphasis on growing by serving the needs of a particular segment, for example, could encourage the business to enter new arenas with unrelated technologies, products, or pro-duction processes. Instead, growth paths usually occur along several di-mensions simultaneously.[10] This can be seen if we superimpose the alter-native *growth arenas* for Acuson Corp., a leading medical ultrasound manufacturer, on top of its *home base*, which describes the company's pres-ent business definition (see Figure 12–2). We can readily see that Acuson has lots of possible directions for growth, although it has chosen to stay tightly focused by limiting itself to medical applications of high-definition ultrasound. Nonetheless, nondestructive materials testing and lithotrypcy (breaking up of kidney stones with sound waves) remain tempting arenas because they use similar hardware, but different software.

This display of the home base of the business, in the context of the feasible growth paths into new arenas, aids strategic thinking in several ways. By focusing on the needs and requirements of distinct customer segments the customer is kept front and center in growth planning. Second, it continually reminds the organization that customers want their needs satisfied or problems solved, and usually have several technologies to choose among. This is certainly true for noninvasive medical diagnoses for which a radiologist can choose X-rays, ultrasound, computerized tomography, or magnetic resonance approaches, depending on the situation. Finally, as a visual framework for communicating assumptions about the present and future scope of the business, this display of growth paths helps isolate fuzzy thinking or potential disagreements within the management team about where the business should be going.

Constraining the Search. Paradoxically, the businesses with the greatest potential are most in need of tight discipline over the choice of growth

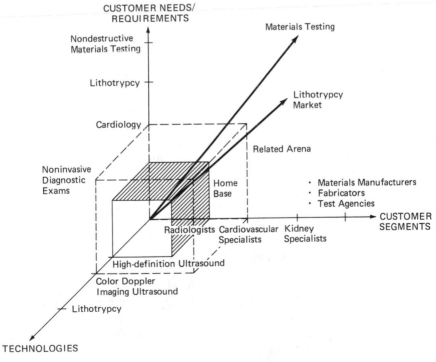

FIGURE 12–2 Growth Paths for Acuson Corp.

path. The lure of new markets, each attractive in their own right and seemingly suited to the core competencies, pulls the management team in many directions. This spreads the resources so thinly that nothing is done well. Meanwhile, tough decisions are shunted aside because the wealth of opportunities encourages the belief that failure is not possible. Priorities are never examined, and a clear strategic direction is never set.

Managers who have survived this challenge contend they were helped most by specifying what they would not do regardless of temptation. For example, one defense supplier defined itself as a designer and manufacturer of high-speed, customized microprocessor-based systems for real-time control and display applications, principally serving military, commercial nuclear, and heavily regulated applications. So far so good! The problem was that its expertise in design, manufacturing, and packaging for harsh environments brought it innumerable new business opportunities. After much soul-searching the management team agreed they would not be:

- a low-cost second source of others' design. These opportunities were always tempting because they meant spreading fixed costs over a bigger revenue base,
- a supplier of electronic warfare, aerospace, or flight-qualified electronic products, or
- a manpower service company.

By rigorously stating what they were not, they succeeded in sharpening their identity.

Generic Growth Paths. These can be displayed in a matrix that combines customer needs and technologies onto one dimension, puts customer segments onto a second, and either geographic scope or stage of value added for the third. New products or markets are new to the business, not necessarily to the world. Thus the attractiveness of moves into new arenas will depend on how well-entrenched the competitors have become, and what advantages the new entrant can bring to dislodge them.

ALTERNATIVE GROWTH PATHS

Most growth strategies at the business level—at least as revealed by what was actually done—follow a mix of the generic growth paths (see Figure 12–3). Within each generic growth path there are many variants, some of them overlapping with other categories. Thus market expansion usually helps gain market share, but often does so by bringing new buyers into the category. However the main alternatives have fairly distinct characteristics.

Market Penetration. Most internal product development programs fit within this category—at least 44 percent by one estimate.[11] These are mostly low-risk improvements or revisions to the present product range, designed to enhance competitive advantages. Depending on whether the business is customer-oriented or competitor-centered, these will be *proactive* moves designed to identify and satisfy changing customer requirements, or *reactive* moves triggered by competitive actions. Tit-for-tat responses are often appropriate for blunting a competitor's advantage gained with new features or levels of performance, but seldom improve the position of the business.

Market Expansion. This is often an attractive growth path because it is less likely to provoke competitive retaliation. Actually this is a family of strategies such as:

- increasing the frequency of usage, by overcoming the barriers to consumption such as inconvenience or high cost. When AT&T wanted to encourage long-distance calling, it provided bonus points to be used to purchase items in a catalog.

- increasing the quantity used, by bundling several products together, or addressing constraints on usage. Low-calorie foods such as salad

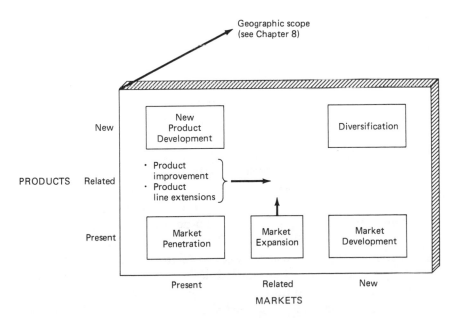

FIGURE 12–3 Generic Growth Paths

dressing or skim milk help overcome the weight concerns that cause people to cut back on eating.

- finding new uses for the product among the present customers. (If these uses are very different, of course, this may be a completely new market.) This is the route 3M has followed with variants on conventional Scotch tape for gift wrap, and reflective tape. Few firms are likely to outdo Arm & Hammer in finding new uses for baking soda. Sales went up by a factor of 10 in a decade as the company persuaded customers that baking soda in a box could be used as a refrigerator deodorizer, a cat-litter deodorant, and a treatment for swimming pools.

Market expansion also means converting nonusers in the served market. This is critical during the early stages of the life cycle when potential buyers haven't tried or adopted the new product category. The resource needs can be considerable: the segments are hard to reach, they are usually price-sensitive so price cuts are needed, and lots of fixed investment and working capital dollars are needed to keep up with growth.

Market Development. Here the intention is to grow by taking existing technologies and products into markets that are completely new to the business. This intention is often thwarted by the substantial risks of unfamiliar markets—making this the least preferred growth path next to full diversification. Indeed, it is often difficult to simply take the present product into a new market without making such major changes that the growth path is a "de facto" diversification.

Despite the considerable risks, growing into new markets has a seductive appeal. On the surface it seems that the existing plant, tooling, and organization can easily accommodate the incremental demand with few incremental costs. These similarities often blind management to even greater differences stemming from distinct servicing needs, different channels, separate stocking and order-fulfillment procedures, and different customer decision-making processes. The story in the following boxed insert is typical of the problems that are encountered.

Product Development. On this path the business grows either by logical extensions of the existing product line (new performance levels, and added features or services) or the addition of related products that appeal to the present customers and take advantage of the firm's distribution coverage, marketing prowess, or brand reputation. Lenox, a maker of fine china, used its high-quality and traditional image and distribution strengths to launch or acquire new lines of jewelry and giftware. Because the company was familiar with the channels and understood the intricacies and rituals of gift buying—and especially weddings—they were able to minimize the

HOW COMPUTRONICS TURNED SUCCESS
INTO FAILURE IN A NEW MARKET

In 1984 Computronics dominated the market for turnkey inventory control systems for jobbers (small distributors) in a major primary industry.[12] The founder of the company had been a jobber, and designed a system that had such widespread support it was endorsed by the industry association.

As the company's share increased, management saw they would have to expand into new markets if growth was to continue. The logical step was to develop a system for the large wholesale distributors in the same industry. A new division was set up to serve the new market. After visiting several warehousing distributors the product specifications were set. Since no one at Computronics had direct experience with this high-end market it seemed easiest to adapt a package from a small software company. After testing the system in several sites, a team of sales reps was hired and a national campaign began.

After three years sales had barely reached the target for the first year. What happened? The postmortem was painful, for the market appeared to be such a good fit to Computronics's skills and experience. This led the company to make a completely erroneous assumption that big warehouses were small jobbers that had grown up. A few cursory field interviews weren't enough to show how misguided this was. Only when the sales reps were trying to sell the new system was it evident how sophisticated the big jobbers had become. Many had developed their own specialized software. Worse, the size of the systems they required made them attractive prospects for IBM and DEC. Computronics's meagerly trained reps were outclassed in this league. In retrospect this was a completely new business, that required building long-term relationships for the sale and support of large ($1/2 million) systems.

Now Computronics is more humble and is soliciting customer inputs from large distributors so the system can be redesigned to better meet their needs.

risks that come from not knowing the market. Since it would have been foolish to develop a jewelry manufacturing capability in-house, the company bought a small but highly regarded supplier.

A recurring theme in studies of new product development is that "me too" products are losers. Unless the business can enter with a significant product advantage it should seriously think about spending the money elsewhere—including putting it in the bank! On the other hand, marrying product development with innovative ways to expand the existing market is at the heart of competitive strategy. As Kenichi Ohmae[13] recently observed in arguing why competition should not come first in making strategy:

> First comes painstaking attention to the needs of customers. First comes close analysis of a company's real degrees of freedom in responding to those needs. First comes the willingness to rethink, fundamentally, what products are and what they do, as well as how best to organize the business system that designs, builds and markets them. Competitive realities are what you test possible strategies against: you define them in terms of customers.

Most companies don't take up this challenge—and consequently don't meet with Yamaha's success in the piano market. Yamaha needed this success, for the market for high-quality pianos they dominated with a 40 percent global share was declining by 10 percent per year. The reasons were clear—people didn't have time to learn to play them, so the existing stock of 40 million pianos was sitting unused and gathering dust as pieces of furniture. Their solution was to develop a new product that offered new value to piano owners. Essentially it is variant on the old piano player, using digital and optical technology to improve performance to concert master levels. For example, it can distinguish 92 different degrees of strength and speed of key touch. Each key stroke can be recorded and reproduced with complete fidelity on a computer disc. With this device retrofitted to an existing piano, live performances can either be recorded or purchased on a prerecorded disk. This product has already seen explosive acceptance in the Japanese market, while creating new markets for discs, and reviving the market for piano tuning.

Diversification. Although diversification is about taking new products into new markets, the real question is how far from home base the prospective opportunity should lure the business. The evidence from the preceeding chapter is compelling; businesses that "stick to their knitting" far outperform those that diversify beyond their core competencies. Unrelated diversification is best left to the corporate parent who may be forced into such a move as part of a major repositioning into growth markets, or for financial reasons that hinge on the potential gains from a restructuring, or as a defense against a takeover. The long-run success of these moves depends on acquiring the assets at a substantial discount to the true value, and having a management team trained in the rigors of turnarounds in unfamiliar situations.

The risks of related diversification must be offset by the promise of competitive advantages that come from exporting the core competencies of the business into new arenas. Enhanced performance is promised through revenue gains, decreased costs, or reduced investment requirements attributable to the commonalities between the present and prospective arenas. Core competencies that can be exported include:

- Technology and development skills. Honda has parlayed an ability to design high-performance engines and drive trains for motorcycles and later cars into effective entries into seemingly unrelated markets such as lawn mowers, marine engines and generators.
- Market access via control of channels has been touted as a rationale for many media mergers. Time, Inc. was attractive to both Warner and Paramount because they could envision how a magazine article could be spun off into a book, a movie, and a TV show that could be sold abroad through their distribution network
- Strong names such as Campbell Soup, Kellogg's, Sunkist, Coca-Cola, Adidas, Head, and so forth may be exportable to new areas so long as the name conjures up strong and positive associations in the different environment. The downside is the dilution of brand equity or outright harm if the performance of the business in the new area is below expectations, or degrades the name.

In theory, any activity a business excels at can be exported to a new arena. In practice these prospective synergies are often illusions, for inevitably the management team contemplating a diversification move won't be familiar with all the key success factors and potential barriers to export. Even when there is the possibility of synergistic exports from other divisions or subsidiaries their managers may be unwilling to cooperate or take the time to ensure they are realized. These risks are likely to be greatest when the diversification relies on internal development. Thus the farther from home base the business intends to go, the more appealing are alliances and acquisitions.

A PROCESS FOR CHOOSING GROWTH PATHS

The myriad of directions that businesses can go in search of growth defy facile generalizations that have any relevance to particular situations. However, there is a straightforward process that a management team can use to clarify its thinking and communicate key assumptions.

Step One: Specify the important dimensions for describing feasible growth paths, as we did for Acuson. On each dimension locate home base, then move out from it to identify other customer groups to serve, other technologies to develop, and other customer applications or needs that could be satisfied. These should be ordered in decreasing similarity to the home base.

Step Two: Select feasible combinations, at the intersections of the new customer groups, technologies, and applications, as arenas to explore.[14] Thus a manufacturer of blending and agitation process equipment for the pulp and paper industry found 12 feasible arenas such as aeration devices (new application) for pulp and paper firms (same customers), using the basic rotary mixing technology already incorporated in its mixers.

Step Three: Screen the arenas jointly for the attractiveness of the market opportunity, and the ability of the business to compete. Arenas can then be displayed on the following nine-block matrix:

The location of each arena in this matrix is less important than the thinking that went into the composite judgments for the two dimensions.

Market attractiveness reflects a number of factors including: (1) the present size of the market, (2) the forecast growth rate, and (3) probable intensity of competition—which in turn considers incumbent rivals, bargaining power of suppliers and customers, ease of entry of new competitors from adjacent markets, and prospects for substitutes. Depending on the size of the firm, the presence of protected segments may be an attractive or unattractive feature of the market.

Ability to compete is a calculated guess about the future prospects for the business if and when it chooses to enter the new arena. This depends on:

- the fit of the key success factors in the new arena with the present competencies of the business
- familiarity with the technology and the market requirements
- prospects for sustainable advantage (which depend on the reactions of the incumbent competitors and other feasible entrants).

Fit and familiarity are related but not identical. It is possible for a business to have a moderately poor fit to either the market or technology despite being quite familiar with them. Thus some features of a new technology may overlap with existing knowledge (for example, the coating of optical lenses and aluminizing semiconductor substrates share many process steps). Similarly, a business may be familiar with a market, while not serving it, because it is a buyer, or has been monitoring it closely with a view to future entry.

If the assessment of fit and familiarity are properly done, new insights may be gained into both the business definition and the core competencies of the organization. Most firms tend to overestimate what they can do, or who they are, and enter arenas where they have little competency. In the mid-seventies the Marriott Corp. defined its business as leisure time. As one executive ruefully admitted later, "From there it was an easy jump from restaurants, contract feeding and hotels to cruise ships and theme parks—aren't theme parks just restaurants with entertainment? And aren't cruise ships floating hotels?" They soon learned, at great cost, that these new ventures required completely different skills and organizations and put them into markets with customers they didn't know and competitors they couldn't understand. Running cruise ships and theme parks was based more on entertainment and pizzazz than the carefully disciplined management of standard service systems that is Marriott's forte.

Step Four: Look for risk-controlling and risk-reducing entry strategies. Attractive market arenas where the business has a medium to poor ability to compete *with its own capabilities* should not be immediately ruled out of bounds. There are many other ways to participate in an arena that is new to the business. The extent of reliance on these alternatives is the last part of the growth strategy to be spelled out for the guidance of management.

METHOD OF PARTICIPATION

What does a business do when it has committed to aggressive growth objectives, needs new markets and new products to perform a number of purposes to support the business strategy, and yet lacks the competencies for internal development of a promising arena? Assume this arena is related by technology or market characteristics to the present business, as otherwise it becomes a diversification move that is the responsibility of corporate management. In other words, the business unit has something to bring to the party, but not enough to mount an entry on its own. Then it has to consider such alternative ways of participating as:

- acquisitions
- licensing agreements
- joint ventures
- marketing agreements
- internal ventures
- educational acquisitions.

Each of these modes is appropriate in some circumstances—but not others. Figure 12–4 is one scheme for specifying the conditions appropriate to each mode. All carry with them significant risks, but these can be controlled with astute management guided by a sound strategy. In this section we'll give a flavor of how these possibilities can support a business growth

Market Familiarity		Base	New Familiar	New Unfamiliar
	New	Joint Ventures	Educational Acquisitions	Educational Acquisitions
	New Familiar	Internal Development or Acquisitions	Internal Ventures or Acquisitions or Licensing	Educational Acquisitions
	Base	Internal Development	Internal Development or Acquisitions or Licensing	Joint Ventures

Technologies or Services Embodied in the Product

FIGURE 12–4 Participation Methods
Source: Adapted from Edward B. Roberts, and Charles A. Berg, "Entering New Businesses: Selecting Strategies for Success," *Sloan Management Review* (Spring 1985), 3–17.

strategy, to show it is important to specify the degree of reliance on each one in advance.

Acquisitions. For managers anxious to take quick action to seize a growth opportunity, this seems the best route. Rather than waiting years to enter a new market at great cost, an acquisition happens in weeks or months. It may be a much cheaper entry strategy than internal development if the key success factors in the new business are intangibles like R&D skills, customer relationships (due to high switching costs), patents, or image.

Yet acquisitions are not a sure thing. Consistently about 60 percent are judged to be failures, by the harsh criterion of eventual divestment.[15] One problem has been fingered by Warren Buffett, in his observations about the recent surge of acquisitions: "(For) many of these acquisitions, managerial intellect wilted in competition with managerial adrenalin. The thrill of the chase blinded the pursuers to the consequences of the catch." In short, most companies paid too much for what they got. This is not surprising, for the market for companies is fairly efficient (in economic terms), which means information is widely available. Efficient markets work to eliminate any above-average profits. If a company has sound management and reasonable prospects the price will be bid up accordingly.

Companies are still justified in paying premiums for attractive candidates if they can add value (by operating the acquired firm in a more cost-effective fashion or giving its products access to new markets), or the acquisition provides essential skills that bolster the acquiring firm's position in its present markets. However, a business stands to gain most from an acquisition if it has a strong base of understanding derived from prior familiarity with the market and technology. Ironically, the more a business needs an acquisition to enter a completely new arena, the less it knows about what it has acquired. This lack of familiarity means the initial valuation may be wrong, and the subsequent integration of firms inappropriate. Too often big firms have acquired small high-technology firms only to find they had stifled the initiative they hoped to bring on board, and eventually lost the key skills.

Educational Acquisitions. These are uneconomic propositions at the outset, because their purpose is to establish a window on an especially attractive technology or market. Large chemical companies have done this to learn about the unfamiliar world of biotechnology. Procter & Gamble bought the Tender Leaf Tea brand to learn about this part of the beverage business. In effect they are buying an option to make a later move, because the first move doesn't commit them to go any farther. If the market sours or the long-run prospects appear unattractive in the light of the new knowledge gained from the acquired firm, there is no need to proceed further. But especially with new technologies, the initial investment is needed in order to know enough to make further investments.

Strategic Alliances. This is both a controversial and increasingly popular growth strategy. Partly it is controversial, because of confusion over what is meant. There is also abundant evidence that some types of alliances—especially traditional joint ventures that see the creation of a third corporation owned by the parents—have limited prospects and create numerous problems.

An alliance as defined earlier is any arrangement that permits mutually beneficial sharing of technologies, skills, or products.[16] It takes many forms, from long-term licensing agreements, to joint ventures and marketing partnerships. Alliances have a special place in a growth strategy when large and small companies join forces to create a new entry. This is not necessarily a joint venture, but could be a marketing agreement where the small company provides the application and the technology, and the large company brings the market coverage and/or manufacturing capability. These alliances work because the contributions are highly complementary. Many of these alliances become unstable in time—especially if the big partner imitates or improves on the technology provided by the small partner, and becomes a competitor.

Internal Ventures. These are set up by the business as separate "skunkworks"—for the purpose of entering different markets or developing radically different products. It is an attractive alternative to internal development if the climate and culture of the business, and emphasis on managing the current offerings, stifle innovations. Recent enthusiasm for this approach traces from the ability of these arrangements to keep and nurture internal entrepreneurs—every company's aspiration in the nineties!

TOWARD A STRATEGIC GUIDANCE SYSTEM

A growth strategy is a statement of intent, used as a compass to direct the entrepreneurial energies and growth aspirations of an organization. It is definitely not a precise roadmap that plots the step-by-step moves a business should make to break into attractive markets and products. Growth strategies also don't remain myopically pointed in the same direction, for new possibilities will continually emerge from the process of learning that is inherent in the trial-and error of R&D, market testing, and eventual success or failure. No organization can afford to stay wedded to a strategy that doesn't reflect what the organization has painfully learned about its own capabilities, its competitors' intentions, and its customers' needs.

A useful growth strategy establishes a broad framework that can adapt to an organization's changing perceptions of where and how it can best compete in the new markets it would like to serve. To ensure all parts of the organization work in concert, the growth strategy should provide a consistent view of the following dimensions:

- growth objectives for the business unit,
- strategic purposes that specify how new products and markets are to support the overall business strategy,
- the size of the risks to be taken,
- growth paths along which opportunities outside the present business definition are to be sought,
- alternative participation strategies to be used to reduce or control the risks of internal development.

This growth framework should offer enough stretching room to exploit the full creative potential of the people in the organization, while discouraging them from pursuing unrewarding competitive arenas. As with any strategy, the primary purpose is to find the best match of internal capabilities and external opportunities.

Issues in Implementing Market-Driven Strategies

THIRTEEN

Choosing Market Strategies

*T*he triumph of this (value-based planning) approach,
sometimes described as the marriage of strategic thinking and
modern financial theory, represents the Eighties' most important
contribution to formal corporate planning.
—WALTER KIECHEL III[1]

Neither the quantity of output nor the bottom line is by itself an
adequate measure of the performance of management and
enterprise. Market standing, innovation, productivity,
development of people, quality, financial results—all are crucial
to a company's performance and indeed to its survival.
—PETER DRUCKER[2]

All strategy alternatives must eventually be tested for their financial attractiveness.[3] This begins the painful process of translating the expectations
and concerns about customer and competitor responses into sales, cost, and
investment forecasts. There are many pitfalls at this stage that can unfairly
compromise a sound strategy or inappropriately favor a flawed strategy.
Some of these pitfalls are traceable to biased judgments about the financial
results of the strategy. Other pitfalls lurk within the valuation method.
There is growing recognition that conventional yardsticks of financial performance, such as return on sales, revenue growth, and earnings are flawed
as guides to action. As a result, these measures are rapidly being replaced
by a new yardstick that judges a market strategy by its ability to enhance
shareholder value.

Rationale for Value-Based Approaches to Choosing Strategies. Adopters
of these approaches accept two basic premises drawn from contemporary
finance theory. The first is that a company's primary obligation is to maximize the returns to shareholders. This is hardly a controversial notion, but

it is difficult to put into practice. Thus we need a second premise which says that the market value of a stock depends on investors' expectations of the cash-generating abilities of each business in the firm. This means that investors willingly invest in a firm only when they expect management can get a better return on their funds than they could get on their own—without exposing themselves to any greater risks. Their minimum expected return is the firm's cost of capital.

These ideas apply neatly to strategy evaluation, since any strategy needing new investment will be justified only if the promised returns are greater than the cost of capital. To account for differences in the timing and riskiness of the financial benefits and up-front costs, the overall value of the strategy is estimated by discounting all relevant cash flows. The best strategy for a business—if there are several to choose among—will create the most value.

The logic of this approach is unassailable. Its acceptance is reinforced by the experience of applying discounted cash flow (DCF) methods to individual capital projects for over 30 years. What is new is the extension to corporate and business strategy evaluation. Most of the enthusiasm in Kiechel's comments is about the benefits of applying DCF notions to corporate restructuring and merger decisions.[4] In order for companies to do this they had to have income statements and balance sheets for each business unit. Once they had this information it was (relatively) easy to extend value analysis to the evaluation of different strategies for each business unit. Increasingly, firms are relying on these approaches to make resource allocation decisions, and so our first objective in this chapter is to show how this can be done.

While value analysis is a step forward in the financial evaluation of business strategies, it is no panacea. The inherent complexity of the process means there is lots of latitude for misuse and misleading signals. Worse, it may drive out sound strategic thinking. As Drucker reminds us at the outset of this chapter, strategy has many ingredients that contribute to the bottom line and no strategy analysis method should deflect us from that reality. Ultimately, shareholder value is created only when a sustainable advantage is created. From this perspective shareholder value analysis plays a critical—but supportive—role in the quest for the best strategy.

THE PROCESS OF VALUING MARKET STRATEGIES

There are numerous valuation methodologies,[5] but all share three basic features. First, they rely on cash flows, so estimates of value are not distorted by the accounting conventions that afflict ROI. Second, the equity or shareholder value of a business unit is arrived at by discounting the forecast cash flows by the risk-adjusted cost of capital. Third, strategies are evaluated on the likelihood that strategic investments will deliver returns greater than the cost of capital.

Cash flows are especially important at the business level, because it is at this level in the organization where it is most obvious that net earnings are not the same as the cash generated by a strategy. Suppose a business maintains market position by allowing customers increasingly long periods to pay. Even though accounting profits are realized, the business may not have enough cash inflow to pay for the increase in working capital as well as other investments. Rapid sales growth may turn a business into a heavy cash consumer. A distributor of medical lasers recently filed for bankruptcy, after a year in which sales trebled. Although reported earnings were high, the accounts receivable grew even faster. The company found itself so short of cash, because of this surge in working capital needs, that it had to write down its receivables, which eliminated most of the next year's earnings. This was a dramatic evaporation of shareholder value, but any business that persistently needs more cash than it generates is eating into shareholder value.

STEPS IN THE VALUATION PROCESS

The raw material is the forecast of annual operating cash flows for each strategy alternative, summarizing the sales, profit, working capital, and fixed capital investment consequences for a particular environmental scenario. Different scenarios for inflation, market growth, and so on during the planning period will have different cash flow forecasts.

The shareholder or equity value the business is expected to achieve when it chooses the strategy alternative has three components: (1) the present value (PV) of cash flows during the planning period, (2) a "residual" value which is the present value of the cash flows received after the end of the planning period, less (3) the market value of debt assigned the business.[6]

Total shareholder   = PV_a (cash flow in years 1 to t)
value   +
                           PV_b (residual value in year t)
                           —
                           market value of debt

This total shareholder value is also equivalent to the initial shareholder value (also called the prestrategy value), plus the value created by the proposed strategy. The initial value is essentially what the business is worth today, without taking any account of the value created by prospective investments.

$$
\begin{aligned}
\text{Total shareholder} \quad &= \quad \text{Initial value} \\
\text{value} \quad & \qquad \quad + \\
& \qquad \quad \text{Value created} \\
& \qquad \quad \text{by strategy}
\end{aligned}
$$

Strategy alternatives can then be compared for value creation potential by subtracting the initial value from the total shareholder value for each alternative. The best alternative creates the most value per dollar of investment (VROI).

$$
\text{VROI} = \frac{\text{value created by a strategy}}{\text{PV (projected incremental investment required by the strategy)}}
$$

When VROI is zero, the strategy yields only the cost of capital and there is no increase in shareholder value. The relative size of a positive VROI tells us the productivity of the investments in working and fixed capital necessary to implement the strategy.

The valuation procedure for each strategy alternative typically traces the following steps:

Step 1: Forecast the annual operating cash flows during the planning period (3 to 5 years)

Step 2: Calculate a risk-adjusted cost of capital for the business (this is weighted to reflect the proportion of debt and equity capital)

Step 3: Discount the operating cash flows back to their present value (PV_a), where:

$$
PV_a = \sum_{i=1}^{t} \frac{A_i}{(1 + R)^i}
$$

and

$$
\begin{aligned}
t \quad &= \quad \text{planning period in years,} \\
R \quad &= \quad \text{risk-adjusted cost of capital, and} \\
A_i \quad &= \quad \text{net after-tax cash flow in year } i
\end{aligned}
$$

$$A_i \quad = \quad \text{pre-interest, pretax operating profit}$$
$$\times \quad (1 - \text{income tax rate})$$
$$+ \quad \text{depreciation}$$
$$- \quad \text{incremental investment in fixed and working capital}$$

Step 4: Estimate the residual value at the end of the planning period, and discount it back to the present (PV_b)

Step 5: Compute the total value of the strategy alternative by summing the present values of future cash flows and the residual value.

$$= PV_a + PV_b$$

Step 6: Compute the initial or prestrategy shareholder value of the business.

Step 7: Value created by the strategy = (total value of strategy alternative) − (the initial value of the business)

Different strategies may have quite different patterns of value creation, or may actually destroy value, as shown below:

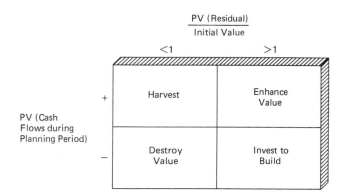

The distinction between present values during and after the planning period is crucial to an understanding of the long-run nature of the value creation process within a business unit. For most businesses, only a small part of the total value will come from cash flows during the next five years. In one long-run study of 620 businesses in the PIMS data base, more than 30 percent of the businesses were found to be net cash users during the entire five-year planning period.[7] The study also confirmed the propensity of American managers for near-term results, as more than half the businesses had positive cash flows at the expense of a reduction in long-term value.

This rather bland recitation of the valuation steps obscures numerous judgment calls, and yields hard numbers that give an unwarranted aura of precision. Three variables are especially vulnerable to dubious assumptions: the cost of capital, the residual value, and the initial value.

HOW MUCH SHOULD CAPITAL COST A BUSINESS?

The rate for discounting the cash flow stream of each business unit should be the weighted average of the costs of debt and equity capital. The rate will differ considerably across business units within a single corporation because of differences in their risk exposure and amount of debt needed to finance the assets of the business.

The relative proportions of the cost of debt and equity in the overall cost of capital are determined by the debt capacity of the business. This depends in turn on the profitability of the business, the financial practices in the industry, including use of suppliers' credit, and the need for a borrowing reserve. The cost of debt is the easiest to establish, for it is whatever the parent corporation would pay for new debt, given its capital structure. The cost of old debt is not relevant, as the emphasis is on the costs associated with future investments.

Three components must be incorporated in the cost of equity capital before it reflects the minimum return expected by shareholders: (1) a "real" interest rate that is their compensation for making a risk-free investment, (2) further compensation for expected inflation, and (3) a risk premium to offset the possibility that the actual results will fall short of expectations.

The risk premium is usually the most difficult to estimate. The task is straightforward in theory: according to the capital asset pricing model[8] the premium should be correlated with the volatility of the stock price movements. This is not practical with business units, since they have no publicly traded stocks, so analysts have to resort to indirect methods such as finding surrogate publicly traded firms. Good surrogates are hard to find, so risk is usually gauged by looking at past variability in earnings, the size of differences between projected and actual earnings, and the susceptibility of future earnings to environmental changes.

HOW MUCH RESIDUAL VALUE HAS BEEN CREATED?

This question is critical, for the residual is usually the largest portion of the total value. Just how big a portion will depend on the length of the planning period, the strategy during the planning period, and assumptions about competitive dynamics after the planning period.

The planning period should be long enough to include the time to implement a change in strategy, such as a new product launch, and observe the results in the market. If the strategy is to build a market position aggressively by launching new products and spending on R&D and new facilities, the market share gains are usually at the expense of negative or negligible cash flows throughout the planning period. Virtually all the value is gained by exploiting the strengthened position after the planning period ends. Conversely, a manage-for-current-earnings or harvest strategy will generate significant cash flows during the planning period at the expense of an eroded residual value at the end of the period.

Whether the planning period is 3, 5, or 10 years, most managers agree that beyond the end of the period the future is too murky to forecast. How can they be expected to arrive at a meaningful residual value for their business when they are least able to see clearly? Both popular answers to this question—the "perpetuity" approach and the market value multiple approach—are controversial and may yield widely varying estimates that undermine one's confidence in the whole process.

The Perpetuity Approach.[9]   The rationale for this approach is that any business able to generate returns above the cost of capital will eventually attract competitors. Their entry will drive profitability down to the minimum acceptable (or cost of capital) rate. By the end of the planning period, the business will be earning only the cost of capital on an average new investment. Once the rate of return has dropped to this level, it can be shown that period-by-period differences in cash flows do not alter the value of the business. Consequently these future flows can be treated as through they were a "perpetuity" or an infinite stream of identical cash flows. Because the present value of any financial perpetuity is the annual cash flow divided by the rate of return, it follows that:

$$\text{residual value} = \frac{\text{perpetuity cash flow}}{\text{cost of capital}}$$

The attractiveness of the "perpetuity" method stems from the simplifying assumption that any cash flows from investments made after the end of the planning period can be ignored because they will not change the value of the firm. It obscures a more troublesome assumption that the annual cash flows will be maintained at the same level they reached at the end of the planning period. This assumption is likely to be unreasonable in any given situation for it ignores differences in the sustainability of size or access advantages that are the basis for superior profit performance.

Investment Multiple Approach. Here the residual value is obtained by multiplying the book value of investment at the end of the planning period, times an estimate of the market to book ratio.

The fact that business units do not have market values because they do not issue their own common stock is not an insuperable problem. Several consulting firms and corporations have developed statistical models that explain company market to book value (M/B) ratios as a function of characteristics of the company and its strategy. A representative model found that the most important determinants of M/B ratios for companies were recent return on equity, growth, spending on R&D, and the interest coverage ratio. These variables can be used with the numbers for each business to estimate the M/B ratio for that business at the beginning or the end of the planning period.

In empirical tests at the company level, the market value multiple approach clearly outperforms the perpetuity approach. Gale and Swire found that value creation estimates based on M/B ratios correlated far better with actual shareholder value creation (i.e., stock price appreciation plus dividends).[10]

Nonetheless, M/B ratios are a rather uncertain instrument for comparing strategy alternatives for a business unit. Book values are susceptible to many distortions because of the reliance on arbitrary accounting interpretations used to apply depreciation to historical costs. Whether the added accuracy of the M/B value multiple can compensate for the increased complexity is also debatable. Adopters of value-based planning methods constantly juggle simplicity and management acceptance versus accuracy.[11] If the models become too complex and incorporate variables that line managers do not believe they control, those managers may begin to feel victimized.

WHAT IS THE INITIAL (PRESTRATEGY) VALUE?

This value is the benchmark against which managers compare the shareholder value of a new strategy to decide whether value has been created. It is the current value of the business, assuming no additional value is created by any prospective investments. This is another of the convenient, if unrealistic, assumptions used to make the method more tractable. It means the annual cash flows can be treated as a financial perpetuity, in which case the present value is the cash flow from the most recent period divided by the cost of capital. If this approach is not palatable, the market value multiplier using an estimated market to book ratio could be used.

The prestrategy value concept does not mesh well with the more realistic notion of a momentum strategy. The latter yields a forecast of financial and market outcomes predicated on maintaining the present scope and thrust of the strategy, with adjustments for anticipated trends in market demand and events such as competitor exits and entries. A momentum strategy is purely reactive; the only investments are those needed to maintain the present strategy as the market evolves. Some of these investments, such as adding new plant capacity to keep up with market growth, should add shareholder value. Though this possibility does not seem to be countenanced by the usual interpretation of prestrategy value, it should always be considered as an alternative to the perpetuity approach. Of course, introducing strategic and environmental considerations into the baseline forecast of value creation opens up many more possibilities for subjectivity and bias.

VALUE ANALYSIS IN ACTION

A multinational consumer products firm recently used value-based planning methods to guide the choice among several strategies for a problem product line in one of its U.S. divisions. The product line had only a small share of a large but mature packaged food category. For several years the operating margins and net profit had failed to meet management expectations.

The product was "vended"; the division did not manufacture the product, though it did provide some manufacturing support to the vendor. The division had complete discretion on how the product line should be marketed.

In February 1987 the issue of unsatisfactory earnings and an after-tax Return on Net Assets (RONA) of less than 3.0 percent was brought to the fore by a distributor request for a one-time promotional allocation of $85,000, which would have virtually eliminated the operating profit for the year. Because the current strategy was so unsatisfactory, the question was what strategy should be pursued in the future.

To address this question, the division's management team initially developed three distinct product strategy alternatives: (1) a status quo strategy in which the division would basically maintain its current level of support for the product line, (2) a build strategy in which the division would commit sufficient resources to take some market share away from competitors, and (3) a harvesting strategy that would gradually withdraw resource support from the product line. Later, corporate management requested that a sell strategy be developed (i.e., sell the product line as a going concern). The "value" associated with the sell strategy was used as a yardstick against which to evaluate the results of the status quo, build, and harvest strategies.

For each product strategy alternative, the management team prepared a competitive scenario within which the firm would achieve a certain level of sales revenue given specific marketing and operational "programs" and overhead commitments. Each strategy entailed a number of variable marketing and manufacturing cost elements (outside manufacturing, some aspects of warehousing, selling commission, etc.), nonvariable marketing expense elements (advertising, home office marketing, and field selling), and nonvariable or fixed expense elements. From these programs and their projected performance results in terms of margins, profits, inventory, receivables, and accounts payable, the division was able to develop an income statement and balance sheet for the specific product line as shown in Tables 13–1 and 13–2, respectively. The income statement and a balance sheet provided the raw data needed to prepare a cash analysis statement for each strategy type as shown in Table 3–3.

At a cost of capital of 12 percent, the operating cash flows were discounted to provide a cumulative net present value of the cash flow stream as shown in Table 13–4. This cost of capital of 12 percent was determined by taking the "risk-free rate," that is, the yield available from government securities, and adding a risk premium that the firm had calculated for firms in its industry and an incremental risk element of one and a half points, which division managers felt was warranted because of the small size of the division (in comparison with the large competitors in this industry segment).

The initial prestrategy value of the business and the residual values were calculated by the perpetuity method, that is, operating cash flows were discounted by the cost of capital. The prestrategy value of $306,000 was based on a continuation of the 1986 after-tax profit of $30,000 and no significant changes in working capital.

The value contributed by each strategy then was calculated in the usual way by subtracting the prestrategy value from the sum of the present values as shown in Table 13–5. The low value contributed by the status quo strategy ($636,000) in relation to the selling value and the inability of the firm to generate additional value by building or harvesting the product line resulted in a decision by the division's managers to try to sell the business. On the basis of some assumptions about the potential value of the product line that some competitors could realize from manufacturing savings and marketing, distribution, and overhead efficiencies, using a value-based analysis, the division managers believed the company could sell the product line for approximately one times current sales or $1,800,000.

Table 13-1 Income Statement for Status Quo Strategy
($ in thousands; % of sales)

	1986 Actual		1987 Budget		1988 Forecast		1989 Forecast		1990 Forecast		1991 Forecast	
	$	%	$	%	$	%	$	%	$	%	$	%
Sales	1905	100.0	1832	100.0	1900	100.0	1950	100.0	1975	100.0	2000	100.0
Total variable costs	1526	80.0	1431	78.1	1475	77.6	1514	77.6	1533	77.6	1552	77.6
Marginal income	379	19.9	401	21.9	425	22.4	436	22.4	442	22.4	448	22.4
Total advertising	0	0.0	85	4.6	0	0.0	0	0.0	0	0.0	0	0.0
Home office marketing	35	1.8	33	1.8	34	1.8	35	1.8	36	1.8	36	1.8
Field selling	95	5.0	92	5.0	48	2.4	49	2.5	49	2.5	50	2.5
Total marketing	129	6.8	201	11.4	82	4.3	84	4.3	85	4.3	86	4.3
Contribution after mktg.	250	13.1	191	10.4	344	18.1	353	18.1	357	18.1	362	18.1
Allocated corporate exp.	88	4.6	84	4.6	87	4.6	90	4.6	91	4.6	92	4.6
Manufacturing mgmt.	38	2.0	37	2.0	38	2.0	39	2.0	40	2.0	40	2.0
R&D	50	2.6	50	2.7	25	1.3	25	1.3	25	1.2	25	1.2
Fixed warehousing	15	.8	15	.8	15	.8	16	.9	16	.9	16	.9
Total nonvariable exp.	191	10.0	186	10.1	166	8.7	169	8.7	171	8.6	173	8.6
Operating profit	59	3.1	6	.3	178	9.3	183	9.4	186	9.4	189	9.4
Total tax	29	1.5	3	.1	67	3.5	69	3.4	70	3.5	71	3.5
Net profit after tax	30	1.6	3	.2	111	5.8	114	5.8	115	5.8	117	5.8

Source: Tables 13–1 to 13–5 are from George S. Day and Liam Fahey, "Valuing Market Strategies," *Journal of Marketing* 52 (July 1988), 45–47.

Table 13-2 Balance Sheet for Status Quo Strategy
($ in thousands; % of total assets)

	1986 Actual		1987 Budget		1988 Forecast		1989 Forecast		1990 Forecast		1991 Forecast	
	$	%	$	%	$	%	$	%	$	%	$	%
Receivables-trade (net)	267	20.0	256	20.5	266	20.8	273	21.3	277	21.7	280	22.2
Inventories (net)	837	62.6	783	62.6	821	64.4	842	65.8	853	67.1	864	68.4
Total current assets	1104	82.5	1039	83.2	1087	85.3	1115	87.2	1130	88.9	1144	90.6
Fixed assets (gross)	350	26.2	350	28.0	350	27.5	350	27.3	350	27.5	350	27.7
Less: accumulated depreciation	117	8.7	140	11.2	163	12.8	186	14.5	209	16.4	232	18.4
Fixed assets (net)	233	17.4	210	16.8	187	14.7	164	12.3	141	11.1	118	9.3
Total assets	1337	100.0	1249	100.0	1274	100.0	1279	100.0	1271	100.0	1262	100.0
Accounts payable	114	8.5	107	8.6	111	8.9	114	8.8	115	9.0	116	9.2
Total accrued	7	.5	1	.5	17	1.3	18	1.4	18	1.4	18	1.4
Total current liabilities	121	9.0	108	8.6	127	10.0	131	10.2	132	10.4	134	10.6
Total liabilities	121	9.0	108	8.6	127	10.0	131	10.2	132	10.4	134	10.6
Retained earnings	1216	90.9	1141	91.3	1146	90.0	1149	89.8	1138	89.5	1128	89.3
Net liabilities and equity	1337	100.0	1249	100.0	1274	100.0	1279	100.0	1271	100.0	1262	100.0

Table 13-3 Cash Flow Analysis of Status Quo Strategy

$ in Thousands

	1987 Budget	1988 Forecast	1989 Forecast	1990 Forecast	1991 Forecast
Net profit after taxes	3	111	114	116	117
Plus: depreciation expense	23	23	23	23	23
Funds from operations after tax	26	134	137	139	140
Plus: increase in accounts payable	(7)	3	3	1	1
Increase in tax payable	(6)	16	1	0	0
Less: increase in accounts receivable	(11)	10	7	4	4
Increase in inventories	(54)	38	22	11	11
Cash flow from operations	78	106	112	126	128

Table 13-4 Cash Flow and Shareholder Value for Status Quo Strategy (using a cost of capital of 12%)

$ in Thousands

Year	Cash Flow	Present Value Cash Flow	Cum. PV Cash Flows	Present Value of Residual Value	Cum. PV CF + PV Residual Value	Increase in Value
1987	78	70	70	583	653	347
1988	106	84	154	736	890	237
1989	112	80	234	677	911	21
1990	126	80	314	613	927	16
1991	128	73	386	556	942	15
						636

Table 13–5 Valuation Summary for Product Line—
Status Quo Strategy
(5-year forecast)

	$ in Thousands
Cumulative PV cash flows	386
Present value of residual value	556
Shareholder value (PV)	942
Less: prestrategy shareholder value	306
Value contributed by strategy	636

WHY VALUE ANALYSIS IS NOT STRATEGY ANALYSIS

Any strategy alternative—if it is to win in the market—must create a competitive advantage. If the strategy doesn't win in the market, no shareholder value will be created. A sound strategy must have both ingredients and be evaluated for its ability to satisfy both criteria. This assumes there is shared understanding within the management team on how the two concepts relate. Frequently this is not the case.

TWO VIEWS OF STRATEGY

Although shareholder value analysis and strategy analyses that seek evidence of advantage are ostensibly about the same thing—identifying the best strategy alternatives—they are neither synonymous nor equivalent. Instead they differ markedly on almost every attribute. Not only do they employ different conceptions of value, but they speak to different reference groups, pertain to different markets, use different levels of analysis, address different decision variables, and emphasize different measures. In short, they view the purpose of strategy from fundamentally different vantage points.

	Strategy Analysis	Shareholder Value Analysis
Purpose of Strategy	Establish superior value in eyes of customer and/or gain lowest delivered cost	Maximize returns to shareholders
Reference Group	Customers and competitors	Shareholders or proxies (4,000 + investment managers)
Decision Variables	Inputs (resources and skills) and Intermediate outcomes (e.g., Market share, relative costs)	Revenue Costs Investments Capital structure
Level of Analysis	Business unit Product-market segments	Firm and business unit (investment centers)
Basis of Measurement	Customer perception of benefits Comparison with competitors Cost analysis Management judgments	Share prices NPV of cash flows Market/book ratios

These differences mean it is possible to achieve one kind of value at the expense of the other. An industrial materials firm enhanced its value to customers by markedly improving after-sales service while keeping prices at competitive levels. Initial gains in share were realized, but the extra cost of the service program washed out the profit gains. Several competitors soon responded with similar programs. When the market finally settled down, the market share gain was held, but the cost of defense meant profitability actually dropped. While the customers won, there was no creation of shareholder value for the suppliers.

Conversely, it is possible to boost the share price by undermining the competitive position of the business. Schlitz tried this in the early seventies, when it reduced brewery labor per barrel, switched to low-cost hops, and shortened the brewing cycle by 50 percent. This worked in the short run, as consumers were slow to react to the degradation of quality and costs were the lowest in the industry. The stock market applauded the gains in return on equity, and by 1974 the stock price had risen to $69.

By 1976 complaints mounted, and share began slipping. The culmination of the decline in customer value was a decision to destroy 10 million bottles of "Flaky" beer. In retrospect the quality perception was already degraded, and despite efforts in 1978 to restore quality, Schlitz never recovered. By 1981 its market position had dropped from no. 2 to no. 7. The stock price dropped even further, hitting a $5.00 bottom, as Wall Street registered its distaste.

The moral of both these stories is that in the long run, customer value and shareholder value converge. This is no consolation if both settle at a depressed level because of earlier miscalculations. The cure for this problem is to ensure the forecasts of cash flows realistically reflect the probable performance of the strategy alternative. For many reasons this may not happen.

MISLEADING SIGNALS FROM VALUE ANALYSIS

The critical link between strategy analysis and value analysis is the transformation of the hopes, fears, and expectations of competitive advantage in the verbal statement of a strategy into cash flows. This means reliance on forecasts of all sorts: cash inflows require forecasts of sales volumes, product mix, and unit prices, while cash outflows use projections of cost elements, working capital requirements, and investment commitments. The difficulties inherent in these forecasts are legendary. Unfortunately, once the forecasts have been made—and encoded in a spreadsheet in someone's personal computer—they take on a life of their own. Too quickly we forget the numbers are only as good as the underlying assumptions about the risks and rewards from a strategy. This is the philosopher's fallacy of misplaced concreteness: the numbers serve as a substitute for an understanding of the underlying competitive context.

But, we ask, why should the cash flow numbers lead us astray? We get a clue from statisticians who have identified two errors of statistical inference. They distinguish errors that result in an alternative being accepted when it should have been rejected, from the opposite error of rejecting an alternative when it should have been accepted. There is also the lurking possibility of a third type of error that happens when the problem is wrongly specified. These endemic errors have close counterparts in value analysis, such as:

- overvaluing the strategy alternative, which raises the probability of choosing the wrong alternative,
- undervaluing the alternative, and rejecting a sound strategy, or

- missing the value potential, by not even analyzing the best alternative.

OVERVALUING THE STRATEGY ALTERNATIVE

Forecasts are often afflicted with unwarranted optimism—which is different from the enthusiastic belief in the merits of a strategy that will mobilize an organization. The result is that cash inflow estimates are too high, because competitive countermoves or customer resistance are not properly anticipated, and/or forecasts of cash outflows are too low, because costs and delays are underestimated.

An industrial products firm planned to regain its leadership position in one market niche by radically revamping its product line. A number of new product features were added and the performance of all items in the product line was greatly enhanced. A significant sales increase was forecast. Although the firm realized a 15 percent increase in sales in the first year of the new program, competitors retaliated by introducing superior products. Sales fell below previous levels.

Why is the translation of strategic moves into cash flow forecasts likely to be biased upward?

First, there is a *natural bias*[12] in forecasts of future events stemming from information availability, anchoring, and selective perception processes. The availability bias arises because evaluations of strategic alternatives are likely to be dominated by facts and opinions that are easy to retrieve. Evidence of the past success of a strategy often is given more weight than qualitative assessments of future threats. Decision makers also tend to "anchor" on a particular outcome they believe will occur. This outcome dominates their thinking and suppresses consideration of uncertainties. As a result, downside risks may be understated. Selective perception occurs because the anticipation of what one expects influences the information one actually attends to; conflicting evidence may be disregarded.

The second source of bias is endemic in financial analyses that use an investment maintenance strategy as the baseline. This alternative often is assumed to be synonymous with a continuation of the status quo. Little attention is given to how competitive behavior, or prices and returns, would change under this maintenance condition. Similar simplifying assumptions may be made about strategic alternatives, to the effect that prices will move and market shares will behave as they have in the past. Price levels, however, may be depressed by too much added capacity or low-cost-capacity additions that displace high-cost facilities. These problems are accentuated when competitors are making similar capacity changes.

A third threat to validity arises from *opportunism.*[13] People are inclined to be self-interest-seeking and may hold back information they could use to their own advantage. If needed budget allocations would be threatened by mentions of lurking doubts about, say, competitive behavior or ability to achieve cost reductions, those doubts will not be fully factored into the forecasts of risks or rewards.

Operating managers aren't alone in putting an optimistic spin on their forecasts. In one large electronics firm, it was customary for the CFO's office, using "rough estimates" of sales and costs associated with likely product introductions provided by division management, to develop cash flow, profitability, and value analyses. Without consulting any other group in the firm, the CFO then presented one new product possibility to the CEO's office. The CEO recommended speeding up the project, and if necessary, committing more resources to it.

When the data that had been presented to the CEO were later examined by the relevant marketing and manufacturing groups, a number of major problems were discovered: the sales estimates were grossly exaggerated—at best, the product would not reach the market for two years beyond the date projected in the original estimates; the product would put the firm in direct competition with some competitors that it was now trying to avoid, one result of which might be to jeopardize sales of current products; the costs involved in putting in place the requisite production facilities were severely underestimated; and, major questions were raised as to whether the firm had sufficient in-house technology to fully develop the product.

As a result of the consequent revisions to the data, the CEO's office found that the cash flow projections were much less favorable and that the product was likely to diminish, rather than enhance, shareholder value.

UNDERVALUING THE STRATEGY ALTERNATIVE

Two important classes of investment strategies fare poorly when put under the value lens—yet both are often critical to building and sustaining a competitive advantage.

Investing in Innovation as a Future Option. Unprofitable investments made in potentially attractive markets or technologies are likely to be undervalued or even ignored. These investments are options because the first investment move does not commit the business to proceed further.[14] If the market is found to be unattractive, the business can stop after the initial investment and cut its losses. The primary justification for the initial investment is that participation in the new area enables the business to learn enough to make sensible further investments. For example, large chemical companies buy small biotechnology start-up firms to gain knowledge about an unfamiliar technology and thus become better informed about future opportunities. Retailers are advised to make a small-scale acquisition in a new country or unfamiliar region so they can learn the purchasing and competitive practices before making a major commitment.

Options are intangible assets and in growth markets may account for a large portion of the value of a business. Unfortunately, discounted cash flow procedures cannot properly value conditional opportunities and understate the attractiveness of new growth areas to the company. This is a serious limitation of the method, exacerbated by the tendency to overstate the long-term risk of new ventures. Informally, managers appear to recognize the value of options and try to avoid letting their judgments be overruled by incomplete financial criteria.[15] Presumably the financial markets also exercise this kind of judgment to recognize the importance of future growth options, because growth stocks consistently sell with high price/earnings multiples.

Still, management must be alert to the possibility they are hamstringing the company's growth by imposing too high a risk hurdle. One European electronics business in an industry that was rapidly consolidating, in anticipation of tariff barriers dropping in 1992, found it was losing out to its competitors in the race for acquisitions because its parent had assigned it a risk hurdle that was much higher than the competition, and unwarranted for the risk.

Investing to Hold Customers. The crux of the problem is that you can put a figure on losing customers, but not on what it is worth to hold them. Some companies find they have to eschew formal financial evaluations. This was the tack taken by Cone Drive Operations in justifying a $2 million investment in a computer-integrated manufacturing system. When the decision was made this manufacturer of heavy-duty gears was facing severe profit pressure, inventory costs were climbing, and customers were unhappy because deliveries were routinely late. With sales volume of only $26 million, a big investment couldn't possibly be justified through cost savings alone. But there was no direct accounting for intangibles such as better quality, faster time to market, quicker order processing, and higher customer satisfaction. In retrospect, they made the right move, and new business and nonlabor savings paid back the investment in just one year. More important, the company held its customer base.

VALUING THE "WRONG" STRATEGY

Value analysis works best when there are meaningful alternatives to choose among. When managers have already committed to a strategy—because it satisfies their needs, or fits their assumptions best—they may subvert this requirement by fabricating a "straw man" alternative to make their preferred strategy look good.

Premature Closure. A less overt problem, with similar results, seems to happen when the "maintenance" or "steady as we go" strategy shows it can deliver acceptable value. This undermines the incentive to look further.

Senior management in a large manufacturing firm undertook a review of one business that had experienced declining sales and profits for several years. The business held about 10 to 15 percent of a market dominated by three major competitors.

As part of the analysis to see whether the business could be turned around, the management team identified a set of distinct strategy alternatives including "business as usual," investment in product development, and divestment. The team carefully articulated what each strategy would entail, estimated revenues and costs for each, and then determined the value contribution of each alternative. The management team concluded that selling the business far surpassed any other strategy alternative in terms of value creation.

The business was sold to a foreign enterprise. The purchaser immediately initiated a strategy that had not received any serious consideration by the original owner. New management drastically reduced the size of the sales force but maintained the same coverage with considerably less call frequency, almost entirely eliminated the advertising and promotion budgets, avoided price competition, and dramatically sliced corporate overheads. In less than a year the new owner had a handsome profit stream.

Creeping Inconsistency. To visualize this problem, try to introspect your typical behavior with a personal computer, and a spread-sheet program that computes cash flows. The agility of these programs permits—even encourages—tweaking the numbers. "Let's see what happens when market growth is 1 percent higher . . . how above a better gross margin . . . maybe we can cut working capital . . ." By the time the analyst has done this for several hours, the results may be completely disconnected from the original strategy projections. It may not even be clear what strategy is being analyzed, because treating variables one at a time introduces inconsistencies and compromises the integrity of the strategy.

FINDING A ROLE FOR VALUE ANALYSIS

The need for value analyses has been created by the increasingly corrosive influence of traditional capital-budgeting methods on long-run competitive performance. Many CEOs are beginning to agree with J. Tracy O'Rourke, chief executive of Allen-Bradley, who says, "We have been trapped in a system of evaluating our financial investments in a short-term tactical way . . . . [If] you are going to reposition the company with a new philosophy to get quantum jumps in quality and productivity, traditional models don't give you any answers." He was reacting to a 1986 study by the National Association of Accountants that found 70 percent of corporations surveyed said they demanded that new investments pay for themselves within three years.

Conventional project-discounting techniques also may jeopardize the ability of a business to compete.[16] Consider two firms in the same price-sensitive industry. Alpha invests in a new manufacturing process that promises to cut costs significantly. Meanwhile, the Delta company rejects the investment project as being insufficiently profitable because it has a higher hurdle rate. However, new equipment has now put the Alpha company in a position to compete aggressively for share by lowering prices. Indeed, it is compelled to do so to get high production volumes for maximum efficiency. The Delta company, with its outdated equipment, is at a significant competitive disadvantage. Not only are its costs higher, but the competitor's price reductions have so reduced profitability prospects that any investments to upgrade facilities or improve service are now even less attractive. Further deferral of investment means continued erosion of market share. This trap has been sprung on Delta because of the implicit assumption of project-discounting techniques that investment decisions are reversible; if one delays an investment it can still be made at a later date with no penalty other than that implied by the discount rate. In reality, the lost ground may be much more expensive to recapture at a later date and may be impossible to regain if the competitor is entrenched with the customers and under pressure to maintain utilization of large-scale facilities.

Are Value-Based Planning Methods a Solution? Delta's plight stems from a myopic project-oriented approach to capital budgeting that ignores the damage to competitive advantage from not investing. A successful turnaround will require investments in a set of projects that make up an overall change in strategy. Some of these projects probably will not yield returns above the corporate hurdle rate, yet they must be funded.

The necessary shift in investment focus from projects to strategies is aided by the adoption of value-based planning methods. These methods will not only ensure that strategically critical projects are funded, but also help to avoid investments in high-yield projects that are embedded in unattractive strategies.

Whether the value-based approaches will identify the best alternative depends on the quality of the input assumptions, especially residual value and risk. These two assumptions have more influence on the results than any other factors and are also the most prone to bias. There is a real irony in the dependence of value-creation forecasts on the size of the residual value at the end of the planning period when by definition the future is only dimly visible.

In light of the dependence of value estimates on the quality of assumptions, a business would be unwise to use the results as the ultimate arbiter of strategic decisions. The methods would be better used as a defensible framework for sensitivity analysis of key assumptions. How much change in the cash flow forecasts, risk levels, or residual value would be needed to change the decision? Whether this scenario is realistic depends on an understanding of the competitive situation, the prospects for sustainable advantage, and the ability of the business to execute the strategy. This approach shifts the analysis back to where it belongs, to an understanding of the determinants of economic value—the strategic fundamentals.

In summary, adopters of value-analysis methods should

- fund strategies, not projects,
- seek sensitivities, and
- emphasize strategic fundamentals.

Value ultimately is created by actions that enhance and sustain the competitive advantage of the business in the markets it elects to serve. No method of resource allocation can be permitted to distract managers from this reality.

FOURTEEN

Building a Market-Driven Organization: The Key to Competing Effectively

Finally the single most important thing to remember about any enterprise is that there are no results inside its walls. The result of a business is a satisfied customer, . . . inside an enterprise there are only cost centers. Results exist only on the outside.

—PETER DRUCKER[1]

Just about every company thinks of itself as market oriented. It's confident it has the strength to compete with the wolf pack, but in reality it's often weak and tends to follow the shepherd.

—BEN SHAPIRO[2]

Marketing is far too important to leave to the marketing department.

—DAVID PACKARD

These quotes sum up the final challenge for organizations seeking to compete more effectively. On the one hand it is an article of faith—and a basic premise of this book—that successful businesses are driven to be responsive to market requirements and anticipate changing conditions. Yet the bulk of the evidence suggests that management of most big businesses—and many that are not so big—don't know how to energize their organizations to be market-driven.[3] Worse, as Shapiro suggests, many of these managers may be deluding themselves by believing they are better than they are. Eventually, of course, reality intrudes as customers are won away by more astute rivals.

Fortunately the trial-and-error learning of many organizations that are striving to become market-driven, and some noteworthy success stories like McDonald's, Marriott Hotels, Frito-Lay, Rubbermaid, Disneyland, and Nordstrom, have slowly coalesced to give a coherent picture of a truly market-driven organization. The first purpose of this chapter is to create this picture along four key dimensions: beliefs, skills and values, organization structures, strategy development processes, and supporting programs. This sets the stage for a more difficult question: How does an organization become market-driven? The answer will be derived from a four-step process designed to build this "invisible asset" into the organization.

PERSPECTIVES ON MARKET-DRIVEN ORGANIZATIONS

At the heart of a market-driven organization is a deep and enduring commitment to a philosophy that the customer comes first, embodying Drucker's dictum that the purpose of a business is to attract and satisfy customers at a profit. Leading-edge firms express this philosophy in similar ways:

- Customers are first, employees second, shareholders third, and the community fourth (H. B. Fuller, a St. Louis adhesives manufacturer)
- The customer is at the top of the organization chart (Scandinavian Airlines System)
- Love the customer more than the product
- Our mission is to find needs and fill them, not make products and sell them.

Even hard-nosed technology firms like Tektronix, a maker of sophisticated test instruments, have become adherents. According to their president, "(The objective is) for Tektronix to become market/customer needs driven by 1990. . . . (Tektronix) is a damn good product driven company. If we're so good, how come our sales are flat? My answer to that is because we're not close enough to our customers . . . we must help our customers become more successful. The customer is our reason for being here. Customer satisfaction is the basis of our legitimacy."

Being customer-oriented is a necessary—but not a sufficient—condition, for on its own it won't assure superior performance that comes from outperforming the competition. Thus market-driven organizations must meet a dual standard: keep close to the customer, and ahead of the competition. This broader orientation pervades the assessments of the competitive position relative competencies, and performance of the business, to continually challenge any tendency to complacency.

A market-driven organization has:

- commitment to a set of processes, beliefs, and values that permeate all aspects and activities, that are
- guided by a deep and shared understanding of customers' needs and behavior, and competitors' capabilities and intentions, for the purpose of
- achieving superior performance by satisfying customers better than the competitors.

This definition tells us what it means to be market-driven. But how did the firms that exhibit these traits achieve and sustain this orientation? In all cases they made appropriate moves along four interlocking dimensions: shared beliefs and values, organization structures and systems, strategy development processes, and supporting programs. The essence of these four dimensions is captured in the framework of Figure 14–1. The payoff is an off-the-balance sheet "invisible asset," embodied in superior skills in understanding and satisfying customers. This is arguably the most sustainable of all competitive advantages, because it takes a long time to put in place, and is so difficult to imitate.

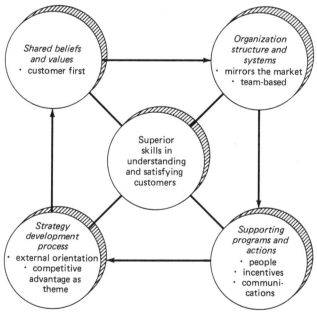

FIGURE 14–1 Dimensions of Market-Driven Management

BELIEFS AND VALUES

Within a market-driven firm, all decisions start with the customer and the anticipated opportunities for advantage. The entire organization then follows through to insist on providing superior quality and service on the customer's own terms. These basic values are continually supported and reinforced by the actions of senior managers who go out of their way to demonstrate concern for their customers. As one understated manager of British Airways (perhaps the most successful international airline turnaround of the past decade) said, "it's a matter of amended focus." At one time this airline's convenience took precedence over the customer's. If it was more advantageous for crews to fly a certain route late in the morning, that's how the schedule would be arranged. Now planes are mostly scheduled to arrive and depart when the customers want them to.

The second hallmark of a market-driven company is attention to service at every level of the value chain. This includes all internal activities, for workers who treat one another well serve customers better. Even the production line workers appreciate that the customer they must satisfy is the next person on the assembly line or processing stage. With these values paramount, it is natural to view channel members as customers and partners and not simply conduits for reaching markets. This notion is often lost on firms that have a different orientation or haven't become completely market-driven. A large poultry firm found that their fully cooked chickens had strong customer acceptance, but rejection by the grocery trade. Retailers complained the sale expiration date came too soon after the chicken was delivered so they refused to stock it. Now the firm has shifted its product and packaging focus to consider the needs of the trade, while spending more time listening to meat managers and communicating their product plans to them.[4]

Third, market-driven firms are intensely competitive: they watch competitors closely, become paranoid about disclosing moves prematurely, calibrate their performance against the "best of breed," and celebrate wins against competitors. Consider Rubbermaid, the maker of kitchen products, rated as one of the top five most admired corporations for four years running. It makes a fetish out of listening to its customers in a continuing quest for new products. Yet, to avoid disclosing its plans Rubbermaid never test markets. Instead it relies on user panels, awareness studies, and diaries that consumers fill out with notations on their problems and usage behavior.[5]

A good litmus test of a market-driven firm is a willingness to obsolete one of their successful products with a new generation of the same product, or even a new technology. This is admittedly very difficult to do, for the decision is made when the successful product is finally yielding hard-earned profits that are a reward for past sacrifices and investments. The short-run temptations to capture more of these profits are resisted by the longer-run realization that the competition will seize on their delay to wrest away market leadership. However, the greater the commitment to fixed assets the greater the reluctance to obsolete these assets, even in the face of a successful competitive attack. Why else were the U.S. tire companies so slow to react to the threat to their bias-belted tire plants from the long-wearing radial tires introduced by Michelin?

Market-driven managers also don't assume their customers are kings who always know what they want. Of course, there are markets where lead users are articulate about their problems and the solution they want, in advance of the business seeing the opportunity. But more often there is a gap between what is wanted, and what would be preferred if it were available. As Levitt has argued,[6] a high-value, globally standardized product will rapidly shift preference structures away from locally customized products. The key is to pay attention to the underlying requirements and problems faced by the customers and innovate to offer better ways to satisfy them. The Japanese have continually demonstrated this ability, even in the demanding German auto market. They succeeded with a well-known global formula:[7] offer reliable cars at a good price to deliver superior value. This didn't seem an especially promising strategy at the outset, for their cars had a boxy configuration designed to meet American tastes rather than the aerodynamic lines preferred by Germans. Worse, the cars weren't built to handle the high speeds of the autobahns. They eventually prevailed by listening closely to customers, learning from their mistakes, and adapting to the specific needs of the German market. To participate in the competitive arena they gave their cars better suspension and steering for a smoother ride at high speeds. They also aggressively seized market opportunities that fit their global capabilities. Environmental protection was becoming a highly charged issue, and Japanese cars were already equipped with exhaust controls while German makes were lagging. Also minivans and four-wheel drive vehicles had become popular, but German auto makers had few models to offer. To overcome customer skepticism about reliablity, the Japanese offered much longer warranties. Thus the globally standardized product was able to override the advantages of local makers, because they offered superior value while exhibiting customer sensitivity.

ORGANIZATION STRUCTURE AND SYSTEMS

The primary purposes of the organization structure are to support market-driven values and behavior and reinforce desired behavior across the business. This means ensuring the people closest to the customers have adequate power and authority to get their job done. If they have little or no influence on the design of products, the level of service, the resources to be spent on marketing, or the payment credit that will be extended, they will not be effective. Various structural remedies are usually prescribed to overcome the problems.

Above all, the structure must mirror the segmentation of the market, so that responsibilities for serving each major market segment are well-defined. Functionally organized firms with large families of semirelated products are especially disadvantaged because no one has the responsibility to be an advocate of a customer group or prospective market category. But when the firm is organized around markets their distinct requirements are highlighted, and packages of products can be developed to meet these requirements. To facilitate this move the supporting systems must be aligned so that revenue, cost, and share information reflect competitive performance within a segment.

McGraw-Hill shifted to a market-focused organization structure in 1986 to overcome the stifling effects of the old organization on product development.[8] Previously books (for trade and college markets), magazines (such as *Business Week* and *Byte*), and statistical services (including Standard & Poor's which rates corporate bonds, and F. W. Dodge which tracks construction activity), were housed in separate divisions. The new organization created 19 multimedia market focus groups, each following a specific industry such as construction, transportation, and health care. Teams of editors and researchers identify the information needs of the market they serve and then create data bases to satisfy these needs. The common data bases are designed to spawn new communications vehicles, from specialty print publications to on-line services for customers with personal computers.

The purpose of a market-driven organization structure is to focus all functional activities and decisions around market opportunities and issues. Then each jurisdiction deals directly with the others and shares common information about customer needs, competitive capabilities, and current market performance. A complete restructuring may not be necessary for task forces, project teams, or integrated new product development groups can often achieve the same ends. These organization devices encourage open dialogue, greatly speed decision making, and assure commitment. Contrast this to the effect of functional walls that create serial communication processes. An aspiring global audio equipment maker used its local dealers to define customer requirements in each country market. These results were compiled and sent to the manufacturing division at headquarters, who then passed the information to the sales planning group. This group drafted a plan based on this information and sent it to the chief designer. Each group in the chain summarized the information in their own terms, so the message that eventually reached the designers was often garbled. When the organization is structured like this to impede and filter critical market feedback, the remote functions will set their own agenda, which will not likely be meeting the needs of customers.

STRATEGY DEVELOPMENT

Market-driven firms eschew formula-driven, inflexible systems that are barely concealed preludes to the preparation of annual budgets. Instead they operate with adaptive approaches that encourage strategic thinking, build organizational commitment, and provide a keen and flexible sense of direction. Each of the four distinctive features of these approaches has been introduced earlier in this book—what follows is a summary of these features as they apply to the task of becoming market-driven.

Information. Planning is an empty exercise unless well grounded in appropriate information about customers, segment trends, social and technological changes, distributors, and competitors, that can clearly illuminate where the business has an edge or a disadvantage. Many firms resist spending the time and money to interview customers, collect competitive intelligence, and track market performance, preferring to rely on their own judgment. This violates several precepts of market-driven behavior. First, there is no way to be sure these judgments are valid portrayals of competitive reality, rather than historical recollections or wishful thinking. Second, being market-driven begins with painstaking attention to the needs of customers, for out of this understanding comes product and service innovations that can beat competitors, not just match them. Third, the market information has to be widely disseminated in order to assure consistency of understanding and action by the management team. This won't happen when the information is the province of one or two people who keep it to themselves.

Process. Effective planning is adaptive and participative. Planning processes of market-driven organizations are designed with these two needs paramount. Adaption is facilitated by astute blending of information from top-down and bottom-up sources, directed to helping the organization learn how to cope with a changing environment. Here learning means the process by which management teams modify and expand their shared mental models of their market and their relative capabilities.[9] The context for learning is a participative process, largely occurring in multifunctional teams where operating managers debate and resolve strategic issues and select the strategic options.

Theme. Unless the dialogue within a planning team has an integrating and energizing theme or vision all functions can commit to, planning efforts will be frustratingly unfocused, creating a sterile environment in which individual functional agendas and internal thinking prevail. When the dialogue focuses on competitive advantage, and proposed actions are tested for their ability to provide superior customer value, improve relative costs, or preempt competitors, the focus is necessarily external.

Resource Allocation. Despite the recent enthusiasm for funding strategies that promise to increase shareholder value, many businesses still hew rigidly to mechanistic discounted cash flow analyses of discrete projects. Those projects that pass muster have met the hurdle rate. The danger is that benefits that are hard to quantify, such as quality improvements or more responsive service, that are vital to making the business competitive, will be overlooked. Most senior executives will protest they don't make their investment decisions so myopically. Unfortunately, their people at the plant level who are in the position to propose or block the projects usually haven't heard the message and won't act until the numbers are right. The solution is to get these people involved in the strategy, so projects can be understood in a broader competitive context, and then eliminate the stultifying levels of project review by pushing capital spending decisions well down in the organization.

SUPPORTING PROGRAMS AND ACTIONS

The fourth dimension is surely the most important. Unless every action is consistent with a customer-first orientation and supports the strategic thrust, nothing lasting will happen. There may be a brief flurry of excitement as new strategic directions and values are proclaimed but old habits will soon prevail.

There are many ways to achieve this reinforcing and supportive behavior where it counts—at the point of contact between the customer and the organization. To Jan Carlzon of SAS, the Scandinavian airline, these are the "million moments of truth." Some especially effective actions and programs are described in the next section.

BECOMING MARKET-DRIVEN

Some organizations are market-driven, but many more are aspirants. The aspirants believe it is "a good thing," but are uncertain how to proceed or have been disenchanted because of failures with past efforts.[10] Most often their frustration stems from unrealistic expectations. They thought marginal changes, a few management workshops, and proclamations of intent would suffice, when they should have been mounting a wide-ranging and fundamental change in their culture. The degree to which market-driven behavior is embedded in the corporate culture—those shared values and beliefs that give members of an organization meaning and provide them with rules for behavior—is being increasingly recognized.[11] Programs and processes for change have to match the magnitude of the cultural transformation if they are to have any chance of success.

Nowhere has the central role of culture been more evident than with AT&T. For decades the Bell system was considered to be extraordinarily service-oriented. The product was affordable, new service was readily available, and repairs were quick. However, the definition of good versus acceptable service was based largely on a long-standing mission of providing ubiquitous and affordable service; customers were seldom queried on what they wanted. Bell prospered with this internal orientation so long as they were in a monopoly environment. With the advent of competition their customers have viable alternatives, so AT&T has had to become market-driven to keep these customers satisfied. The shift has been painful and drawn-out, because it ran counter to a culture that said "treat everyone the same," then rewarded people for meeting internal goals such as making a certain number of repairs a day, and used a nonparticipative management system that imposed standard practices and inhibited individual efforts to solve customer problems.

Staying Market-Driven. If changing is difficult, so is maintaining a market-driven orientation. We saw in Chapter 6 that firms have difficulty maintaining a balanced perspective toward customers and competitors, especially when competitive pressures force reactive responses. Ironically, success in satisfying customers creates its own problems. As growth comes the old ways of staying tuned to customers and responsive to market shifts that once worked so well start working less well in an expanded organization. Procedures and functions begin to proliferate and ossify and sensitivity deteriorates. There is also a danger that success will breed arrogance and over-confidence that leads to the damaging belief that "we know better than the customer" while underestimating their competitors' capabilities. Becoming market-driven is an ongoing activity, that begins with a broad-based change program.

DESIGNING THE CHANGE PROGRAM

Lessons on how to become market-driven can be drawn from several sources. The experience of firms that have attempted such a change alert us to what to avoid, while offering insights into effective interventions. Unfortunately too few success stories have been adequately documented for clear and unambiguous patterns to emerge.[12] But much can be learned from adapting the lessons for strategic change that have been applied throughout this book. These yield specific guidelines for designing a workable program:

- Change is most likely to be initiated by a major crisis or an adverse shift in the environment that exposes flaws in the firm's approach to customers.
- Deeds count for more than words. Only ruthless consistency of actions with top-management statements over long periods of time will bring lasting change.
- Strategy implementation is more about commitment than correctness. Excellent implementation is based on shared understanding, communication, and teamwork that yield personal motivation. With commitment to a basically sound strategic direction, the details of the strategy will be refined and improved during implementation.
- Action plans and programs are more about coordination than control. Without individual accountabilities, resource priorities, and schedules, a plan is merely an aspiration left to individual discretion. There is no way to avoid conflicts or unnecessary duplication.
- Measurement is essential to recognizable achievement. Strategies and programs need quantified objectives that define how they are to be accomplished during a time period. Monitoring of progress against these measures allows learning and suggests improvements.

A change program incorporating these guidelines has four distinct steps:

Step One: Assess the present orientation of the business, and identify the barriers to becoming market-driven.

Step Two: Demonstrate top-management commitment to a more market-driven orientation.

Step Three: Align the strategy with the structure and human resources.

Step Four: Encourage and reward market-driven behavior at all levels of the organization.

ASSESS THE CURRENT ORIENTATION: STEP ONE

The purpose of this step is to answer three questions:

- What do our customers think of us relative to the competition?
- What do we, as a management team, think of our performance as an organization? Are we market-driven, and if not, where do we fall short?
- What are the barriers to becoming more market-driven?

Customer Perceptions. Often the crisis that impels a business to reexamine its orientation is a complaint by an influential customer, the unexpected loss of a major account, or an abrupt decline in share. Then it is mandatory to find what lies behind these shocks. But why wait for a crisis? Proactive firms will head off potential problems before they get beyond correction. The survey procedure described in Chapter 7, for breaking a stalemate in a commodity industry, is widely applicable. There are more informal means such as focus groups or customer workshops where big customers are invited to give their views, identify problems, and compare the firm with their best suppliers, regardless of product or service. Many firms with a large service business such as appliance repair, credit cards, or retail banking, are using a recently devised standard measure of service quality to identify customer expectations and their experience with the providers of the service.[13]

Regardless of how the customer's views are injected into the process, two rules must be observed if the results are to have an impact. First, there is no substitute for first-hand contact with customers by all members of the management team: R&D, manufacturing, and field service. Until everyone has heard the complaints and frustrations there will not be a pervasive sense of urgency. Second, there is nothing to be gained from collective delusion. This is an ever-present risk with managers who have grown up believing their firm excels, and refusing to acknowledge change. Customers may abet this tendency by holding back so as to not offend. To minimize this risk, some form of objective information should be collected by a third party, who is not identified with the sponsoring client.

Management Judgments of Effectiveness. After confronting reality—as defined by the target customers—the management team needs to review its performance on each of the four dimensions of a market-driven organization. Here it is essential to be frank and self-critical, by using high standards of performance as the benchmark. Only with openness will there be a basis for a dialogue about what it means to be market-driven.

A useful aid to management thinking is a standard questionnaire that defines each of the four dimensions in term of the differences between internally oriented (or technology- or engineering-driven), and market-driven behavior. Exhibit 14–1 is one way to contrast the two orientations:[14]

Exhibit 14-1 Attributes of Market-Driven Behavior

Market-Driven Businesses	*Internally Oriented Businesses*
Segment by customer applications and economic benefits received by the customer	Segment by product
Know the factors that influence customer-buying decisions; focus on a package of values that includes product performance, price, service, applications	Assume that price and product performance/technology are the keys to most sales
Invest in market research and systematic collection of sales reports to track market changes and modify strategy	Rely on anecdotes and have difficulty disciplining the sales force to provide useful reports
Treat marketing investments in the same way as R&D investments	View marketing as a cost center with little of the value associated with an investment
Communicate with the market as a segment	Communicate with customers as a mass market
Talk about customer needs, share, applications, and segments	Talk about price performance, volume, and backlogs in orders
Track product, customer, and segment P&Ls and hold junior managers responsible for them.	Focus on volume, product margins, and cost allocations among divisions; junior managers not held accountable due to the "political" nature of allocations
See channels as extensions of sales force and partners in serving users	Think of distribution channels as conduits
Know the strategy, assumptions, cost structure, and objectives of major competitors	Know competitive product features
Management reviews spend as much time on marketing and competitive strategy issues as on R&D, sales, and human resources	Marketing not reviewed outside of budget time

It is normal for members of the management team to disagree—sometime sharply—on how well their firm is performing on these key decisions. This reflects different frames of references, recent experiences with customers, and their functional backgrounds. One computer-services firm found so much variation in top-management judgment, that it had to conclude it really didn't know what it meant to be market-driven. For some years it had served large-scale captive customers, and happily concentrated on the technical problems of response times and memory enhancement. With the displacement of its mainframe computing capacity by distributed computing systems controlled by its customers the firm found itself thrust into an unfamiliar search for a new strategy to serve new markets. The survey of its marketing capabilities was a catalyst for a major educational program, followed by numerous other interventions to change the culture without losing the firm's technical prowess.

Barricades to Market-Driven Behavior. A realistic appraisal of the firm's capability should recognize the numerous internal obstacles—barricades—that misdirect people toward internal concerns, and have to be overcome in an action plan. A number of possibilities have been identified:[15]

- short-sighted preoccupation with immediate sales results, that often leads to defensive and reactive behavior.
- individual inability to act. This is often traceable to a mismatch of skills and organizational needs. In one firm the marketing and salespeople were condescendingly called "peddlers," because of their strong tactical sales orientation and seeming inability to contribute to resolving broader strategic issues.
- absence of leadership. Here the presumptive leaders lack credibility or credentials, may demand politically acceptable solutions, or be unable to bring the management to a market-driven consensus.
- limited strategic planning processes, without mechanisms to stimulate, nurture, and distribute new ideas.
- ineffective or nonexistent communications that hinder a shared understanding of competitive strategies.
- restrictive organizational structures that were designed in an earlier era of success and fit an out-of-date strategy.
- stifling cultures that tend to make managers and employees suspicious of ideas outside the status quo. Such cultures often develop as the rules of conduct and practice thought to be behind a firm's earlier success are codified into operating standards and expectations.

Many of these barricades are engrained in the conventional wisdom—

making them very difficult to dislodge by someone steeped in the history of the business, especially when the business is performing adequately. There is no sense of urgency or pressure to improve in this setting, and future threats can always be discounted. The challenge of change management is to insert a sense of urgency and dissatisfaction with the tried and true rules of thumb before a crisis demands a response. This can only be done from the top of the business. Otherwise commitment will be limited to lip service.

DEMONSTRATE TOP-MANAGEMENT COMMITMENT: STEP TWO

If a market-driven organization is like an engine, then leadership is the fuel that starts it and keeps it running. The CEO or division general manager must make a clear and continuing commitment to putting the customers first. This commitment is mainly signaled by deeds and time spent. Words have their place, but if they are not consistent with actual behavior the rest of the organization will soon learn the real priorities and behave accordingly.

The biggest problem with making leadership a necessary condition to market-driven behavior is that the same prescription applies to all other areas of organization change. Articles and studies on areas as diverse as ethical behavior and implementation of new manufacturing systems all conclude that change begins at the top. So how does the beleaguered CEO allocate scarce time and energy? Skimpy evidence suggests that most CEOs are unwilling or unable to back up their words—or even their deepest beliefs about the importance of staying close to the customers—with an investment of time. Consider the Exhibit 14–2, drawn from a study of 236 CEOs of Fortune 1,000 companies, that contrasts the importance of eight business activities with their current level of involvement. It is striking and discouraging to see that financial planning is the dominant activity, as many critics have long suspected.

How can top managers signal their commitment, and successfully persuade the entire organization that the firm's performance hinges on satisfying target customers better than the competition? The answer depends on the style of the CEO, the magnitude of the change in values and beliefs, and the past history of efforts to change. However, the following actions have been found to deliver a "customers first" message fluently through the organization:

- an enthusiastic emphasis on superior quality of service and customer relations, with occasional direct interventions to help solve a customer's problems.

- time spent visiting customers and listening aggressively for their point of view and an insistence that all senior managers spend time with these customers.

- an emphasis on customer and market issues—trends, needs, requirements, opportunities for advantage—during strategy reviews. This needs to be supported with a willingness to invest resources in deeper understanding of customers and competitors.

- an insistence on calibrating the performance of the business in serving the target customers against the "best of breed," and then understanding why these competitors excel.

A useful platform for these actions is a high-profile marketing steering committee, that includes senior functional managers. This may be the best body to mount a thorough assessment of the present orientation, and design programs to overcome the barricades to change. Side benefits are the building of top-level commitment to change based on a shared understanding of the benefits.

Exhibit 14–2 CEO Concerns and Priorities
(% of CEOs answering yes)

	"Is this function very important to corporate growth and profit?"	*"Do you have considerable involvement with the following functions?"*
Financial planning	57%	46%
Customer relations	57	14
Production/manufacturing	42	9
New product development	41	8
Research and development	36	7
Labor relations	28	5
Personnel management	26	5
Market analysis	24	3

Source: Richard T. Hise and Stephen W. McDaniel, "American Competitiveness and the CEO—Who's Minding the Shop," *Sloan Management Review* 30 (Winter 1988), 49–55.

ALIGN STRATEGY, STRUCTURE, PEOPLE, AND PROGRAMS: STEP THREE

Top-management leadership is essential to galvanize a business to become market-driven, and then develop a strategic direction that all functions and activities can coalesce behind. Unity of purpose with functional behavior is the watchword at this stage.

A good place to start is with a market-driven positioning theme that gives the business an identity in the market, and the customers a reason to buy. Market-driven implementation programs that involve new organizational arrangements, new or improved skills and capabilities, and significant program investments are all tested for their congruence with this positioning theme.

In Chapter 7 we saw how a major ingredient supplier made a strategic decision to reposition itself to "act as [a] partner in the effective management of your requirements." To implement this new theme the management team identified four effort priorities, each with supporting action programs:

1. Ensure company-wide understanding and support of the positioning theme. Representative actions were to: have each functional department develop "customer impact statements" describing how they could improve customer relations, create measurement standards to track performance, build specific obligations into the position descriptions, and mount a major internal communications effort.

2. Manage the customer base more intensely by: developing a "top-to-top" selling program, improving the knowledge of segment requirements, and restructuring the sale force to establish separate industrial and retail specialist groups.

3. Upgrade the quality of sales representation by: investing in training, improving selling aids, and revamping the compensation plan to encourage selling to reach gross margin rather than volume targets.

4. Develop program opportunities that would enhance the positioning theme, including introducing an array of price protection devices, investment in electronic data interchange with key customers, and so forth.

While these programs were dictated by the unique needs of this firm, some elements of the most popular market-driven realignments were employed: reorganizing and human resource development.

Redesigning the Organization Structure. A frequent impediment to market-driven thinking and strategies is a product-oriented organization and supporting systems. There may or may not be separate sales and marketing organizations, but otherwise each major function in the business is responsible for all products and all markets. More often there will be a separate marketing function to carry out product planning, communications, research, pricing, and so on. If there are many product families in the business, separate product managers may be assigned to each. This is an easy system to administer, since communications are straightforward. These organizations tend to be competitor-centered, and measure success relative to competition with a strong emphasis on cost position. In practice the sales and R&D departments have the greatest influence on strategy, and the customer's voice is muffled in the aggregation of market segments. With divergent needs and fragmenting markets this can be dangerous.

By contrast, market-driven organizations align sales and marketing toward markets. Instead of product managers, there are focus market managers with responsibility for all products sold to each target segment, and each salesman is responsible for selling all products to a distinct customer segment. There are significant advantages to this approach. The customer's problems and needs dominate the strategy dialog. Also new products proposed by lead customers as a solution to their problems have higher visibility. The market managers must have a broader perspective on the business, which helps develop them as managers. The drawbacks are that individual products are harder to manage, for there is no single champion for that product within the organization. There is also the possibility that emerging customer segments for existing products may be overlooked. Some of these drawbacks can be overcome with team-based organization approaches.

Building Teams. Even Procter & Gamble, the longtime advocate of powerful and autonomous brand managers, has discovered the virtues of teams. No longer do brand managers operate like mini-czars, but are being assigned to teams with the manufacturing, sales, and research managers they once outranked. These changes have been necessitated by the increasing power of retailers, the proliferation of new consumer products, and new classes of consumers—singles, the elderly, and working couples—outnumbering the at-home housewives that used to make up a reasonably homogeneous mass market. Teams are credited with speeding product launches in half the usual time, and preventing costly mistakes, because a much broader range of solutions is available. To ensure decisions are market-driven, P&G has also introduced category managers, who oversee entire groups of related products and emphasize cooperation, not competition among brands.

The advantages of teams in bringing a market perspective to all decisions has been credited by DuPont as a major reason for the success of StainMaster stain-resistant carpet. To develop the StainMaster fiber, which is sold to mills that weave it into carpet, a six-member team of marketing, R&D, and finance people was appointed.[16] They were told to ask themselves constantly, "How does what we're doing affect the customer?" The team members spent three years coordinating closely with retailers and mill operators by regularly asking them for suggestions about pricing and how to communicate the benefits of the new carpet.

There is no question that teams take longer to make decisions, and make it more difficult for individual conributors to stand out. But ultimate effectiveness is greatly enhanced by creating informed and committed team members who can then move their functional areas far more quickly and confidently to market.

Recruiting, Developing, and Deploying Personnel. Reorganizing won't work if seasoned marketers aren't available to fill the new positions, and all levels of the organization aren't closely attuned to the necessity of satisfying customers.

Ideally people with proven marketing capability and orientation will be found within the organization and assigned to new positions that let them use their talents. Alternatively it may be necessary to recruit senior people. This usually doesn't work unless the outsider is brought in at a high level. Perhaps the most dramatic recruitment came when Steve Jobs, then president of Apple Computer, realized his firm wouldn't survive unless it could learn to be market-driven, rather than engineering-oriented. This led to the successful hiring of John Scully away from PepsiCo. But a track record will be of little value in the new setting unless the newcomer can win the respect of the other functions, and understands the key success factors in the new market. Product managers from consumer packaged goods companies are often unable to make this transition to unfamiliar environments especially if they don't get the depth of support they have been given in the past.

Training is a useful vehicle for shifting the values and skills of all levels of the organization toward a customer-orientation. This training must ensure that everyone knows why it is important to change, and can recognize superior performance. If training groups include people from all functions, then it is possible to discuss the application of the concepts from a number of vantage points. This is turn will reduce later resistance to changes in systems and rewards.

ENCOURAGE AND REWARD MARKET-DRIVEN BEHAVIOR: STEP FOUR

When managers and their unit-level employees are rewarded for behaving as though the customer comes first, and performance is judged relative to that of competitors, then the remaining skeptics in the organization become believers. But if the skeptics are not convinced that it pays to give obsessive attention to customers and see that bonuses and accolades still go to those who best control costs, increase volume, or manage cash flows by cutting receivables, there is not likely to be a lasting behavior change.

Market-driven managers know that the tried-and-true performance measures such as sales growth and profitability are rewards for past successes, but give little guidance on how well the business is doing to improve customer satisfaction. Better measures are closer to the customer and relative to the competition:

- market share is widely used, but to be fully useful it should track share within each target segment.
- customer satisfaction measurements, especially those obtained from external and objective sources, are less used. This is unfortunate for they offer insights into the performance of each customer-contact activity such as sales, repairs, delivery, billing, and warehousing, beyond the performance of the product or service. Without such information it is difficult to uncover sources of customer discontent.
- complaint measures—in conjunction with information on their handling—are critical, but often haphazardly collected and interpreted. This is curious in light of the persistent evidence that the majority of unhappy customers who have their complaints properly resolved will buy again, whereas only 19 percent of those whose complaint wasn't resolved will buy again.[17]

Good tracking information on these key measures will tell top management whether their programs to change the organization are working and if not, why not. Their ability to make improvements will be strengthened if some part of the compensation of each manager and each unit or department depends on its progress in satisfying the customer. This may be the clearest signal top management can make that they are serious about the transformation.

TOWARD MARKET-DRIVEN STRATEGIES

All three of the integrating themes woven through this book have converged in this final chapter to complete the picture of organizations that can self-confidently aspire to achieve superior performance in the market arenas they have elected to serve.

Market-driven strategies serve these winners by giving focus and direction to the skills and resources they have acquired. There is a single-minded emphasis on creating and recreating positional advantages in both cost and customer value. Superior customer value is achieved with some combination of superior quality and service, faster responsiveness, and closer relationships with channels and customers. The rewards are market share dominance, superior profitability and optimistic growth prospects which are the necessary conditions for the creation of shareholder value.

Winning competitors have learned how to instill a pervasive external orientation. They are able to maintain a high level of customer and competitor consciousness throughout their organization, and especially in the important nooks and crannies where the real work gets done. When everyone understands the importance of putting the customer first, while staying ahead of the competition, they have a reason for doing their jobs. Then "quality" becomes an understood dedication rather than an imposed dictum, "fast response" a meaningful motivation rather than a mechanical metric, "market share" an earned result rather than a warlike target, and "self-managed teams" are mechanisms for improvement rather than a comfortable indulgence.[18]

Finally, there is a commitment to thinking and planning processes that harness the power of bottom-up understanding of customers and competitive realities with top-down vision and leadership. A powerful vision is a shared intention that creates a winning atmosphere throughout the organization. By focusing attention on a desired leadership position, measuring progress against that achievement, and continually seeking new ways to gain competitive advantage by serving customers better, the actions and aspirations of the organization are given meaning.

Notes

CHAPTER 1

Managing in Turbulent Markets

1. Patricia Sellers, "Why Bigger Is Badder at Sears," *Fortune* (December 5, 1988), 79–84.

2. Alan Zakon and Richard Winger, "Consumer Draw: From Mass Markets to Variety," *Management Review* (April 1987), 20–27.

3. J. A. Sousa De Vasconcellos e Sá and D. C. Hambrick, "Key Success Factors: Test of a General Theory in the Mature Industrial—Product Sector," *Strategic Management Journal* 10 (July–August 1989), 367–383.

4. Pankaj Ghemawat, "Sustainable Advantage," *Harvard Business Review* 64 (September–October 1986), 55–58.

5. George S. Day and David B. Montgomery, "Diagnosing the Experience Curve," *Journal of Marketing* 47 (Spring 1983), 44–58.

6. Frank V. Cespedes, "Channel Management Is General Management," *California Management Review* 31 (Fall 1988), 98–120.

7. "Is Your Company Too Big?" *Business Week* (March 27, 1989).

8. Frederick E. Webster, Jr., *It's 1990—Do You Know Where Your Marketing Is?* (Cambridge, Mass.: Marketing Science Institute, 1989).

9. Kenichi Ohmae, "The Global Logic of Strategic Alliances," *Harvard Business Review* 67 (March–April 1989), 143–154.

10. "Managing Now for the 1990s," *Fortune* (September 26, 1988), 44–94.

11. Amitai Etzioni, *The Moral Dimension* (New York: Free Press, 1988).

12. The typology is described in R. E. Miles and Charles C. Snow, *Organizational Strategy, Structure and Process* (New York: McGraw-Hill, 1978).

13. Roy Stata, "The Role of the Chief Executive Officer in Articulating the Vision," *Interfaces* 18 (May–June 1988), 3–9.

14. "The Quiet Coup at Alcoa," *Business Week* (June 27, 1988), 58–65.

15. The notion of strategic intent as an active management process that starts

with a vision of a desired leadership position, and establishes the criterion the organization will use to assess progress is developed further in Gary Hamel and C. K. Prahalad, "Strategic Intent," *Harvard Business Review* 67 (May–June 1989), 63–76.

16. Ronald Henkoff, "This Cat is Acting like a Tiger," *Fortune* (December 19, 1988), 71–76.

17. Peter F. Drucker, *The Practice of Management* (New York: Harper and Row, 1954).

18. This section draws on Frederick E. Webster, Jr., *Rediscovering the Marketing Concept* (Cambridge, Mass.: Marketing Science Institute, 1988).

19. George S. Day and Robin Wensley, "Marketing Theory with a Strategic Orientation," *Journal of Marketing* 47 (Fall 1983).

CHAPTER 2
Strategies for Competing

1. For more details about Otis Elevator, see OtisLine, HBS Case Services, 9-186-304 (revised August 1986).

2. Peter Drucker, *Management: Tasks, Responsibilities, Practices* (New York, Harper and Row, 1974).

3. Daniel H. Gray, "Uses and Misuses of Strategic Planning," *Harvard Business Review* 64 (January–February 1986), 89–97.

4. A variety of portfolio models are available that display these investment strategies in terms of their suitability for different levels of market attractiveness and business strength. The logic and application of these models are described in George S. Day, *Analyses for Strategic Market Decisions* (St. Paul, Minn.: West Publishing, 1986).

5. Alfred Rappaport, *Creating Shareholder Value: The New Standard for Business Performance* (New York: Free Press, 1986).

6. This section is adapted from George S. Day, "Tough Questions for Developing Strategies," *Journal of Business Strategy* 6 (Winter 1986), 60–69.

7. Robert Heller, *The Super Marketers* (New York: Dutton, 1987), pp. 97–98.

8. Richard O. Mason and Ian I. Mitroff, *Challenging Strategic Planning Assumptions: Theory, Cases and Techniques* (New York: Wiley, 1981).

9. "Jack Welch: How Good a Manager?" *Business Week* (December 14, 1987), 96.

CHAPTER 3
Making Strategic Decisions

1. The distinction between deliberate and emergent strategies has long been

studied by Henry Mintzberg. For a recent update see his article, "Crafting Strategy," *Harvard Business Review* 65 (July–August 1987), 66–79.

2. Bill Saporito, "Scott Isn't Lumbering Anymore," *Fortune* (September 30, 1985).

3. Jay Bourgeois and David Brodwin, "Strategic Implementation: Five Approaches to an Elusive Phenomenon," *Strategic Management Journal* 5 (1984), 241–264.

4. James Brian Quinn, "Technological Innovation, Entrepreneurship and Strategy," *Sloan Management Review* 20 (1979), 19–30.

5. Rosabeth Moss Kanter, *The Change Masters* (New York: Simon and Schuster, 1983).

6. Richard T. Pascale, "Perspectives on Strategy: The Real Story Behind Honda's Success," *California Management Review* 26 (Spring 1984), 47–72.

7. Adapted from John Thackray, "Planning an Avon Turnaround," *Planning Review* (1985), 6–11, and Robert W. Pratt, Jr., "Strategy Development and Implementation—Avon Products, Inc." presentation to the Conference Board's 1986 Strategic Planning Conference, New York City, March 19, 1986.

8. David K. Hurst, "Of Boxes, Bubbles and Effective Management," *Harvard Business Review* 62 (May–June 1984), 78–88.

9. The distinction between the two approaches was earlier made by Steven Wheelwright, "Strategy, Management and Strategic Planning Approaches," *Interfaces* 14 (January–February 1984), 19–33. He used this structure to contrast Texas Instruments and Hewlett-Packard.

10. Richard A. Bettis and William K. Hall, "Strategic Portfolio Management in the Multi-Business Firm," *California Management Review* 24 (Fall 1981), 23–38.

11. Daniel H. Gray, "Uses and Misuses of Strategic Planning," *Harvard Business Review* 64 (January–February 1986), 89–97.

12. Robert H. Waterman, Jr., *The Renewal Factor* (New York: Bantam, 1987).

13. This table is derived from Michael Goold and Andrew Campbell, "Many Best Ways to Make Strategy," *Harvard Business Review* 64 (November–December 1987), 70–76. The profitability data for the three styles are not directly comparable since some firms rely more heavily on acquisitions than others. The most profitable firms overall were in the financial control category.

CHAPTER 4

Adaptive Planning

1. One of the earliest and best descriptions of this normative planning frame-

work is found in Kenneth R. Andrews, *The Concept of Corporate Strategy* (Homewood, Ill.: Irwin, 1965).

2. Sandra D. Kresch, "The Impact of Consumer Trends on Corporate Strategy," *Journal of Business Strategy* 3 (Winter 1983), 58–63.

3. This example is adapted from an extensive analysis of the chain-saw industry in Michael E. Porter, *Competitive Advantage: Creating and Sustaining Superior Performance* (New York: Free Press, 1985), Chapter 13.

4. Adapted from William E. Rothschild, *Putting It All Together: A Guide to Strategic Thinking* (New York: AMACON, 1976).

5. Howard H. Stevenson, "Defining Strengths and Weaknesses," *Sloan Management Review* 17 (Spring 1976), 51–68.

6. William W. Bain, "Competitors and Profits: Staying Close to Customers' Needs," Speech to the Petroleum Equipment Suppliers Association, Marco Island, Florida, April 10, 1984.

7. Gary Jacobson and John Hillkirk, *Xerox: American Samurai* (New York: Macmillan, 1986).

8. Frederick W. Gluck, "Taking the Mystique Out of Planning," *Across the Board* (July–August 1985), 56–61.

9. Margaret A. Stroup, "Questioning Assumptions: One Company's Answer to the Planner's Nemesis," *Planning Review* (September 1986), 10–15.

10. See Robin M. Hogarth and Spyros Makridakis, "Forecasting and Planning: An Evaluation," *Management Science* 27 (February 1981), 115–138.

11. Jane Dutton and Robert B. Duncan, "The Influence of the Strategic Planning Process on Strategic Change," *Strategic Management Journal* 8 (March–April 1987), 103–116.

12. William R. King, "Using Strategic Issues Analysis," *Long Range Planning* 15 (1982), 45–49.

13. James E. Bandrowski, "Orchestrating Planning Creativity," *Planning Review* (September 1985), 18–23, 44–45.

14. Robert H. Hayes, "Strategic Planning—Forward in Reverse?" *Harvard Business Review* 63 (November–December 1985), 111–119.

15. Stroup, op. cit., p. 15.

CHAPTER 5

Understanding Competitive Markets: Their Structures and Attractiveness

1. The investment performance of Warren Buffett, chairman of Berkshire Hathaway, was extraordinary in the tumultuous 1987 market; a $464 million gain in net worth. This was an advance of 19.5 percent in the year, and only slightly below the 23.1 percent annual average he has posted over the past 23 years. See Carol J. Loomis, "The Inside Story of Warren Buffett," *Fortune* (April 11, 1988), 26–34.

2. A fuller discussion of substitution can be found in Michael Porter, *Competitive Advantage: Creating and Sustaining Superior Performance* (New York: Free Press, 1985), Chapter 8 (pp. 273–314), and John L. Forbis and Nitin T. Mehta, "Value-based Strategies for Industrial Products," *Business Horizons* (Summer 1982), 32–42.

3. Reprinted in Robert A. Garda, "A Strategic Approach to Market Segmentation," *McKinsey Quarterly* (Autumn 1981), 16–19.

4. Garda, op. cit.

5. These approaches to segmentation are described in greater detail in Yoram Wind, "Issues and Advances in Segmentation Research," *Journal of Marketing Research* 11 (August 1978), 317–337.

6. Rowland Moriarty and David J. Reibstein, *Benefit Segmentation: An Industrial Application* (Cambridge: Marketing Science Institute, 1982).

7. This example is adapted from Kenichi Ohmae *The Mind of the Strategist: The Art of Japanese Business* (New York: McGraw-Hill, 1982).

8. According to Richard Rumelt, "Theory, Strategy and Entrepreneurship," in David J. Teece, *The Competitive Challenge: Strategies for Industrial Innovation and Renewal* (Cambridge, Mass.: Balinger, 1987), the variance in profitability *within* industries, due to competitive advantage, is three to five times larger than the variance *between* industries due to differences in market attractiveness.

9. This treatment of the five competitive forces follows the original formulation by Michael Porter in his book *Competitive Strategy* (New York: Free Press, 1980).

10. George S. Yip, *Barriers to Entry: A Corporate Strategy Perspective* (Lexington, Mass.: Lexington Books, 1982).

11. Useful background on the air express market can be found in Brian Dumaine, "Turbulence Hits the Air Couriers," *Fortune* (July 21, 1986), 101–106 and "Why Federal Express Has Overnight Anxiety," *Business Week* (November 9, 1987), 62 and 63.

12. These results are adapted with permission from Exhibit 4–10 in Robert D. Buzzell and Bradley T. Gale, *The PIMS Principles: Linking Strategy to Performance* (New York: Free Press, 1987), p. 69.

13. Other aspects of the shake-out phenomenon are discussed in David A. Aaker and George S. Day, "The Perils of High Growth Markets," *Strategic Management Journal* 7 (September–October 1986), 409–422.

CHAPTER 6

Assessing Advantages

1. An early study of the value of a competitive advantage in unattractive markets is William K. Hall, "Survival Strategies in a Hostile Environment,"

Harvard Business Review 58 (September–October 1980), 75–85. Further insights from the PIMS study can be found in Robert D. Buzzell and Bradley T. Gale, *The PIMS Principles: Linking Strategy to Performance* (New York: Free Press, 1987).

2. Portions of this section of the chapter are taken from George S. Day and Robin Wensley, "Assessing Advantage: A Framework for Diagnosing Competitive Superiority," *Journal of Marketing* 52 (April 1988), 1–20.

3. Al Ries and Jack Trout, *Marketing Warfare* (New York: McGraw-Hill, 1986).

4. Tom Peters and Nancy Austin, *A Passion for Excellence: The Leadership Difference* (New York: Random House, 1986).

5. There is growing interest in the profound effects of the ways managers *make* sense of or "enact" their environment, launched by the work of Karl Weick, *The Social Psychology of Organizing* (Reading, Mass.: Addison-Wesley, 1979), and Jeffrey Pfeffer and Gerald Salancik, *The External Control of Organizations: A Resource Dependence Perspective* (New York: Harper and Row, 1978). An empirical test of these ideas can be found in George S. Day and Prakash Nedungadi, "Managed Representations of Competitive Position," University of Toronto (unpublished working paper), 1989.

6. This broadened view of "congenial" controls is well described in Robert H. Waterman, Jr., *The Renewal Factor* (New York: Bantam, 1987).

7. For more details about the McKesson system, see E. Raymond Corey, "The Role of Information and Communications Technology in Industrial Distribution," in Robert D. Buzzell, *Marketing in an Electronic Age* (Cambridge, Mass.: Harvard Business School Press, 1985), pp. 29–51.

8. See Chapter 6 of Buzzell and Gale, op. cit.

9. Bill Saporito, "A Smart Cookie at Pepperidge," *Fortune* (December 22, 1986), 67–74.

10. This insert was adapted from Peter Doyle and John Saunders, "Market Segmentation and Positioning in Specialized Industrial Markets," *Journal of Marketing* 49 (Spring 1985), 24–32.

11. H. Paul Root, "Industrial Market Intelligence Systems: A Source of Competitive Advantage," (Wilmington, Del.: DuPont Company, June 1986).

12. This example was adapted from Robert A. Garda, "Strategic Segmentation: How to Carve Niches for Growth in Industrial Markets," *Management Review* (August 1981), 15–22.

13. John Koten, "Car Makers Use 'Image' Map as Tool to Position Products," *Wall Street Journal* (March 22, 1984), p. 31.

14. A similar notion called market leakage analysis is employed by John A. Weber, *Growth Opportunity Analysis* (Reston, Va: Reston Publishing, 1976).

15. Michael E. Porter, *Competitive Advantage: Creating and Sustaining Superior Performance* (New York: Free Press, 1985), Chapter 4.

16. A detailed and insightful exposition of the value chain can be found in Chapters 3 and 4 of Porter, op. cit.

17. Stuart Gannes, "Americas Fastest Growing Companies," *Fortune* (May 23, 1988), 28–40.

18. Quoted by Waterman, op. cit., p. 156.

19. Gary Willard and Arun M. Savara, "Patterns of Entry: Pathways to New Markets," *California Management Review* 30 (Fall 1987).

20. The identification of "good" competitors is discussed in Porter, op. cit., p. 212.

CHAPTER 7
Deciding How to Compete

1. Patricia Sellers, "How King Kellogg Beat the Blahs," *Fortune* (August 29, 1988).

2. See Lynn Phillips, Dae Chang, and Robert Buzzell, "Product Quality, Cost Position and Business Performance: A Test of Some Key Hypotheses," *Journal of Marketing* 42 (1983), 26–43. Other evidence is reported in Charles Hill, "Differentiation and Low Cost: A Contingency Framework," *Academy of Management Review* 13 (1988), 401–412.

3. These positioning options are analysed in C. Merle Crawford, "A New Positioning Typology," *Journal of Product Innovation Management* 4 (1985), 243–253.

4. This example was adapted with permission from an analysis by David McKinley of Tandem International, Inc., of Toronto, Canada. This firm also made important contributions to the process model used to develop a positioning theme.

5. See Robert D. Buzzell and Bradley T. Gale, *The PIMS Principles: Linking Strategy to Performance* (New York: Free Press, 1987), and especially Chapter 6. Confirming evidence from a selection of businesses under the TRW Corp. umbrella is found in John Grocock, *The Chain of Quality* (New York: Wiley, 1986).

6. "The Push for Quality," *Business Week* (June 8, 1987), p. 135.

7. These dimensions follow closely those proposed by David A. Garvin, *Managing Quality* (New York: Free Press, 1988).

8. This section is drawn with permission from Daryl Wyckhoff, "New Tools for Achieving Service Quality," *Cornell Hotel and Restaurant Administration Quarterly* (November 1984), 78–91.

9. Many of the examples in this section are based on the work of the Boston Consulting Group on time-based management, and in particular Alan Zakon and Richard Winger, "Consumer Draw: From Mass Markets to Variety," *Management Review* (April 1987), 20–27, and George Stalk, Jr., "Time—

The Next Source of Competitive Advantage," *Harvard Business Review* 66 (July–August 1988), 41–51.

10. Brian Dumaine, "How Managers Can Succeed through Speed," *Fortune* (February 13, 1989), 54–59.

11. Joseph L. Brower and Thomas M. Hout, "Fast-Cycle Capability for Competitive Power," *Harvard Business Review* 66 (November–December 1988), 110–118.

12. Theodore Levitt, *The Marketing Imagination* (New York: Free Press, 1983).

13. This analysis of GM draws on several speeches by Maryanne Keller, the well-known auto analyst with Vilas-Fischer Associates.

14. See George S. Day and David B. Montgomery, "Diagnosing the Experience Curve," *Journal of Marketing* 47 (Spring 1983), 44–58, for details of how to undertake experience curve analysis.

15. Bill Saporito, "Heinz Pushes to Be the Low-Cost Producer," *Fortune* (June 24, 1985), 44–54.

16. Many of the ideas in this section, as well as the general value chain framework for cost analysis, were developed by Michael Porter, *Competitive Advantage: Creating and Sustaining Superior Performance* (New York: Free Press, 1985), in Chapter 3.

17. See Walter Guzzardi, "Big Can Still Be Beautiful," *Fortune* (April 25, 1988), 50–60 and "Is Your Company Too Big?" *Business Week* (March 27, 1989), 84–94.

18. Nicholas Vitorich, "Higher Productivity Through Shared Scale," *McKinsey Quarterly*, (Spring 1983), 31–50.

CHAPTER 8
Deciding Where to Compete: Focusing and Sustaining the Advantage

1. Donald K. Clifford Jr. and Richard E. Cavanagh, *The Winning Performance: How America's High Growth, Mid-Size Companies Succeed* (New York: Bantam, 1985).

2. David S. Landes, "Time Runs Out on the Swiss," *Across the Board* (January 1984), 46–55.

3. This example was adapted from George Stalk, "Time—The Next Source of Competitive Advantage," *Harvard Business Review* 66 (July–August, 1988), 41–51. He goes on to describe how the Japanese competitors used the flexible factory concept to break out of the dilemma.

4. Regis McKenna, "Marketing in an Age of Diversity," *Harvard Business Review* 66 (September–October 1988), 88–96.

5. Adapted from Derek F. Abell, *Defining the Business: The Starting Point of Strategic Planning* (Englewood Cliffs, N.J.: Prentice-Hall, 1980).

6. Brian Dumaine, "Japan's Next Push in U.S. Markets," *Fortune* (September 26, 1988), 135–140.

7. Stuart Gannes, "The Riches in Market Niches," *Fortune* (April 27, 1987), 227–230. See also Bro Uttal, "Pitching Computers to Small Business," *Fortune* (April 1, 1985), 95–104.

8. Richard E. Cavanagh and Donald K. Clifford, Jr., "Lessons from America's Midsized Growth Companies," *McKinsey Quarterly* (Autumn 1983), 2–23.

9. For a discussion of activity-based cost accounting, see Robin Cooper and Robert S. Kaplan, "How Cost Accounting Distorts Product Costs," *Management Accounting* (April 1988), 20.

10. The notion of the cost of compromise is developed by Michael Porter, *Competitive Advantage: Creating and Sustaining Superior Performance* (New York, Free Press, 1985), in Chapter 5.

11. An insightful analysis of the reasons a firm might put itself into such a no-win situation can be found in John K. Shank and Vijay Govindarajan, "Making Strategy Explicit in Cost Analysis: A Case Study," *Sloan Management Review* 29 (Spring 1988), 19–30.

12. "Why Tandem Struggles While Its Market Sizzles," *Business Week* (August 22, 1988), 88–89.

13. Landes, op. cit.

14. Robert D. Buzzell and Bradley T. Gale, *The PIMS Principles: Linking Strategy to Performance* (New York: Free Press, 1987).

15. Pankaj Ghemawat, "Sustainable Advantage," *Harvard Business Review* 64 (September–October 1986), 53–58.

16. George S. Yip, *Barriers to Entry: A Corporate Strategy Perspective* (Lexington, Mass.: Lexington Books, 1982).

17. "Industrial Gases: Money from Nothing," *The Economist* (September 10, 1988), 88.

18. This diagram was presented by John Frey in a speech entitled, "Pricing Over the Competitive Cycle," delivered at the 1982 Marketing Conference of the Conference Board.

19. Hiroyuki Itami, *Mobilizing Invisible Assets* (Cambridge, Mass.: Harvard University Press, 1987).

20. William T. Robinson and Claes Fornell, "Sources of Market Pioneer Advantages in Consumer Goods Industries," *Journal of Marketing Research* 12 (August 1985), 305–17, and William T. Robinson, "Sources of Market Pioneer Advantages: The Case of Industrial Goods Industries," *Journal of Marketing Research* 14 (February 1988), 87–94.

21. George S. Day and Jonathan Freeman, "Pioneers that Survive: Managing the Risks of Early Market Entry," in Luis R. Gomez-Mejia and Michael Lawless, editors, *High Technology Management* (JAI Press, 1990).

22. M. T. Flaherty, "Market Share; Technology Leadership and Competition in International Semiconductor Markets," in Richard S. Rosenbloom, editor, *Research on Technological Innovation. Management and Policy* (JAI Press, 1986).

23. Masaki Imai, *Kaizen: The Key to Japan's Competitive Success,* New York, Random House, 1986.

24. See William T. Robinson, "Marketing Mix Reactions to Entry," *Marketing Science* (Fall 1988), and idem, "Marketing Mix Reactions to New Business Ventures," Pimsletter 42 (Cambridge, Mass.: Strategic Planning Institute, 1987).

25. For more extensive discussion of defensive tactics, see Porter, op. cit., Chapter 14.

26. Gary Hamel and C. K. Prahalad, "Strategic Intent," *Harvard Business Review* 67 (May–June 1989), 63–76.

27. George S. Day and David B. Montgomery, "Diagnosing the Experience Curve," *Journal of Marketing,* 47 (Spring 1983), 44–58.

Chapter 9
Gaining Access to Markets

1. Theodore Levitt, "After the Sale is Over," *Harvard Business Review* 61 (September–October 1983), 87–93.

2. Lee Iacocca, *Iacocca* (New York: Bantam, 1985).

3. These channel strategy elements were suggested by Kenneth G. Hardy and Allan J. Magrath, *Marketing Channel Management* (Glenview, Ill.: Scott, Foresman, 1988).

4. Adapted from *Distribution: A Competitive Weapon* (Cambridge, Mass.: The MAC Group, 1985).

5. Howard Sutton, *Rethinking the Company's Selling and Distribution Channels* (New York, Conference Board, 1986).

6. William T. Ross, "Managing Marketing Channel Relationships," Working Paper (85–106) (Cambridge, Mass.: Marketing Science Institute, July 1985).

7. Sutton, op. cit.

8. This section draws on Rowland T. Moriarty and Ursula Moran, "Hybrid Marketing Systems—The Dominant Design for the 1990's," unpublished working paper, Harvard Business School (January 1989).

9. Robert Spekman, "Strategic Supplier Selection: Understanding Long-Term Buyer Relationships," *Business Horizons* (July–August 1988), Gary L. Frazier, Robert E. Spekman, and Charles R. O'Neal, "Just-in-Time Exchange Relationships in Industrial Markets," *Journal of Marketing* 52 (October, 1988), 52–67, and Ivor P. Morgan, "The Purchasing Revolution," *IMEDE Perspectives for Managers* (August 1986).

10. Michiel R. Leenders and David L. Blenkhorn, *Reverse Marketing* (New York: Free Press, 1988).

11. Paul W. Beamish, "Control in Non-Equity Strategic Coalitions," unpublished working paper, University of Western Ontario (February 1988).

12. Faye Rice, "How to Succeed at Cloning a Small Business," *Fortune* (October 28, 1985), 60–66.

13. This section draws from E. Raymond Corey, "The Role of Information and Communications Technology in Industrial Distribution," in Robert D. Buzzell, editor, *Marketing in an Electronic Age* (Cambridge, Mass.: Harvard Business School Press, 1985); Michael Porter and Victor E. Millar, "How Information Gives You Competitive Advantage," *Harvard Business Review* 63 (July–August 1985), 149–60; and Peter Petre, "How to Keep Customers Happy Captives," *Fortune* (September 2, 1985), 42–46.

14. Rowland T. Moriarty, Gordon S. Swartz, and Charles A. Khuen, "Managing Hybrid Marketing Channels with Automation" (Cambridge, Mass.: Marketing Science Institute, 1988).

15. See Susan Segal-Horn and John McGee, "Competition or Cooperation: Strategies to Cope with Retailer Buyer Power," (Oxford: Templeton College Management Research Papers, 1987). They propose a number of specific strategies for dealing with the increasingly one-sided dependency relationship of manufacturers with retailers.

16. Frederick Webster, "Top Management's Concerns about Marketing: Issues for the 1980s," *Journal of Marketing* 45 (Summer 1981), 9–16.

17. Kathryn Rudie Harrigan, *Strategies for Joint Ventures* (Lexington, Mass.: Lexington Books, 1985).

18. Joel Dreyfuss, "Smith Klines Ulcer Medicine 'Holy War,'" *Fortune* (September 19, 1983), 129–136.

19. Elements of this process were developed by Louis W. Stern and Frederick D. Sturdivant, "Customer-Driven Distribution Systems," *Harvard Business Review* 65 (July–August 1987), 34–41.

20. The following example is adapted from Peter R. Dickson, "Distributor Portfolio Analysis and the Channel Dependence Matrix: New Technologies for Understanding and Managing the Channel," *Journal of Marketing* 47 (Summer 1983), 35–44.

21. Phillip McVey, "Are Channels of Distribution What the Textbooks Say?" *Journal of Marketing* 24 (January 1960), 61–64.

22. Applications of the techniques for trade-off analysis of service attribute preferences are described in Phillipe Cattin and Richard R. Wittink, "Commercial Use of Conjoint Analysis: A Survey," *Journal of Marketing* 46 (Fall 1982). A specific technique appropriate for this purpose is found in Paul E. Green, "Hybrid Models of Conjoint Analysis: An Expository Review," *Journal of Marketing Research* (May 1964).

23. Source: Henley Centre for Forecasting, 1984, cited in Segal-Horn and McGee, op. cit.

24. This approach to vertical integration questions is mainly credited to Oliver Williamson, *Markets and Hierarchies: Analyses and Antitrust Implications* (New York: Free Press, 1975).

25. This section draws from Erin Andersen and Barton A. Weitz, "Make-or-Buy Decisions: Vertical Integration and Marketing Productivity," *Sloan Management Review* 27 (Spring 1986), 3–19.

26. A further influence on "make or buy" decisions is environmental uncertainty. We have not included it in this list because the empirical evidence on its effects is very mixed. See George S. Day and Saul Klein, "Cooperative Behavior in Vertical Markets: The Influence of Transaction Costs and Competitive Strategies," in Michael J. Houston, editor, *Review of Marketing* (Chicago: American Marketing Association, 1987).

27. A similar analysis is described in detail in James A. Narus and James C. Andersen, "Strengthen Distributor Performance through Channel Positioning," *Sloan Management Review* 29 (Winter 1988), 31–40.

28. Stern and Sturdivant, op. cit.

CHAPTER 10
Responding to Global Markets

1. Theodore Levitt, "The Globalization of Markets," *Harvard Business Review* 61 (May–June 1983), 92–102.

2. Thomas Hout, Michael E. Porter, and Eileen Rudden, "How Global Companies Win Out," *Harvard Business Review* 60 (September–October 1982), 98–108.

3. Pierre M. Loewe and George S. Yip, *Is It Time to Adopt a Global Strategy?* (Cambridge, Mass.: The MAC Group, 1986).

4. See Michael E. Porter, editor, *Competition in Global Industries* (Boston: Harvard Business School Press, 1986), for the rationale for this definition.

5. This matrix was developed by Hirotaka Takeuchi and Michael E. Porter, "Three Roles of International Marketing in Global Strategy," in Porter, op. cit., pp. 111–146.

6. Gary Hamel and C. K. Prahalad, "Do You Really Have a Global Strategy?" *Harvard Business Review* (July–August 1985).

7. Sources include Bill Saporito, "Black and Decker's Gamble on 'Globalization,'" *Fortune* (May 14, 1984), 39–48, and John Huey, "The New Power at Black and Decker," *Fortune* (January 2, 1989), 89–94.

8. Kenichi Ohmae, *Triad Power* (New York: Free Press, 1985).

9. Marie E. Wicks Kelly and George C. Philippatos, "Comparative Analysis of

the Foreign Investment Practices by U.S.-Based Multinational Manufacturing Firms," *Journal of Business Strategy* 3 (Winter 1982), 19–42.

10. "A Scramble for Global Networks," *Business Week* (March 21, 1988), 140–148.

11. Takeuchi and Porter, op. cit., p. 113.

12. Michael E. Porter, "Competition in Global Industries: A Conceptual Framework," in Porter, *Competition in Global Industries,* op. cit., pp. 15–60.

13. This matrix is adapted from Herbert Henzler and Wilhelm Rall, "Facing Up to the Globalization Challenge," *McKinsey Quarterly* (Winter 1986), 52–68.

14. For further details on these examples, see C. K. Prahalad and Yves L. Doz, *The Multinational Mission* (New York: Free Press, 1987), and John A. Quelch and Edward J. Hoff, "Customizing Global Marketing," *Harvard Business Review* 64 (May–June 1986).

15. Prahalad and Doz, op. cit., Chapter 2.

16. Levitt, op. cit., p. 95.

17. William H. Davidson, *Global Strategic Management* (New York: Wiley, 1982).

18. General Electric Company, *Operating Objectives to Meet the Challenges of the 90's* (Fairfield, Conn.: General Electric Company, March 14, 1988).

19. "Two Hands are Joined in Polypropylene," *Chemical Week* (May 25, 1983), 10–11.

20. This list of benefits is adapted from Michael E. Porter and Mark B. Fuller, "Coalitions and Global Strategy," in Porter, *Competition in Global Industries,* op. cit., pp. 315–343.

21. Ohmae, op. cit.

22. Failure rates are based on studies by Coopers and Lybrand, and McKinsey and Co., as reported in "Corporate Odd Couples," *Business Week* (July 21, 1986), 100–106.

23. J. Peter Killing, "How to Make a Global Joint Venture Work," *Harvard Business Review* 60 (May–June 1982), 124–130.

24. George Taucher, "Beyond Alliances," *IMEDE Perspectives for Managers* 1 (1988).

25. Joseph M. Winski and Laurel Wentz, "Parker Pen: What Went Wrong," *Advertising Age* (June 2, 1986), 1, 60–71.

26. Ruth G. Shaffer, *Building Global Teamwork for Growth and Survival* (New York: Conference Board, 1989).

27. William H. Davidson and Philippe Haspeslagh, "Shaping a Global Product Organization," *Harvard Business Review* 60 (July–August 1982), 125–132.

28. Christopher A. Bartlett, "MNC's: Get Off the Reorganization Merry-Go-Round," *Harvard Business Review* 61 (March–April 1983), 138–146.

CHAPTER 11
Charting New Directions: Conditions for Successful Renewal

1. Richard N. Foster, *Innovation: The Attacker's Advantage* (New York: Summit Books, 1986).

2. Gary E. Willard and Arun M. Savara, "Patterns of Entry: Pathways to New Markets," *California Management Review* 31 (Fall 1987), 1–19. They provided the quote from Miyamoto Musaski, *A Book of Five Rings* (New York: Overlook Press, 1974).

3. Roy Rothwell et al., "SAPPHO Updated—Project SAPPHO Phase II," *Research Policy* 3 (1974), 258–91.

4. For major studies of new produce successes and failures, see M. A. Maidique and B. J. Zirger, "A Study of Success and Failure in Product Innovation: The Case of the U.S. Electronics Industry," IEEE Transactions, *Engineering Management,* EM-31 (November 1984), 192–203, and Robert G. Cooper, "The Dimensions of Industrial New Product Success and Failure," *Journal of Marketing* 43 (Summer 1979), 93–103.

5. Eric von Hippel, *The Sources of Innovation* (New York: Oxford University Press, 1988).

6. Laurence P. Feldman and Albert L. Page, "Principles versus Practice in New Product Planning," *Journal of Product Innovation Management* (January 1984), 43–55.

7. Robert G. Cooper, "The Performance Impact of Product Innovation Strategies," *European Journal of Marketing* (1984), 1–54. See also Robert G. Cooper, *Winning at New Products* (Toronto: Gage Publishing, 1987).

8. Arthur M. Louis, "The Bottom Line on Ten Big Mergers," *Fortune* (May 3, 1982), 84–89.

9. Michael E. Porter, "From Competitive Advantage to Corporate Strategy," *Harvard Business Review* 65 (May–June 1987), 43–59. Another influential study was by Richard Rumelt, "Diversity, Strategy and Profitability," *Strategic Management Journal* 3 (1982), 359–369.

10. Useful sources are George Stalk, Jr., "Time—The Next Source of Competitive Advantage," *Harvard Business Review* 66 (July–August 1988), 41–51, and Christopher Lorenz, "Seizing the Initiative in a Struggle for Survival," *Financial Times* (June 17, 19, 26, and July 3, 1987).

11. Reported in Brian Dumaine, "How Managers Can Succeed through Speed," *Fortune* (February 13, 1989), 54–59. The study was conducted by McKinsey & Co.

12. James Brian Quinn, "Managing Innovation: Controlled Chaos," *Harvard Business Review* 63 (May–June 1985), 73–84, is a strong advocate in this article where he says, "few, if any major innovations result from highly structured planning systems."

13. Hirotaka Takeuchi and Ikujiro Nonaka, "The New New Product Development Game," *Harvard Business Review* 64 (January–February 1986), 137–146.

14. Michael G. Duerr, *The Commercial Development of New Products* (New York: The Conference Board, 1986).

15. Kenneth Labick, "The Innovators," *Fortune* (June 6, 1988), 52–64.

16. Quinn, op. cit., p. 79.

17. The distinction between integrative and segmental approaches has been extensively studied by Rosabeth Moss Kanter, *The Change Masters: Innovation and Entrepreneurship in the American Corporation* (New York: Simon and Schuster, 1983).

CHAPTER 12
Finding the Growth Direction

1. C. Merle Crawford, "Defining the Charter for Product Innovation," *Sloan Management Review* 21 (Fall 1980), 3–12.

2. For details of this study, see Booz, Allen and Hamilton, Inc., *New Products Management for the 1980s* (New York: 1982. However, there is some evidence that this study may be overstating the extent of improvement (see Laurence P. Feldman and Albert L. Page, "Principles versus Practice in New Product Planning," *Journal of Product Innovation Management* [January 1984], 43–55), especially in technology-based firms.

3. "Humbled and More Cautious, Time Inc, Marches On," *Business Week* (February 13, 1984), 62–63.

4. "Masters of Innovation: How 3M Keeps Its New Products Coming," *Business Week* (April 10, 1989), 58–63.

5. The related notion of strategic roles is further developed in Thomas D. Kuczmarski, *Managing New Products* (Englewood Cliffs, N.J.: Prentice-Hall, 1988).

6. Adapted from a talk by John Grey, at a Marketing Science Institute Conference on *Charting New Business Directions: What Role for Marketing?* Cambridge, Mass. (December 1984).

7. This example was derived from an HBS Case Services case by Bob Dolan, on Sealed Air Corp.

8. Peter F. Drucker, *Innovation and Entrepreneurship: Practice and Principles* (New York: Harper and Row, 1985). The Tylenol example is adapted from his discussion.

9. A recently completed two-year study for the National Science Foundation contrasted American and Japanese patterns of technology development. The biggest difference was the Japanese emphasis on spending for improved pro-

cess technology at twice the rate of spending on improved product technology. Among the American firms this proportion was reversed.

10. This methodology for defining new product arenas was developed by Robert G. Cooper, "Strategic Planning for Successful Technological Innovation," *Business Quarterly* 43 (Spring 1978), 46–54.

11. Thomas D. Kuczmarski and Steven J. Silver, "Strategy: The Key to Successful New Product Development," *Management Review* (July 1982), 26–40.

12. Modesto A. Maidique and B. J. Zirger, "The New Product Learning Cycle," *Research Policy* (December 1985).

13. Kenichi Ohmae, "Getting Back to Strategy," *Harvard Business Review* 66 (November–December, 1988), 149–156. The Yamaha example is adapted from this article.

14. A similar process is described in Robert Cooper, *Winning at New Products* (Toronto, Gage, 1987).

15. For a recent study, see Michael E. Porter, "From Competitive Advantage to Corporate Strategy," *Harvard Business Review* 65 (May–June 1987), 43–59.

16. David J. Teece, "Capturing Value from Technological Innovation: Integration, Strategic Partnering, and Licensing Decisions," *Interfaces* (May–June 1988), 46–61.

CHAPTER 13
Choosing Market Strategies

1. Walter Kiechel III, "Corporate Strategy for the 1990's," *Fortune* (February 29, 1988), 34–42.

2. Peter F. Drucker, "Management and the World's Work," *Harvard Business Review* 88 (September–October 1988), 65–77.

3. Portions of this chapter are taken from George S. Day and Liam Fahey, "Valuing Market Strategies," *Journal of Marketing* 52 (July 1988), 45–47.

4. Bernard C. Reimann, "Stock Price and Business Success: What is the Relationship?" *Journal of Business Strategy* 8 (Summer 1987), 38–50.

5. The best-known methodologies are those advocated by the Alcar Group (see Alfred Rappaport, *Creating Shareholder Value: The New Standard for Business Performance* [New York: Free Press, 1986]), and by Marakon Associates (see William W. Alberts and James M. McTaggart, "Value-Based Strategic Investment Planning," *Interfaces* 14 [January–February 1984], 138–51). Other firms such as Strategic Planning Associates, Stern Stewart, and Holt and Co. offer variants on these methodologies.

6. The procedure outlined here generally follows Rappaport, with modification for the initial and residual value.

7. Robert D. Buzzell and Bradley T. Gale, *The PIMS Principles: Linking Strategy to Performance* (New York: Free Press, 1987).

8. Richard Brealey and Stewart Myers, *Principles of Corporate Finance* (New York: McGraw-Hill, 1981).

9. See Rappaport, op. cit.

10. Bradley T. Gale and Donald J. Swire, "The Tricky Business of Measuring Wealth," *Planning Review* 16 (March–April 1988), 14–7, 47.

11. Bala Chakravarthy, Worth Loomis, and John M. Vrabel, "Dexter Corporation's Value-Based Strategic Planning System," *Planning Review* 16 (January–February 1988), 34–41.

12. Robin M. Hogarth and Spyros Makridakis, "Forecasting and Planning: An Evaluation," *Management Science* 27 (February 1981), 115–138.

13. Oliver E. Williamson, *Markets and Hierarchies: Analysis and Antitrust Implications* (New York: Free Press, 1975).

14. Stewart C. Myers, "Finance Theory and Financial Strategy, *Interfaces* 14 (January–February 1984), 126–137.

15. Carl Kester, "Today's Options for Tomorrows Growth," *Harvard Business Review* 62 (March–April 1984), 153–160.

16. Robert H. Hayes and David A. Garvin, "Managing As If Tomorrow Mattered," *Harvard Business Review*, 60 (May–June 1982), 71–74.

CHAPTER 14

Building a Market-Driven Organization: The Key to Competing Effectively

1. Peter F. Drucker, "Management and the World's Work," *Harvard Business Review* 66 (September–October 1988), 65–76.

2. Benson P. Shapiro, "What the Hell is 'Market-Oriented?'" *Harvard Business Review* 66 (November–December 1988), 119–125.

3. See, for example, Frederick E. Webster, Jr., "Top Management's Concerns about Marketing: Issues for the 1980's," *Journal of Marketing* (Summer 1981), 9–16, a study about the incomplete acceptance of the marketing concept and "Business Planning in the Eighties. The New Competitiveness of American Corporations," a study conducted by Yankelovich, Skelly, and White for Coopers and Lybrand in 1984.

4. These examples are drawn from Patricia Sellers, "Getting Customers to Love You," *Fortune* (March 13, 1989), 38–49.

5. Alex Taylor III, "Why the Bounce at Rubbermaid?" *Fortune* (April 13, 1987), 77–78.

6. Theodore Levitt, *The Marketing Imagination* (New York: Free Press, 1983).

7. Thomas F. O'Boyle, "German Pride in Cars Doesn't Stop Japan," *Wall Street Journal* (October 21, 1987), 24.

8. Stuart Gannes, "Marketing Is the Message at McGraw-Hill," *Fortune* (February 17, 1986), 34–37.

9. This aspect of an adaptive process is demonstrated within the Shell Group of companies, by Arie P. DeGeus, "Planning as Learning," *Harvard Business Review* 66 (March–April 1988), 70–74.

10. Webster op. cit.

11. See Rohit Despande and Frederick E. Webster, Jr., "Organizational Culture and Marketing: Defining the Research Agenda," (Cambridge, Mass.: Marketing Science Institute, 1987), and Orville C. Walker, Jr., and Robert W. Ruekert, "Marketing's Role in the Implementation of Business Strategies: A Critical Review and Conceptual Framework," *Journal of Marketing* 51 (July 1987), 15–33.

12. A useful source is William T. Ross, "Developing a Marketing Orientation," the Summary of a Marketing Science Institute Conference held on April 23, 1987.

13. A. Parasuraman, Valarie A. Zeithaml, and Leonard L. Berry, "SERVQUAL: A Multiple-Item Scale for Measuring Consumers' Perceptions of Service Quality," *Journal of Retailing*, (Spring 1988), 13–40.

14. This exhibit is adapted from Michael Nevens, "Marketing Excellence Takes a Commitment," *Electronic Business* (June 15, 1984). Formal checklists can be found in Philip Kotler, "From Sales Obsession to Marketing Effectiveness," *Harvard Business Review* 55 (November–December 1977), 67–75, and B. Charles Ames and James D. Hlavacek, *Market-Driven Management* (Homewood, Ill.: Dow Jones-Irwin, 1989).

15. Arthur Daltas and Philip McDonald, "Barricades to Strategic Marketing Thinking," *Planning Review* (January–February 1987), 8–15.

16. Sellers, op. cit.

17. Patricia Sellers, "How to Handle Customers' Gripes," *Fortune* (October 24, 1988), 88–100.

18. A paraphrase of Ted Levitt, "Making Sense," *Harvard Business Review,* 67 (November–December 1989), 8.

Index